Japan Decides 2021

Robert J. Pekkanen · Steven R. Reed ·
Daniel M. Smith
Editors

Japan Decides 2021

The Japanese General Election

palgrave
macmillan

Editors
Robert J. Pekkanen
Jackson School of International
Studies, University of Washington
Seattle, WA, USA

Steven R. Reed
Faculty of Policy Studies
Chuo University
Tokyo, Japan

Daniel M. Smith
Columbia University
New York, NY, USA

ISBN 978-3-031-11323-9   ISBN 978-3-031-11324-6   (eBook)
https://doi.org/10.1007/978-3-031-11324-6

This Palgrave Macmillan imprint is published by the registered company Springer Nature
Switzerland AG
The registered company address is: Gewerbestrasse 11, 6330 Cham, Switzerland

To my friend Paul, who is always asking me how my book is going.
This one is for you.

—From Robert J. Pekkanen

Steve Reed thanks his coeditors, past and present.

—From Steven R. Reed

To everyone who has lost a friend or loved one in the pandemic.

—From Daniel M. Smith

ACKNOWLEDGMENTS

We are thrilled to produce the fourth in our series of high-quality analyses of general elections for Japan's House of Representatives, following *Japan Decides 2012, 2014,* and *2017.* The global coronavirus pandemic framed Japan's 2021 election, as we and many authors argue in these pages. However, it also posed new challenges for the editorial team and publisher. Through the hard work of our authors, we were able to compile what we believe will be the definitive volume on the October 31, 2021, general election in Japan. We wish to also express our thanks to our stalwart editor at Palgrave Macmillan, Ambra Finotello. She made every one of the many steps in this process easier. This is the first *Japan Decides* volume not to benefit from the intelligence and creativity of one of the inaugural editors, Ethan Scheiner, and we want to thank him for his work in establishing the *Japan Decides* series. Robert thanks Saadia, Sophia, Sarah, Lynn, and John Pekkanen for their support. Steve thanks his coeditors, past and present. Dan thanks John, and the many friends and family members who supported him through a challenging two years.

CONTENTS

NOTES ON CONTRIBUTORS

Amano Kenya is a Ph.D. student in the Department of Political Science at the University of Washington. His research focuses primarily on the intersections of economic institutions and politics, with an emphasis on monetary and fiscal policy, and regulation.

Fahey Robert A. is an Assistant Professor at the Waseda Institute for Advanced Study (WIAS) at Waseda University in Tokyo. His research work focuses on populism, polarization, and the influence of social media on political beliefs and behaviors.

Green Michael J. is Director of Asian Studies and Chair in Modern and Contemporary Japanese Politics and Foreign Policy at Georgetown University's School of Foreign Service and Senior Vice President for Asia and Japan Chair at the Center for Strategic and International Studies. He previously served as Special Assistant to the President for National Security and Senior Director for Asian Affairs on the staff of the National Security Council.

Hamzawi Jordan is a Post-doctoral Research Fellow for the Program on US-Japan Relations at Harvard University. His research focuses on electoral institutions, political parties, and voter behavior.

Harris Tobias is a Senior Fellow for Asia at the Center for American Progress in Washington, D.C. He is the author of *The Iconoclast: Shinzo Abe and the New Japan* (Hurst Publishers, 2020).

Katada Saori N. is a Professor of International Relations and the director of the Center for International Studies at University of Southern California. Her book *Japan's New Regional Reality: Geoeconomic Strategy in the Asia-Pacific* was published from Columbia University Press in July 2020. She has co-authored two recent books: *The BRICS and Collective Financial Statecraft* (Oxford University Press, 2017), and *Taming Japan's Deflation: The Debate over Unconventional Monetary Policy* (Cornell University Press, 2018).

Klein Axel is Full Professor at the Institute of Political Science at Duisburg-Essen University (Germany). He is co-author of *Kōmeitō: Politics and Religion in Japan* (IEAS Berkeley, 2014), has produced the documentary film "Pictures at an Election" (DIJ Tokyo 2008), and has published widely on Japanese politics.

Kubo Hiroki is an Associate Professor of Political Science at Meiji Gakuin University. His research interests include comparative politics, political parties, legislative studies, electoral systems, and political representation. His articles have appeared in *Party Politics, Electoral Studies, Public Choice,* and *Asian Journal of Comparative Politics.*

Kweon Yesola is an Assistant Professor of Political Science at Sungkyunkwan University. Her primary research areas are comparative political economy, political behavior, and public policy with a focus on East Asia. Her recent publication includes the co-authored book, *Democracy under Siege? Parties, Voters, and Elections after the Great Recession* (Oxford University Press, 2020).

Leheny David is a Professor in the Graduate School of Asia-Pacific Studies at Waseda University. His most recent book is *Empire of Hope: The Sentimental Politics of Japanese Decline* (Cornell University Press, 2018).

Lee Yeon Ju is the Korea Foundation-Song Family Assistant Professor in Korean Business and Economics at Georgetown University's Walsh School of Foreign Service. Her research examines the political origins and consequences of economic inequality and development with a focus on Japan and East Asia.

Lipscy Phillip Y. is an Associate Professor in the Department of Political Science and Munk School of Global Affairs & Public Policy at the University of Toronto, where he is also Chair in Japanese Politics & Global Affairs and Director of the Centre for the Study of Global Japan. He is the author of *Renegotiating the World Order: Institutional Change in International Relations* (2017) and co-editor of *Japan under the DPJ: The Politics of Transition and Governance* (2013) and *The Political Economy of the Abe Government and Abenomics Reforms* (2021).

Lukner Kerstin is Managing Director of the Alliance for Research on East Asia Ruhr (AREA Ruhr), a joint research and teaching institute of the Universities of Duisburg-Essen and Bochum, Germany. Her research focuses on Japan's foreign and security policy. She is co-author of *Reluctant Warriors: Germany, Japan, and Their U.S. Alliance Dilemma* (Brookings Institution Press, 2020).

Maeda Ko is an Associate Professor of Political Science at the University of North Texas. His research interests center on elections, party competition, and political institutions. His work has appeared in journals such as the *Journal of Politics, British Journal of Political Science, Comparative Political Studies,* and *Electoral Studies.* He serves as an editor of the *Japanese Journal of Political Science* and an associate editor of the *Journal of Elections, Public Opinion, and Parties.*

Maeda Yukio is Professor at the Institute of Social Science at the University of Tokyo. His research focuses on Japanese political behavior and public opinion. He has served on a Japanese local committee for major international surveys, including the Comparative Study of Electoral Systems, the Asian Barometer Survey, and the World Value Survey.

McClean Charles T. is the Japan Foundation CGP Postdoctoral Associate at Yale University's Council on East Asian Studies. Previously, he was the Toyota Visiting Professor at the University of Michigan's Center for Japanese Studies and a Postdoctoral Associate at Harvard University's Program on US-Japan Relations. His research focuses on the politics of age and aging, institutions, representation, social policy, and Japan.

McElwain Kenneth Mori is Professor of Comparative Politics at the Institute of Social Science, University of Tokyo. His research focuses on comparative political institutions, most recently on differences in constitutional design across countries. His work has been published in a number of journals and edited volumes, including *American Journal of Political Science, Journal of East Asian Studies, Social Science Japan, Chūō Kōron,* and the *Journal of Japanese Studies.* He also serves as Editor-in-Chief of *Social Science Japan Journal,* published by Oxford University Press, and is a board member of the UTokyo Center for Contemporary Japanese Studies.

McLaughlin Levi is an Associate Professor at the Department of Philosophy and Religious Studies, North Carolina State University. He is co-author of *Kōmeitō: Politics and Religion in Japan* (IEAS Berkeley, 2014) and author of *Soka Gakkai's Human Revolution: The Rise of a Mimetic Nation in Modern Japan* (University of Hawai'i Press, 2019), as well as numerous book chapters and articles on religion and politics in Japan.

Nemoto Kuniaki is a Professor of Political Science at Musashi University, Japan. His research interests cover electoral systems, parties and party systems, and legislative politics. His articles have appeared in *British Journal of Political Science*, *Comparative Political Studies*, *Electoral Studies*, and *Party Politics*.

Pekkanen Robert J. is Professor at the University of Washington (USA). He has published twelve earlier books on politics, most recently including *Party Personnel Strategies* and *The Oxford Handbook of Japanese Politics*. His work has appeared in *American Political Science Review*, *British Journal of Political Science*, *Comparative Political Studies*, and other journals.

Reed Steven R. is Professor of Modern Government at Chuo University (Emeritus). He has recently published *Political Corruption and Scandals in Japan* with Matthew M. Calrson (2018). He has published in the *British Journal of Political Science* and the *American Journal of Political Science* as well as numerous other academic journals.

Rehmert Jochen is a Post-doctoral Research Fellow at the Department of Political Science at the University of Zurich, Switzerland. His research revolves around the topics of candidate selection and coalition governments and has been published in *Comparative Political Studies*, *Political Behavior*, and the *Japanese Journal of Political Science*.

Sharpe Michael Orlando is an Associate Professor of Political Science at York College of the City University of New York and an Adjunct Research Scholar at Columbia University's Weatherhead East Asian Institute. His research interests concern the politics of migration, immigrant political incorporation, and political transnationalism in the Netherlands, Japan, and around the world. His first book, *Postcolonial Citizens and Ethnic*

Migration: The Netherlands and Japan in the Age of Globalization, was published by Palgrave MacMillan in 2014. He is currently completing his second book manuscript *The Politics of Racism and Antiracism in Japan.* His other research investigates Japan as an emerging migration state as well as the paid voluntary return of migrants and their families and implicit boundary making in liberal democracies. He is currently a member of the Association of Asian Studies Northeast Asia Council Distinguished Speakers Bureau.

Smith Daniel M. is the Gerald L. Curtis Visiting Associate Professor of Modern Japanese Politics and Foreign Policy in the Department of Political Science and School of International and Public Affairs at Columbia University. He is the author of *Dynasties and Democracy: The Inherited Incumbency Advantage in Japan* (Stanford University Press, 2018).

Steel Gill is Professor in political science at the Institute for the Liberal Arts, Doshisha University. Her research has mainly focused on public opinion and political behavior, including research on young people in Japan and Britain. Her recent publications include *What Women Want: Gender and Voting in Japan, Britain, and the United* States (2022) and the edited volume *Beyond the Gender Gap in Japan* (2019).

Thies Michael F. is an Associate Professor of Political Science, University of California, Los Angeles (USA). He is co-author (with Frances Rosenbluth) of *Japan Transformed: Political Change and Economic Restructuring* (2010) and his work on elections, parties, coalitions, and policymaking in Japan, and other advanced democracies has appeared in top political science journals and edited volumes.

Vekasi Kristin is an Associate Professor in the Department of Political Science and School of Policy and International Affairs at the University of Maine. Her research focuses on trade and investment strategies in changing geopolitical environments, economic security, and the political risk management of supply chains. She specializes in Northeast Asia, and her book *Risk Management Strategies of Japanese Companies in China* (Routledge 2019) explores how Japanese multinational corporations mitigate political risk in China.

Yanai Yuki is an Associate Professor in the School of Economics and Management at the Kochi University of Technology and Research Fellow in the Graduate School of Law at Kobe University. He conducts research on the comparative political economy of elections, redistribution, and political institutions.

ABBREVIATIONS

POLITICAL PARTIES

CDP	Constitutional Democratic Party of Japan (Rikken Minshutō)
Daichi	New Party Daichi (Shintō Daichi)
DP	Democratic Party (Minshintō)
DPJ	Democratic Party of Japan (Minshutō)
Hope	Party of Hope (Kibō no Tō)
HRP	Happiness Realization Party (Kōfuku Jitsugen Tō)
Ishin	Japan Ishin no Kai (Nippon Ishin no Kai)
JCP	Japanese Communist Party (Nihon Kyōsantō)
Kokoro	Party for Japanese Kokoro (Nippon no Kokoro)
Kōmeitō	Kōmeitō
LDP	Liberal Democratic Party (Jiyū Minshutō)
Reiwa	Reiwa Shinsengumi
SDP	Social Democratic Party (Shakai Minshutō)
TF	Tokyoites First (Tōmin Faasuto no Kai)

NEWSPAPERS

Asahi	Asahi Shinbun
Mainichi	Mainichi Shinbun
Nikkei	Nihon Keizai Shinbun
Sankei	Sankei Shinbun
Yomiuri	Yomiuri Shinbun

OTHER ABBREVIATIONS

ASEAN	Association for Southeast Asian Nations
COVAX	COVID-19 Vaccines Global Access
CPTPP	Comprehensive and Progressive Agreement for Trans-Pacific Partnership
DNLW	Dually Nominated List Winner
DPRK	Democratic People's Republic of Korea
FOIP	Free and Open Indo-Pacific
FPTP	First-Past-The-Post Electoral System
HC	House of Councillors
HR	House of Representatives
KPI	Key Performance Indicator
MP	Member of Parliament (or Diet Member, DM)
ODA	Official Development Assistance
PR	Proportional Representation
QUAD	Quadrilateral Security Dialogue
SDF	Self-Defense Forces
SEA-IP region	Southeast Asian/Indo-Pacific region
SMD	Single-Member District
TPP	Trans-Pacific Partnership
WHO	World Health Organization

LIST OF FIGURES

LIST OF TABLES

CHAPTER 1

Introduction: Japan's Coronavirus Election

Robert J. Pekkanen, *Steven R. Reed, and Daniel M. Smith*

This book analyzes the background and results of the October 31, 2021, general election for Japan's House of Representatives (HR). This is the fourth volume of *Japan Decides*, following our analyses of the general elections of 2012, 2014, and 2017 (Pekkanen et al. 2013, 2016, 2018). Each previous volume analyzed an election in which Abe Shinzō led the Liberal Democratic Party (LDP) to an overwhelming victory, in coalition with Kōmeitō. This volume also follows an LDP-Kōmeitō victory, but not an overwhelming one and one in which Abe was not the LDP leader for the first time in a decade. Perhaps more significantly, this is the

R. J. Pekkanen (✉)
Jackson School of International Studies, University of Washington, Seattle, WA, USA
e-mail: pekkanen@uw.edu

S. R. Reed
Faculty of Policy Studies, Chuo University, Tokyo, Japan

D. M. Smith
Columbia University, New York, NY, USA
e-mail: dms2323@columbia.edu

R. J. Pekkanen et al. (eds.), *Japan Decides 2021*,
https://doi.org/10.1007/978-3-031-11324-6_1

1

first (and we hope only) Japanese HR election held during the coronavirus (or COVID-19) pandemic. For that reason, this election will be of broad comparative interest to scholars trying to make sense of the political consequences of the global pandemic. We make our own arguments about how the coronavirus pandemic affected the 2021 election in Japan in the conclusion to this volume.

In the chapter that follows this Introduction, Robert J. Pekkanen and Steven R. Reed provide more background and context to the election. The chapter touches on several events on which later chapters will focus, such as the coronavirus pandemic, the reorganization and campaign of the opposition parties, the transitions in LDP leadership from Abe to Suga Yoshihide to Kishida Fumio, and the Tokyo Olympics and Paralympics, but also sets the political stage through a discussion of the 2019 House of Councillors (HC) election that preceded the fall 2021 HR election.

The third chapter, by Ko Maeda, argues that the results of the 2021 election seem superficially comparable to those of 2012, 2014, and 2017, with the LDP-Kōmeitō coalition maintaining a majority and the opposition remaining fragmented. However, the chapter also identifies important differences in this 2021 election. First, the single-member district (SMD) races are becoming more volatile. Several veteran incumbents lost seats they had held for a long time. Second, Nippon Ishin no Kai (Ishin) more than tripled its seats and further fragmented the opposition camp. Third, the largest opposition Constitutional Democratic Party (CDP) and several smaller opposition parties coordinated candidate nominations in SMDs and gained many districts previously held by the LDP. Yet, the CDP's dismal performance in the proportional representation (PR) tier of the mixed-member electoral system led to its overall loss in this election. The performance of the opposition parties is also taken up later in the volume, as the next three chapters consider political parties more specifically.

The first of these and the fourth chapter in the volume, by Kuniaki Nemoto, focuses on the LDP's internal party presidential election and candidate nomination processes to analyze how the party prepared to stay in power before the 2021 election. With the new presidential election process, the party was able to replace an unpopular leader (Suga) just before the election, although it did not choose the most popular contender (instead choosing Kishida). Using various tools at the party's disposal, such as internal polls and the PR tier, the LDP tried to minimize the fragmentation of the conservative vote, although ultimately it took place in 12 districts and the LDP lost to the opposition in five of them. Overall, the LDP was able to avoid a major loss, even though it was not able to increase its seats.

In Chapter 5, Robert J. Pekkanen and Steven R. Reed analyze the opposition. They trace the evolution of the opposition parties from their situation in late 2017 following the 2017 election. At that time, the major opposition parties included the Party of Hope as the third largest party after the collapse of the Democratic Party of Japan (DPJ), but by the 2021 election, that party effectively no longer existed. The creation and destruction of the persistently fragmented opposition is a major theme in Japanese politics and of this chapter. The chapter also examines the coordination among four parties on the left—the CDP, Japanese Communist Party (JCP), Social Democratic Party (SDP), and Reiwa Shinsengumi—which it argues was successful. Finally, the authors speculate on the future of the opposition in Japan.

The sixth chapter returns to the governing coalition, this time examining Kōmeitō. Axel Klein and Levi McLaughlin argue that, in October 2021, Kōmeitō solidified its importance as a coalition partner to the LDP and its influential place within the national government. The chapter details how the party navigated its election campaign between contrasting demands from the LDP and members of Sōka Gakkai, the lay Buddhist organization that founded Kōmeitō in 1964 and remains the party's, and Japan's, most potent vote-gathering bloc. It highlights the ways through which Kōmeitō promoted social welfare initiatives in response to the COVID-19 pandemic, how it mitigated the rise of Ishin in western Japan, and how its historic links to the People's Republic of China may grow in importance as tensions rise in the region. The chapter also considers the impact of scandals among its members, an overall trajectory of lowered vote counts, and how changes underway within Sōka Gakkai may shape Kōmeitō's future and affect LDP electioneering and policymaking.

Following these three introductory chapters and the three focusing on the main set of political parties, the volume proceeds with five chapters that consider contemporary party politics in Japan from different angles: Abe's legacy, candidate selection, generational change in leadership, party switching, and ministerial selection.

The first of these is written by Tobias Harris and focuses on the legacy of one of Japan's most dominant political figures, Abe Shinzō. After resigning as prime minister and leader of the LDP in September 2020, it was unclear what role Abe would play in Japanese politics. However, as the LDP approached another leadership election in 2021—and as the general election approached—Abe returned to prominence as a king-maker, using his media presence and his clout within the LDP to influence first the party's presidential election and then the policy choices of the new government of Prime Minister Kishida. This chapter describes the sources of Abe's power after leaving the premiership and details the ways in which he used his power to influence the government's agenda during the first months of Kishida's government.

Chapter 8, authored by Jochen Rehmert, examines candidate selection. The 2021 general election saw one of the highest levels of legislative turnover in recent elections. Yet, this was not due to the coordination of candidates by parties of the progressive opposition, but rather to the nomination practices and outcomes in the LDP and Kōmeitō. While the LDP had to replace several resigning incumbents and remove several others who were tainted by scandals, Kōmeitō's internal selection rules forced a partial rejuvenation of its roster. In addition, both the governing parties and the opposition saw conflicts over nominations within their own ranks. The LDP was especially plagued by intraparty conflicts over nominations after several incumbents from other conservative parties joined the party prior to the election. Socio-demographically, candidates remain overwhelmingly male and close to retirement age.

In Chapter 9, Charles McClean examines generational change and continuity in Japan's political leadership. Young people are underrepresented in most political institutions, and Japan's House of Representatives is no exception. While a few young challengers managed to capture national headlines by defeating much older incumbents, the 2021 election otherwise featured the fewest candidates and elected members of parliament (MPs) under 40 years old in decades. McClean explores the causes and consequences of this decline in young people running for office. He finds that candidates under 40 were significantly more likely than older candidates to say that they would prioritize education, childcare, and employment if elected; were more supportive of strengthening Japan's defense capabilities; and were more positive toward enacting bills to recognize same-sex marriage and promote LGBT awareness. These patterns suggest that reforms aimed at increasing the number of young legislators could have significant consequences for the policies that get debated and ultimately implemented by the parliament.

In the tenth chapter, Jordan Hamzawi turns his lens on the phenomenon of party switching in Japan. In the two decades since electoral reform, Japan's party system has been in constant flux. After a slow build toward a predominantly two-party system, politics are currently dominated by the LDP and its coalition partner Kōmeitō, with an ever-changing roster of opposition parties vying for the place of challenger. The 2021 election continued the recent state of political (non)competition as opposition parties were unable to make a dent in the LDP's sizeable majority. While there are numerous contributing factors that explain Japan's anemic party competition, Hamzawi focuses on how candidates navigate their partisan affiliation. He finds that candidates, particularly candidates from the opposition, follow a pattern of switching from weak parties to new parties, preferring the potential of a new party over the issues with existing ones. Instead of slowly building strength with a roster of seasoned candidates, Japan's opposition parties constantly collapse in on themselves because of candidate choices.

In the final chapter on party politics, Hiroki Kubo examines how and why ministers are selected in Japanese cabinets under the three most recent prime ministers. Kubo analyzes the outcomes of cabinet portfolio allocation, comparing LDP faction seat shares and the percentage of cabinet portfolios each secured in the six cabinets formed since 2017. His analysis reveals that: First, there is overall proportionality between faction seat shares andcabinet portfolios; second, there is nevertheless a relative advantage enjoyed by the prime minister's faction and the large main factions; and third, independent LDP members are not disadvantaged in portfolio allocation. In terms of seniority, relatively young MPs have been included in the cabinet. In addition, the Kishida cabinet features three female MPs, accounting for 15% of cabinet members. We return to the broader issue of women's representation in Japan later in the volume.

After these chapters on party politics, we turn to the campaign for the next four chapters—on public opinion with a focus on COVID-19, social media, youth turnout, and how COVID-19 affected the election results.

Chapter 12 is authored by Yukio Maeda and investigates public opinion. The 2021 election results surprised journalists and pollsters in Japan. This chapter explains why the LDP outperformed expectations by examining media polls and coverage of three prime ministers from 2017 to 2021. Abe struggled to respond to the novel coronavirus while also dealing with conventional corruption allegations. His successor, Suga, initially received high approval ratings as people expected him to manage the pandemic better than Abe. However, these expectations became a liability when COVID-19 cases surged while Japan was hosting the

Summer Olympics. When Kishida succeeded Suga, COVID-19 cases were rapidly declining, and the LDP subsequently won a victory in the 2021 election. Underestimating the impact of the public's shifting views of the government's pandemic response may account for much of the gap between election predictions and actual results.

Robert A. Fahey in Chapter 13 examines social media and the election campaign. Since the use of social media in election campaigns was made legal in 2013, platforms such as Twitter and Facebook have been widely adopted by candidates in Japan's elections. This chapter examines how social media platforms were used in the 2021 election, looking at which candidates and parties chose to engage most heavily in online campaigning, and at the issues, policies, and narratives which the various parties' candidates focused on in their social media messaging. LDP candidates focused on the government's track record and the success of the COVID-19 vaccination program, while mainstream opposition candidates' online messaging largely focused on pocketbook and family issues. The chapter concludes with an analysis of the Twitter follower networks of both candidates and major media organizations, providing insight into the extent of affective polarization on social media during the 2021 election period.

In Chapter 14, Gill Steel looks at youth turnout in the election, showing that the various mobilization efforts had very little effect on young people's participation. She claims that the LDP has depressed young people's engagement with politics in the various ways the party (and through it, the state) depoliticizes politics. As part of this governing strategy of depoliticization, the state has limited citizens' opportunities for participation and has cultivated, or mandated, an atmosphere of depoliticization that discourages citizen interest and engagement. The state does so through depoliticizing schools, broadcasting, restricting youth political activities, campaigning, and curtailing NPOs (nonprofit organizations). Depoliticization means that young people do not receive political information and cues from elites that impart a sense of the excitement of politics or the legitimacy of political conflict through mainstream channels.

Chapter 15 again returns to a theme of this volume, the influence of the coronavirus pandemic on the election. Here, Michael F. Thies and Yuki Yanai examine the impact of COVID-19 on voting behavior. When the pandemic began, Japan's parliamentary term had passed its halfway point; the next general election was due before late autumn 2021. An autumn 2020 election seemed likely, to slipstream in the wake of the Tokyo Summer Olympics. When COVID-19 forced a year's postponement of the Games, the government put off the election as well, gambling for good news before the term ran out. Voters were largely dissatisfied with the government's pandemic response, and many opposed staging the Olympics at all. In the event, no post-Olympics boost materialized. But dramatic improvements in COVID-19 outcomes in the few weeks between the election announcement and voting day led most voters to focus on the economy instead, just in time for the gamble to pay off. Nonetheless, the authors do find that urban prefectures with higher death rates were less likely to support the ruling LDP, and interestingly, more likely to support upstart Ishin.

After these four chapters on the campaign, we turn to a deeper analysis of the issues framing the election—from coronavirus policy to foreign policy to the Olympics. These ten chapters dig into the issues that dominated Japanese politics in the years, months, and weeks leading up to the vote, in order to provide a rich understanding of the background context of the 2021 election.

The first of these chapters, by Phillip Y. Lipscy, provides a deep analysis of Japan's COVID-19 response policy. What features of Japan's COVID-19 response stand out, and how are they best explained? Lipscy argues that the Abe model of governance critically shaped both the strengths and weaknesses of the Japan model of COVID-19 response. Japanese officials have often promoted the Japan model as exemplary of how to manage the pandemic without sacrificing fundamental democratic values and civil liberties. However, key features of the model—such as an emphasis on macroeconomic growth, avoidance of harsh lockdowns, and making scientific experts the public face of the response—were compatible with how former Prime Minister Abe governed Japan throughout his tenure. The chapter also places Japan's COVID-19 response in comparative, cross-national context: Relative to other G7 countries, Japan stands out for relatively low cases and deaths per capita, but the numbers must be interpreted with caution and are largely in line with those of regional peers. The chapter concludes with an early assessment of the COVID-19 response under the first six months of Prime Minister Kishida.

In Chapter 17, Kenya Amano and Saori N. Katada take on the central questions of macroeconomic policy. Highly accommodative monetary policy during nine years of Abenomics allowed fiscal expansion to become the center of the Japanese government's COVID-19 stimulus and the further economic measures were the primary issue facing the 2021 election. Under monetary constraints, the economic policy choice among Japan's conventional growth strategy, distribution, and fiscal discipline creates a trilemma, whereby the government can pursue only two of these three goals. In this election, the LDP-Kōmeitō coalition managed to straddle between distribution and growth strategy, while exploiting the policy space for the opposition parties. Although the coalition maintained its electoral majority, the inroads made by Ishin, Reiwa, and the Democratic Party for the People (DPP) whose campaigns neglected fiscal discipline in favor of both growth and distribution foreshadows the challenge against the Japanese government's future fiscal health.

In Chapter 18, Yeon Ju Lee investigates income inequality and the election. The chapter examines how income inequality began to receive attention from politicians and voters before the 2021 election. While income inequality has dominated the political agenda in numerous countries around the world, it has not been a politically salient issue in Japan even though it has been increasing since the 1980s. However, income inequality became politically visible to voters and politicians as the COVID-19 pandemic further strained the already stagnant economy, having a direct impact on people, especially those who were less well off. Both ruling and opposition parties responded to the public dissatisfaction by introducing measures to address income inequality in their party platforms, including Prime Minister Kishida's vision of "New Capitalism" to promote simultaneous growth and distribution.

In Chapter 19, Yesola Kweon furthers the investigation of a critical topic: women's representation. This chapter examines women's representation in Japanese politics and the Japanese economy. In the economic realm, Womenomics implemented under the Abe regime made several meaningful improvements in women's labor participation, especially for those who have children. However, little progress was made in terms of the gender wage gap and gender disparities in high-quality job employment. The COVID-19 pandemic also had a disproportionate impact on women, parents, and those with non-regular jobs. This, in turn, led to lower trust and confidence in the government and its policy responses to the pandemic. The latter half of the chapter considers gender representation in politics. The 2021 election saw a decrease in the number of women representatives. As with previous elections, the ruling LDP had the smallest share of female candidates and elected women legislators.

The chapter examines both supply-side and demand-side factors in order to explain the lagging representation of women in Japanese politics.

In the next chapter, Michael Sharpe analyzes the issue of Black Lives Matter (BLM) as well as its broader context in Japan. Although BLM was more in the background of Japan's 2021 election, compared to the 2020 election in the United States, it brought important issues of race and racism into the national conversation. The chapter argues that BLM in Japan follows a long pattern of ambivalence around race as the world's first non-white modern power. BLM in Japan has been successful in highlighting the notions and attitudes that perpetuate antiblack racism but has fallen short in joining concerted action among newer and older excluded groups under an antiracist banner. Sharpe discusses BLM Japan's immediate impact, Japan's racial gymnastics, the complexities of black admiration and antiblack racism, and finally what BLM tells us about race, racism, and coalition building possibilities. As Japan opens to immigration, the realities of old and new racisms will increasingly take center stage, with antiracist collective action and policy innovations becoming critical to Japan's future development as a liberal democracy.

Another crucial issue for Japanese democracy is constitutional revision. In Chapter 21, Kenneth McElwain explores the surprisingly muted role that constitutional revision played in the 2021 election. While former Prime Minister Abe had evinced a personal commitment to amending the constitution during his tenure, his initiatives stalled due to disagreements between the LDP and its coalition partner, Kōmeitō, and conflicting priorities among LDP backbenchers. The COVID-19 pandemic further limited opportunities for serious deliberation of constitutional change, and Abe's resignation left the issue with no cheerleader to push it onto the legislative agenda. Given the lower priority placed on constitutional issues by Abe's successors, opposition parties also saw less reason to make protection of the constitution a centerpiece of their election manifestos. As a result, for the first time since the 2012 election, constitutional change became an afterthought in the campaign, with less than 10% of voters seeing it as a policy priority.

Chapter 22 widens the lens to the international dimension of COVID-19. Kerstin Lukner asks: Can we identify an explicit "COVID-19 foreign policy" in Japan, despite the absence of such an issue as a campaign topic in the 2021 general election? The chapter scrutinizes the way Tokyo has been coping with the COVID-19 crisis at the bilateral, regional, and multilateral levels as well as the rationales behind its responses. Lukner argues that apart from backing the fight against the pandemic specifically in its own neighborhood, Japan's actions have been primarily guided by its strategic competition with China—that is, the intention to increase its regional influence by means of COVID-19-related health diplomacy.

In Chapter 23, Michael Green investigates broad questions of Japan's foreign policy. The 2021 election came at a time of major activism in Japanese foreign and security policy but no candidate for the leadership of the ruling LDP, nor the leaders of the major opposition parties, challenged the broad strategic trajectory set by former Prime Minister Abe. Voters appeared to understand that Abe's focus on strengthening the US-Japan alliance, deepening the US-Japan-India-Australia "Quad," investing in infrastructure and resilience in developing Asia, and increasing deterrence capabilities vis-à-vis China together constituted the necessary elements of a strategy to secure Japanese interests at a time of growing geopolitical friction. Yet while there was no debate about new directions in national security, the election debates did foreshadow some of the major decisions the Kishida government will face in the coming years, from technology decoupling to development of strike capability for the Self-Defense Forces.

In the next chapter, Kristin Vekasi focuses on the role of China in Japan's election. In 2021, parties across the political spectrum were overtly critical toward China's human rights record, foreign policy, policy toward Taiwan, and especially its territorial posture in the East China Sea. Her analysis of candidate statements and party manifestos finds few voices within the electorate or among political candidates arguing for deeper engagement or a conciliatory policy toward China. Even economic policy, typically a stabilizing element of the relationship, is increasingly reflecting a more securitized orientation, as reflected in Japan's proposed Economic Security Bill and ministerial-level economic security position. Vekasi argues that the LDP's electoral victory may presage a more hawkish China policy and increased defense spending. However, this prediction must be tempered with the moderating influence of the LDP's long-time coalition partner, Kōmeitō, which alone put forward a more positive vision for the future of Japan–China relations.

The Tokyo Olympics of 2020 (held in summer 2021) made headlines for years in Japan and across the world. In Chapter 25, David Leheny analyzes the event. Even before the COVID-19 pandemic made their staging an unprecedented challenge, the 2020 Summer Olympics and Paralympics had already been politically controversial, with initial public skepticism giving way to more widespread enthusiasm, though dotted with opposition given the wastefulness and corruption associated with recent Games. The long delay in the Games, the public health risks associated with even spectator-less events, a series of astonishingly embarrassing gaffes and revelations, and the collapse of projected economic benefits all contributed to the possibility that they would be costly to the ruling LDP in the 2021 election. Leheny describes the politics surrounding the Games and their role in the 2021 election, particularly the challenges associated with turning a major, controversial news story into a winning issue for either the ruling parties or the opposition.

After these twenty-five chapters analyzing the election from a variety of angles, the three editors of this book contribute a short overview of the election. In this, they argue that the coronavirus pandemic profoundly shaped the 2021 election by framing it as a competency election. This probably hurt the CDP, but Ishin benefited as "competent" due to its perception of regional success. The timing of the successful vaccine rollout probably also influenced the way the pandemic affected the vote, this time benefiting the LDP which might not have fared as well had the election been held before the vaccine arrived.

References

Pekkanen, Robert J., Steven R. Reed, and Ethan Scheiner (eds.). 2013. *Japan Decides 2012: The Japanese General Election*. Palgrave Macmillan.

Pekkanen, Robert J., Steven R. Reed, and Ethan Scheiner (eds.). 2016. *Japan Decides 2014: The Japanese General Election*. Palgrave Macmillan.

Pekkanen, Robert J., Steven R. Reed, Ethan Scheiner and Daniel M. Smith (eds.). 2018. *Japan Decides 2017: The Japanese General Election*. Palgrave Macmillan.

CHAPTER 2

Japanese Politics Between 2017 and 2021

Robert J. Pekkanen ⓘ *and Steven R. Reed*

It was four long years from Japan's October 22, 2017, election to its October 31, 2021, election. It is relatively rare for the House of Representatives to reach its full term (most recently in 2009 during the global financial crisis), but the circumstances were clearly exceptional with a worldwide pandemic disrupting societies and economies in a perhaps unprecedented fashion (see Lipscy 2022; Lukner 2022; Amano and Katada 2022; Thies and Yanai 2022). Even though its effects were really felt on starting in 2020, the coronavirus or COVID-19 pandemic is the dominant feature of the 4 years from 2017 to 2021. Other major events occurred in this period for Japan, notably the Tokyo Olympics (postponed to 2021 from 2020 by the pandemic; see Leheny 2022); the accession of a new emperor (Reiwa) in 2019; and, the "Trump shocks" to Japan's foreign policy (see Green 2022). In this chapter, we focus on some more

R. J. Pekkanen (✉)
Jackson School of International Studies, University of Washington, Seattle, WA, USA
e-mail: pekkanen@uw.edu

S. R. Reed
Faculty of Policy Studies, Chuo University, Tokyo, Japan

© The Author(s), under exclusive license to Springer Nature Switzerland AG 2023
R. J. Pekkanen et al. (eds.), *Japan Decides 2021*,
https://doi.org/10.1007/978-3-031-11324-6_2

explicitly party politics aspects of these developments. We discuss the 2019 House of Councillors election results; the rise of the Constitutional Democratic Party (CDP) as the main opposition party (see also Pekkanen and Reed 2018, 2022); and Liberal Democratic Party (LDP) Prime Minister Abe Shinzo and his successors (see also Harris 2022; Nemoto, 2022). We also note for the record the accession of Emperor Reiwa on May 1, 2019 (which is not discussed elsewhere in this volume) succeeding his father, the Heisei Emperor after the latter's abdication.

2019 HOUSE OF COUNCILLORS RESULTS

After the October 22, 2017, House of Representatives general election, PM Abe was riding high (see Pekkanen et al. 2018 for analysis). His LDP had taken a supermajority of 291 seats in a decisive rout. The opposition was in disarray, with the main opposition party, the Democratic Party of Japan (DPJ) splintering into a more liberal CDP and more conservative Party of Hope (Hope), with a few legislators retaining the DPJ label (Pekkanen and Reed 2018). Ishin continued as a small conservative opposition party, and Komeito continued as the junior partner in the coalition with the LDP (see Klein and McLaughlin 2018). Support for Abe in the polls was high and he had already compiled a track record that would make him arguably the most influential postwar Prime Minister. His first major political test following the 2017 election came in 2019, with the regular summer election for the House of Councillors . The LDP won the July 21, 2019, HC election, marking the last in a string of six Abe electoral victories (HR 2012 , 2014 , 2017; HC 2013 , 2016, 2019), although of course Kishida would continue the run in 2021 (HR) (and the LDP won the 2010 HC election). These 2019 HC electoral results led one respected observer to detect a return to one-party dominance (Jain 2020).

The HC uses a different electoral system than the HR to elect its HC members. Elections are regularly held every three years for half of the chamber (124 in 2019), with the other half being elected three years later. Besides the fixed and staggered timing for elections, the HC differs from the HR in that the HC combines a prefectural tier (usually SNTV MMD) and an open-list PR tier, where voters can vote for a party or a candidate (and not a SMD tier and closed list PR bloc tier). District magnitude in the prefectural tier varies from 1 to 6 (Tokyo is the only 6, and there are two single seats representing two prefectures each) for 74 total members in 45 districts. Table 2.1 provides the seat outcomes in the HC election for each party. In the end, the LDP won 57 of the 124 seats being contested, putting its overall total in the HC at 113. This meant its seat total was slightly down as a result of the election, but the LDP would still control the chamber, presaging the results of the 2021 election. With Komeito pulling in 28 seats, the coalition had a solid majority in the chamber. The Party of Hope had been extinguished, losing its only seat. The CDP was the second largest party at 32 seats, up 8 from its pre-election total. In several ways, the 2019 HC election was consistent with the results of the 2021 election.

Japan's HC open-list proportional representation (OLPR) feature, introduced in 2001, allows voters to choose not only a party but also a candidate (Reed 2021). Voters cast a single vote. They may cast it either for a party or for a candidate. All candidates must be on a party list. The number of seats allocated to a party is determined by the sum of the party vote and the vote for all of the candidates on its list. Seats won by the party are then allocated to candidates in the order of the number of personal votes they received. The key to winning a seat is, first and foremost, to get nominated by a large party. Few voters go to the trouble of writing a candidate's name on the ballot and simply vote for a party. Between 2001 and 2016, the average percentage of voters who went to the trouble to vote for a candidate was 28%.

Winning candidates are often sponsored by large interest groups. A "sponsored" candidate is one chosen by the interest group. The group asks a party to nominate their candidate but takes responsibility for electing her. Parties, of course, are delighted to nominate a candidate with a high probability of victory based on voters who might not even support the party otherwise. The primary support groups for both CDP

Table 2.1 Seats in HC 2019 election by party

	LDP	CDP	Komeito	DPP	Ishin	JCP	Hope	Other	Total
Pre-election	123	24	25	23	13	14	1	15	245
After 2019 election	113	32	28	21	16	13	0	22	245
District	38	9	7	3	5	3	0	9	74
PR	19	8	7	3	5	4	0	3	50

Source Ministry of Internal Affairs and Communications, Japan

and DPP are labor unions. When the Democrats split, unions were forced to choose which party they would ask to nominate their candidate. The choices they made recreated the split between the two socialist parties and labor federations of the era that preceded the 1994 reforms.

Table 2.2 shows the votes and seats won by the parties in the PR tier in 2019. The CDP won 7,917,719 votes and eight seats in the PR tier. Unions sponsored five candidates for the CDP and all won seats. Their votes totaled 689,719 providing 8.9% of the party's total vote but 47.3% of its candidate votes. The DPP won 3,481,053 votes and three seats, both less than half of the CDP totals. The contrast is even greater if one examines the number of votes received by the party: The CDP received almost three times the DPP vote. Unions sponsored five of candidates for the DPP and those candidates won all three of the seats available but two of their union candidates failed to secure seats. Union sponsored candidates delivered 1,101,812 votes to the DPP, 1.7 times more than union sponsored candidates provided the CDP. The religious group *Risshō Kōseikai* (RK), which had been supporting the Democrats since the 2000 election, also sponsored a candidate and had him nominated by the DPP winning 143,467 votes but no seat. The union sponsored candidates provide 31.7% of the DPP's total vote and 84.3% of its candidate vote. Including RK, sponsored candidates provided 34.2% of the DPP's total vote and 91.1% of its candidate vote.

The threshold of victory for candidates running on the CDP ticket was 73,787 while that for the DPP was 256,928. Toshiba and Japanese Association of Metal, Machinery and Manufacturing Workers (JAM) candidates failed to win a seat because the DPP did not command enough support in the general public and both would have won if they had run for the CDP. The difference is due to the percentage of CDP and DPP voters who voted for the party instead of the candidate, 84.6% for the CDP and

Table 2.2 PR seats and votes by party in the House of Councillors 2019 election

	LDP	CDP	Komeito	DPP	Ishin	JCP
PR seats	19	8	7	3	5	4
PR share	35.4%	15.8%	13.1%	7%	9.8%	9%
PR votes	17,712,373	7,917,719	6,536,336	3,481,053	4,907,844	4,483,411

Source Ministry of Internal Affairs and Communications, Japan

Table 2.3
Organization-sponsored
candidates in the HC
2019 election

Organization	Votes	Party
UA Zensen	260,324	DPP
JAW	258,507	DPP
Electrical power workers	256,928	DPP
Toshiba	182,586	DPP (defeated)
Jichiro	157,848	CDP
JTU	148,309	CDP
JPGU	144,751	CDP
NTT	143,472	CDP
JAM	143,472	DPP (defeated)
Private RR	104,339	CDP

Source Authors' analysis

62.5% for the DPP. The DPP attracted few party votes and depended heavily on the candidate votes. Table 2.3 shows the votes received by candidates sponsored by organizations in the HC 2019 election.

The CDP retained more of the 2016 Democratic vote than the DPP. The DPP did better in rural than urban municipalities. Both parties did better in those municipalities that experienced less of a decline in turnout (95% of municipalities experienced a drop in turnout). Having a candidate running in the prefecture increases the vote of both parties as does having an incumbent in either house of the Diet. The presence of a Communist candidate in the prefecture reduces the DPP but not the CDP vote. The Liberal vote in 2016 increases the CDP vote but not the DPP vote despite the fact that Ozawa Ichirō, the Liberal leader, chose to join the DPP. The Liberals appear to follow their policy preferences and not their leader. Until Ozawa's decision, he and the party had been against nuclear power plants and in favor of cooperating with the JCP.

HOPE AND AFTER: THE OPPOSITION

The chapter on the Opposition covers this ground in more detail (Pekkanen and Reed 2022), but the outlines are important for setting the stage for this election volume. In the run-up to the 2017 election, the Democratic Party of Japan (DPJ), reconstituted as the Democratic Party (Minshintō) imploded in spectacular fashion, marking the effective demise of the second most successful party in Japanese political history (Pekkanen and Reed 2018). Lawmakers streamed from the party into the

Party of Hope, led by insurgent Tokyo Governor Koike Yuriko. On the heels of a decisive victory in the Tokyo Metropolitan Assembly as Tokyoites First (Tomin Faasuto), Koike turned her local party national as the Party of Hope. Fear was a better description for the emotions that this transformation engendered in both the DPJ and the LDP.

The DPJ suffered a string of defections to Hope, and the party leader Maehara Seiji seemed ready to dissolve the party in order to be absorbed by Hope. However, more progressive DPJ legislators balked at joining the Party of Hope—largely because of a (perceived or real) litmus test on security issues) (Pekkanen and Reed 2018, p. 87) Instead, led by Edano Yukio, they formed the Constitutional Democratic Party of Japan. In the 2017 election, the CDP placed second and Hope placed third. The failure of Hope and the relative success of the CDP (Pekkanen and Reed 2018, pp. 86–89) left the conservative opposition in disarray. After the dust settled, some of Hope's candidates defected to the CDP, many formed a new conservative opposition party they called the DPP, five candidates to the right of the LDP who had been affiliated with Kokoro (previously the Party for Future Generations) changed their name yet again, this time retaining Koike's label, Hope, and a few chose no party at all. DPP support in the polls was zero. In November 2020, DPP leader Tamaki Yuichiro signaled that the DPP was no longer interested in cooperating with the other opposition parties by using his question time and not mentioning the Science Council scandal (a scandal embroiling PM Suga, who didn't appoint six professors to the advisory council, because, it was alleged, of their political views). He also began talks with Ishin and the LDP on constitutional revision. Heading into the 2021 election, the leading opposition party was clearly the CDP with 110 seats, a progressive alternative to the LDP. The Japanese Communist Party led the other smaller opposition parties, but held only a dozen seats. Ishin held 11 and the DPP 8.

ABE AND AFTER: 2020 RESIGNATION AND REPLACEMENTS

The Abe administration from the 2012 elections through the 2014 and 2017 elections delivered consecutive landslide victories. Abe became the most powerful prime minister in Japan's postwar history (see Lipscy and Hoshi 2021; Harris 2020). He also became its longest serving prime minister, before his eventual resignation in September 2022. The Abe administration maintained relatively high cabinet support rates between elections and successfully enacted bold policy initiatives, some of which had been sitting on the LDP's back burner since the 1960s. Each of our three previous volumes documented and analyzed these successes (Pekkanen et al. 2013, 2015, 2018). During this period, Abe can lay claim to being the most successful LDP prime minister in history.

After 2017, however, Abe's support rates dropped and he announced he would resign in August 2020 for health reasons much like he had in 2007. He was replaced in September 2020 by Suga Yoshihide who began with high expectations reflected in his cabinet support rates which soon evaporated, much like Abe's first term and both of the LDP prime ministers who succeeded him (Fukuda Yasuo and Aso Taro). Like Koizumi Junichiro in 2005, Abe in 2020 proved to be a hard act to follow. Suga's popularity dropped (Maeda 2022) and he would be out in a year—very much like Fukuda Yasuo after he succeeded Abe in 2007–2008. Suga soon demonstrated continuity with the Abe administration, declaring his commitment to revising the constitution, his support continued to be based on the same reasons, i.e., there is no alternative, continuing to stonewall any questions about scandals even when most of the public did not believe he had explained properly, and soon had a new scandal of his own, the Science Council of Japan scandal, very much in the same mold as Abe's scandals. The LDP wanted to hold an election in 2020, while Suga had the highest support rates he was ever likely to see. However, Komeito had just emerged from an internal lockdown to protect their members from COVID-19 and to protect Soka Gakkai from charges of spreading COVID-19 (Klein and McLaughlin 2022). Suga agreed to put COVID-19 first and wait until 2021. As a result, he would not be PM when the election was held (see Nemoto 2022).

In December 2020, Suga admitted defeat and canceled his Go To Travel (subsidized domestic travel and accommodations to promote domestic tourism) over the holidays. On the same day, an NHK poll showed a drop in cabinet support of 14 points and a 17 point increase in non-support. A Yomiuri poll showed a 29 point drop in support rates, tying Aso for the worst record. They also noted one difference between Aso and Suga: The LDP led the DPJ in support 37% to 23% but the LDP lead the CDP by 47% to 4%. There still is no alternative. One difference: When Abe was unpopular, the problem was trust in Abe himself (Maeda and Reed). When Suga's approval fell, the reason given for non-support was policy, almost certainly referring to COVID.

In April 2021, Suga ordered the dumping of diluted but contaminated water from the Fukushima nuclear power plant. Perhaps even worse for him, there were three by-elections in April 2021 all won by the opposition. Losing in Nagano was normal but the other two losses were responses to corruption scandals. In Hokkaido, the incumbent had resigned and the LDP did not field a candidate. In Hiroshima, the incumbents had been convicted of election law violations and, though the LDP fielded a candidate, neither local LDP assembly members nor prominent LDP leaders were able to participate because they had been implicated as well. In both the latter cases, turnout dropped drastically because the LDP was unable to mobilize its supporters. These by-elections set off some warning bells in the LDP.

Then, in July 2021, The LDP gained seats but performed well under expectations in the Tokyo Prefectural Assembly election. This was the same election in 2017 in which the LDP was drubbed by Tokyoites First. The only good news for the LDP was that Komeito shifted their support from Tokyoites First to the LDP. CDP-JCP cooperation also worked very well. The CDP almost doubled its seats.

A third electoral warning bell rang in August 2021 for the LDP when the candidate that received Suga's full support lost the Yokohama mayoral election finishing far behind the candidate supported by the CDP and JCP. The LDP did surveys of each district for a general election that indicated that the party would win 240 seats, a loss of 40 but still a majority with Kōmeitō. However, it also found that many LDP candidates were on the cusp of losing. Under these circumstances, Suga announced his resignation and the search was on for his replacement.

On September 29, 2021, the LDP held its party presidential election (Nemoto 2022). The leading candidates were Kishida Fumio (who won), Kōno Tarō (who was most popular with the public), Takaichi Sanae (who had Abe's backing and a sterling hawk's profile), and Noda Seiko. Ishiba Shigeru had declined to run. Kishida Fumio won the election and was duly also elected as Japan's Prime Minister. However, he saw only a modest bump in support—hardly a huge honeymoon period (Maeda 2022). This set the stage for the election of October 31, 2021, analyzed in this volume.

BIBLIOGRAPHY

Amano, Kenya, and Saori Katada. 2022. "Economic Policy Trilemma: Macroeconomic Politics in the 2021 Election." In Robert J. Pekkanen, Steven R. Reed, Daniel M. Smith (eds.), *Japan Decides 2021: The Japanese General Election.* New York: Palgrave Macmillan.

Green, Michael. 2022. "Foreign Policy and Defense Issues in Japan's 2021 Election." In Robert J. Pekkanen, Steven R. Reed, and Daniel M. Smith (eds.), *Japan Decides 2021: The Japanese General Election.* New York: Palgrave Macmillan.

Harris, Tobias. 2020. *The Iconoclast.* Hurst: New York.

Harris, Tobias. 2022. "Abe's Legacy." In Robert J. Pekkanen, Steven R. Reed, and Daniel M. Smith (eds.), *Japan Decides 2021: The Japanese General Election.* New York: Palgrave Macmillan.

Jain, Purnendra. 2020. "Japan's 2019 Upper House Election: Solidifying Abe, the LDP and Return to a One-Party Dominant Political System." *Asian Journal of Comparative Politics* 5 (1): 23–37.

Klein, Axel, and Levi McLaughlin. 2018. "Komeito 2017: New Complications." In Robert J. Pekkanen, Steven R. Reed, Ethan Scheiner, and Daniel M. Smith (eds.), *Japan Decides 2017: The Japanese General Election.* New York: Palgrave Macmillan.

Klein, Axel, and Levi McLaughlin. 2022. "Kōmeitō in 2021: Strategizing Between the LDP and Sōka Gakkai." In Robert J. Pekkanen, Steven R. Reed, and Daniel M. Smith (eds.), *Japan Decides 2021: The Japanese General Election.* New York: Palgrave Macmillan.

Leheny, David. 2022. "The Olympics in the 2021 Election." In Robert J. Pekkanen, Steven R. Reed and Daniel M. Smith (eds.), *Japan Decides 2021.* New York: Palgrave Macmillan.

Lipscy, Phillip Y., and Takeo Hoshi (eds.). 2021. *The Political Economy of the Abe Government and Abenomics Reform.* New York and London: Cambridge University Press.

Lipscy, Phillip Y. 2022. "Japan's Response to the COVID-19 Pandemic." In Robert J. Pekkanen, Steven R. Reed, and Daniel M. Smith (eds.), *Japan Decides 2021: The Japanese General Election.* New York: Palgrave Macmillan.

Lukner, Kerstin. 2022. "Covid-19: The International Dimension." In Robert J. Pekkanen, Steven R. Reed, and Daniel M. Smith (eds.), *Japan Decides 2021: The Japanese General Election.* New York: Palgrave Macmillan.

Maeda, Yukio., and Reed, Steven R. 2021. "The LDP under Abe." In Takeo Hoshi & Phillip Lipscy (eds.), *The Political Economy of the Abe Government and Abenomics Reforms,* 87–108. Cambridge: Cambridge University Press. https://doi.org/10.1017/9781108921145.004

Maeda, Yukio. 2022. "Public Opinion and COVID-19." In Robert J. Pekkanen, Steven R. Reed, and Daniel M. Smith (eds.), *Japan Decides 2021: The Japanese General Election*. New York: Palgrave Macmillan.

Nemoto, Kuniaki. 2022. "How the Liberal Democratic Party Avoided a Loss in 2021." In Robert J. Pekkanen, Steven R. Reed, and Daniel M. Smith (eds.), *Japan Decides 2021: The Japanese General Election*. New York: Palgrave Macmillan.

Pekkanen, Robert. J., and Steven R. Reed. 2018. "The Opposition: From Third Party Back to Third Force." In Robert J. Pekkanen, Steven R. Reed, Ethan Scheiner, and Daniel M. Smith (eds.), *Japan Decides 2017: The Japanese General Election*. New York: Palgrave Macmillan.

Pekkanen, Robert J., and Steven R. Reed. 2022. "The Opposition in 2021: A Second Party and a Third Force." In Robert J. Pekkanen, Steven R. Reed, Daniel M. Smith (eds.), *Japan Decides 2021: The Japanese General Election*. New York: Palgrave Macmillan.

Pekkanen, Robert J., Steven R. Reed, and Ethan Scheiner (eds.). 2013. *Japan Decides 2012: The Japanese General Election*. New York: Palgrave Macmillan.

Pekkanen, Robert J., Steven R. Reed, and Ethan Scheiner (eds.). 2015. *Japan Decides 2014: The Japanese General Election*. New York: Palgrave Macmillan.

Pekkanen, Robert J., Steven R. Reed, Ethan Scheiner, and Daniel M. Smith (eds.). 2018. *Japan Decides 2017: The Japanese General Election*. New York: Palgrave Macmillan.

Reed, Steven R. 2021. "Japanese Electoral Systems Since 1947." In Robert J. Pekkanen and Saadia M. Pekkanen (eds.), *The Oxford Handbook of Japanese Politics*. New York: Oxford University Press.

Thies, Michael F., and Yuki Yanai. 2022. "Did COVID-19 Impact Japan's 2021 General Election?" In Robert J. Pekkanen, Steven R. Reed, Daniel M. Smith (eds.), *Japan Decides 2021: The Japanese General Election*. New York: Palgrave Macmillan.

CHAPTER 3

The 2021 Election Results: Continuity and Change

Ko Maeda

Prime Minister Kishida Fumio dissolved the House of Representatives (HR) on October 14, 2021, and set the election date for October 31. Unlike the last two general elections in 2014 and 2017 that were early elections, the legislators who served until this dissolution almost completed their four-year terms. Also, unlike the last two elections, Abe Shinzō was no longer the prime minister. The ruling coalition went into this election with a prime minister who took office only 10 days before the dissolution.

This was the ninth HR election conducted under the mixed-member majoritarian electoral system introduced in the 1994 electoral law reform. At stake were all 465 seats of the chamber. The single-member district (SMD) tier elects 289 members, and the proportional representation (PR) tier fills 176 seats from 11 regional districts. Each voter casts two ballots, one for each tier.

K. Maeda (✉)
University of North Texas, Denton, TX, USA
e-mail: Ko.Maeda@unt.edu

The ruling coalition of the Liberal Democratic Party (LDP) and Kōmeitō, as always, coordinated candidate nominations in SMDs so that no district would have candidates from both parties. The LDP fielded candidates in 277 SMDs and Kōmeitō in nine. The three districts that did not have a candidate from either of them (Tokyo 15th, Kanagawa 1st, and Nara 3rd) had incumbent legislators who were close to the LDP but ran as independent candidates.[1] Thus, each of the 289 SMDs of the country had one candidate who represented the LDP-Kōmeitō coalition either officially or implicitly.

The largest opposition Constitutional Democratic Party (CDP) sought cooperation with other opposition parties to form a unified front to compete against the coalition. On September 8, leaders of four opposition parties—the CDP, the Japanese Communist Party (JCP), the Social Democratic Party (SDP), and Reiwa Shinsengumi—agreed on policy principles, and the four parties then worked to coordinate candidate nominations (See Rehmert 2022). Two opposition parties, the Democratic Party for the People (DPP) and Nippon Ishin no Kai (hereafter referred to simply as "Ishin"; it is also known as the Japan Innovation Party), did not join this four-party alliance. Yet, the DPP did not field its candidates in the districts where there was a CDP incumbent and vice versa.

The approval rate of the Kishida cabinet was 40.3% according to Jiji Tsushin's survey conducted on October 8 to 11.[2] Right before the last general election in 2017, the cabinet approval rate was 37.1%.[3]

Table 3.1 shows the results of the election, juxtaposed with the 2017 election for comparison. The ruling coalition reduced their combined seat share from 67.3% to 63.0% (including ex-post nominations). Although the coalition won a two-thirds majority in every general election since 2012, it failed to do so this time. The largest opposition CDP won 96 seats. Although it may seem like a major gain from 54 in 2017, the party's seat share in fact declined from what it had right before the election (109 seats).[4] The JCP and the SDP also reduced their seats. The biggest winner of this election was Ishin, which more than tripled its seats.

Voter turnout was 55.9%, according to the official report by the Ministry of Internal Affairs and Communications. That was an increase from 53.7% in 2017, but still the third-lowest turnout among the postwar HR elections. The number of female HR members declined slightly from 47 (10.1% of the total seats) in 2017 to 45 (9.7%) in this election. The

Table 3.1 Votes and seats in the 2017 and 2021 general elections

		LDP	Kōmeitō	CDP	Ishin	JCP	SDP	Hope	Others	Indep.	Total
SMD (2017)	Candidates	277	9	63	47	206	19	198	44	73	936
	Total votes	26,500,777	832,453	4,726,326	1,765,053	4,998,932	634,770	11,437,601	211,252	4,315,028	55,422,193
	Average vote %	49.9%	48.2%	39.1%	19.6%	12.7%	17.4%	30.1%	2.5%	30.8%	
	Seats	215	8	17	3	1	1	18	0	26	289
PR (2017)	Total votes	18,555,717	6,977,712	11,084,890	3,387,097	4,404,081	941,324	9,677,524	729,207		55,757,552
	Vote %	33.3%	12.5%	19.9%	6.1%	7.9%	1.7%	17.4%	1.3%		100%
	Seats	66	21	37	8	11	1	32	0		176
Total (2017)	Seats	281	29	54	11	12	2	50	0	26	465
	Seat %	60.4%	6.2%	11.6%	2.4%	2.6%	0.4%	10.8%	0.0%	5.6%	100%

(continued)

Table 3.1 (continued)

		LDP	Kōmeitō	CDP	Ishin	JCP	SDP	DPP	Reiwa	Others	Indep.	Total
SMD (2021)	Candidates	277	9	214	94	105	9	21	12	36	80	857
	Total votes	27,626,235	872,931	17,215,621	4,802,793	2,639,631	313,193	1,246,812	248,280	222,368	2,269,168	57,457,033
	Average vote %	50.2%	48.8%	40.5%	25.7%	12.6%	17.5%	29.9%	10.4%	3.1%	14.3%	
	Seats	187	9	57	16	1	1	6	0	0	12	289
PR (2021)	Total votes	19,914,883	7,114,282	11,492,095	8,050,830	4,166,076	1,018,588	2,593,396	2,215,648	900,181		57,465,979
	Vote %	34.7%	12.4%	20.0%	14.0%	7.2%	1.8%	4.5%	3.9%	1.6%		100%
	Seats	72	23	39	25	9	0	5	3	0		176
Total (2021)	Seats	259	32	96	41	10	1	11	3	0	12	465
	Seat %	55.7%	6.9%	20.6%	8.8%	2.2%	0.2%	2.4%	0.6%	0.0%	2.6%	100%

Notes: The number of single-member district (SMD) candidates for the parties are officially nominated candidates. They do not include independent candidates implicitly affiliated with a party. Some of those independents were elected and obtained an ex-post nomination. Including ex-post nominations, the LDP in 2017 won 284 seats, the CDP in 2017 won 55, and the LDP in 2021 won 261

Party abbreviations: LDP Liberal Democratic Party; *CDP* Constitutional Democratic Party; *Ishin* Nippon Ishin no Kai; *JCP* Japanese Communist Party; *SDP* Social Democratic Party; *Hope* Party of Hope; *DPP* Democratic Party for the People; *Reiwa* Reiwa Shinsengumi

Source: Ministry of Internal Affairs and Communications

percentage of women is higher among the PR winners (11.9%) than among the SMD winners (8.3%).[5]

ISHIN'S RISE

Ishin's sudden rise is perhaps the biggest story of this election. Ishin as a national party was originally founded in 2012 and has gone through several organizational changes (Reed 2013; Pekkanen and Reed 2016, 2018). Osaka is Ishin's birthplace and stronghold, and Ishin has been dominating Osaka's local politics. Yet, it had not been successful in increasing its popularity outside of the Kinki region (Reed et al. 2013). In the 2017 election in which Ishin did not perform well, out of the 11 total seats Ishin won, eight were from the Kinki region (three SMDs in Osaka and five PR seats in the Kinki region district).

Although Ishin was the sixth largest party in the 2017 election, it became the third largest in this 2021 election, winning 41 seats (16 SMD seats and 25 PR seats). Yet, its popularity and strength are still heavily concentrated in Osaka. Figure 3.1 shows the vote shares of Ishin's SMD candidates in their districts, broken down by geographical groups (Osaka, Kinki region except for Osaka, Tokyo, and all others).[6] Each circle is an SMD, and an X mark shows the average Ishin vote share in each group. It is clear that Ishin candidates in Osaka performed much better than the rest. Ishin ran its candidates in 15 of Osaka's 19 SMDs, and all of them won their districts with 49.1% of votes on average.[7] However, outside of Osaka, Ishin ran 79 candidates but won only one district (Hyogo 6th, which is near Osaka). Ishin's contrasting performance in Osaka and elsewhere is also seen in the magnitude of vote change from the last election. In Osaka's 15 SMDs, Ishin candidates' vote share improved by 12.0 percentage points on average. In contrast, outside of Osaka, in the 19 SMDs where Ishin had its candidates in both 2017 and 2021, Ishin's average vote share increase was 7.6 percentage points.

In the PR tier, Ishin's national vote share improved from 6.1% to 14.0%. In the Kinki region district, Ishin's vote share (33.9%) was higher than any other party, and the party won 10 seats. This was a much better performance than the last election in the same region (18.3% and 5 seats). Ishin's gain was more modest outside of Kinki, but Ishin's PR votes increased in almost all prefectures.[8] On average, of 41 prefectures outside of Kinki, Ishin's PR vote share in 2017 was 4.0%, but it went up to 9.0%.

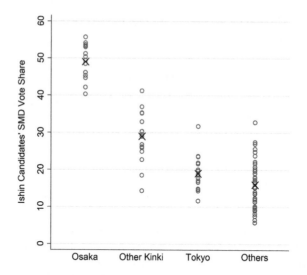

Fig. 3.1 Vote share of Ishin SMD candidates

Where did Ishin's gain come from? Did Ishin win votes from the LDP-Kōmeitō coalition or from the other opposition parties? This is a question better answered with survey data that are not yet available. But an aggregate-level analysis indicates a certain pattern. Figure 3.2 is a triangular plot that shows prefecture-level PR vote changes from 2017 to 2021. For each prefecture, PR votes are divided into three groups: Ishin, LDP-Kōmeitō, and all others. The closer to the lower-left vertex in the graph, the higher Ishin's vote share was. Likewise, the closer to the lower-right vertex, the higher the combined vote share of the LDP and Kōmeitō was, and the top vertex is for all the other parties. Each prefecture is represented by a line with a dot at one end. The location of a dot shows the composition of the votes in the 2021 election, and the other end of the line is for the 2017 election.

It is noticeable in Fig. 3.2 that several prefectures such as Osaka and Hyogo made a significant move toward the lower-left vertex. In those prefectures, Ishin gained a large share of votes, and both the LDP-Kōmeitō duo and the CDP-led opposition parties lost greatly. Except for those, most prefectures are clustered near the right side of the triangle, moving downwards. In those, both Ishin and the LDP-Kōmeitō duo improved their vote shares (the LDP and Kōmeitō's combined vote share

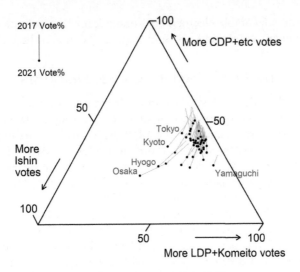

Fig. 3.2 Prefecture-level PR vote change, 2017–2021

increased in 38 of the 47 prefectures). The opposition parties other than Ishin were the main losers in the PR tier.

In an exit poll conducted by Kyodo News, among the voters who consider themselves to be independents, 21% voted for Ishin in the PR tier, which is a marked improvement from 2017 when only 9% of those independents voted for Ishin in PR (*Mainichi*, October 31, 2021, online edition). In contrast, the independents' support for the CDP declined from 31% in 2017 to 24% in 2021, according to the same exit poll. Sunahara and Zenkyo (2022) point out that Ishin was able to attract relatively young voters in urban areas in this election. It appears that many anti-LDP/Kōmeitō voters who would normally vote for the center-left, mainstream opposition party (the Democratic Party of Japan, or the DPJ, in the past and the CDP in 2017) switched their vote choice to Ishin in this election. It is uncertain at this point whether Ishin's triumph in this 2021 election is a temporal phenomenon or a sign of a long-term trajectory. Ishin's future as a national party depends greatly on whether it can develop a nationally recognized leader (Sunahara and Zenkyo 2022). If Ishin can succeed in solidifying its national presence and attracting a large portion of voters who are critical of the LDP-Kōmeitō government, that would create a favorable electoral environment for the coalition in which anti-government votes would be split between Ishin and the CDP.

THE LDP'S FALL IN URBAN DISTRICTS

As shown earlier, the LDP secured 55.7% of the total seats in this election. Even though the party controls far more than a simple majority, it was clearly sub-par performance for the LDP, which had been winning 60% of seats in each election since its return to power in 2012.[9] The LDP's loss came from the SMD tier where it lost 28 seats from the last election. In contrast, the party gained 6 seats in the PR tier. The LDP's 72 seats in the PR tier is its highest number since 2005.

Figure 3.3 shows the winning percentages of the LDP's SMD candidates since 2012, broken down by levels of urbanization. Urbanization is measured by the percentage of residents who live in census-defined "densely inhabited districts." This variable is hereafter referred to as the DID%. I calculated each SMD's DID% based on the 2015 census data with the help of the detailed population data broken down by electoral districts compiled and published by Akira Nishizawa.[10] In Fig. 3.3, urban SMDs are where the DID% is above 90. The middle SMDs' DID% is between 90 and 50, and rural ones have DID% that is below 50. Each of the three groups includes roughly a third of the total SMDs.

Fig. 3.3 Winning percentage of the LDP's SMD candidates

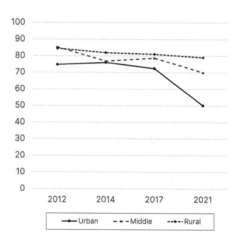

The LDP has always been stronger in rural areas since its foundation, and its varying strength in urban and rural districts has been observed in recent elections as well (Scheiner et al. 2018). Figure 3.3 indicates that the LDP's strength in its rural base is still present; 79% of the LDP candidates who ran in rural districts won their SMDs in this election. In contrast, the winning percentage in urban districts sharply declined to 50%. It is partly because all LDP candidates in Osaka lost to Ishin's candidates. Yet, that was not the only reason. The LDP candidates' winning rate in urban districts while excluding Osaka is still 59%, which is significantly lower than the rate in 2017 (73%).

Who defeated LDP candidates in those urban SMDs? Out of the 60 urban SMDs won by the LDP in 2017, the LDP was able to hold 37 seats. The rest were won by the opposition: the CDP took 13, and Ishin won 10. The LDP's losses happened in both senior members' districts and junior members' districts, and there is no statistically significant difference between the LDP's winners and losers in terms of their seniority status. Some of the LDP heavyweights who were defeated in their urban SMDs in this election include Ishihara Nobuteru (Tokyo 8th) and Amari Akira (Kanagawa 13th), who had served 10 and 13 terms, respectively.

Overall, the LDP was able to hold 77% of the SMDs it won in the last election. This percentage is significantly lower than usual (91% in 2014 and 90% in 2017).[11] At the same time, however, in this 2021 election, the LDP won 30% of the SMDs it did not win in the last election, which is more than usual (18% in 2014 and 28% in 2017). These numbers indicate that SMD competition is becoming more volatile than before. Investigating why this is the case is an important question for future research.

The CDP's Dilemma and Debacle

Edano Yukio founded the CDP right before the 2017 election, and he was the face of Japan's opposition for the last four years as the leader of the largest opposition party (see Pekkanen and Reed 2018). Edano apparently had high hopes going into this election. On September 7, Edano announced seven policy issues that would be decided upon "in the first cabinet meeting of an Edano cabinet."[12]

However, Edano faced a difficult tactical decision before this election: his party's relationship with the JCP. Whether and how to work with the JCP is a perennial question for Japan's center-left and left-wing parties (see Maeda 2017, 2018). The JCP is small, but it has loyal supporters thinly spread out across the country. When the JCP runs its own district candidates, which it routinely did in all districts in the past, anti-LDP votes are split, helping the LDP. Yet, when a center-left party works closely with the JCP, it risks alienating moderate voters who dislike the JCP.

Caught in this dilemma, Edano and his CDP leadership chose to work with the JCP. As mentioned at the beginning of this chapter, the CDP signed a policy agreement with three other opposition parties, the largest of which being the JCP. Further, Edano met with the JCP leader Shii Kazuo on September 30, and the two agreed that the JCP would not formally join an Edano cabinet as a coalition member party but would play a supporting role for it (*Sankei*, September 30, 2021, online edition). Presumably, Edano thought he struck a delicate balance by announcing that the JCP would not join his cabinet. But the Edano-Shii agreement was fiercely criticized by Yoshino Tomoko, the president of the Japanese Trade Union Confederation, or *Rengo*, the country's largest labor organization. She said at a press conference on October 7 that it was "impossible" ("*arienai*" in Japanese) that the JCP would play a supporting role for a CDP-led government even from outside of the cabinet (*Nikkei*, October 7, 2021, online edition). Predictably, the LDP also attacked the CDP for its willingness to work with the JCP, even while coming up with a term "Constitutional Communist Party" by combining the names of the CDP and the JCP (*Sankei*, October 26, 2021, online edition).

Did cooperating with the JCP help or hurt the CDP electorally? This question was repeatedly raised after the election by the news media and political pundits. Ultimately, the true answer to this question is never known because the exact consequence of the CDP-JCP cooperation must be examined against the counterfactual scenario of *how many seats the CDP would have obtained if it had not cooperated with the JCP*. It is not adequate to compare districts where opposition parties successfully nominated a unified candidate and districts where such coordination failed. Such a comparison potentially suffers from a selection bias problem that stems from the possibility that the parties worked harder to coordinate candidate nominations in their "target" districts where they thought they would have a realistic chance to defeat the LDP's candidate.

While keeping the limitations in mind, let us see what observed data can tell us. I ran a regression analysis employing district-level electoral results of the 2017 and 2021 elections. The dependent variable is the change in the percentage-point margin between the top opposition candidate (Ishin candidates are excluded) and the candidate of the LDP-Kōmeitō coalition in SMDs. The margin is coded in such a way that it takes a positive value if an opposition candidate earned more votes than a coalition candidate and a negative value if a coalition candidate won more votes. For example, in the Tokyo 8th district in 2017, a CDP candidate was defeated by the LDP veteran Ishihara (mentioned earlier) with a margin of −9.2 percentage points. In 2021 in the same district, the CDP candidate won with a margin of 11.3 percentage points. In this district, the change in the opposition-coalition margin from 2017 to 2021 is 20.5, indicating a major improvement of the opposition. A negative value for this variable means that a candidate of the LDP-Kōmeitō coalition performed better and widened the gap with the top opposition candidate.

In this analysis, SMDs where opposition candidates won in 2017 are excluded so that we can focus on the SMDs held by the coalition which the opposition tried to flip. Further, SMDs where pro-LDP independent candidates obtained more than 20% of votes in either election are excluded. The number of SMDs that remain in the data is 217. The main independent variable is a dummy variable that indicates successful opposition cooperation in 2021. This variable takes the value of one for SMDs that had multiple opposition candidates (excluding Ishin candidates but including opposition-leaning independent candidates who won more than 20% of votes) in 2017 but had one in 2021 and zero otherwise. The following five control variables are also included:

- The DID% variable explained earlier. This variable measures the degree of urbanization.
- A dummy variable that indicates Ishin's entry. This variable takes the value of one if the SMD did not have an Ishin candidate in 2017 but had one in 2021, and zero otherwise.
- The vote share of the top opposition candidate (excluding Ishin) in 2017.
- The number of terms the coalition's candidate previously served.
- Whether the coalition's candidate was a Kōmeitō candidate.

Table 3.2 shows the results of the estimation. Model 1 includes all 217 observations discussed above. The main independent variable has a coefficient of 5.739 which is statistically significant. This means that the top opposition candidate narrowed the vote-share margin with the LDP/Kōmeitō candidate by, on average, 5.7 percentage points in the SMDs where opposition parties successfully nominated a unified candidate in 2021 (but did not in 2017), in comparison with the rest of the SMDs. The DID% variable has a positive and statistically significant coefficient, indicating that the opposition candidates gained more in urban districts than in rural ones. The top opposition candidates' vote share in 2017 is negative and statistically significant. This is expected because if an opposition candidate performed well in 2017, there is not much room for improvement.

Model 2 repeats the same analysis with a smaller set of observations. In Model 2, the SMDs where a JCP candidate was the sole opposition candidate in either election were excluded. Those districts are not comparable with others because a JCP candidate typically does not attract many non-JCP supporters (except in Okinawa where there is a unique tradition of

Table 3.2
Determinants of SMD vote change

	(1)	(2)
Opposition cooperation	5.739***	9.657***
	(1.693)	(1.621)
DID%	0.105***	0.080***
	(0.033)	(0.030)
Ishin new candidate	−1.226	0.163
	(1.986)	(1.754)
Top opposition votes 2017	−0.238***	−0.258***
	(0.086)	(0.090)
Coalition candidate terms	0.427	0.573
	(0.292)	(0.297)
Komeito candidate	−3.566	−2.427
	(2.291)	(2.756)
Intercept	−1.775	−1.017
	(4.184)	(4.359)
# of observations	217	175
R-squared	0.155	0.295
St. error of regression	11.53	9.74

Notes Models estimated with OLS. Robust standard errors are in parentheses. *** $p < 0.01$, ** $p < 0.05$, * $p < 0.1$

opposition cooperation).[13] The main independent variable's coefficient goes up to 9.657 in Model 2. While it is necessary to recognize the limitations of this kind of analysis discussed above, the regression analysis presented here reveals a rather large difference in the opposition's electoral performance between the SMDs where the opposition nominated a unified candidate and the rest of the SMDs. Sugawara's (2022) statistical analysis on the electoral data also indicates a positive effect of opposition cooperation in SMDs. His study shows that, among others, when the JCP withdraws its candidate from an SMD, the main opposition candidate's vote share increases by about 8 percentage points on average.

In fact, out of the 57 SMDs the CDP won in this election, about half of them (28) are districts the LDP won in 2017 (and none of those 28 districts had a JCP candidate this time). The CDP was, to some extent, successful in gaining seats from the LDP in the SMD tier, and the LDP in this election lost an unusually large number of SMDs, as discussed earlier. This electoral change might not have happened if the opposition parties had not cooperated. After all, it is hard to argue that the CDP suffered a defeat in SMDs because it won 57 districts in this election, which is the same as the total number of SMDs the CDP, Hope, and opposition-leaning independents won in the last election.

Instead, what caused the overall loss of the CDP's seats was its dismal performance in the PR tier. Its 20.0% PR vote share in this election was an underachievement, considering that the CDP in 2017 obtained 19.9% and an additional 17.4% was won by Hope, a large portion of which has since joined the CDP. Also note that the DPJ, before defeating the LDP in 2009, was constantly receiving well above 20% of PR votes (26.1% in 2000, 37.4% in 2003, and 31.0% in 2005).

Unlike SMD races in which candidates' personal popularity and parties' cooperation in individual districts can make differences, PR vote share more directly reflects a party's overall strength. In this sense, the CDP's failure in the PR tier in this election clearly reveals that it was not popular enough to become the country's ruling party. In an October 2021 survey, the percentage of respondents who said they supported the CDP was only 3.8% (see footnote 2). In hindsight, with that level of party popularity, it was simply impossible for the CDP to defeat the LDP. Both Sugawara (2022) and Sunahara and Zenkyo (2022) point out that the CDP's main problem in this election was its low party popularity.

However, that does not necessarily mean Edano should not have talked about what an Edano cabinet would do in office. As the leader of the largest opposition party, he basically had no choice but to run a campaign to win power. Not doing so would have been seen as defeatism, and he would have been severely criticized from within his party. He nevertheless resigned as the party leader after the election, having failed to fulfill a goal that was impossible to achieve in the first place.

Another source of unpleasant news for the CDP is the aging of its supporters. According to an exit poll conducted by Kyodo News, the CDP's support is higher among older people and lower among the youth (*Nikkei*, November 1, 2021, online edition). Although the CDP is the most popular party among the elderly population above 60, its popularity among the people below 40 is about a half of the LDP's. If the CDP cannot change its course and attract younger voters, it will not be able to become a viable challenger to the LDP.

Conclusion

On the surface, this 2021 election result may seem comparable to the last three elections. After all, the LDP-Kōmeitō coalition maintained a comfortable majority while the opposition stayed fragmented. However, as I discussed in this chapter, major changes are taking place. First, SMD races are becoming more volatile. The LDP lost an unusually large number of districts it won in the last election, especially in urban areas. But the LDP was also able to gain more new districts than it usually does. Some prominent politicians of both the LDP and the opposition lost their seats which they had kept for a long time. Why this happened is not clear. But if this trend continues, there will be fewer safe seats of incumbents, and a large-scale electoral change may happen when parties' popularity shifts.

Second, even though the opposition continues to be fragmented, it is more so than before. This election produced an ironic result for opposition parties in the sense that the CDP and the JCP cooperated with each other but reduced their seat shares while Ishin made a major gain without working with other parties. Ishin will most likely maintain its course and keep criticizing other opposition parties. With Ishin being large and antagonistic, Japan's opposition is more deeply divided than ever. The CDP and Ishin will be vying to claim the status as the country's main opposition party that can attract floating voters when the government becomes unpopular.

Third, and more broadly, if Ishin can continue winning like it did in this election and further increase its popularity outside of its base in Osaka, that would fundamentally transform the structure of Japan's party system. For the last two decades, the country's party system was characterized by bilateral competition between the LDP-Kōmeitō duo on the right-wing side and various opposition parties on the left-wing side, with Ishin (and other now-defunct third-force parties) occupying a niche position for the last decade. Yet, if Ishin can break out of its niche status and become a mainstream party, the bilateral structure will be replaced by trilateral party competition between Ishin, the LDP-Kōmeitō coalition, and other opposition parties led by the CDP.

Competition within the opposition, namely the rivalry between the CDP and Ishin, will be the most crucial issue in Japan's party politics in 2022 and beyond. Meanwhile, the LDP will be able to focus on governing with a renewed mandate without facing serious challenges from the opposition. The LDP's dominant status in politics remains unshaken for now.

NOTES

1. Two of them were elected in this election and received ex-post endorsements from the LDP.
2. https://www.jiji.com/jc/article?k=2021101500722, accessed on December 14, 2021.
3. https://www.crs.or.jp/backno/No721/7210.htm, accessed on December 14, 2021. See Yukio Maeda (2022) for more on public opinion.
4. In September 2020, a majority of DPP legislators and some independent politicians joined the CDP, and the CDP was re-established as a new party with the same name. In a legal sense, the CDP in 2017 and the CDP in 2021 are different parties.
5. See Kweon (2022) for more on gender issues.
6. District-level electoral results were provided by Yuki Yanai.
7. Osaka's 3rd, 5th, 6th, and 16th districts are where Kōmeitō always fields its candidates. Ishin has never nominated its candidate in any of those four districts. Presumably, Ishin consciously avoids direct confrontation with Kōmeitō in Osaka (see Klein and McLaughlin 2022).
8. Prefecture-level PR vote data are taken from the official report of the Ministry of Internal Affairs and Communications.
9. Nemoto (2022) explains how the LDP was able to minimize its loss by its leadership selection and candidate nomination.

10. https://home.csis.u-tokyo.ac.jp/~nishizawa/senkyoku/, accessed on October 10, 2021.
11. The percentages for 2014 and 2017 were calculated while excluding redistricted SMDs.
12. https://cdp-japan.jp/news/20210907_2039, accessed on December 29, 2021.
13. The JCP has been winning the Okinawa 1st district since 2014 while cooperating with other opposition parties. That is the only district in the country where a JCP candidate has won since 2000.

References

Klein, Axel, and Levi McLaughlin. 2022. "Kōmeitō in 2021: Strategizing Between the LDP and Sōka Gakkai." In Robert J. Pekkanen, Steven R. Reed, and Daniel M. Smith (eds.), *Japan Decides 2021: The Japanese General Election*. Palgrave Macmillan.

Kweon, Yesola. 2022. "Women's Representation and the Gendered Impact of COVID-19 in Japan." In Robert J. Pekkanen, Steven R. Reed, and Daniel M. Smith (eds.), *Japan Decides 2021: The Japanese General Election*. Palgrave Macmillan.

Maeda, Ko. 2017. "Explaining the Surges and Declines of the Japanese Communist Party." *Asian Survey* 57(4): 665–689.

Maeda, Ko. 2018. "The JCP: A Perpetual Spoiler?" In Robert J. Pekkanen, Steven S. Reed, Ethan Scheiner, and Daniel M. Smith (eds.), *Japan Decides 2017: The Japanese General Election*, 93–106. New York: Palgrave Macmillan.

Maeda, Yukio. 2022. "Public Opinion and COVID-19." In Robert J. Pekkanen, Steven R. Reed, and Daniel M. Smith (eds.), *Japan Decides 2021: The Japanese General Election*. Palgrave Macmillan.

Nemoto, Kuniaki. 2022. "How the Liberal Democratic Party Avoided a Loss in 2021." In Robert J. Pekkanen, Steven R. Reed, and Daniel M. Smith (eds.), *Japan Decides 2021: The Japanese General Election*. Palgrave Macmillan.

Pekkanen, Robert J., and Steven R. Reed. 2016. "From Third Force to Third Party: Duverger's Revenge?" In Robert J. Pekkanen, Steven R. Reed, and Ethan Scheiner (eds.), *Japan Decides 2014: The Japanese General Election*, 62–71. New York: Palgrave Macmillan.

Pekkanen, Robert J., and Steven R. Reed. 2018. "The Opposition: From Third Party Back to Third Force." In Robert J. Pekkanen, Steven S. Reed, Ethan Scheiner, and Daniel M. Smith (eds.), *Japan Decides 2017: The Japanese General Election*, 77–92. New York: Palgrave Macmillan.

Reed, Steven R. 2013. "Challenging the Two-Party System: Third Force Parties in the 2012 Election." In Robert J. Pekkanen, Steven R. Reed, and Ethan

Scheiner (eds.), *Japan Decides 2012: The Japanese General Election*, 72–83. New York: Palgrave Macmillan.

Reed, Steven R., Ethan Scheiner, Daniel M. Smith, and Michael F. Thies. 2013. "The 2012 Election Results: The LDP Wins Big by Default." In Robert J. Pekkanen, Steven R. Reed, and Ethan Scheiner (eds.), *Japan Decides 2012: The Japanese General Election*, 34–46. New York: Palgrave Macmillan.

Rehmert, Jochen. 2022. "Candidate Selection for the 2021 General Election." In Robert J. Pekkanen, Steven R. Reed, and Daniel M. Smith (eds.), *Japan Decides 2021: The Japanese General Election*. Palgrave Macmillan.

Scheiner, Ethan, Daniel M. Smith, and Michael F. Thies. 2018. "The 2017 Election Results: An Earthquake, a Typhoon, and Another Landslide." In Robert J. Pekkanen, Steven S. Reed, Ethan Scheiner, and Daniel M. Smith (eds.), *Japan Decides 2017: The Japanese General Election*, 29–50. New York: Palgrave Macmillan.

Sugawara, Taku. 2022. "Yato kyoto wa fuhatsu dattanoka." *Sekai*. January. 214–225.

Sunahara, Yosuke, and Masahiro Zenkyo. 2022. "Shokyokuteki shiji de yakushin shita Nippon Ishin no Kai." *Chuo Koron*. January. 130–137.

PART I

Party Politics

CHAPTER 4

How the Liberal Democratic Party Avoided a Loss in 2021

Kuniaki Nemoto

In 2021, the ruling Liberal Democratic Party (LDP) was able to retain a comfortable majority with 261 seats out of the 465 lower-house seats in total. But it was still a loss for the LDP, as the party won 284 seats in the 2017 election and had 276 seats when the House of Representatives (HR) was dissolved. This chapter analyzes how the LDP was able to avoid a major loss, even as it was unable to increase its seats. In doing so, it focuses on two aspects: How the party selected its new leaders; and how the party prevented independent conservative candidates from pulling away votes from its nominees in district races.

There are many factors that explain why the party won or lost, so this chapter is not meant to offer any deterministic account. On the positive side, the LDP benefited from the fragmentation of the opposition, as explained by Pekkanen and Reed (2022). The main opposition Constitutional Democratic Party (CDP) formed a united front with extreme

K. Nemoto (✉)
Musashi University, Tokyo, Japan
e-mail: knemoto@cc.musashi.ac.jp

© The Author(s), under exclusive license to Springer Nature Switzerland AG 2023
R. J. Pekkanen et al. (eds.), *Japan Decides 2021*,
https://doi.org/10.1007/978-3-031-11324-6_4

leftists, including the Japan Communist Party (JCP), but moderate opposition parties refused to join the electoral coalition and competed over the same anti-LDP vote. On the negative side, as Yukio Maeda (2022) describes, Suga Yoshihide, who resigned as the prime minister and the LDP's leader just before the election, was very unpopular. He was unable to keep the momentum of the previous Abe administration, which won national elections six consecutive times, since his countermeasures to the COVID-19 crisis drew heavy criticisms.

That said, the analysis below on the presidential selection and candidate nomination processes reveals that the LDP made conscious efforts to minimize its electoral loss, if not perfectly. Under the latest rule for the LDP's presidential selection process, grass-roots party members (*tōin* and *tōyū*) are now allowed to have exactly the same voting power as Diet members, so that the party can choose a popular leader who can improve its image and therefore mobilize votes. In 2018 and 2020, the party was able to choose leaders who were expected to bring stability and continuity to the party, while in 2021, members were able to exert pressure on an unpopular leader to step down. Moreover, as also explained by Rehmert (2022), in the broader nomination process for candidates, now the party applies stricter control over candidates to maintain party unity and minimize electoral loss. Using its internal polls, the proportional representation (PR) tier of the electoral system, and even threats, the party tried to prevent the rise of conservative independents whose candidacies could benefit the opposition.

Presidential Selection

The basic structure of the LDP's presidential selection process traditionally had two stages (Nemoto et al. 2014; Nemoto 2021). In the first round, Diet members and two or three delegates from each of the prefectural chapters would cast votes. If no candidate won an outright majority in the first round, this would be followed by a second round majority run-off, in which only Diet members could cast votes for one of the top-two candidates. If the party president resigned in the middle of his or her term, the party could use an emergency clause to skip the first round and simply hold a majority run-off election, in which Diet members and one delegate from each of the 47 prefectural chapters would be able to cast votes. Although there have been some short-lived experiments, such as the introduction of a primary in 1978, this basic structure remained intact up until the era of the prime minister Koizumi Junichirō.

Combined with the very personalistic single, nontransferable vote (SNTV) electoral system used for the HR until 1994, the LDP's presidential selection process did not function as a mechanism to choose a strong, popular leader who could affect the country's policy direction. Rather, it was more or less a competition over office perks, as the constitution bestows the prime minister the exclusive power to appoint cabinet ministers. Factions spent literally billions of yen to buy out other factions' headcounts and formed unstable coalitions of convenience before voting.

Such days were gone following the 1994 electoral reform to the mixed-member majoritarian (MMM) system, at least in theory. Since winning elections under the new electoral system requires a strong party president that can build a popular party image, the LDP reformed its presidential selection process to match the new reality, by gradually expanding the voting power of grass-roots party members (*tōin* and *tōyū*). Under the latest rule put into effect in 2014, *tōin* and *tōyū* have exactly the same number of votes as Diet members in the first round.[1] *Tōin* and *tōyū* must be a Japanese citizen aged 18 or older, and needs to pay the party membership fee of 4000 yen for two or more years in order to participate in the presidential selection. In addition, 47 prefectural chapters are now allowed to participate in the second round, which was previously open only to Diet members. The emergency clause was also reformed, such that each of the 47 prefectural chapters now has three votes.

The new rule was applied to the 2018 selection for the first time, since the previous one in 2015 had only one candidate: Abe Shinzō. With the voting power of *tōin* and *tōyū* ever increasing, three would-be contenders—incumbent Abe, Ishiba Shigeru, and Kishida Fumio—put an emphasis on regional trips to shore up local supporters (Yomiuri, May 21, 2018). Kishida, the then Chairperson of the Policy Affairs Research Council who eventually gave up running for the 2018 selection, in an attempt to raise his profile across the country, had meetings with prefectural chapters almost every weekend (Yomiuri, May 21, 2018). Ishiba, a major competitor against Abe in 2012, also tried to gain momentum by making frequent visits to local areas to expand his name recognition among *tōin* and *tōyū* (Asahi, January 9, 2018), since most of the factions, including the biggest Hosoda faction and Secretary-General Nikai Toshihiro's faction, decided to back incumbent Abe well before the race started. Even Abe as incumbent took time out from his official trips to meet with the LDP's local assembly members (Yomiuri, May 21, 2018). This is somehow surprising, given that he was backed up by most of the factions and an opinion poll before voting showed that 59% of LDP supporters picked Abe as the next leader, while Ishiba was chosen by 20% (Asahi, June 25, 2018). In April, Abe visited Osaka, Hokkaido, Shiga, and Saitama, where Ishiba had more votes from *tōin* and *tōyū* in the 2012 selection (Yomiuri, July 22, 2018).

The result of the selection in September 2018 is shown in Table 4.1. Clearly, Abe looked invincible, partly because many Diet members and *tōin* and *tōyū* might have wanted his leadership to continue. By the time of voting, he built his image as "a party president who can win the elections" (*senkyo ni tsuyoi sōsai*) (Asahi, January 9, 2018). In addition, more than 70% of his supporters considered diplomacy and security, economy, and disaster recovery as important policy issues when making voting decisions (Yomiuri, September 17, 2018), suggesting that he was preferred by those who wanted stability and continuity.

The 2020 selection took place in a completely different environment. All of a sudden, Abe announced in August 2020 his intention to resign due to a recurrence of his chronic illness, ulcerative colitis, in the midst of the COVID-19 pandemic crisis. This was a great shock to the party. Abe won the sixth national election for the upper house in 2019 and set the new record as the longest serving prime minister ever. Partly because of his popularity among voters, the LDP changed its rule in 2017 to extend the term limit of the party president from two three-year terms to three. The LDP's Secretary-General Nikai Toshihiro even suggested from time to time that the party might change its rule to extend the presidential term limit to four terms (Nikkei, February 22, 2019).

Secretary-General Nikai decided to use the emergency clause to determine Abe's successor. That is, the party decided to bypass the two-round process in which *tōin* and *tōyū* would have the same voting power as Diet members. Nikai and other leaders said that there was no time to create a political vacuum in the middle of the COVID-19 disaster (Asahi,

Table 4.1 The result of the 2018 presidential selection		*Diet members*	Tōin *and* Tōyū	*Total*
	Abe	329	224	553
	Ishiba	73	181	254

August 30, 2020). That would mean that there would be only a one-shot run-off, in which 394 Diet members and 47 prefectural chapters would be able to participate, with each of the Diet members and each of prefectural chapters having one and three votes, respectively. It was also decided that the party would sponsor no local rally, in order to avoid the spread of the virus (Yomiuri, September 4, 2020, Evening Edition). Ishiba complained, since he won 45% of the *tōin* and *tōyū* votes in the previous selection (Nikkei, August 31, 2020). More than 140 junior Diet members, including the then environment minister Koizumi Shinjirō, also demanded the first round, saying that skipping the first round to ignore *tōin* and *tōyū* would harm the legitimacy of the selection process and worsen the image of the party (Asahi, August 31, 2020, Evening Edition).

Now that the presidential selection would be held using the emergency clause, Suga Yoshihide decided to run. As he had served as the Abe administration's Chief Cabinet Secretary for more than seven years, many members expected that the party under his leadership would bring stability and continuity (Yomiuri, August 31, 2020). As the Nikai faction announced its support for Suga, other factions joined the bandwagon (Asahi, September 1, 2020). According to an Asahi poll, 49% of the LDP supporters preferred Suga, while only 23% picked up Ishiba as a next leader (Asahi, September 4, 2020). The same poll also suggested that more people preferred stability and continuity, as 45% of the respondents would like a next leader to continue the Abe administration's policy directions.

Thus even before the race officially started, Suga was expected to win. But still, three candidates—Suga, Ishiba, and Kishida this time—tried to meet with local assembly members from various prefectures to make their presence visible. This is because the LDP encouraged each prefectural chapter to decide at its own discretion how many of its three votes would go to which candidate (Nikkei, September 2, 2020, Evening Edition). Except Akita, where Suga was born, the other 46 prefectures decided to hold primaries in allocating their three votes to candidates (Yomiuri, September 8, 2020, Evening Edition). The three candidates and their aides seemed to believe that regardless of how Diet members would vote, it might be possible to appeal to every *tōin* and *tōyū* and expand their support networks, which in turn would influence the decision of Diet members (Yomiuri, September 9, 2020, Evening Edition).

As shown in Table 4.2, the 2020 Presidential Selection resulted in Suga's landslide victory. As in 2018, the selectorate might have preferred

Table 4.2 The result of the 2020 presidential selection

	Diet members	Prefectural chapters	Total
Suga	288	89	377
Kishida	79	10	89
Ishiba	26	42	68

stability and continuity—perhaps even more so in midst of the pandemic crisis. Noticeable is the fact that Suga won 63% of the prefectural chapters' votes. Of the LDP's 47 prefectural chapters, 27 said they would prefer the continuation of the Abe administration's policy directions (Asahi, September 12, 2020). Suga might have been considered as the best successor of Abe.

Although it started with a very high approval ratio of 74% (Nikkei, September 18, 2020), the Suga administration became very unpopular in less than one year, with its approval ratio hovering around 34% in July 2021 (Nikkei, July 27, 2021) and 28% in August (Asahi, August 10, 2021). As explained in Leheny (2022), although the administration hoped the Tokyo Olympics would work as a catalyst to improve its popularity, a majority of Japanese citizens believed the Olympics was unsafe and unsecure (Asahi, August 10, 2021). As Lipscy (2022) and Thies and Yanai (2022) show, the administration's countermeasures to the COVID-19 were perceived to be largely unsuccessful: The Go To Travel campaign, a stimulus package targeted at the local tourism industry, had to be canceled in December 2020, with the spread of the virus; the state of COVID-19 emergency was declared in Tokyo in July 2021 and expanded to 19 other prefectures in July and August; and new infection cases hit a record high at more than 25,000 in August.

Thus, although Suga reportedly wanted to dissolve the lower house by September and win the election to stay in power, such a strategy became highly risky. With the approval ratio of Suga steadily declining, the LDP kept losing elections: by-elections for the lower house and the upper house in April; elections for the Tokyo Metropolitan Assembly in July; and the Yokohama mayoral election in August. Some junior members demanded a change in the leadership, saying that it would be difficult to compete in the coming election with Suga at the head of the party (Asahi, August 28, 2021). Reportedly, an internal opinion poll conducted in August by the LDP revealed that more than 60 members would not get reelected under Suga's leadership (Asahi, September 10, 2021).

Against this background, Suga decided on September 3 not to run for the coming presidential selection (Asahi, September 3, 2021, Evening Edition). In the political vacuum created by his sudden resignation, four contenders decided to run for the party presidency: Kishida Fumio, Kōno Tarō, Takaichi Sanae, and Noda Seiko. Since the next lower election constitutionally needed to be held by November 2021, members, especially junior ones, wanted whoever would be the most popular among voters and helpful in improving the image of the party and their reelection chances (Asahi, September 6, 2021). A consortium composed of the LDP's junior members, *Tōfū Isshin no Kai,* demanded the party presidential selection should not be held behind the closed doors and members should be able to select their own leader independent from factions' interests (Asahi, September 12, 2021). Factions, except the Kishida faction, decided not to support any specific candidate at least in the first round (Asahi, September 16, 2021).

Unlike the previous selections in 2018 and 2020, there was no clear frontrunner in the race. A poll revealed that Ishiba, who used to be popular among *tōin* and *tōyū* in the previous selections, was in fact less popular than Kōno, who had a significant presence as the minister responsible for vaccination (Yomiuri Shimbun September 7, 2021). Thus Ishiba gave up running and instead supported Kōno, who was popular among voters with 41% of *tōin* and *tōyū* choosing Kōno as a next leader (Yomiuri, September 20, 2021), but his maverick stance was "absolutely unacceptable" among veteran members (Asahi, September 6, 2021). Meanwhile, although Kishida and Takaichi lagged behind in terms of support from *tōin* and *tōyū,* they were more popular among Diet members: Kishida secured headcounts from his own faction's 46 members and veterans; and Takaichi was backed by Abe and many of his Hosoda faction. As none of the candidates was likely to win a majority in the first round, Kishida and Takaichi agreed to form a coalition in the second majority run-off (Asahi, September 29, 2021, Evening Edition).

Given the uncertainty of the race, the contenders stepped up every effort to shore up *tōin* and *tōyū* votes. Given that the party decided not to sponsor any local rallies like the previous selection (Asahi, September 17, 2021, Evening Edition), from time to time, all the contenders tried to have online meetings with LDP supporters and local assembly members (Yomiuri, September 20, 2021). Previously unseen was the proactive use of social networking services: Kishida started to respond to citizens' opinions on Twitter, and Takaichi resumed her Twitter account for the first

Table 4.3 The result of the 2021 presidential selection

First round	Diet members	Tōin and Tōyū	Total
Kishida	146	110	256
Kōno	86	169	255
Takaichi	114	74	188
Noda	34	29	63
Second round	Diet members	Prefectural chapters	Total
Kishida	249	8	257
Kōno	131	39	170

time in more than two years to increase followers (Yomiuri, September 18, 2021). They should have been influenced by tech-savvy Kōno, whose Twitter account boasted more than 2.4 million followers as of September 2021.

The 2021 presidential selection chose Kishida as the LDP's new leader, as shown in Table 4.3. As expected, Kōno won the most *tōin* and *tōyū* votes, but he was less popular among Diet members. Kishida gained broad support from both Diet members and *tōin* and *tōyū*. The coalition of Kishida and Takaichi worked well in the second round, as most of the supporters for Takaichi seemed to vote for Kishida.

Kishida's new administration started with the mediocre approval ratio of 45% (Asahi, October 8, 2021, p. 3). This was better than Suga's 28% in August, but still not very high. Campaigning for the 2021 election, one LDP member said, "I feel no headwinds, but no tailwinds either" (Asahi, October 15, 2021, p. 2). In retrospect, this statement was right: The LDP did not lose, partly because it was able to replace the unpopular prime minister; and the LDP did not win, partly because it failed to select the candidate most popular among the general Japanese voters.

NOMINATIONS

The LDP has long practiced a de facto policy of "*kateba Jimintō*," or "If you win, you are LDP" (Reed 2009). That is, even if a candidate does not have a nomination from the LDP, as long as you win in an election, you will be accepted to the party. The LDP used to and still does give an ex post nomination (*tsuika kōnin*) after an election to a candidate running as an independent and winning a seat—sometimes by defeating an LDP incumbent! Reed (2009) calls such independents Liberal Democratic Independents (LDIs). Former LDIs include even a former prime minister, Mori Yoshirō.

LDIs flourished under the pre-reform SNTV system, because the system made the impact of party label significantly weak. According to Thayer (1969), a nomination from the LDP to was worth about 10,000 votes, compared to 79,806 votes that an average candidate would need to win a seat (Nemoto et al. 2014). Thus as long as candidates had powerful personal vote mobilization networks, or *kōenkai*, they gave it a try. On top of that, because factional headcounts mattered much in the presidential selection process, factional bosses sometimes implicitly supported LDIs to outcompete other factions' candidates in the same districts, in an attempt to expand their factions (Nemoto et al. 2014). Between 1958 and 1990, as many as 44 LDIs ran on average (Smith and Reed 2018).

In theory, the reform from SNTV to MMM should be expected to reduce *hoshu bunretsu* or multiple conservative candidates competing over the same vote. Note that *hoshu bunretsu* necessarily took place under the pre-reform system, since a majority-seeking party like the LDP had to nominate multiple candidates in the same district. But now a party nominates only one candidate representing the party in a single-member district (SMD). Voters vote for a candidate as an agent for a party. Thus party label is much more important and running as an independent should be discouraged. Indeed, as shown in Fig. 4.1, *hoshu bunretsu* has been declining, although it never disappeared. Between 1996 and 2009, on average, 34 districts had *hoshu bunretsu*. Beginning from the 2012 election, *hoshu bunretsu* rapidly declined to only nine districts in 2017.

The LDP needs to prevent *hoshu bunretsu*, since it could result in *tomodaore*, or candidates from the same camp losing to other parties. Let us take an example of Kanagawa 4. In 2014, Asao Keiichirō ran as an independent and won a seat. Before the 2017 election, Asao joined the LDP to apply for a nomination from the party. The Kanagawa prefectural chapter balked, since the district had another incumbent from the LDP, Yamamoto Tomohiro, who was elected through the PR tier of the electoral system. The chapter said nominating Asao would cause a serious fission inside the local organization (Asahi, September 27, 2017) and demanded no other candidate than Yamamoto should get a nomination or a rank in the party's PR list (Asahi, September 30, 2017). Asao still

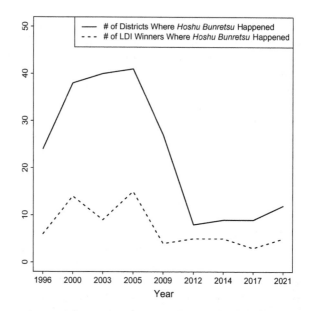

Fig. 4.1 Number of districts where *Hoshu Bunretsu* happened and number of LDI winners where *Hoshu Bunretsu* happened, 1996–2001 (*Source* Smith and Reed [2018] and the author's analysis)

ran as an LDI, but as a result of the conservative vote being split to Asao and Yamamoto, an opposition candidate won a seat.[2]

As shown in Table 4.4, *hoshu bunretsu* was possible in 23 districts in the 2021 election. As also explained in Rehmert (2022), the LDP has three strategies in preventing *hoshu bunretsu*. First, it can simply use the old practice of letting candidates run as independents and guaranteeing a winner *tsuika kōnin* (Reed 2009). This strategy is called *Fukuoka Hōshiki* (Fukuoka method), which is thus named since in the 2016 by-election for Fukuoka 6, the LDP did not nominate any candidate but just let two LDIs run and gave *tsuika kōnin* to Hatoyama Jirō, the winner (Yomiuri, February 6, 2019). In the 2021 election, *Fukuoka Hōshiki* was used in Tokyo 15, where Kakizawa Mito and Imamura Hirofumi applied for LDP nominations.[3] Kakizawa won and was accepted to the LDP with *tsuika kōnin*. Given that this strategy is very risky, since an opposition candidate may benefit from *hoshu bunretsu* and win, the party now seems to use the second and third strategies more often.

Table 4.4 Districts where *Hoshu Bunretsu* was possible in 2021

	District incumbent	Zombie incumbent[1]	Contenders for LDP nomination	LDP nomination
Hokkaido 7	Itō Yoshitaka		Itō Yoshitaka Suzuki Takako	Itō Yoshitaka
Gunma 1	Omi Asako		Omi Asako Nakasone Yasutaka	Nakasone Yasutaka
Tokyo 15	(Open seat)	Kakizawa Mito	Kakizawa Mito Hirofumi Imamura	None
Kanagawa 4	Waseda Yuki (CDP)	Yamamoto Tomohiro	Yamamoto Tomohiro Asao Keiichirō	Yamamoto Tomohiro
Niigata 2	Washio Eiichirō	Hosoda Ken'ichi	Washio Eiichirō Hosoda Ken'ichi	Hosoda Ken'ichi
Niigata 5	Izumida Hirohiko		Izumida Hirohiko Mori Tamio	Izumida Hirohiko
Fukui 2	Takagi Tsuyoshi	Saiki Takeshi (Hope)	Takagi Tsuyoshi Yamamoto Taku	Takagi Tsuyoshi
Shizuoka 5	Hosono Gōshi		Hosono Gōshi Yoshikawa Takeru	Yoshikawa Takeru
Osaka 3	Satō Shigeki (Komeito)		Yanagimoto Akira	None
Hyogo 1	Moriyama Masahito		Moriyama Masahito Takahashi Shingo	Moriyama Masahito
Okayama 3	Abe Toshiko		Abe Toshiko Hiranuma Shōjirō	Abe Toshiko
Hiroshima 4	Shintani Masayoshi		Shintani Masayoshi Nakagawa Toshinao	Shintani Masayoshi
Yamaguchi 3	Kawamura Takeo		Kawamura Takeo Hayashi Yoshimasa	Hayashi Yoshimasa
Tokushima 1	Gotōda Masazumi		Gotōda Masazumi Fukuyama Mamoru	Gotōda Masazumi
Ehime 4	(Open seat)		Hasegawa Junji Sakurauchi Fumiki	Hasegawa Junji

(continued)

Table 4.4   (continued)

	District incumbent	Zombie incumbent[1]	Contenders for LDP nomination	LDP nomination
Kochi 2	Hirota Hajime (CDP)	Yamamoto Yūji	Ozaki Masanao Yamamoto Yūji	Ozaki Masanao
Fukuoka 5	Harada Yoshiaki		Harada Yoshiaki Kunihara Wataru	Harada Yoshiaki
Nagasaki 4	Kitamura Seigo		Kitamura Seigo Segawa Mitsuyuki	Kitamura Seigo
Kumamoto 2	Noda Takeshi		Noda Takeshi Nishino Daisuke	Noda Takeshi
Miyazaki 1	Takei Shunsuke		Takei Shunsuke Wakitani Noriko	Takei Shunsuke
Kagoshima 1	Kawauchi Hiroshi (CDP)		Miyaji Takuma Yasuoka Hirotake	Miyaji Takuma
Okinawa 1	Akamine Seiken (JCP)	Kokuba Kōnosuke Shimoji Mikio (Ishin)	Kokuba Kōnosuke Shimoji Mikio	Kokuba Kōnosuke

[1]A zombie incumbent refers to a candidate who lost in the 2017 election in the district but survived on the PR tier

Source Author's analysis

The second strategy is to use the PR tier. The LDP utilizes its internal polls to give nominations to winnable candidates in SMDs (Nikkei, October 16, 2021). Candidates deselected are instead given good ranks on the PR list if they are electorally competitive, while electorally vulnerable candidates are given hopeless ranks. In 2021, 10 candidates gave up running on their SMDs and instead ran as pure-PR candidates. Some SMD incumbents, such as Omi Asako from Gunma 1 and Washio Eiichirō from Niigata 2, were preferentially treated on the lists with the first ranks, perhaps because they won the last elections with comfortable margins. Meanwhile, Kawamura Takeo, a ten-term incumbent in Yamaguchi 3, was forced to resign. Kawamura was challenged by Hayashi Yoshimasa, a five-term member of the House of Councillors, who wanted to switch to the HR. Kawamura gave in, since Hayashi was able to collect endorsements from all of the 26 Yamaguchi Prefectural Assembly members from the LDP and all of the four mayors in the district (Asahi, July 16, 2021).[4]

The third strategy is to threaten a candidate. For instance, in Fukuoka 5, a former Fukuoka Prefectural Assembly member, Kurihara Wataru, planned to run as an LDI to challenge Harada Yoshiaki, an incumbent in the district. Some local supporters demanded Harada, aged 77, should be replaced by younger Kurihara. The party headquarters intervened, proposing that Harada would run in the 2021 election, while Kurihara would run in the next. To Kurihara, this message from the party meant that if Kurihara still chose to run as an independent, the LDP would purge him (Yomiuri, October 16, 2021). That is, even if Kurihara would win as an independent, the LDP would not welcome him with *tsuika kōnin* and he would have to face an official LDP challenger a couple of years later. Thus Kurihara gave up the idea of running.[5]

Thus all in all, in 23 districts where *hoshu bunretsu* was possible, the LDP was able to prevent it in 11 of them by using the three strategies above. In the remaining 12 districts where *hoshu bunretsu* happened, five LDIs won seats. Winners include high-profile candidates such as: Hosono Gōshi in Shizuoka 5, a seven-term veteran incumbent who defected from the Party of Hope; Hiranuma Shōjirō in Okayama 3, the son of Hiranuma Takeo, who was expelled in 2005 from the LDP but kept retaining his seat with his strong *kōenkai*; and Mitazono Satoshi in Kagoshima 2, a former Kagoshima prefectural governor. The LDP won two districts in Hiroshima 4 and Ehime 4, but it lost to the opposition in five districts where LDIs took away some conservative votes from its candidates.[6]

Given that just letting LDIs run and giving *tsuika kōnin* to whoever wins is such a risky strategy, the LDP should not be happy about welcoming LDI winners to the party now. Worse, the strategy could also encourage future LDIs to run and challenge LDP incumbents. After the 2021 election, only one candidate was given *tsuika kōnin* (Kakizawa Mito), while one was later admitted to the LDP (Hosono Gōshi) and one joined the LDP's *kaiha*, or legislative faction (Hiranuma Shōjirō). A member of the LDP's Shizuoka prefectural chapter was indignant, saying, "Even though Hosono did whatever he wanted to, it is shameful for the LDP to say, 'You can join the party'" (Asahi, November 13, 2021). Although Mitazono wanted to join the LDP after the election, the Kagoshima prefectural chapter said, "Probably that would not happen" (Asahi, November 3, 2021).

CONCLUSION

This chapter focused on the LDP's presidential selection and candidate nomination processes to analyze how the party got prepared to stay in power before the 2021 election. With the new presidential selection process, the party was at least able to replace an unpopular leader before the election, although it did not choose the most popular one. Using various tools at disposal, such as internal polls and the PR tier, the party tried to minimize *hoshu bunretsu*, although ultimately it took place in 12 districts and the party lost to the opposition in five of them. So overall, the LDP was able to avoid a major loss, while it was not able to increase its seats.

NOTES

1. Votes from *tōin* and *tōyū* are allocated to candidates using the d'Hondt method.
2. Yamamoto was able to retain a seat through the PR tier. Exactly the same drama took place in 2021.
3. Kakizawa lost the SMD race in 2017 with a nomination from the now defunct Party of Hope but survived on the PR tier. He left the party in 2018 to become an independent. Imamura was a former lower-house member (2012–2014) from the Japan Restoration Party on the PR tier. He switched to the LDP in 2015 and unsuccessfully ran in 2017.
4. In exchange, Kawamura's son was given the 32nd rank on the Kitakantō PR bloc and lost.
5. Despite Kurihara's concession, Harada lost to an opposition candidate in 2021.
6. They are Yamamoto Tomohiro in Kanagawa 4, Izumida Hirohiko from Niigata 5, Moriyama Masahiro in Hyogo 1, Takei Shunsuke in Miyazaki 1, and Kokuba Kōnosuke in Okinawa 1.

REFERENCES

Leheny, David. 2022. "The Olympics in the 2021 Election." In Robert J. Pekkanen, Steven R. Reed, and Daniel M. Smith (eds.), *Japan Decides 2021: The Japanese General Election*. Palgrave Macmillan.

Lipscy, Phillip Y. 2022. "Japan's Response to the COVID-19 Pandemic." In Robert J. Pekkanen, Steven R. Reed, and Daniel M. Smith (eds.), *Japan Decides 2021: The Japanese General Election*. Palgrave Macmillan.

Maeda, Yukio. 2022. "Public Opinion and COVID-19." In Robert J. Pekkanen, Steven R. Reed, and Daniel M. Smith (eds.), *Japan Decides 2021: The Japanese General Election*. Palgrave Macmillan.

Nemoto, Kuniaki. 2021. "Japan's Liberal Democratic Party: Changes in Party Organization under Shinzō Abe." In Robert J. Pekkanen and Saadia M.

Pekkanen (eds.), *The Oxford Handbook of Japanese Politics*. Oxford: Oxford University Press.

Nemoto, Kuniaki, Robert Pekkanen, and Ellis Krauss. 2014. "Over-Nominating Candidates, Undermining the Party: The Collective Action Problem Under Sntv in Japan." *Party Politics* 20: 740–750.

Pekkanen, Robert J., and Steven R. Reed. 2022. "The Opposition in 2021: A Second Party and a Third Force." In Robert J. Pekkanen, Steven R. Reed, and Daniel M. Smith (eds.), *Japan Decides 2021: The Japanese General Election*. Palgrave Macmillan.

Reed, Steven R. 2009. "Party Strategy or Candidate Strategy: How Does the Ldp Run the Right Number of Candidates in Japan's Multi-Member Districts?" *Party Politics* 15: 295–314.

Rehmert, Jochen. 2022. "Candidate Selection for the 2021 General Election." In Robert J. Pekkanen, Steven R. Reed, and Daniel M. Smith (eds.), *Japan Decides 2021: The Japanese General Election*. Palgrave Macmillan.

Smith, Daniel M., and Steven R. Reed. 2018. "The Reed-Smith Japanese House of Representatives Elections Dataset." V1 ed: Harvard Dataverse.

Thayer, Nathaniel B. 1969. *How the conservatives rule Japan*. Princeton: Princeton University Press.

Thies, Michael, and Yuki Yanai. 2022. "Did COVID-19 Impact Japan's 2021 General Election?" In Robert J. Pekkanen, Steven R. Reed, and Daniel M. Smith (eds.), *Japan Decides 2021: The Japanese General Election*. Palgrave Macmillan.

Newspaper Articles

Asahi, September 27, 2017. "Kaku Tō no Ugoki, Kappatsuka." Yokohama edition. p. 29.

Asahi, September 30, 2017. "Jimintō Kenren ga Honbu ni Yōseibun." Yokohama edition. p. 25.

Asahi, January 9, 2018. "'Posuto Abe' Shiwasu no Omowaku." p. 1.

Asahi, June 25, 2018. "Tsugi no Sōsai, Shushō 30% de Shui." p. 2.

Asahi, August 30, 2020. "Syōryaku, Tōnai ni Iron." p. 3.

Asahi, August 31, 2020. Evening Edition. "Shū Ake Nagatachō, Ugoki Kyū." p. 1.

Asahi, September 1, 2020. "Sōsaisen, Senryaku ni Gosan." p. 2.

Asahi, September 4, 2020. "Tsugi no Shushō, Fusawashii no wa." p. 1.

Asahi, September 12, 2020. "Chihō, Korona Keizai Taisaku wo Yōbō." p. 4.

Asahi, July 16, 2021. "Shūin Yamaguchi 3-ku, Jimin Mapputatsu." p. 4.

Asahi, August 10, 2021. "Gosan, Seiken Fuyō no Kibakuzai." p. 3.

Asahi, August 28, 2021. "Kishida-shi, Tō Sasshin Zenmen." p. 4.

Asahi, September 3, 2021, Evening Edition. "Suga Shushō, Sōsaisen Shutsuba Sezu." p. 1.

Asahi, September 6, 2021. "Wakate Giin, 'Kao' Shina Sadame." p. 3.

Asahi, September 10, 2021. "Nikai-shi 'On Shirazu.'" p. 1.

Asahi, September 12, 2021. "Seiken wa Gōin? 'Wakate' Kikikan." p. 3.

Asahi, September 16, 2021. "Kaku Habatsu, Irei no Jishu Tōhyō." p. 1.

Asahi, September 17, 2021, Evening Edition. "Yūzei sezu, Onrain de Tōronkai." p. 1.

Asahi, September 29, 2021, Evening Edition. "Sōsaisen, Kecchaku he." p. 1.

Asahi, October 8, 2021. "Semaru Shūinsen, 2-hosen Kokuji." p. 3.

Asahi, October 15, 2021. "Goshūgi Kitai vs. Kyōto Kyōka." p. 2.

Asahi, November 3, 2021. "Jimin Iri no Ikō, Tōsen no Mitazono-shi ga Shimesu." Kagoshima edition. p. 21.

Asahi, November 13, 2021. "Mushozoku Tōsen Giin, Jimintō he Zokuzoku Nyūtō." p. 4.

Nikkei, February 22, 2019. "Posuto Abe ha Abe-shi?" p. 4.

Nikkei, August 31, 2020. "Shin Shushō Senshutsu, Raigetsu 17-nichi nimo." p. 1.

Nikkei, September 2, 2020, Evening Edition. "Sōsaisen, 14-nichi Tōkaihyō Kettei." p. 1.

Nikkei, September 18, 2020. "Kan Naikaku Shijiritsu 74%, Hossoku Ji 3-banme no Takasa." p. 1.

Nikkei, July 27, 2021. "Shijiritsu 'Kiken Suiiki' Chikaduku." p. 4.

Nikkei, October 16, 2021. "Jimin 'Kateru Kōho' Yūsen." p. 2.

Yomiuri, May 21, 2018. "Tōinhyō Haya Sōdatsusen." p. 3.

Yomiuri, July 22, 2018. "Jimin Sōsaisen 4-nin ga Iyoku." p. 3.

Yomiuri, September 17, 2018. "Gaikō Keizai de Abe-shi Shiji." p. 3.

Yomiuri, February 6, 2019. "Hinpatsu Suru Hoshu Bunretsu Sono 2." p. 4.

Yomiuri, August 31, 2020. "Hosoda Asō Ha Dōkō Kagi." p. 3.

Yomiuri, September 4, 2020, Evening Edition. "Sōsaisen Chihō Yūzei Okonawazu." p. 1.

Yomiuri, September 8, 2020, Evening Edition. "Jimin Sōsaisen Kokuji." p. 1.

Yomiuri, September 9, 2020, Evening Edition. "Suga-shi Kōmu de Zaikyō." p. 1.

Yomiuri, September 7, 2021. "Ishiba-shi Tōin Hyō Yūsei Kuzureru." p. 2

Yomiuri, September 18, 2021. "Sōsaisen, Kisou Hassinryoku." p. 1.

Yomiuri, September 20, 2021. "Jimin Sōsaisen Tōin Hyō." p. 1.

Yomiuri, October 16, 2021. "Shūinsen Kōtairon Osae Zengiin Jimin Kōnin Kecchaku." p. 31.

CHAPTER 5

The Opposition in 2021: A Second Party and a Third Force

Robert J. Pekkanen⬥ *and Steven R. Reed*

Elsewhere, one of us has referred to the transformations of the opposition camp in Japan as "telenovela-like" (Pekkanen and Pekkanen 2015). Since the outcome of the 2017 election, what would normally pass for quite dramatic developments have rocked the opposition in Japan. However, these have not drawn the attention they merit, perhaps because they pale beside the drama of the 2017 election—when two brand new parties flared into existence just before the election and placed second (Constitutional Democratic Party of Japan, or CDP) and third (Party of Hope) in the election results. The rise of these two parties also signaled the demise of the Democratic Party of Japan (DPJ), arguably the second most successful party in Japanese political history. The larger of those

R. J. Pekkanen (✉)
Jackson School of International Studies, University of Washington, Seattle, WA, USA
e-mail: pekkanen@uw.edu

S. R. Reed
Faculty of Policy Studies, Chuo University, Tokyo, Japan

R. J. Pekkanen et al. (eds.), *Japan Decides 2021*,
https://doi.org/10.1007/978-3-031-11324-6_5

two parties, the CDP, is the standard bearer for the opposition today. The other of those parties is essentially gone from Japanese politics (although the half life of failed parties is long in Japan). In many countries, the disappearance of the third largest party would be a dramatic event. By the standards of Japan's opposition parties, however, it seems to hardly elicit much attention.

In this chapter, we review developments in the opposition both in the longer period of 2017–2021 and in the immediate run up to and including the 2021 election. As always, there is a lot going on. In the 2017–2021 period, the third largest party, Hope, imploded and left a rump party, the Democratic Party for the People (DPP). The second largest party after the 2017 election, the CDP, absorbed many former Hope members and solidified its place as the main opposition party. In the run up to the election, the CDP closely coordinated with the Japanese Communist Party (JCP) to an unprecedented degree. Despite this, the CDP came away from the election disappointed, and party leader Edano Yukio resigned. The surprise opposition "winner" of the election was Ishin, a conservative party that drew heavy support around its Osaka base. This sets the stage for potential further turmoil and probably pushes back the clock on the chance an "opposition" party can defeat the LDP at the polls.

The Opposition 2017–2021: Disappearance of Hope, Consolidation Around CDP

Scheiner and Thies (2022:183) summarize the record of Japanese opposition parties as follows: "… opposition parties in Japan have failed at an alarming rate for more than half a century." They then go on to divide the history of opposition into three distinct periods: (1) opposition as protest (1955–1989), (2) opposition as alternative government (1989–2012), and (3) opposition as irrelevant (2012–present).

Period 1 was the era of LDP predominance. The transition from period 1 to period 2 began with the LDP loss of the House of Councillors (HC) and was spurred by the electoral reform of 1994 which introduced an electoral system featuring single-member districts (SMDs). The opposition parties quickly learned the most obvious lesson of the new system: a divided opposition loses. This lesson is simply a way of stating Duverger's Law or recognizing the incentives for opposition to consolidate into a single candidate in a single-member district (SMD) and has been rammed home at each election since the first in 1996. The transition to period three was caused by the failure of the Democratic Party of Japan (DPJ) in government and the opposition fragmentation that followed. Facing a divided opposition, the LDP was able to reestablish predominance without increasing their vote totals.

Duverger's Law is working in Japan but that law applies only to elections in single-member districts, not to other elections nor to policy. Thus, even in their fragmented state, the opposition parties managed to present a single challenger to the LDP in every House of Councillors single-member district in both 2016 and 2019 while continuing to compete among themselves elsewhere. Fragmentation occurs *between* elections and is caused by disagreements over policy and strategy. The conservative opposition seeks a party that proposes "realistic" policy proposals which, in practice, means policies that the LDP might adopt. Progressives, on the other hand, seek an opposition party that challenges the LDP on the issues. In other words, progressives want to offer voters a choice while conservatives want to offer an echo. Conservatives refuse to cooperate with the JCP while progressives have developed a close relationship with that party.

Soon after the 2017 election, the Party of Hope disintegrated. Its failure followed a pattern of conservative opposition party failure (Pekkanen and Reed 2018: 89). The fifteen Democrats who refused to join Hope (and perhaps would never have been accepted by that party anyway) and formed the CDP representing the progressive wing (particularly on security issues—the "constitutional" in the party name is a nod to Article 9) had fared quite well, gaining 40 new seats and (at 55) surpassing Hope by five seats. The 2019 HC election was another victory for the LDP but the progressive CDP fared much better than the conservative DPP (see Pekkanen and Reed 2022). The progressive opposition was represented by the CDP, the Social Democratic Party of Japan (SDP), and the JCP; and, the conservative opposition by the DPP and Ishin. As the parties prepared for the next election, the force of Duverger's Law led to merger negotiations between the CDP and the DPP. These negotiations resulted in the bulk of the DPP joining the CDP. The CDP thus emerged as the undisputed leader of the opposition camp. All four progressive parties cooperated in the Diet and fielded a single candidate in many electoral districts. The CDP in 2021 thus offered the largest and most unified alternative to the LDP since the DPJ in 2009. Everything pointed to the emergence of a more competitive party system up until the votes were counted. An aspect of the mixed-member electoral system which had never had a major impact on election outcomes (PR tier) upset all predictions giving the LDP another win.

The opposition parties managed to cooperate and even merge with the CDP under the pressure of the approaching election but the potential for yet another fragmentation remained. First, some of those joining the CDP did not do so because they had learned that a conservative strategy cannot defeat the LDP but simply because the CDP represented a safe ship in the approaching electoral storm. They obeyed Duverger's Law during the election with no intention of following a progressive strategy or the CDP policy platform after the election.

Second, the labor unions that support the DPP have no interest in shifting their support to the CDP. These unions are unwilling to cooperate with the JCP and do not support many of the progressive policies of the CDP. In the 2019 upper house election five unions sponsored candidates for the CDP and five others sponsored candidates for the DPP. Union sponsored candidates delivered 1,101,812 votes to the DPP, 1.7 times more than the 689,719 votes union sponsored candidates provided the CDP. Union sponsored candidates provided 31.7% of the DPP's total PR vote and 84.3% of those who chose to vote for a candidate rather than a party. Union sponsored candidates running for the CDP won a total of 689,719 votes, providing 8.9% of the party's total vote and 47.3% of its candidate votes. However, PR seats in the HC are allocated on the basis of the total PR vote, the sum of the number of voted for the party and those who voted for a candidate nominated by a party. Union candidates nominated by the CDP won five seats while those nominated by the DPP won only three. Several of the DPP candidates who refused to join the CDP were those dependent upon unions for their votes. Some of the DPP unions preferred cooperation with the LDP to cooperation with the CDP and the JCP. The clearest case is the Toyota union, the largest union in Japan Auto Workers and a major player in Aichi politics, refused to endorse any CDP candidates except those who were union members.

THE 2021 ELECTION AND THE OPPOSITION

There are three main points to discuss with relation to the election results. First, the CDP lost several seats—down to 96 from 110. Second, the CDP had very effective coordination with the JCP. Third, Ishin did surprisingly well, zooming from 11 seats to 41. So, the results were not great for CDP, but were surprisingly good for Ishin. Our interpretation of this is that Ishin got a bump for Governor Yoshimura Hirofumi's handling of the coronavirus pandemic in Osaka. This at least distracts from, and possibly sets back significantly, the consolidation of the opposition around the CDP. Without Ishin's good showing, the main headlines for the opposition on November 1, 2021, would possibly have been about the success of the opposition coordination effort. So, our view is that this election is reminiscent of the failure of the New Frontier Party (NFP) in 1998. The NFP rose as a big opposition party seemingly capable of competing with the LDP in a 2+ party system and setting a pattern of alternation in power. However, the party splintered due to internal divisions and disbanded before it could ever win an election. The formation and then dissolution of the NFP set back the clock, as it were, for the rise of the DPJ challenge and successful 2009 DPJ election. It is possible that CDP will not follow a similar trajectory to take power. After all, few predicted the rise of Ishin or the Party of Hope's ephemeral burst of success.

The CDP: Japan's Second Party

The big loser in the 2021 election was the CDP. Despite expectations of major gains, the CDP lost 14 seats. The LDP lost seats, too, but was able to declare victory and hold a "stable majority." To rub salt in the wound, a rival opposition party did very well as, despite being largely ignored, Ishin gained 30 seats. Both these gains and losses were concentrated in the PR tier. The CDP gained 9 SMDs but lost 23 PR seats while Ishin gained 13 SMD seats and 17 PR seats. Ishin's SMD gains were all in its home base in Osaka and were easily explained by the popularity of their governor. The PR gains and losses were harder to explain.

The CDP strategy was successful in the SMDs. Not only did it gain 9 seats but ran very close races in many more. The CDP PR winners averaged a ratio of votes to winner's votes (sekihairitsu) of 93.2%, at least 25 of them presenting a serious challenge to the winning LDP candidate. If it were not for the PR tier results, the CDP would have made a strong case for "just one more push." However, something went seriously wrong with their PR strategy.

The explanation that surfaced in media commentary in Japan is that many voters chose the opposition candidate in the SMD but could not bring themselves to write CDP on their PR ballot. They chose instead neither right nor left by voting Ishin. Voters shied away from the CDP because it was cooperating with the JCP. Commentators conclude that the CDP has to stop cooperating with the JCP and move toward the center. The problem with this interpretation is that it endorses the strategy that has failed repeatedly since 2012. We find little evidence of a JCP allergy in the SMD races. Reports make it clear that the LDP featured red-baiting in their campaigns in two districts, Kagawa 1st and Kanagawa 13th. In both districts, the CDP candidate won. In Kanagawa the LDP loser was Amari Akira, secretary-general of the LDP.

So what did go wrong with the CDP PR vote? A definitive explanation will have to await analyses of data not yet available but one serious difference between 2019 and 2021 is the abbreviations of the party name used by the CDP. In 2019, it was *rikken* (in hiragana) but in 2021 it was *minshuto* (in Chinese characters), the abbreviation used by the DPP in both elections. Two parties with the same abbreviation was confusing at the least. Asahi reports that over 100,000 votes wrote *minshu* on their ballots and, as the law prescribes, these votes were divided between the CDP and the DPP in proportion to their verified votes.

Edano Yukio resigned as CDP party leader after the 2021 election to take responsibility for the showing. He was replaced by Izumi Kenta in November 2021.

The SDP

The SDP has no future in national elections but it has a strong base in several prefectures and unions and in local government. That base resists joining the CDP. However, as the election approached some prefectural branches of the SDP moved toward merger (Asahi 6 November 2020). The SDP organization is concentrated in Kyushu where the CDP is weak. Oita is particularly important. The unions that support the SDP, most notably the local and prefectural government employee union Jichirō, are firmly in the CDP camp nationwide. The SDP was one of the four opposition parties to engage in electoral cooperation, along with CDP, JCP, and Reiwa Shinsengumi.

Reiwa Shinsengumi

Reiwa Shinsengumi is a new party founded in 2019 by actor-turned-politician Yamamoto Tarō. "Reiwa" is the reign name of the current

Emperor, and "shinsengumi" is a group from the end of the Tokugawa shogunate. Reiwa Shinsengumi is usually viewed as a progressive populist party. In the year of its formation, the party entered the legislature after winning two seats in the 2019 HC election. The party took party in the four-party opposition party cooperation arrangement in the HR 2021 election. Reiwa ran in 12 districts (and listed 21 candidates in PR), winning no districts but taking 3 PR seats on 3.86% of the party vote—including Yamamoto Tarō in the Tokyo bloc. Gill Steel (2022) discusses Reiwa's campaign strategies for young voters. After the 2021 election, the party remained very small and faces an uncertain future.

The JCP

The DPP and the unions that support it both reject any cooperation with the JCP. Both the CDP and DPP tried to walk a tightrope in order to keep the opposition unified, obeying Duverger's Law, but the reality is that the CDP had to choose between the DPP and the JCP. The electoral calculus makes it clear that the JCP is the more attractive partner. The JCP won 1,002,358 more votes in PR than the DPP in the 2019 House of Councillors election, had more support in the polls, and an infinitely stronger organization. The JCP thus had more votes and was expected to be capable of delivering a higher percentage of that vote them to the CDP while the DPP and its unions have fewer votes and were much less likely to deliver them to the CDP.

In the 2021 election, the JCP delivered 82% of their votes to the CDP even though the CDP delivered only 46% of their votes to the JCP (Yomiuri Shinbun, November 1, 2021). The JCP is willing to participate in this asymmetric exchange because even 47% is an improvement over previous elections. Relationships between the JCP and the opposition candidates who have experienced cooperation have grown warmer. Between the 2014 and 2017 general elections the mean JCP thermometer reading of Democratic candidates (defined as those candidates who ran in 2014 or were slated to run for *Minshinto* in 2017) rose from 27.5 to 43.6 according to the UTAS candidate surveys. Those who were nominated by the CDP rose to 54.1 and for those who ran as independents to 51.2 but those nominated by Hope in 2017 remained low at 34.2.[1] "When the opposition candidate looked out at their crowds, they saw JCP supporters and members of the various citizens' groups that had demanded a single opposition candidate. Naturally, they felt the need to address their concerns" (Interview by author with Tamura Tomoko, JCP Vice-Chair, Tokyo, Japan, February 19, 2020).

The Democratic Party for the People

The Democratic Party for the People is a conservative party that emerged out of the chaos of the 2017 election, which saw the rise of the Party of Hope and the splintering of the Democratic Party (DPJ) into the liberal Constitutional Democratic Party and those mostly conservative members who joined the Party of Hope. The rump Democratic Party and the Party of Hope then merged to form the Democratic Party for the People in 2018 (DPP, sometimes also abbreviated DPFP). The DPP rapidly returned to its conservative strategy. In September 2020, most of the DPP members left to join the CDP. However, some members (14) remained, led by Tamaki Yuichiro. This rump DPP retained the DPP party name. The opposition, which included the DPP until that party split, had cooperated in attacking the LDP for their repeated scandals but after the split, party leader Tamaki Yuichiro stopped participating (Yomiuri Shinbun, October 10, 2020). In some ways, the DPP stopped being an opposition party. In July 2021, Tamaki doubled down on the issue of cooperation with the JCP by declaring that Communism is a form of totalitarianism. The JCP responded by nominating candidates in two districts with a DPP. The DPP remained a small conservative party after the results of the 2021 election, winning 5 PR seats (on 4.51%) and 6 district seats.

The Third Force Opposition: Ishin

Ishin is a local party with a solid base in Osaka but has not been able to extend its presence beyond Osaka and the neighboring prefectures. Ishin did not participate in any of the joint opposition talks, taking neither a pro-LDP nor a pro-opposition side. They were led by a popular governor who delivered an overwhelming victory in Osaka prefecture, defeating the LDP every district while leaving Komeito candidates unchallenged. Their strategy outside the Kinki bloc was to run candidates in as many districts as possible to attract PR votes ("contamination"). This works but is normally an extremely inefficient way of winning PR seats. A party must nominate many SMD candidates who have no chance of winning the

SMD in order to win one or two PR seats. In this election, the strategy proved wildly successful.

One should not, however, jump to the conclusion that Ishin's PR strategy worked. None of Ishin's SMD candidates outside of the Kinki bloc came close to winning their SMD. The average sekihairitsu of their PR winners outside of Kinki was 51.4%, meaning that they won about half the vote of the winning candidate. Many of their PR winners came in third in their districts. Ishin remains a local party. Its PR victories outside the Kinki bloc give it a chance to establish something more solid but may also prove ephemeral.

Given the popularity of Ishin's Osaka Governor Yoshimura on the coronavirus issue, it is possible that Ishin simply got a "covid bump" that will not be repeated. However, Ishin will probably misinterpret the bump as signaling future success. This, in turn, could delay opposition consolidation and give the LDP a more secure grip for a few elections.

THE FUTURE OF THE OPPOSITION

First and foremost, we can argue that the CDP was not irrelevant. They fought the LDP toe-to-toe in the SMDs. The LDP and many of their candidates are perfectly aware that they have been challenged and are responding to that challenge. The future of the CDP will be largely determined by the new leader. If they follow the advice of the political commentators and abandon cooperation with the JCP, the LDP may well be safe for the next several elections. However, the CDP maintained their intention to analyze the data before deciding on their next steps.

The DPP has made its choice by working with the Ishin fraction in the Diet. The conservative opposition will be led by the Ishin-DPP group until the next election. Ishin has a chance to build a base outside of the Kinki bloc but also face serious problems. One of the biggest is the dearth of leadership in the Diet. The party leader is the mayor of the city of Osaka and their most popular leader is the governor of Osaka Prefecture. Having the most popular figure in the party outside of the Diet was one factor in the failure of Hope.

We would also like to point out that these election results would have been very unlikely in different electoral systems. Although Ishin's regional strength could have led to some local victories even in SMD, the overall results would probably look different. The framing for electoral

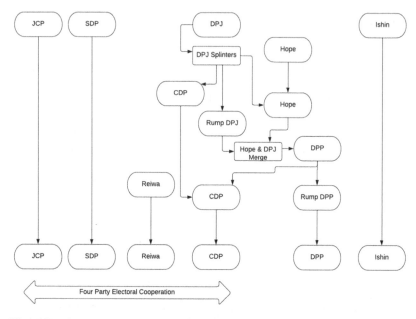

Fig. 5.1   Opposition parties 2017 to 2021

cooperation with the JCP would also have been substantially different (Fig. 5.1).

NOTE

1. Calculated from UTAS data 2019 "Shuyō seitō ha dō hennka shita ka? ("How have the Main Parties Changed?" https://www.asahi.com/senkyo/asahitodai/asahitodai15nen/?iref=pc_extlink).

REFERENCES

Pekkanen, R. J., and Pekkanen, S. M. (2015). More About Abe: Japan in 2015. *Asian Survey*, (February 2016), 56(1): 34–46.

Pekkanen, R. J., and Reed, S. R. (2018). The Opposition: From Third Party back to Third Force. In Robert J. Pekkanen, Steven R. Reed and Daniel M. Smith, (Eds)., *Japan Decides 2017* Palgrave Macmillan, (pp. 77–92).

Pekkanen, Robert J. and Steven R. Reed. (2022). "Japanese Politics between 2017 and 2021." In Robert J. Pekkanen, Steven R. Reed and Daniel M. Smith, (Eds.), *Japan Decides 2021: The Japanese General Election*. Palgrave Macmillan.

Scheiner, Ethan and Michael F. Thies. 2022. "The Political Opposition in Japan." In Robert J. Pekkanen and Saadia M. Pekkanen, (Eds.), *The Oxford Handbook of Japanese Politics*. New York: Oxford University Press.

Steel, G. (2022). "Are the Kids Alright? Young People and Turnout in Japan." In Robert J. Pekkanen, Steven R. Reed and Daniel M. Smith, (Eds)., *Japan Decides 2021* Palgrave Macmillan.

CHAPTER 6

Kōmeitō in 2021: Strategizing Between the LDP and Sōka Gakkai

Axel Klein and *Levi McLaughlin*

The religion Sōka Gakkai (SG) wields political influence by ensuring that Kōmeitō, the party it founded in 1964, remains in coalition with the Liberal Democratic Party (LDP). This arrangement suits the LDP because Gakkai members, especially those within its Women's Division (*joseibu*), have long been Japan's most potent vote-gatherers. Kōmeitō trades Gakkai-gathered votes LDP politicians need to keep their seats for a place in government and LDP approval of policies that benefit SG supporters. Most of Kōmeitō's policy demands match the quotidian needs of Sōka Gakkai's Women's Division; these policies also appeal more broadly to Japan's homemakers and others who prioritize families and social welfare. But keeping Gakkai supporters engaged in electioneering is a demanding task. Both coalition parties must contend with ways SG

A. Klein (✉)
Institute of East Asian Studies, Duisburg-Essen University, Duisburg, Germany
e-mail: axel.klein@uni-due.de

L. McLaughlin
North Carolina State University, Raleigh, NC, USA

© The Author(s), under exclusive license to Springer Nature Switzerland AG 2023
R. J. Pekkanen et al. (eds.), *Japan Decides 2021*,
https://doi.org/10.1007/978-3-031-11324-6_6

members assess Kōmeitō and the LDP politicians following foundational party (and religious) principles and the moral guidance of Sōka Gakkai's honorary president Ikeda Daisaku (1928–). Kōmeitō leaders have refined a remarkable ability to retain their party's role as casting vote in the national government by negotiating between the contrasting demands of Gakkai supporters and the LDP. They justify their many compromises to their SG base by emphasizing Kōmeitō's effect on mitigating the LDP's most intransigent impulses and their party's "power to actualize" (*jitsug-enryoku*) policies that benefit supporters' everyday lives while, at strategic moments, they remind the LDP of the extent to which it relies on Gakkai votes (cf. Klein and McLaughlin 2022).

This chapter considers how Kōmeitō leaders navigated between the LDP and Sōka Gakkai to improve their party's standing in the 2021 LH (or HR) election. We discuss what events after the 2017 general election and the lead-up to the 2021 race tell us about Kōmeitō's survival as a junior coalition partner, its crucial importance to the LDP, the effect on the party of changes within SG, and how it is likely to operate in the near future.

LIFE AS A JUNIOR COALITION PARTNER: SEEKING STABILITY AMIDST TURMOIL

A publication issued by Kōmeitō in October 2019 that reflected on twenty years in coalition affirmed the party's role as a pivot (*kaname*) for reforms and political stability. The party's retrospective emphasized political stability as a core strength and praised Japan for its "unrivalled economic and social stability" among industrialized democracies (Kōmei STH 2019: 59). "Stability" (*antei*) remains the party's hallmark, and the 2021 campaign indicated the continuity of this core principle. Party representatives and its SG supporters alike routinely emphasize the importance of staying the course with the coalition, and they regard their party's stable alliance with the majority LDP as a justification for Gakkai members' continued political engagement (Kōmei KI 2022: 2–8). The 2019 reflection recapitulated the standard Kōmeitō justification that it is only by being in power that a political party can implement the policies at "the core of its existence" (Kōmei STH 2019: 59).

Kōmeitō's policies between the 2017 and 2021 general elections continued to be geared toward Sōka Gakkai's Women's Division. Better education at lower costs, commitment to child support, increased support for elder care and family health care, and other family subsidies took up a majority of Kōmeitō's election manifestos, campaign literature, and space on party websites. The onset of the COVID-19 pandemic saw Kōmeitō emphasize another reliable policy instrument: cash disbursements. In April 2020, the party supported a decision made by Prime Minister Abe Shinzō to provide a 100,000-yen (~US$1000) payment to every Japan resident. In October 2020, it supported a 20,000-yen (~US$200) gift to all high school seniors, and during the 2021 election campaign Kōmeitō promised families another 100,000-yen per child eighteen years of age and younger.

These plans received approbation, but other Kōmeitō policies and strategic decisions proved unpopular with both the LDP and SG. After losing to Ishin candidates in local elections in the Kansai region in April 2019, for example, Kōmeitō agreed to vote in favor of Ishin's plan to transform Osaka from a prefecture and city into a unified metropolitan area in exchange for Ishin's guarantee to not run in six LH SMDs where Kōmeitō would field candidates (*Asahi*, October 22, 2020).[1] Supporting Ishin's "One Osaka" (*Ōsaka-to kōsō*) objective reversed Kōmeitō's 2015 position, when the first referendum on the Osaka merger took place, and left local Gakkai members dismayed about the party to which they had pledged generations of local-level support. This policy reversal also angered the Osaka-level LDP, which opposed the planned merger. Ishin's project was rejected by the 2019 referendum, leaving Kōmeitō's allies disenchanted. In retaliation, city council member and Liberal Democrat Yanagimoto Akira announced his intention to run in autumn 2021 as an independent against Kōmeitō's Sato Shigeki in Osaka 3; the LDP ultimately defused the conflict by fielding him as a PR candidate two weeks before the LH election (*Asahi*, October 10, 2021; October 16, 2021).

Kōmeitō sparked some conflict with the LDP through attempts to push legislation for its core constituency. After weeks spent supporting a 100,000-yen payment to every resident to address the financial impact of the COVID-19 pandemic (Kōmei GH 2020: 20–21, 27), the LDP leadership, including future Prime Minister Kishida Fumio, announced in spring 2020 a 300,000-yen allowance for 13 million households that had lost income due to pandemic shutdowns. Spurred by "perhaps the worst-ever criticism from our voter base" (Yamaguchi Natsuo according to Gotō et al. 2020), the Kōmeitō leader alerted then-PM Abe of the potential consequences at the ballot box. Yamaguchi convinced Abe to adopt Kōmeitō's 100,000-yen measure and to make the unprecedented move of changing a supplementary budget bill that had already received Cabinet approval. At an April 17, 2020 press conference, Abe apologized and took responsibility for the confusion over the support payment policy (ibid.; cf. Lipscy 2022).

The fact that Kōmeitō prevailed in this conflict does not mean that it enjoys policy dominance over the LDP. It instead shows that Kōmeitō can, in exceptional cases, remind its coalition partner that its electoral fate depends upon not angering Sōka Gakkai supporters. These instances can temporarily strain Kōmeitō's relationship with Liberal Democrats, and they exact a price at the negotiation table. In most cases, Kōmeitō avoids dramatic confrontations and seeks to win over LDP factions and otherwise promote its objectives in an incremental fashion. One example of this approach is Kōmeitō support for the right for spouses to keep separate family names after marriage (*Nikkei*, July 18, 2021). At present, Japanese law only recognizes marriage between heterosexual couples, and the Japanese Civil Code and family registration laws require that both spouses share a family name (Toyoda 2020); in almost every case, the wife takes her husband's name. Kōmeitō and a percentage of LDP members support doing away with this obligation, while conservatives within the LDP and in other parties resist this change (*Asahi*, October 14, 2021; cf. Kweon 2022).

It is worth noting that Kōmeitō's support for separate-surname legislation corresponds with recent administrative shifts within SG. In April 2021, the Gakkai administration announced that its Young Women's and Married Women's Divisions would be merged on November 18 (the anniversary date of SG's founding in 1930) into a single Women's Division (*Seikyō Shinbun*, April 30, 2021). This bureaucratic adjustment recognized the stark reality of Japan's low marriage rate (*The Asahi Shinbun*, January 4, 2021), changing Japanese attitudes toward marriage, likely shifts in Gakkai adherent numbers, and a related need to separate marital status from the core identities of the women adherents who power the religion's vote-gathering campaigns.

As a junior coalition partner, Kōmeitō's opposition to the LDP on selected issues requires that it capitulate to its senior partner in many other intra-coalition negotiations. From 2018, Kōmeitō cooperated with the LDP to support the "Integrated Resort Law" to allow for the operation of casinos in Japan, even though Women's Division members voiced opposition. Kōmeitō's capacity to mollify its vote-gathering base may have been aided by a long-term favorable relationship between Kōmeitō and

Abe's successor, Suga Yoshihide (*Asahi*, September 28, 2020). Perceived warm relations with PM Suga may have also helped Kōmeitō convince LDP supporters to back Saitō Tetsuo as a candidate during tumult over Hiroshima 3 (see below) and to appease its supporters as the coalition parties adjusted the income limit below which Japanese 75 years of age and older were to be exempted from a hike in co-payments for medical bills from 10 to 20%. Tensions surrounding this shift led Suga and Yamaguchi to set up joint project teams for policy coordination in January 2021. These were intended to function as the ruling parties' "policy making structure" and to help avoid escalating disputes between both sides (*Yomiuri*, January 17, 2021).

KŌMEITŌ LINKS TO CHINA: AN IMPORTANT CONDUIT IN TENSE TIMES

In recent elections, Kōmeitō has not treated foreign policy as a top priority, and its campaign literature now contains little more than non-specific pacifist appeals. However, the party distinguishes itself by maintaining close relations with government of the People's Republic of China, and long-standing connections between Kōmeitō and PRC leaders remain a key conduit between both countries (Harris and McLaughlin 2021). From 1971, negotiations by Kōmeitō politician Takeiri Yoshikatsu with Premier Zhou Enlai produced the template for diplomatic normalization in 1972, and Ikeda Daisaku, then third Sōka Gakkai president, met with Zhou in 1974, inspiring lasting Gakkai/PRC bonds that have seen generations-long cultural and educational exchanges. Cheng Yonghua, Chinese ambassador to Japan from 2010 to 2019, studied at Sōka University from 1975, one of six students who were among the first to come from the PRC to Japan after normalization, and many other influential connections have been fostered between the Gakkai, its affiliated party, and the People's Republic (*Asahi*, May 7, 2019).

In the lead-up to the 2021 general election, the PRC continued its crackdown on democracy activists in Hong Kong, maintained "re-education" camps for Uyghurs in Xinjiang, sent repeated sorties over the Diaoyu/Senkaku islands, and increased naval incursions around Taiwan and the South China Sea. While the LDP criticized the Chinese regime, Kōmeitō mostly kept silent.[2] Party head Yamaguchi addressed China's human rights record for the first time at a press conference on October 7, reportedly because of pressure from LDP Diet members who accused him of pandering to the PRC (*Sankei*, October 26, 2021). While the LDP may take its cue from U.S. criticism of China, Kōmeitō will continue to provide a back channel as tensions rise (cf. Vekasi 2022).[3]

KŌMEITŌ'S 2021 CAMPAIGN

The two major elections held before the 2021 HR election foreshadowed vote losses for Kōmeitō. Even though the party called the 2019 HC election a "victory based on voters' trust" and pointed to its unprecedented seat count (14), it achieved this result with one million fewer PR votes than it gained in 2016 (a drop of 13.7%). In summer 2021, the Metropolitan Tokyo election again confirmed Kōmeitō's ability to predict its national-level voter turnout. All 23 of Kōmeitō's Tokyo candidates were elected, but the party received 100,000 fewer votes than its 2017 count, losing an average of 13.5% in each district (Fig. 6.1).

When official campaigning for the LH started on October 19, 2021, Kōmeitō fielded nine candidates in SMDs and 44 on the party's eleven PR lists. It abandoned Kanagawa 6 after scandals plagued one of its rising

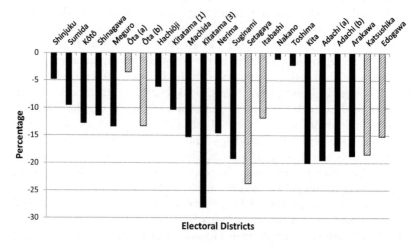

Fig. 6.1   2021 Tokyo metropolitan election. Kōmeitō's 2021 losses as a percentage of 2017 total in all electoral districts (lighter columns indicate those districts where the Kōmeitō candidate changed) (*Source* Public Broadcaster NHK at www.nhk.or.jp/senkyo/database/togisen/2021/ [accessed February 4, 2022])

stars, Toyama Kiyohiko. He had been a bearer of hope for this highly competitive electoral district, but resigned in February 2021, having been heavily criticized, notably by fellow Gakkai adherents, for taking part in clandestine Diet member excursions to hostess clubs in Tokyo's posh Ginza district during an intense period of the pandemic state of emergency. Toyama's fall from grace embarrassed Gakkai members, who had treated him as a vehicle for carrying out *f-tori* (or *f-hyō*), the religion's practice of gathering "f" (friend) votes for Kōmeitō and its allies from non-member friends and relatives.[4] As a consequence, the party decided to support Furukawa Naoki, an LDP city council member and the first Liberal Democrat to run in Kanagawa 6 since the beginning of the LDP-Kōmeitō coalition in 1999, rather than selecting a Kōmeitō alternate.

A corruption case involving Liberal Democrats in Hiroshima provided Kōmeitō with compensation. Kōmeitō insisted on fielding a candidate in Hiroshima 3, the former SMD of Kawai Katsuyuki, Justice Minister under Abe, who in June 2021 was sentenced to three years in prison for vote-buying to secure a seat for his wife Anri in the 2019 HC election (*Asahi*, June 18, 2021). The Hiroshima branch of the LDP and Kishida Fumio, who has represented Hiroshima 1 in the LH since 1996, sought a replacement from within their own ranks, but Kōmeitō asserted that the Kawais' corruption scandal made it impossible for the party and its voters to support a Liberal Democrat in this district. Kōmeitō negotiated with the LDP to field Saitō Tetsuo, the 69-year-old Minister of Land, Infrastructure, and Transport; he was moved from Kōmeitō's party list to Hiroshima 3. The LDP's Hiroshima branch protested at first, but after considering how other LDP candidates would suffer if they lost Gakkai voter support, its regional supporters gave in (*AERA*, March 8, 2021). Saitō won the seat with more votes than Kawai had gained in 2017.

Priorities in Kōmeitō's 2021 manifesto remained the same as those for the 2017 election: education, child support, economic support for SMEs, disaster preparedness and response, and a portfolio that otherwise centered on social welfare. As was the case in 2017, Kōmeitō's 2021 manifesto dedicated scant attention to constitutional issues. In the 20-page version, titled "Major Policies" (*Jūten seisaku*), constitutional concerns did not appear at all, and in the small-print 72-page "Policy Compilation" (*Seisakushū*), "On the Constitution of Japan" only appeared on the second-to-last page, as a short section that reprised Kōmeitō's proposed "adding to the constitution" (*kaken*) approach, a stance the party has advanced consistently while in coalition as an alternative to LDP proposals for wholesale replacement of constitutional text (cf. Mori McElwain 2022). With regard to Article 9, the manifesto stated without elaboration that Kōmeitō is still "prudently discussing" the subject (*Seisakushū* 2021: 70). The biggest difference to the 2017 manifesto was a promise to take a clear position on "politics and money." The two counter-measures it proposed were limited to not paying salaries to politicians who have criminal convictions and to keep the Diet member salary cap at 80% for the duration of the pandemic in order to show solidarity with the people of Japan (ibid.: 16).

In their campaign speeches, Kōmeitō candidates emphasized that their party had been the key force behind the push for free COVID-19 vaccinations for all Japan residents. Their speeches were otherwise notable for lambasting opposition parties as secretive and unreliable. Framing the Constitutional Democratic Party as if it were the Democratic Party of Japan of a decade ago, Kōmeitō candidates reminded voters of the "irresponsible Democratic government" that was in power from 2009 to 2012, and even though predictions indicated that the LDP-Kōmeitō coalition would retain an LH majority, Kōmeitō campaigners stressed that this election was about "choosing a government" (*seiken sentaku*). Kōmeitō candidates also reprised their critiques of the Japanese Communist Party, their party's arch rival (Abe and Endo 2014).

While candidates and the press dedicated attention to a revival of Japan's domestic "GoTo Travel" campaign (which PM Suga pushed even as COVID-19 case numbers surged) and promotion of a unified social security ID called the "My Number Card," it was Kōmeitō's proposed 100,000-yen payment for each household member 18 years and younger that gained the most attention. Kōmeitō's "future support allowance" (*mirai ōen kyūfu*) was an election promise the LDP did not endorse; it was in line with cash benefits promised by most of the opposition parties and contrasted with the LDP proposal. After the election, the LDP tried to force a Kōmeitō compromise by offering 50,000-yen in cash and another 50,000 as a voucher to be issued at a later date, and to enforce an income limit on disbursements. Because of high administration costs a split payment would have entailed, 99.6% of all local governments eventually paid a lump sum of 100,000-yen (*Tokyo Shinbun*, January 14, 2022).

As in other campaigns, Kōmeitō delivered implicit criticism of the LDP as it staked its own claims. Praise for Kōmeitō's Covid management implied that the LDP had done too little too slowly, Kōmeitō's promise to fight money politics was pitched primarily at the wrongdoings of Liberal Democrats, and the party's (albeit modest) stances on constitutional reform emphasized policy contrasts with the LDP. When the LDP included a hike in defense spending in its manifesto, Yamaguchi suggested that "the populace will not understand" [this allocation of resources] (*Asahi*, October 16, 2021), and the LDP's demand for an alternative to Kōmeitō's promised "future support allowance" was explained by Kōmeitō with reference to the recalcitrance of its coalition partner. Party statements simultaneously referred to the LDP as a reliable coalition partner and as "the government" that obstructed progress with delays and unwanted compromise. Kōmeitō rhetoric thus tended to position the party and its supporters as underdogs embattled by hegemonic forces, in spite of their advantageous position at the heart of government.

ELECTION RESULTS

In *Japan Decides 2017*, we explained that dissatisfaction among Gakkai members was reflected in the LH election results (Klein and McLaughlin 2018: 73). The 2021 election indicated that the party mitigated some of its supporters' concerns. The campaign was of course affected by pandemic-era conditions, but an almost 70% national vaccination rate and comparatively low Covid case numbers across Japan in autumn 2021 appear to have allowed Sōka Gakkai to mobilize with an efficacy comparable to that of its pre-pandemic campaigns. Kōmeitō's PR vote numbers increased slightly from 6.9 to 7.1 million (Fig. 6.2), and Fig. 6.3 shows that Kōmeitō candidates improved their advantage over their strongest competitors in six out of eight SMDs. Cooperation with Ishin in Kansai allowed both parties to win all seats in Osaka. Because Reiwa had overlooked a detail in election regulations, Kōmeitō gained another PR seat and ended up with 32 Diet members. As in 2014 and 2017, around 7% of unaffiliated voters cast their ballot for Kōmeitō, according to *Asahi* exit polls (*Asahi*, November 1, 2021). The negative association between overall turnout and Kōmeitō's seat share persisted and proved once again that low overall turnout is beneficial to parties with a well-organized voter base (Fig. 6.4).

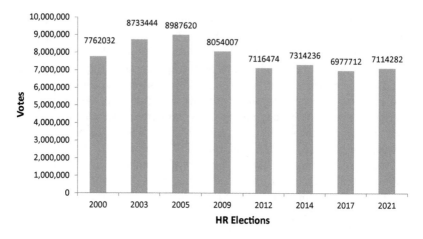

Fig. 6.2 Kōmeitō's PR votes in House of Representatives Elections (2000–2021) (*Source* Ministry of Internal Affairs and Communications at https://www.soumu.go.jp/senkyo/senkyo_s/data/shugiin/ichiran.html [accessed February 4, 2022])

Conclusion: The Status Quo, and Changes on the Horizon

Kōmeitō's PR vote numbers remained stable (+1.9% compared to 2017) and it gained three seats in the general election, assuring its Cabinet seat (with Saitō Tetsuo's reappointment) and its influence over policymaking. Among the 189 Liberal Democrats who won their SMD races in October 2021 (72.4% of all LDP seats), 17 came first by a margin of 5% or less, and 46 won with a plurality rather than a majority of their district's votes (Smith 2021). Given the estimate that Kōmeitō provides LDP candidates with approximately 20,000 votes in each SMD, the LDP's continued dependence on Kōmeitō to retain its command of the Diet was further cemented in 2021.[5] There was no policy issue between 2017 and 2021 as contentious to Gakkai supporters as the security legislation passed by the Diet in September 2015, and a relatively low number of intra-coalition disputes reduced the potential for conflict between the LDP and SG. However, Gakkai member hostility to corruption and misbehavior by LDP and Kōmeitō politicians seems to have grown during the pandemic,

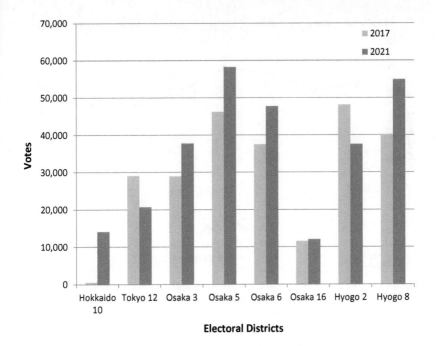

Fig. 6.3 Kōmeitō candidates' lead in SMDs over their strongest competitors (2017 and 2021) (*Source* Ministry of Internal Affairs and Communications at https://www.soumu.go.jp/senkyo/senkyo_s/data/shugiin/ichiran.html [accessed February 4, 2022])

increasing pressure on both parties when it comes to candidate selection (cf. Rehmert 2022).

It remains to be seen how Kōmeitō's alliances and electoral agreements will play out under the Kishida administration. Its relationship with Ishin in Osaka is likely to prove strategically important so long as popular discontent with the governing coalition, and left-wing parties in the opposition, feeds groundswell support for Ishin. Kōmeitō was the only competitor in Kansai able to counter Ishin, which surged to a third-place finish in the Diet, gaining 30 LH seats and claiming every seat in Osaka prefecture, save four where they had agreed to not run against Kōmeitō.

Kōmeitō is a veteran navigator of contrasting prime ministerial regimes, but it remains unclear if the party will establish smooth relations with

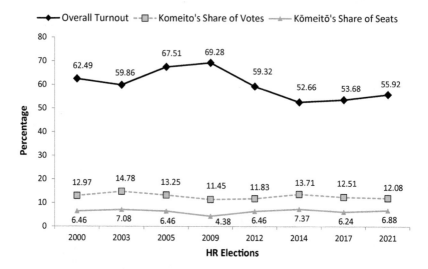

Fig. 6.4 Overall turnout and Kōmeitō vote and seat share (*Source* Ministry of Internal Affairs and Communications at https://www.soumu.go.jp/senkyo/sen kyo_s/data/shugiin/ichiran.html [accessed February 4, 2022])

Kishida. In contrast to Suga, Kishida does not have a history of close ties to Kōmeitō. This may complicate LDP efforts to communicate with its junior partner; the loss of Hiroshima 3 and disagreements over some COVID-19 policies may have also negatively affected Kishida's view of Kōmeitō and its position within the coalition. Yamaguchi has shown Kishida Kōmeitō's willingness to compromise on the issue of Japan's capability to destroy missiles in enemy territory (*Kyōdō Tsūshin*, January 9, 2022), signaling potential coalition rapprochement on security issues. However, talks between the secretary generals of the coalition parties on February 2, 2022, did not see them reach their customary agreement to endorse one another's candidates (LDP in SMDs, Kōmeitō in MMDs) in the forthcoming summer 2022 UH election (*Asahi*, February 4, 2022). And while it waited for the LDP to finalize its UH candidates, SG announced it would offer recommendations not based on party but "chiefly on the basis of the [candidate's] character" (*jinbutsu hon'i*), thereby adopting an electoral strategy the religion had not announced to its members since 1994 (*Yomiuri*, February 1, 2022).

Kōmeitō is seeing a changing of the guard. Party leader Yamaguchi is slated to be replaced in 2022, and Ōta Akihiro and Inoue Yoshihisa, both in their mid-seventies, were among seven senior Kōmeitō politicians who did not seek re-election in 2021. It is also likely that the near future will see the end of the lifetime of Ikeda Daisaku. He has not been seen in public since May 2010, but his followers nonetheless celebrated his 94th birthday on January 2, 2022. With his death will come a reckoning for the Gakkai's affiliated party, which relies to a great extent on adherents' personal loyalty to Ikeda as a primary means to inspire campaigning for Kōmeitō, and for the governing coalition as a whole. Kōmeitō's, and possibly the LDP's, continued electoral strength will be significantly affected by changes on the horizon within Sōka Gakkai.

NOTES

1. Former Osaka governor and Ishin party founder Hashimoto Tōru also spoke on television about the deal between Kōmeitō and Ishin (https://twitter.com/osakatokosono/status/1322944828401876992?s=20, accessed January 1, 2022).
2. The unwillingness of the party to take an open stand against China was exemplified by its decision to let only one first-term HC member join in May 2021 when 83 Diet members from all parties formed the Nonpartisan Parliamentary Association for Reconsidering Human Rights Diplomacy. Even the Japanese Communist Party condemned the Chinese regime, while Kōmeitō did not (*Shinbun Akahata*, July 1, 2021).
3. In a January 1, 2022 speech, Yamaguchi Natsuo proposed the establishment of a permanent regional framework resembling the OECD that would include the PRC, the USA, ASEAN member states, India, Japan, and South Korea, in order to maintain communication channels between member countries and to deescalate potential conflict. This idea was not accompanied by any PR initiative, nor was it picked up in the party's media. https://www.youtube.com/watch?v=TnFlvW1pKMo (accessed January 18, 2022).
4. Personal communication with former Kōmeitō Diet member Ueda Isamu (November 22, 2021) and interview with two SG members (February 24, 2021). Footage of Toyama on stage at a May 3, 2017 event organized by the nationalist lobby organization Nippon Kaigi recirculated as the scandal unfolded, further stoking the ire of Gakkai supporters. See https://www.nipponkaigi.org/activity/archives/9895 (accessed January 1, 2022).
5. Hirasawa Katsuei, member of the Lower House for the LDP since 1996, estimated Sōka Gakkai's support for LDP candidates to be around 20,000 votes on average (Klein interview, November 11, 2010). Journalists in

Japan report similar numbers (*Shūkan Asahi*, December 12, 2014, 18; *Asahi*, December 21, 2019; *Japan Times*, December 29, 2019).

References

Abe, Yuki and Masahisa Endo. 2014. "Kōmeitō's Uncertain Decades Between Politics and Religion." In George Ehrhardt, Axel Klein, Levi McLaughlin, and Steven R. Reed (eds.), *Kōmeitō. Politics and Religion in Japan*, pp. 83–112. Berkeley, CA: Institute of East Asian Studies.

Smith, Daniel M. 2021. "Resolved: The Lower House Election is a Warning Sign for the LDP." https://www.csis.org/analysis/resolved-lower-house-election-warning-sign-ldp (accessed December 31, 2021).

Gotō, Tadashi, Yasuhiro Yamada and Taishi Shimizu. *NHK seiji magajin* [NHK Politics Magazine], April 22, 2020. https://www.nhk.or.jp/politics/articles/feature/34154.html (accessed December 31, 2021).

Harris, Tobias, and Levi McLaughlin. 2021. "The Small Pacifist Party That Could Shape Japan's Future." *Foreign Policy*, November 4, 2021. https://foreignpolicy.com/2021/11/04/komeito-ldp-japan-elections-defense-policy-china/ (accessed January 31, 2022).

Klein, Axel, and Levi McLaughlin. 2018. "Kōmeitō 2017: New Complications." In Robert Pekkanen, Steven R. Reed, Ethan Scheiner, and Daniel M. Smith (eds.), *Japan Decides 2017*, pp. 53–76. London: Palgrave Macmillan.

Klein, Axel, and Levi McLaughlin. 2022. "Kōmeitō: The Party and Its Place in Japanese Politics." In Robert J. Pekkanen and Saadia M. Pekkanen (eds.), *The Oxford Handbook of Japanese Politics*, pp. 201–222. London: Oxford University Press.

Kōmeitō KI (Kōmeitō Kikanshi Iinkai, ed.) 2022. *Kōmei*, vol. 193, January 2022.

Kōmei GH (Kōmei Gurafu Henshūbu, ed.). 2020. *Komei Graphic Autumn 2020*. Tokyo: Kōmeitō.

Kōmei STH (Kōmei Shinbun Tōshi Hensanhan, ed.). 2019. "Renritsu 20-nen-me no jikō seiken" [The LDP-Kōmeitō Government in the Twentieth Year of the Coalition]. *Kōmei*, Vol. 166, October 2019, 57–65.

Kweon, Yesola. 2022. "Women's Representation and the Gendered Impact of COVID-19 in Japan." In Robert J. Pekkanen, Steven R. Reed, and Daniel M. Smith (eds.), *Japan Decides 2021: The Japanese General Election*. Palgrave Macmillan.

Lipscy, Phillip Y. 2022. "Japan's Response to the COVID-19 Pandemic." In Robert J. Pekkanen, Steven R. Reed, and Daniel M. Smith (eds.), *Japan Decides 2021: The Japanese General Election*. Palgrave Macmillan.

Mori McElwain, Kenneth. 2022. "Constitutional Revision in the 2021 Election." In Robert J. Pekkanen, Steven R. Reed, and Daniel M. Smith (eds.), *Japan Decides 2021:The Japanese General Election*. Palgrave Macmillan.

Rehmert, Jochen. 2022. "Candidate Selection for the 2021 General Election." In Robert J. Pekkanen, Steven R. Reed, and Daniel M. Smith (eds.), *Japan Decides 2021: The Japanese General Election*. Palgrave Macmillan.

Seisakushū [Policy Compilation]. 2021. www.komei.or.jp/komeipolicy/ (accessed January 1, 2021).

Toyoda, Etsuko. 2020. "Japan's Marital System Reform: The *fūfubessei* Movement and Individual Rights." *The Asia-Pacific Journal: Japan Focus*, Vol. 18 Issue 3, No. 3 (June 25, 2020). https://apjjf.org/2020/13/Toyoda.html.

Vekasi, Kristin. 2022. "China in Japan's 2021 Election." In Robert J. Pekkanen, Steven R. Reed, and Daniel M. Smith (eds.), *Japan Decides 2021: The Japanese General Election*. Palgrave Macmillan.

CHAPTER 7

Abe's Legacy

Tobias Harris

As Kishida Fumio unveiled his leadership team after winning the Liberal Democratic Party's presidency on September 29, Azumi Jūn, a senior opposition lawmaker, delivered a blunt assessment: "The Abe cabinet now has Mr. Kishida's face on it."[1]

Kishida had won the LDP's leadership handily, but his victory depended heavily on Abe Shinzō and the party's right wing (see Nemoto 2022). His new party executive was dominated by Abe's allies. Amari Akira, a longtime Abe supporter, was named secretary-general. Takaichi Sanae, who Abe had backed in the leadership race, returned to lead the Policy Research Council, which she previously led under Abe. Fukuda Tatsuo, a member of Abe's faction, became head of the general affairs council. Asō Tarō left the finance ministry after nine years to become the LDP's vice president. While the cabinet lineup was marginally more balanced, members of Abe's faction and other allies received important portfolios, including Chief Cabinet Secretary Matsuno Hirokazu,

T. Harris (✉)
Center for American Progress, Bethesda, MD, USA
e-mail: tharris@americanprogress.org

Minister of Economy, Trade, and Industry Hagiuda Kōichi, and Minister of Defense Kishi Nobuo, Abe's younger brother.

Polls suggested that the public shared Azumi's judgment. Not only were Kishida's initial approval ratings the lowest for a new prime minister in more than a decade, but there was evidence to suggest that widespread beliefs of Abe's influence over the Kishida government weighed on its popularity. A *Mainichi Shimbun* poll conducted in early October found that fifty-nine percent felt that Abe's and Asō's influence were a disadvantage for the government.[2] With the general election looming, the LDP lawmakers fretted about what these numbers meant for their chances (Y. Maeda 2022).[3]

However, the relationship between Kishida and Abe became more nuanced than it first appeared. Kishida was not wholly subservient to the former prime minister, but Abe had thrust himself back into the arena and was determined to use all of the tools at his disposal—his faction, the party's right wing and its allies in the press, and his bully pulpit—to pressure Kishida to build on his policy achievements. He is determined to continue his life's work of remaking the LDP so that it will pursue policies to boost Japan's economic and military prowess and foster national pride. To govern, Kishida has had to manage his relationship carefully with a man who is simultaneously the leader of the LDP's largest faction, a respected global statesman, and the LDP's "conservative-in-chief," the leader of what is effectively the party's single largest ideological bloc. From the beginning of his premiership, it was clear that managing Abe would be one of the greatest challenges that Kishida would face as he pursued a durable administration of his own.

ABE AS KINGMAKER

Abe's resurgence began as the end of Suga's term approached in summer 2021. Kishida had thrown his hat into the ring promising party reform, and trained his fire squarely on Nikai Toshihiro, LDP secretary-general and key Suga ally. Suga for his part was increasingly desperate to secure his position as party president. LDP lawmakers, facing a general election before the end of the year, fretted that their fortunes were bleak. COVID-19 case numbers were surging to their highest levels yet, and Suga's approval ratings were dropping (Y. Maeda 2022).

With his chances of securing a new term fading, Suga appealed to party leaders for help, recognizing that his best chance of survival would be if party bosses, particularly faction leaders, threw their weight behind him and stymied Kishida's insurgent campaign. He announced that he would reshuffle the party executive before the leadership race—replacing Nikai with a fresher face—and then call a snap election before the LDP election. If the leading factions approved and offered high-profile members to serve under Suga, it would be a vote of confidence, complicating Kishida's bid. If they declined, Suga could be facing near-certain defeat.

As Suga tried to stitch together a coalition to support his reelection, Abe's influence grew. He was increasingly viewed as the de facto leader of the Hosoda faction, which, as the party's largest, would play a critical role in the vote. Together with his ally Asō, head of the second largest faction, Abe's vote could be decisive. Suga may have felt encouraged when, after a brief meeting with Kishida, Abe declined to endorse Kishida, who had once been viewed as his likeliest successor.[4] Suga perhaps had reason to hope for Abe's support, not only having served as chief cabinet secretary for the entirety of his second administration but also having committed to continuing Abe's policies as prime minister.

However, Abe and the other party leaders withheld their support, and, on September 3, the prime minister bowed out of the race.[5] For the first time since leaving the premiership, Abe demonstrated the power he could wield over the direction of the party. Playing this role may not have been his first choice—as Suga's approval ratings slumped during the spring of 2021, Nagatacho was abuzz with speculation that Abe would seek the LDP's leadership again—but he did not hesitate when the opportunity arose to unseat Nikai, who Abe and Asō had increasingly opposed, and replace an increasingly unpopular party president.[6]

ABE IN THE LEADERSHIP ELECTION

It quickly became apparent that Abe's turn against Suga was not motivated solely by concern for the LDP's electoral prospects. In the suddenly open race for the party leadership, Abe signaled he was more animated by ideology than by a purely pragmatic political calculus.

The day after Suga's announcement, reports emerged that Abe was preparing to throw his weight behind Takaichi Sanae.[7] Takaichi, a strident conservative who had been one of Abe's most loyal supporters and served in several party and cabinet posts during his second premiership, was an unlikely contender for the leadership. After all, although Takaichi signaled her intention to run before Suga's exit, it was unclear whether she would even be able to secure the twenty endorsements needed to run. In a *Nikkei Shimbun* poll in late August, she was an afterthought. Asked who should be the next leader, only three percent of respondents cited Takaichi, good for seventh place after Kōno Tarō, Ishiba Shigeru, Kishida, Suga, Koizumi Shinjirō, and Abe himself. Among LDP supporters, her support was four percent.[8]

Nevertheless, despite this inauspicious beginning, Takaichi played an important role in the outcome. Although she only finished third in the first round of voting—missing the runoff—she surpassed Kōno in voting among LDP lawmakers, dealing a major blow to the popular favorite who was widely expected to win the first round. Instead, Kishida surpassed Kōno by one vote, all but ensuring his victory.

Takaichi played this role, which dramatically raised her profile and has positioned her for another run in the future, thanks largely to Abe. Takaichi not only had no difficulty securing the twenty endorsements needed, but Abe also fought on her behalf within the Hosoda faction. Although Takaichi had once been a member, the faction's leadership was not necessarily disposed to back her. Hosoda Hiroyuki, the titular leader, preferred Kishida. However, thanks to Abe's influence, the party's largest faction informed its members that they could vote for either Kishida or Takaichi in the first round, in a stroke boosting her prospects, particularly since other factions also struggled to unite behind a single candidate.

As the campaign began, Abe emerged as a master strategist organizing Takaichi's campaign, drumming up support from lawmakers across the party, particularly from junior lawmakers—the so-called Abe children elected in 2012 and thereafter—anxious about the general election.[9] She gained in the polls. Her support among the LDP's lawmakers surged, to the point that Kishida's camp—and Abe's allies—grew alarmed that she would pass Kishida and advance to runoff against Kōno, which, they feared, would ensure Kōno's victory.

Takaichi, meanwhile, outlined a platform that would continue Abe's programs. She was the most hawkish candidate on China. She stressed the need for constitutional revision and called for strong policies to confront growing emergencies. In short, her commitment to the "new conservative" program that Abe has pursued since the beginning of his career was not in doubt, and in fact she may have been less willing to compromise those ideals than Abe had been as prime minister. (For example, early in the campaign she issued an unambiguous pledge to worship at Yasukuni Shrine as prime minister.[10])

Abe likely had strategic reasons for backing Takaichi, who, even with his backing, was a long shot to win the LDP leadership. Abe, after all, was determined to prevent his longtime rival Ishiba and, after Ishiba declined to run, Kōno from winning the party leadership.[11] Nevertheless, with Abe's support, Takaichi could play a spoiler. If she could consolidate the support of conservative lawmakers, she could prevent any candidate from securing a first-round majority and therefore enable Abe to extract concessions from the frontrunners on policy and personnel. Takaichi's presence in the race also ensured a wider airing to the ideas of the party's conservative wing.

At the same time, the Takaichi threat may have forced Kishida to run more to the right than he might otherwise have done. As the heir to the LDP's moderate wing, leader of the Kōchikai, the faction founded by Ikeda Hayato, he had once boasted of his differences with Abe.[12] As he said in 2017, "The prime minister is conservative, dare I say, a hawk. I am liberal, a dove."[13] While it is possible that the leadership race's rules and factional politics would have forced to Kishida to the right regardless, Kishida knew he needed the right wing's support to prevail. As a result, he made several high-profile concessions to conservatives. He pledged to support constitutional revision along the lines outlined by Abe in 2017; suggested he would take a harder line toward China on human rights; called for updating the national security strategy and other fundamental defense documents (see Green 2022); and voiced his opposition to female succession to the throne.[14] He also declined to endorse separate surnames for spouses or same-sex marriage (see Kweon 2022).[15] While conservatives may not have entirely trusted Kishida, these concessions likely made it easier for Kishida to become their second choice.[16]

Accordingly, on the day of the LDP election, Kishida and Takaichi pledged to back each other in a final round against Kōno, perhaps the final blow to Kōno's chances.[17]

The Balance Shifts

The perception that Kishida was Abe's puppet only deepened during the general election campaign, particularly after the LDP's manifesto was unveiled. As the party's policy chief, Takaichi was responsible for the manifesto. It was immediately apparent that she had lifted entire sections from her leadership campaign manifesto, while dropping some of Kishida's signature proposals.[18] The economic policy section, for example, included sections on "crisis management investment" and "growth investment" as the pillars of the post-election growth strategy, literally using the same phrases as Takaichi did during the leadership campaign.[19]

Abe himself played a modest role in the general election campaign. His thirty-eight campaign appearances on behalf of LDP candidates were less than some other party heavyweights, and at least half of his appearances were on behalf of present or future members of his faction. Among those candidates he supported who belonged to other factions, most had some connection to Abe through conservative political organizations or belonged to the Asō faction.[20]

However, although Kishida entered the campaign laboring under perceptions that Abe dominated his government, the outcome of the general election shifted the balance of power in Kishida's favor. By limiting the LDP's losses to fifteen seats despite forecasts that it could lose dozens, Kishida showed his party that he could be an election winner. After the general election, he also enjoyed a belated bump in his approval, making him one of a handful of prime ministers in recent history whose approval ratings rose during their first three months.[21] While public approval can be fluid, Kishida's chances of survival had improved, particularly if he could lead the LDP to victory in the 2022 upper house elections.

Political capital in hand, Kishida set about bolstering his leadership. It was a stroke of fortune that he had to replace Amari as secretary-general, after Amari became the first sitting secretary-general to lose his constituency (although he was revived via proportional representation). He replaced Amari with Motegi Toshimitsu, a political heavyweight in his own right whose faction backed Kishida strongly in the leadership race. Motegi helmed the third-largest faction, had leadership ambitions of his own, and, while he served in Abe's cabinets in multiple posts, he was by no means an Abe lieutenant in the way that Amari was. Revealingly, Abe had reportedly lobbied for Takaichi to succeed Amari, but was rebuffed.[22]

Then, to replace Motegi as foreign minister, he tapped Hayashi Yoshimasa, a lawmaker from Yamaguchi prefecture belonging to Kishida's faction. Hayashi's appointment not only showed that Kishida could bring his own allies into key posts, it was also a pointed message to Abe. Hayashi and Abe are longtime personal rivals, dating back to competition between their fathers under the old multi-member electoral system.[23] After years of trying, Hayashi finally succeeded in jumping from the House of Councillors to the House of Representatives in 2021, boosting his profile as a potential contender for the premiership. Elevated by Kishida, he could also threaten Abe's influence in his own backyard.[24] Abe and Asō appealed to Kishida not to appoint him, and the right wing mobilized against his appointment, citing his chairmanship of the Japan–China Friendship Association as evidence that he would be too conciliatory toward China. But Kishida, undaunted by this opposition, brought Hayashi into the cabinet.

The Hayashi appointment was a turning point in Kishida's relationship with Abe. It was harder to claim that Kishida was simply Abe's puppet. Instead, after the general election, Kishida was looking for opportunities to expand his personal authority at the former prime minister's expense, even as he seemingly recognized that he could not easily defy Abe due to the strength of his faction and his influence as an opinion leader.

ABE AS OPINION LEADER

During Kishida's belated honeymoon, Abe returned to his old role as the LDP's most prominent and vocal conservative. But he would no longer be an upstart princeling taking aim at the LDP's establishment (Harris, 2020). He had become the establishment, as the leader of both the largest faction and of its most cohesive ideological movement. The two roles are not necessarily distinct. "We will together strive to pass on to the next generation a Japan that has pride," he said at a party marking the turnover of the *Seiwa-kai* from Hosoda faction to Abe faction. "Doesn't the Seiwa-kai stand at the forefront of debates on constitutional revision? We will fulfill this responsibility as the largest policy group in the party."[25]

Accordingly, his public comments on policy issues sought to prevent any drift from his longstanding vision or his administration's policies. Ironically, in fulfilling this role, Abe may be trying to push Kishida away from the kind of pragmatic compromise—for example, Abe's diplomatic outreach with Beijing—that often characterized Abe's own tenure, compromises Abe could make precisely because his brand of conservatism faced little intra-party resistance.

On the most important question facing the Kishida government—how to manage Japan's relationship with China as tensions between the United States and China worsen and as China's military activities around Japan have increased—Abe has been vocal in calling on Kishida to take a hard line toward Beijing (see Vekasi 2022). The shift from Abe's limited rapprochement began in earnest under Suga, who, for example, used a joint statement with U.S. President Joe Biden to criticize China's behavior more explicitly than any previous bilateral document.[26]

The foreign policy position he has advanced has three major pillars. First, Abe wants the Kishida government to build on his and Suga's efforts in strengthening ties not just with the United States but also with other regional partners. "Japan, positioned as a frontline country [between the United States and China] must be at the core of taking leadership and strengthening cooperation with like-minded countries," he said in an interview with the *Nikkei Shimbun*.[27] Perhaps most notably, he wants these efforts to expand to include Taiwan, which, as he argued in a speech recorded for the Prospect Foundation, a Taiwanese think tank, could be a potent partner for defending democracy, human rights, and the rule of law.[28]

Second, Abe wants the Kishida government to adopt a more confrontational approach to China's human rights abuses and its military activities around Taiwan. Abe used the diplomatic boycott against the 2022 Winter Olympics in Beijing launched by the United States, Canada, and other advanced industrial democracies to pressure the Kishida government on human rights issues, calling for Japan to take a leading role in organizing the boycott. In December 2021, as the Kishida government was deliberating on whether to join the boycott, Abe used media and other public appearances to amplify pressure from other lawmakers on the government to make a quick decision to join the boycott. "Japan should exercise leadership in sending a political message to China," he said in a December 13 appearance on NTV."[29] The following day, representatives from three parliamentary groups on China-related human rights issues, whose leaders included Takaichi and Abe ally Shimomura Hakubun, delivered a petition to the prime minister formally calling for a boycott.[30] After Kishida decided not to send any government officials to Beijing, Abe met with the prime minister and gave his approval.[31]

Perhaps Kishida would have reached this decision without pressure from the LDP's right, but from the beginning of the debate, Abe and his allies had the upper hand. It was broadly accepted that Japan must signal its disapproval regarding China's human rights practices, particularly after the United States announced its boycott. Though a comparatively minor issue in the Japan–China relationship, the diplomatic boycott nevertheless illustrated the pressure that Abe and his allies could bring to bear on Kishida in China policy.

Finally, with the Kishida government preparing to update major national security documents in 2022, including the National Security Strategy, the National Defense Program Guidelines, and the Mid-Term Defense Program, Abe has also used his bully pulpit to stake out a maximally hawkish position ahead of those deliberations. In his interview with *Nikkei*, he praised the ¥770 billion in defense spending included in the Kishida government's FY2021 supplemental budget, but suggested that it was not enough. He argued that the U.S.-Japan alliance is as important to the military balance in the Indo-Pacific region as NATO was in Europe during the Cold War, and that Japan must therefore contribute far more to the conventional military balance with China. Most notably, he argued extensively in favor of Japan's acquisition of strike capabilities—one of the major questions in the defense debate—by suggesting that if Japan were attacked and looked to the United States to retaliate on its behalf, it would be a crisis for the alliance.[32] He also demonstrated his ability to shape the defense policy agenda after Russia's invasion of Ukraine in February 2022, when he singlehandedly prompted the LDP to conduct a debate on an arrangement to "share" nuclear weapons with the United States despite Kishida's own misgivings about nuclear weapons.[33]

What is striking about these remarks is that whereas in the past Abe and other defense hawks framed their proposals as necessary responses to North Korea's growing arsenal, Abe's call for greater military power is now explicitly framed as a response to China. As Abe said in remarks to Taiwan's Institute for National Policy Research in December 2021, "A Taiwan emergency is a Japan emergency."[34] In these comments, Abe likely previewed the talking points that he and his allies will use as the Kishida government proceeds with its policy review.

Abe's role as a policy advocate has not been limited to national security. He has also sought to safeguard the legacy of Abenomics, his program for reviving Japan's economy. "[Kishida] should not change the fundamental direction [of economic policy] from 'Abenomics.' The markets are also expecting this," he said in a TV Tokyo appearance in December 2021.[35] While Kishida campaigned on a vision of a "new Japanese capitalism," in the early months of his term, there were few signs of a fundamental break with Abenomics, whether on expansionary monetary and fiscal policy, state-led industrial policy, or an interventionist incomes policy (see Amano and Katada 2022).

However, Abe's defense of Abenomics masks the extent to which his own thinking has changed since he left office. During his premiership,

Abe tried to strike a balance on fiscal policy. He would pursue fiscal stimulus in the near term, while eyeing fiscal consolidation over the longer term. After leaving office, however, he has virtually abandoned the pretense of a commitment to reducing the government's fiscal burden.

Indeed, even as Kishida has been careful not to break with the former prime minister's economic program, Abe has become increasingly vocal in his support for heterodox fiscal policy ideas. In a speech in December 2021, he directly attacked a controversial essay by Ministry of Finance Administrative Vice Minister Yano Kōji published in the monthly journal *Bungei Shunjū* in October 2021 that excoriated politicians for wasteful spending and warned that Japan was a Titanic headed for a fiscal iceberg. "If Japan were the Titanic," Abe argued, "there would be no people buying bonds issued by the Titanic."[36] Instead, Japan's debt, which surged during the pandemic as the government used deficit spending to finance emergency stimulus, is fine because the Bank of Japan (BOJ)—a "national subsidiary"—now bears the bulk of outstanding debt, meaning the government owes money to itself.

Whether this situation is sustainable, Abe's conservative allies increasingly share this position. During her campaign, for example, Takaichi said that fiscal rules should be suspended so that the government can boost investment in strategic industries (Takaichi 2021). She has also used her position as policy chief to institutionalize fiscal heterodoxy. She struck a blow against the LDP's deficit hawks by renaming the party's Fiscal Reconstruction Promotion Headquarters—established in 2015 by Inada Tomomi, another Abe protégé, when she was policy chief, and elevated into a headquarters when Kishida was policy chief—into the Fiscal Policy Examination Headquarters and appointing conservative Nishida Shōji as its chair, with Takaichi and Abe as senior advisers.[37] Nishida has for several years been the LDP's leading proponent of Modern Monetary Theory, which, among other things, argues that a sovereign borrower borrowing in its own currency cannot default, making his appointment is another sign of the mainstreaming of heterodox fiscal policy.[38]

Abe and Takaichi claimed victory when Kishida announced a stimulus package that totaled a record ¥55.7 trillion, which followed a meeting between Abe and Kishida in which he urged the prime minister to provide at least ¥30 trillion in fiscal stimulus to help Japan's economic recovery.[39] Whether Abe's pressure is truly responsible for the size of the stimulus package—with an upper house election in 2022, Kishida had his own reasons for a larger stimulus—the LDP's right wing will continue to argue on behalf of greater spending and against fiscal consolidation. The fiscal policy headquarters is already considering a proposal not just to delay Japan's target for achieving a primary fiscal surplus again but to drop the primary fiscal surplus as a target altogether.

As with China policy, Abe and his conservative allies are shaping the boundaries of acceptable policy discourse within the LDP. Abe's bully pulpit enables him to amplify his ideas and overwhelm ideological rivals, whether proponents of a more stable relationship with China or a fiscal consolidation. This, in turn, could limit Kishida's freedom of action as prime minister.

Conclusion

In a radio interview on January 3, 2022, Kishida spoke warmly of his relationship with Abe. "I have a lot of advice, starting with foreign policy, for which I am extremely grateful," he said. "I would of course like to continue to make efforts to maintain a friendly relationship, including a factional relationship."[40]

As Kishida aims for a long-term administration of his own, Abe's influence is inescapable. He leads the LDP's largest faction. He commands not just domestic media attention but also global media attention in a way that even the prime minister might struggle to match. And he is the leader of a conservative ideological bloc whose members span the party's factions and occupy key posts in the Kishida cabinet and the LDP executive. The former prime minister's power is not absolute—Kishida's national security policy review, for example, will likely show that LDP junior coalition partner Kōmeitō's power remains considerable—but the fact remains that Abe enjoys tremendous power to shape what is politically possible for the prime minister. Far from acting as an august and remote shadow shogun, Abe is squarely in the political arena, waging on ongoing battle to reshape the LDP—and Japan—according to his vision.

Notes

1. *News 24*, October 1, 2021, "'Kishida-san no kaoshita Abe naikaku' jinji ni hamon," https://www.news24.jp/articles/2021/10/01/04948798.html, accessed March 2022.

2. *Mainichi*, October 5, 2021, "Kishida naikaku no shijiritsu 49% Amari-shi kiyō 'hyōka seza' 54% honshi yoron chōsa," https://mainichi.jp/articles/20211005/k00/00m/010/142000c, accessed March 2022.
3. *Jiji*, October 15, 2021, "Teichō sutaato, shūinsen e fuan Kishida naikaku ni Abe-Asō-shi no kage ichiji Jiji yoron chōsa," https://www.jiji.com/jc/article?k=2021101500986&g=pol, accessed March 2022.
4. *Asahi*, August 31, 2021, "Sōsaisen Abe-shi no dōkō shōten Kishida-shi, Takaichi-shi ga shūha," https://digital.asahi.com/articles/DA3S15027343.html, accessed March 2022.
5. *Nishi Nippon Shimbun*, September 4, 2021, "'O-mae to isshō ni shizumerarenedarō' taijin hyōmei zenya, '2A' kara shushō ni san kudari han," https://www.nishinippon.co.jp/item/n/795598/, accessed March 2022. It is also possible that Abe and Asō quietly urged Kishida to challenge Suga. See: Tase Yasuhiro, "Tanmei ni owatta Suga Seiken," *Nippon.com*, October 6, 2021, https://www.nippon.com/ja/in-depth/d00761/, accessed March 2022.
6. *Friday*, May 25, 2021, "Abe saisai tōban taibō ron no shussho ha 'hotondo honnin to sono shūhen' no bukimi," https://friday.kodansha.co.jp/article/182641, accessed March 2022. On Abe and Asō's struggle against Nikkai, see Yora Masao, "The 3A-2F War: The Veiled Election-Year Struggle Inside the LDP," *Nippon.com*, August 18, 2021, https://www.nippon.com/en/in-depth/d00727/, accessed March 2022.
7. *Nikkei*, September 4, 2021, "Abe zen-shushō, Takaichi-shi wo shien no ikō jimin sōsaisen," https://www.nikkei.com/article/DGXZQOUA040UN0U1A900C2000000/, accessed March 2022.
8. *Nikkei*, August 29, 2021, "'Tsugi no sōsai' shui wa Kōno-shi 2-i Ishiba-shi, jimin shijisō ha shushō," https://www.nikkei.com/article/DGXZQOUA290ED0Z20C21A8000000, accessed March 2022.
9. *Nishi Nippon Shimbun*, September 26, 2021, "Fukusō damedashi, wakate ni denwa kōsei…Takaichi-shi shien 'gunshi' Abe-shi no shini," https://www.nishinippon.co.jp/item/n/806330, accessed March 2022.
10. *Sankei Shimbun*, September 3, 2021, "Takaichi-shi, shushō shūnin ato mo Yasukuni sanpai keizoku e," https://www.sankei.com/article/20210903F36Z3JGL5VOUZG46FFBPBBXHZY/?176149, accessed March 2022.
11. Although conservative media outlets would accuse Kōno of being soft on China and criticize his opposition to nuclear power, Abe's opposition to Kōno—who joined forces with Ishiba and Koizumi Shinjirō, another Abe antagonist—may have been as much about personality clashes and who controls the levers of power in the party as about policy and ideology. All three are known for their independent streaks and their broad popularity, which could reduce their dependence on Abe and his allies.

12. Tobias Harris, October 4, 2021, "Fumio Kishida's Principles Are About to Be Put to the Test," *Foreign Policy*, https://foreignpolicy.com/2021/10/04/fumio-kishida-new-japanese-prime-minister-ldp/, accessed March 2022.

13. *Asahi*, August 10, 2017, "'Abe-shushō ha taka-ha, watashi ha hato-ha' jimin-Kishida seichō kaichō," https://digital.asahi.com/articles/ASK8B4 1J7K8BUTFK00D.html, accessed March 2022.

14. *Sankei*, September 8, 2021, "Jimin sōsaisen Kishida-shi intabyuu jyokei tennō 'hantai,'" https://www.sankei.com/article/20210908-UYGHAJ YVB5KMTCD7HUURUX5ZG4, accessed March 2022.

15. *Sankei*, September 27, 2021, "Kishida, Takaichi-shi dōseikon ni shinchō Kōno, Noda-shi ha 'bessei' sansei," https://www.sankei.com/article/202 10927-VFNB7AG2NJMVTO6FYMX6IQ2FGQ, accessed March 2022.

16. Leading right-wing commentator Sakurai Yoshiko, for example, published a column in the *Sankei Shimbun* upon Kishida's elevation to the premiership in which she acknowledged his concessions to the right wing but said he needed to do more to disown the Kōchikai tradition, which she blames for burdening postwar Japan with constraints on its power. See *Sankei Shimbun*, October 4, 2021, https://www.sankei.com/article/202 11004-E5YDWPGBZ5IQZKCY6DRX7WOAEI, accessed March 2022.

17. *Sankei*, September 29, 2021, "Kessen tōhyō de no kyōtō Kishida, Takaichi ryōjinei ga seishiki gōi," https://www.sankei.com/article/202 10929-WCUAUSVYTNP7ZCKYIE62RJDI7I, accessed March 2022.

18. *Mainichi*, October 13, 2021, "Jimin kōyaku 'Takaichi-iro' koku sōsaisen toki no shuchō fundan," https://mainichi.jp/articles/20211013/ddm/005/010/102000c, accessed March 2022.

19. See Takaichi's manifesto at https://jimin.jp-east-2.storage.api.nifcloud.com/sousai21/pdf/takaichi_sanae.pdf. At a speech in Hyogo prefecture, she reportedly boasted that criticisms that the LDP manifesto was just her manifesto were correct. See https://news.yahoo.co.jp/articles/06b 26a3983597cf638008753a5aa84400f43f515.

20. Data on Abe's campaign appearances available at https://www.jimin.jp/election/results/sen_shu49/speech/index2.html?id=100360.

21. *Nikkei*, December 27, 2021, "Kishida Seiken sankagetsu, irei no shijiritsu jōshō shihanseiki de 3-reime," https://www.nikkei.com/article/DGX ZQOUA261BN0W1A221C2000000, accessed March 2022.

22. News Post Seven, November 8, 2021, "Kishida shushō to hibana chirasu Abe-shi, tenteki-Hayashi Yoshimasa-shi no gaishō kiyō soshi ni ugoita," https://web.archive.org/web/20211107223425/https://news.yahoo.co.jp/articles/06b26a3983597cf638008753a5aa84400f43f515, accessed March 2022.

23. *Nikkei*, December 27, 2021, "Tsugi no shushō e kurigae, 'Sanin no kabe' koenanori Hayashi Yoshimasa," https://www.nikkei.com/article/DGXZQOUA120UY0S1A211C2000000, accessed March 2022.
24. It is also possible that the next round of redistricting could eliminate one of Yamaguchi's four districts, which could pit Abe and Hayashi against each other directly.
25. *Nikkei*, November 11, 2021, "30 nenburi no Abe-ha 'Hokoriaru Nippon hikitsugu," https://www.nikkei.com/article/DGXZQOUA113G L0R11C21A1000000, accessed March 2022.
26. The White House, April 16, 2021, "U.S.-Japan Joint Leaders' Statement: "U.S.—JAPAN GLOBAL PARTNERSHIP FOR A NEW ERA," press release, https://www.whitehouse.gov/briefing-room/statements-releases/2021/04/16/u-s-japan-joint-leaders-statement-u-s-japan-global-partnership-for-a-new-era, accessed March 2022.
27. *Nikkei*, December 1, 2021, "Abe Shinzō moto shushō no intabyuu zenbun," https://www.nikkei.com/article/DGXZQOUA01C3O0R01C 21A2000000, accessed March 2022.
28. The Prospect Foundation, December 13, 2021, "2021 Taiwan-US-Japan Trilateral Indo-Pacific Security Dialogue_Keynote Speech_Shinzo Abe," YouTube, https://youtu.be/XaZrlkRm7S8, accessed March 2022.
29. *Nikkei*, December 14, 2021, "Abe-shi, gaikō boikotto 'Nippon ga riidaashippu wo,'" https://www.nikkei.com/article/DGXZQOUA13CHS0T 11C21A2000000, accessed March 2022.
30. *Nikkei*, December 14, 2021, "Peikin gorin 'gaikō boikotto wo' gi-ren ga shushō ni yōsei," https://www.nikkei.com/article/DGXZQOUA1462 U0U1A211C2000000/?n_cid=SNSTWP&n_tw=1639480826, accessed March 2022.
31. *Asahi*, December 24, 2021, "Abe moto shushō 'dōshi-kuni no senretsu ni kuwawatta' 'gaikō boikotto' wo hyōka," https://digital.asahi.com/articles/ASPDS44Y4PDSUTFK00B.html, accessed March 2022. Takaichi, however, criticized how long it took Kishida to decide and questioned the decision to send Japan Olympic Committee president Hashimoto Seiko, a sitting member of the House of Councillors. See Fuji News Network, December 28, 2021, "gaikō-teki boikotto 'osokatta,'" https://web.archive.org/web/20211228092025/https://www.fnn.jp/articles/-/291974, accessed March 2022.
32. *Nikkei*, December 1, 2021, "Abe Shinzō moto shushō no intabyuu zenbun," https://www.nikkei.com/article/DGXZQOUA01C3O0R01C 21A2000000, accessed March 2022. This line of argument is a marked departure from the understanding that the United States is the "spear" and Japan the "shield" in the relationship. It also marks a shift away from a focus on the ability to strike "enemy bases," as he argued that

the focus should instead be on "counterattack" or "strike" capabilities broadly defined.

33. *Nikkei*, March 11, 2022, "'kaku kyōyū' giron, jimin de fujō bei no shiyō handan ni kanyo," https://www.nikkei.com/article/DGXZQOUA08DP 90Y2A300C2000000/, accessed March 2022.

34. Abe Shinzō Channel, December 1, 2021, "Keynote speech – Impact Forum," YouTube, https://www.youtube.com/watch?v=qkwCMattztQ, accessed March 2022.

35. *Sankei*, December 26, 2021, "'Abenomics no hōkō kaeru beki de ha nai' Abe-shi," https://www.sankei.com/article/20211226-FSUT6BCE7 BJFNNZWAMZXY2XYS4/, accessed March 2022.

36. *Asahi*, December 16, 2021, "Abe moto shushō 'Nippon ga taitanikku nara kokusai wo kau hito ha inai,'" https://digital.asahi.com/articles/ ASPDH7DFXPDHUTFK02Z.html, accessed March 2022.

37. *Asahi*, December 1, 2021, "Zaisei giron no saikō komon ni Abe moto shushō – Saiken-ha ha fūzen no tomoshibi," https://digital.asahi.com/ articles/ASPD172ZZPD1UTFK00J.html, accessed March 2022.

38. On Nishida as Japan's foremost advocate of MMT, see Megumi Fujikawa, "'We're Already Doing It': Japan Tests Unorthodox Economic Doctrine," *Wall Street Journal*, 15 May 2019, https://www.wsj.com/ articles/were-already-doing-it-japan-tests-unorthodox-economic-doctrine-11557912602, accessed March 2022. Takaichi echoed MMT arguments in her rebuttal to Yano's essay, arguing among other things that Japan cannot default on its debt since it borrows in its own currency, a common argument in Modern Monetary Theory.

39. Yusuke Takeuchi, "Kingmaker Abe behind push for Japan's supersize stimulus," *Nikkei Asia*, 20 November 2021, https://asia.nikkei.com/ Politics/Kingmaker-Abe-behind-push-for-Japan-s-supersize-stimulus, accessed March 2022.

40. *Jiji*, January 4, 2022, "'Abe-shi to yūkō kankei tsuduketai' Kishida-ha kakudai ni shinchō – shushō," https://www.jiji.com/jc/article?k=202201 0300297&g=pol, accessed March 2022.

References

Amano, Kenya, and Saori Katada. 2022. Economic Policy Trilemma: Macroeconomic Politics in the 2021 Election. In *Japan Decides 2021: The Japanese General Election*, eds. Robert J. Pekkanen, Steven R. Reed, Daniel M. Smith. New York: Palgrave Macmillan.

Green, Michael J. 2022. Foreign Policy and Defense Issues in Japan's 2021 Election. In *Japan Decides 2021: The Japanese General Election*, eds. Robert J. Pekkanen, Steven R. Reed, Daniel M. Smith. New York: Palgrave Macmillan.

Harris, Tobias. 2020. *The Iconoclast: Shinzō Abe and the New Japan*. London: Hurst Publishers.

Kweon, Yesola. 2022. Women's Representation in Japan. In *Japan Decides 2021: The Japanese General Election*, eds. Robert J. Pekkanen, Steven R. Reed, Daniel M. Smith. New York: Palgrave Macmillan.

Maeda, Yukio. 2022. Public Opinion and COVID-19. In *Japan Decides 2021: The Japanese General Election*, eds. Robert J. Pekkanen, Steven R. Reed, Daniel M. Smith. New York: Palgrave Macmillan.

Nemoto, Kuniaki. 2022. How the Liberal Democratic Party Avoided a Loss in 2021. In *Japan Decides 2021: The Japanese General Election*, eds. Robert J. Pekkanen, Steven R. Reed, Daniel M. Smith. New York: Palgrave Macmillan.

Takaichi, Sanae. 2021. *Utsukushiku, tsuyoku, seichō suru kuni he: Watashi no 'Nihon no keizai kyōjinka keikaku.'* Tokyo: Wac Bunko. Kindle.

Vekasi, Kristin. 2022. China in Japan's 2021 Elections. In *Japan Decides 2021: The Japanese General Election*, eds. Robert J. Pekkanen, Steven R. Reed, Daniel M. Smith. New York: Palgrave Macmillan.

CHAPTER 8

Candidate Selection for the 2021 General Election

Jochen Rehmert

For the 2021 general election, eight parliamentary and ten extra-parliamentary parties nominated a total of 1,051 candidates, slightly down from the 1,180 candidates who ran in the 2017 general election. Out of these 1,051 candidates, 416 (40%) were incumbent members of the House of Representatives (HR). An additional 84 (8%) were former members of the HR prior to the 2017 general election, attempting a comeback in 2021. 368 candidates (35%) were running for the first time, while 183 (17%) had run (unsuccessfully) at least once before. Most candidates (59%) ran as dual-listed candidates in the mixed-member majoritarian (MMM) electoral system, i.e., competing in one of the 289 single-member districts (SMD) and simultaneously on a party-list in one of the eleven proportional representation blocs (PR). Only 233 (22%) candidates competed in an SMD without a PR nomination, while 195 (19%) candidates were nominated solely on the party-list. Table 8.1

J. Rehmert (✉)
Department of Political Science, University of Zurich, Zurich, Switzerland
e-mail: rehmertjochen@gmail.com

103

Table 8.1 Parties and candidates in the 2021 general election

	LDP	Kom	CDP	JCP	Ishin	DPP	Reiwa	SDP	Other	Total
Incumbents	252	21	105	12	10	7	1	0	8	416
	75%	40%	44%	9%	10%	26%	5%	0%	6%	40%
Former incumbents	12	4	29	8	15	3	2	0	11	84
	4%	8%	12%	6%	16%	11%	10%	0%	5%	8%
New candidates	59	16	74	43	46	13	13	9	95	368
	18%	30%	31%	33%	48%	48%	62%	60%	71%	35%
Recurring candidates	13	12	32	67	25	4	5	6	19	183
	4%	23%	13%	52%	26%	15%	24%	40%	14%	17%
SMD-only	25	9	1	90	0	0	0	0	108	233
	7%	17%	<1%	69%	0%	0%	0%	0%	81%	22%
Dual-listed	252	0	213	15	94	21	12	8	8	623
	75%	0%	89%	12%	98%	78%	57%	53%	6%	59%
PR-only	59	44	26	25	2	6	9	7	17	195
	18%	83%	11%	19%	2%	22%	43%	47%	1%	19%
Female	33	4	44	46	14	8	5	9	24	187
	10%	8%	18%	35%	15%	30%	24%	60%	18%	18%
Median Age	57	53	53	53	51	53	51	66	52	54
Total	336	53	240	130	96	27	21	15	133	1,051

Notes Party abbreviations: LDP = Liberal Democratic Party; Kom = Kōmeitō, CDP = Constitutional Democratic Party; JCP = Japanese Communist Party; Ishin = Ishin no Kai; DPP = Democratic Party for the People; Reiwa = Reiwa Shinsengumi; SDP = Social Democratic Party. Other includes: The party fighting against NHK in the trial for violating Article 72 of the Attorney Act (30 candidates); No Party to Support (2); New Party Yamato (4); Japan First Party (4); New Party Kunimori (2); as well as five other parties each with one candidate as well as 80 independents

presents an overview of the type of candidates nominated by the eight parties represented in the HR at the time of its dissolution.

Table 8.1 also highlights that despite recent legislation calling for parties to "make their best effort" to address the gender inequality in electoral politics, the blatant underrepresentation of women continues. Without stipulating any benchmarks or legal consequences, the rather toothless *Act on Promotion of Gender Equality in the Political Field* (passed in 2018) has not helped to improve the sorry state of women's representation so far. Only 18% (187) of all candidates in 2021 were women—no improvement over the 2017 numbers when 209 women were nominated, equally accounting for 18% of all candidates that year. The situation is particularly skewed for the governing parties—though by no means limited to them—which taken together have nominated only 37 women (on gender representation, see Kweon, this volume).

With 96 fresh faces to enter the HR, legislative turnover increased over previous elections. While turnover in 2014 stood at 9% and at 12% in 2017, the 96 newly elected candidates in 2021 account for 21% of the HR's 465 seats. This number can be attributed especially to the strong showing of Ishin no Kai (27 newcomers) but also to the Liberal Democratic Party (LDP) nominating newcomers in a series of safe districts vacated by LDP incumbents (32 newcomers overall). Several of these newcomers were selected following open recruitment (e.g., Rehmert, 2021). Yet, the increase in turnover did not improve the representation of women or younger generations. Only 8% (20 from 258) of newly elected LDP are women and only 5% (12 from 258) are 40 or younger (on younger politicians, see McClean, this volume). The relatively high share of newcomers in Kōmeitō (28%) can be traced to its internal rules of deselecting incumbents too old or too long in office. Its tendency to compete mainly on the PR tier allowed for the party leadership to enforce its rules more effectively compared, for instance, with the internal rules regarding deselection in place in the LDP (see also Smith, 2013).

However, the uptake in legislative turnover should not obscure the high reelection rates for incumbents of all parties. Incumbents indeed enjoyed very high reelection rates, ranging from the highest of 95% for Kōmeitō incumbents to the lowest rate of 67% for the Japanese Communist Party (JCP). 87% of LDP incumbents were reelected, as were 80% of Ishin no Kai incumbents and 70% of Constitutional Democratic Party (CDP) incumbents. Compared to the dire expectations in the run-up to the election, the eventual outcome certainly came as a relief to many LDP incumbents and its leadership. With a series of scandal-invoked resignations, intra-party as well as intra-coalition competition over nominations and the rising menace of an unified opposition, the LDP entered the election period with several headaches (on the LDP, see Nemoto, this volume).

Conflict Over Nominations in the Governing LDP and Kōmeitō

Over the summer several LDP incumbents declared they were not seeking reelection. While a few did so of their own will, others resigned over scandals. Among the voluntary retirees are Shiozaki Yasuhisa (Ehime 1st), Yamaguchi Taimei (Saitama 10th) and Kawasaki Jirō (Mie 2nd). All three bequeathed their districts to their sons who successfully continue their family's political dynasties (cf. Smith, 2018). Other voluntary retirees include such veteran lawmakers as Ōshima Tadamori (Aomori 2nd), Yamamoto Kōzo (Ehime 4th), Ibuki Bunmei (Kyoto 1st), and Takemoto Naokazu (Osaka 15th)—all above the age of 74. Hase Hiroshi (Ishikawa 1st) and Okonogi Hachirō (Kanagawa 3rd) resigned to run for Governor of Ishikawa and Mayor of Yokohama, respectively.

However, other incumbents resigned after being implicated in one of several scandals. Matsumoto Jun (Kanagawa 1st), Tanose Taidō (Nara 3rd), and Ōtsuka Takashi (Osaka 8th) resigned from the LDP to take responsibility for late night drinking in a bar in Tokyo's upscale Ginza district during a Coronavirus-induced nationwide state of emergency. While Matsumoto and Tanose both ran as independents, only Tanose was elected. Three other incumbents including Akimoto Tsukasa (Tokyo 15th), Katsunuma Shigeaki (Miyagi 5th), and Shirasuka Takaki (Chiba 13th) had to resign and may face legal consequences for their involvement in a bribery scandal revolving around Integrated Resorts, that may exclusively house international casinos on Japanese ground. Others resigned over cases of sexual harassment (Ishizaki Tōru, who switched to Ishin no Kai instead), implications in the Akita Foods Inc. scandal (Yoshikawa Takamori and Nishikawa Kōya) or for violating the Public Offices Election Law, including Sugawara Isshū (Tokyo 9th) but also Kawai Katsuyuki (Hiroshima 3rd), whose case caused major discord between the LDP and its long-term partner, Kōmeitō (on Kōmeitō, see Klein and McLaughlin, this volume).[1]

The source for the tensions between the coalition partners was a vote-buying bribery scandal of unprecedented scale with Kawai Katsuyuki at its center. In order to help his wife Anri's campaign for the 2019 House of Councillors (HC) election, Kawai was found to have distributed around 29 million Yen (roughly $250,000) to almost 100 prefectural and local politicians in exchange for their support and mobilization. Eventually, Kawai resigned his seat in the HR in April 2021 and began serving his three-year prison sentence in June 2021. With the LDP's image tainted by bribery, an imprisoned former incumbent and an open seat in Hiroshima 3rd, Kōmeitō began pushing to establish their own Saitō Tetsuo as candidate in the district. However, with the LDP's Hiroshima branch in the hands of the Kishida faction, which was eager to recover from the loss of their affiliate Mizote Kensei in the 2019 HC election, no side was about to back down. Eventually, the LDP accepted the nomination of Saitō after warnings by Kōmeitō to withhold their electoral support for all candidates of the Kishida faction in the general election (cf. Liff and Maeda, 2019). Ironically, a similar switch in candidates took place in Kanagawa 6th when the Kōmeitō incumbent resigned over the Ginza club affair and the LDP successfully established their candidate in the district for the first time since 1996. Both parties emphasized their electoral cooperation despite these spats and chairman Yamaguchi Taimei (LDP) as well as then-PM Suga Yoshihide announced in June 2021 that the LDP endorsed all nine of Kōmeitō's SMD candidates. This was a strong signal for the coalition by the LDP, as these recommendations are usually given only after the HR's dissolution (*Mainichi*, June 4 & 11, 2021).

Nonetheless, the LDP also saw competition over nominations within their own ranks. Although nominations within the LDP have traditionally been local affairs, since the electoral reform of the mid-90s there has been a tendency toward greater centralization, especially with more influence for prefectural branches (e.g., Asano, 2006). Some prefectural party branches have also tried to unseat renomination-seeking incumbents, as happened in Tokushima and Yamaguchi with the nomination of Governor Iizumi Kamon and Hayashi Yoshimasa, member of the HC, for Tokushima 1st and Yamaguchi 3rd, respectively. Iizumi eventually announced he would not run, opening the way for incumbent Gotōda Masazumi to receive the party's endorsement and ending the nomination row which had been smoldering since April (*Mainichi*, October 2, 2021). In Yamaguchi, however, incumbent Kawamura Takeo was less fortunate when—under pressure from his prefectural party—he appealed unsuccessfully to the party leadership in Tokyo. He lost the nomination to Hayashi, who went on to win the district (*Mainichi*, October 2, 2021). Not only is outright deselection of this kind a rare occurrence in the LDP (or most parties for that matter), it moreover contradicts one of the party's internal rules for endorsements.

The main rule guiding the nomination practices of the LDP is the simple and general priority for incumbents. This rule of primacy for incumbents, however, receives some qualifications from two other rules. The first rule is to withhold nominations from those candidates who have previously failed to win their district two times in a row. Although it appears to only affect unsuccessful candidates it does in fact extend to the so-called *zombie* incumbents, i.e., dual-listed candidates who have competed unsuccessfully in their districts but who were "resurrected" through the party-list provision under the MMM system (e.g., Pekkanen et al., 2006). Secondly, the primacy of incumbency is modified by setting a (soft) age limit, which applies only to nominations on the party-list. Specifically, incumbents as well as first-time candidates who have passed the age of 73 shall not receive any party-list nomination and may therefore only compete in the SMDs. In the run-up to the election, all three guidelines have been emphasized by either Yamaguchi Taimei, chairman of the election committee of the LDP under PM Suga (*Mainichi*, November 11, 2021) or by Amari Akira, the short-lived secretary-general under PM Kishida Fumio (*Mainichi*, October 5, 2021). As exemplified by the deselection of Kawamura in Yamaguchi above, the party adheres to these rules to varying degrees. While the age limit was ignored in only three instances, 24 out of the 25 *zombie* incumbents who have lost their districts at least twice in a row were nominated again.

Moreover, despite the clear priority for incumbents several districts were in danger of *hoshu bunretsu*, i.e., a division in the conservative forces due to multiple LDP or LDP-leaning candidates seeking nomination. In the case of Miyazaki, the prefectural LDP branch was hesitant to endorse Miyazaki 1st incumbent Takei Shunsuke over a suspected hit-and-run incident. Former assemblywoman Wakatani Noriko sensed an opportunity to run, but eventually the LDP gave the endorsement to Takei (with a nod to the priority rule). Rather than back down, Wakatani ran as independent, enabling CDP first-timer Watanabe Sō to narrowly win the district. Luckily for Takei, his narrow defeat qualified him for one of the party-list seats. The danger of *hoshu bunretsu* further became a fierce reality in the districts of Hiroshima 4th, Kanagawa 4th, and Shizuoka 5th. In these cases, the priority rule for incumbents was less clear, as in all three cases current and former incumbents competed over nominations. In Hiroshima, incumbent Shintani Masayoshi had to face off against former incumbent Nakagawa Toshinao but was able to comfortably defend his district. Somewhat lucky was *zombie*-incumbent Yamamoto Tomohiro in Kanagawa 4th, who was not only facing CDP incumbent Waseda Yuki but also former incumbent Asao Keiichirō. Yamamoto came out third and retained his *zombie*-seat thanks to the LDP's strong showing in Minami Kanto. In Shizuoka 5th, the LDP had two incumbents. Yoshikawa Takeru, who ran unsuccessfully in 2017 but entered parliament through his list position in 2019 as replacement for the resigning Tabata Tsuyoshi, and district incumbent Hosono Gōshi, who began to court the LDP in 2019 after leaving the defunct Party of Hope. Gōshi dwarfed his competition with a comfortable 25% vote margin and joined the LDP after the election.

Quite often the LDP has avoided *hoshu bunretsu* by using top-list positions to appease some of the incumbents. In 2021, these cases include Hokkaido 7th, where a stand-off between Itō Yoshitaka and Suzuki Takako was resolved by nominating her on top of the list; Gunma 1st, where Omi Asako received the top rank and Nakasone Yasutaka the district; or Niigata 2nd, where Washio Eiichirō was nominated on the top rank and Hosoda Kenichi received the district nomination. Other districts in which the party-list was used to avoid *hoshu bunretsu* include Tochigi 2nd, Kochi 2nd, and Saitama 7th (cf. Rehmert, 2022). This incumbent-surplus was often due to the combination of having two types of them—directly elected and *zombie*-elected incumbents of the same district—and the LDP's practice of post-election nominations for successful independents and in-switching from other conservative outfits, such as the Party of Hope. Yet, this practice of preferential treatment through promising list positions also came under fire from incumbents in marginal districts (*Asahi*, October 6, 2021). The LDP typically ranks all dual-listed candidates on the same list rank. While district winners are then taken off the list, the remaining candidates are then re-ordered following how close their defeat in the district was. Depending on the number of PR seats the party wins, the "best losers" then may still enter the HR as a *zombie*-elected MP. Obviously, the more top ranks above the bracket of dual-listed candidates the LDP hands out, the less "competitive ranks" (Reed and Di Virgilio, 2011) remain as safety-net for marginal incumbents, many of whom feared the dynamics of a coordinated opposition (see the later discussion in this chapter).

Candidate selection within Kōmeitō, in contrast, was overall much smoother despite an imminent generational change. The greater centralization in selection allowed the party leadership to enforce its own age and term limit for nominations without much backlash from the incumbents themselves. According to these rules, incumbents above the age of 69 and those in office for longer than 24 years shall not be nominated again, unless there is a strong request from the local community for renomination, a lack of replacement, or the incumbent in question is central for party management. Out of ten incumbents affected, six resigned voluntarily,[2] while the other four all received exemptions from these rules based on their role for the party; Saitō Tetsuo (69), Secretary-General; Kitagawa Kazuo (68), vice party-leader; Ishii Keiichi (63), acting Secretary-General; and Satō Shigeki (62), chair of the election strategy committee. The last three are still below the age limit, but each has been serving in the HR for more than 24 years (*Mainichi*, July 21, 2020).

Coordination of the Progressive Opposition

In the run-up to the general election, the opposition underwent several significant changes. With speculations about a snap election simmering at least since 2019, the more progressive forces among the opposition started calling for presenting voters a serious alternative to the LDP by unifying the notoriously fragmented opposition. As the largest opposition party, the CDP was best positioned to become the focal point for this endeavor. After absorbing a group of independents led by Okada Katsuya, former leader of the Democratic Party (DP), the next goal for Edano Yukio, leader of the CDP, was to join hands with the Democratic Party for the People (DPP), led by Tamaki Yūichirō. The DPP itself came to live as the merger of the more conservative Party of Hope[3] and the conservative wing of the now-defunct DP. Despite the ideological discrepancies between the CDP and the DPP and after hard-fought negotiations, both parties eventually agreed to merge and to retain the name Constitutional Democratic Party, with Edano becoming or rather remaining its leader with 107 votes from the 149 Diet members of the new party (*Mainichi*, September 10, 2020). However, a conservative minority around Tamaki refrained from joining the more liberal CDP. One month later, the Social Democratic Party (SDP) also voted to merge with the CDP— which a majority of the party's member did. Again, however, party leader Fukushima Mizuho opposed the merger and remained in the SDP. Nevertheless, these mergers were an achievement for the opposition. Now, the CDP could enter the 2021 election with 113 incumbent MPs, double the number of MPs elected for the CDP in 2017. Yet, the process of unifying the opposition was not complete.

For truly presenting a viable alternative to and challenging the LDP rule, the CDP had to seek the electoral cooperation with other smaller parties, including the DPP but also the ones left of the center, to avoid splitting the opposition vote. What such unified opposition can achieve became apparent in a series of by-elections, first for three seats of the Diet held in April 2021 (one for the HR, two for the HC) and then for two seats of the HC on October 24th—only a week before the actual vote on October 31. In four out of these five by-elections, the unified candidate supported by the CDP, the DPP/, the JCP, and the SDP triumphed over the LDP. Only for the vacant HC seat in the conservative stronghold of Yamaguchi did the LDP candidate prevail. Yet, for the general election, cooperation among the opposition and fielding unified candidates across hundreds of districts was less straightforward and a bumpier road than these victories may suggest.

Paramount to a successful coordination among the opposition parties was an agreement between Edano's CDP and the JCP. Despite having no realistic chance of winning, the JCP typically nominates candidates in all districts, oftentimes considered as spoiling the success of more viable opposition candidates (Maeda, 2018). Reaching an agreement with the JCP to not compete against the CDP was thus of central importance. Moreover, a more comprehensive agreement might even have the potential for the CDP to take advantage of the JCP's local party machines to mobilize voters. Hence, to strengthen this nascent electoral alliance, the CDP and the JCP—along with the remainder of the SDP and the newly established left-populist Reiwa Shinsengumi—agreed on a common policy platform for the upcoming election on September 8, including for instance the repeal of the 2013 state secret laws and the 2015 security laws passed by the LDP. Yet, progress on candidate coordination was slower. On the very day of signing the agreement, the JCP promised to not run candidates in 93 out of the 105 SMDs in which CDP incumbents planned to compete. The CDP in turn agreed to not field candidates in four out of five districts held by the JCP. For the majority of districts, cooperation remained elusive (*Japan Times*, October 13, 2021).

One month later, on October 12 and with the election date in sight, the CDP was set to field candidates in 214 SMDs. Among the four left-leaning parties (CDP, JCP, SDP, and Reiwa) the goal was to have a unified candidate in about 200 SMDs. Yet, despite their prior agreement, the strongest competition was taking place between the CDP and the JCP. Although both parties promised to not field candidates against their respective incumbents, several districts were still plagued by a lack of coordination (*Mainichi*, October 13, 2021). Moreover, while the advantage of fielding a common candidate appears to be obvious for both parties, the CDP clearly stood to benefit the most from such cooperation, being the more competitive (and less reviled) party of the two. For the JCP, however, the advantage was less clear-cut. As it was typically the JCP that withdrew their candidates, voices within the JCP were trying to raise its price and demanding more concessions this time around (cf. Maeda, 2018, p. 103). Moreover, the electoral incentives for the JCP under MMM make it attractive for the party to maintain as many candidates as possible. As voters in Japan have two votes to cast—one for a district candidate and one for a party—it is commonly assumed that the pure presence of a party's candidate in a given district tends to boost the party's PR vote share as well (known as "contamination"). This makes it worthwhile for parties operating under a mixed-member system to nominate candidates even in futile districts hoping that doing so will boost their party vote share (e.g., Ferrara et al., 2005).

For the CDP, cooperation with the Communists comes at a price. Not only was a unified candidate possible in only a third of all SMDs, the JCP with its many antisystem positions is widely seen as uncoalitionable and has in fact never participated in any coalition (Pekkanen and Reed, 2018, p. 81). Entering into such a frank cooperation thus came with the risk of alienating other potential partners. The DPP, for example—with 7 incumbents—did not join the four-party agreement out of protest over cooperating with the JCP, but nonetheless showed a willingness to do so bilaterally with the CDP. The DPP and CDP agreed to not challenge their respective incumbents. However, more importantly, roughly 60% of voters were skeptical about the agreement with the JCP, as was the Japanese Trade Union Confederation (Rengo), on whose support—reportedly seven million members-strong—many CDP candidates rely. The greatest concern for many is the potential role of the JCP in case of a CDP-led majority after the election. Pledges made by Edano that the JCP will never formally join the cabinet and will instead merely support a CDP-led government did not appear to have successfully alleviated these concerns (*Mainichi*, September 30, 2021).

Nonetheless, with the HR dissolution approaching coordination received new momentum. All four signatory parties made concessions and withdrew some of their candidates, sometimes in spectacular fashion. Yamamoto Tarō, leader of Reiwa, announced his intention on October 8 to run in Tokyo 8th only to withdraw three days later after receiving pushback from local activists and the CDP whose candidate Yoshida Harumi has been doing the groundwork for her candidacy in the district for years. In total, Reiwa withdrew 8 of their previously announced SMD candidacies (including that of Yamamoto), the SDP withdrew one, the JCP withdrew 24 candidates and the CDP only two. Overall, despite the ups and downs the progressive opposition managed to nominate a unified candidate in 217 out of 286 districts. A coordination success, but

arguably an electoral failure with the CDP and JCP being the only opposition parties to lose seats—though mainly in the PR tier (on the electoral
results, see K. Maeda, this volume).

CONCLUSION

As in the years before, the 2021 general election did not improve the
representation of women in the HR nor did it result in a significant rejuvenation of the political elite. Despite the increase in legislative turnover,
women and younger generations remain heavily underrepresented in the
HR. The main culprit for these dismal numbers is the major party's nomination practices with strong local influence and the primacy for old male
incumbents. Given the electoral hegemony of the LDP, tangible changes
may only occur once the party tackles and reforms its recruitment.

As for the opposition, the unexpectedly bad showing after the effort
of unifying its candidates is likely to cause some soul-searching about
whether and how to cooperate in the future. Especially the relations with
the JCP as the most controversial partner among the progressive opposition will come under scrutiny again. The stunning success of Ishin no Kai
may be due to regional idiosyncrasies, but they may also suggest a dislike
for an opposition (partly) carried by the JCP.

NOTES

1. Klein and McLaughlin also cover the background of the regional-level
   cooperation between Kōmeitō and Ishin no Kai in Osaka. In fact, in the
   2021 election Kōmeitō and Ishin did not field any candidates against each
   other. For cooperation among the opposition see the later discussion in the
   text.
2. Including Inoue Yoshihisa (74), Masuya Keigo (70), Ishida Noritoshi (70),
   Takagi Michiyo (69), and Tomita Shigeyuki (68), who had spent 25 years
   in the HR. Ōta Akihiro (74) resigned voluntarily citing health issues.
3. Founded by Koike Yuriko, Governor of Tokyo, the party was reinstated in
   October as Tomin First no Kai and announced on the 4th that they would
   compete the general election, only to redact that statement two weeks later
   realizing the little time to organize.

References

Asano, Masahiko. 2006. *Shimin Shakai ni okeru Seido Kaikaku: Senkyo Seido to Kouhosha Rikuruuto* [System Reform at the Level of Civil Society: Electoral Reform and Candidate Recruitment]. Tokyo: Keio University Press.

Ferrara, Federico, Erik S. Herron, and Misa Nishikawa. 2005. *Mixed Member Electoral Systems: Contamination and Consequences*. New York: Palgrave Macmillan.

Liff, Adam P. and Ko Maeda. 2019. "Electoral Incentives, Policy Compromise, and Coalition Durability: Japan's LDP-Komeito Government in a Mixed Electoral System." *Japanese Journal of Political Science* 20(1):53–73.

Maeda, Ko. 2018. The JCP: A Perpetual Spoiler? In *Japan Decides 2017. The Japanese General Election*, ed. Robert J. Pekkanen, Steven R. Reed, Ethan Scheiner and Daniel M. Smith. Palgrave Macmillan, 93–106.

Pekkanen, Robert J., Benjamin Nyblade and Ellis S. Krauss. 2006. "Electoral Incentives in Mixed-Member Systems: Party, Posts, and Zombie Politicians in Japan." *American Political Science Review* 100(2):183-193.

Pekkanen, Robert J. and Steven R. Reed. 2018. The Opposition: From Third Party Back to Third Force. In *Japan Decides 2017. The Japanese General Election*, ed. Robert J. Pekkanen, Steven R. Reed, Ethan Scheiner and Daniel M. Smith. London: Palgrave Macmillan, 77–92.

Reed, Steven R. and Aldo Di Virgilio. 2011. Nominating Candidates Under New Rules in Italy and Japan: You Cannot Bargain with Resources You Do Not Have. In *A Natural Experiment on Electoral Law Reform. Evaluating the Long Run Consequences of 1990s Electoral Reform in Italy and Japan*, ed. Daniela Giannetti and Bernard Grofman. New York: Springer, 61–76.

Rehmert, Jochen. 2021. "Behavioral Consequence of Open Candidate Recruitment." *Legislative Studies Quarterly* 46(2):427–458.

Rehmert, Jochen. 2022. "Coordinating Nominations: How to Deal with an Incumbent Surplus after Electoral Reform." *Japanese Journal of Political Science* 23(1):55–72.

Smith, Daniel M. 2013. Candidate Recruitment for the 2012 Election: New Parties, New Methods ... Same Old Pool of Candidates? In *Japan Decides 2012. The Japanese General Election*, ed. Robert J. Pekkanen, Steven R. Reed and Ethan Scheiner. London: Palgrave Macmillan, 101–122.

Smith, Daniel M. 2018. *Dynasties and Democracy: The Inherited Incumbency Advantage in Japan*. Stanford: Stanford University Press.

CHAPTER 9

Generational Change or Continuity in Japan's Leadership?

Charles T. McClean

One of the most surprising outcomes of the 2021 election was the fact that a number of young challengers managed to unseat much older, long-entrenched incumbents. In a result that grabbed headlines nationwide, the Constitutional Democratic Party of Japan's (CDP) Futori Hideshi (44) won in Kanagawa 13th District over the Liberal Democratic Party's (LDP) Amari Akira (72), who became the first LDP secretary-general to lose a single-member district (SMD) contest. Likewise, in Iwate 3rd District, the LDP's Fujiwara Takashi (38) defeated the CDP's Ozawa Ichiro (79), arguably one of Japan's most influential politicians and a former president of the now-defunct Democratic Party of Japan (DPJ). It was Ozawa's first constituency loss in over 50 years since his first election in 1969. Although Amari and Ozawa still secured seats in the House of Representatives via the proportional representation (PR) component of Japan's hybrid electoral system, the SMD victories by these young

C. T. McClean (✉)
Yale University, New Haven, CT, USA
e-mail: charles.mcclean@yale.edu

R. J. Pekkanen et al. (eds.), *Japan Decides 2021*,
https://doi.org/10.1007/978-3-031-11324-6_9

politicians were stunning. In response, Amari resigned his post as LDP secretary-general.

Were these victories by young candidates indicative of widespread generational change in the 2021 election? Or were they merely outliers in an election that otherwise continued the status quo, with mostly older politicians dominating Japanese politics?

While this chapter highlights a few reasons to be optimistic about the next generation of leaders in Japan, the overall results point to the 2021 election as a step backward for youth representation from both a historical and comparative perspective. Candidates for the House of Representatives did range significantly in age, from 25 (the legal age of eligibility) to 86. However, the election also featured the lowest percentage of candidates (9.4%) and members of parliament (MPs) (4.9%) under 40, highest average age among candidates (54.2) and MPs (55.5), and highest percentage of candidates (9.2%) and MPs (9.0%) age 70 or older in decades (for more on candidate selection, see Rehmert 2022). With less than 5% of elected MPs under 40,[1] Japan now ranks second to last in the OECD in youth representation, ahead of South Korea (3.7%) and just below the United States (6.7%) but far behind the OECD average (23.7%) and group leader Italy (42.7%) (Inter-Parliamentary Union 2021).

The relatively small and declining number of young politicians in Japan is concerning for several reasons. For one, there may be a "vicious cycle" of youth political participation, where a relatively low number of young candidates reinforces, and is reinforced by, low youth turnout and low youth interest in politics (Stockemer and Sundström 2018). In other words, if young people do not see politicians as anything like them— for instance, because the average politician is much older—then they may become less interested in electoral politics and less willing to turn out to vote (Pomante and Schraufnagel 2015). Thus, the increasingly short supply of young people running for office could be one driver of the declining youth turnout in Japanese elections (for other drivers, see Steel 2022).

Another concern, and the focus of this chapter, is that the shortage of young politicians may limit the extent to which young people's opinions are represented in the policymaking process. Research shows that younger people have distinct policy preferences from older people on a wide range of issues, including education, childcare, immigration, employment, gender equality, and environmental protection (Wattenberg 2007).

Without more young people serving in public office, there is a risk that the policies enacted by mostly older politicians will largely ignore the wishes of younger generations (McClean 2020, 2021).

Using data from the UTokyo-Asahi Survey (UTAS), which surveyed nearly every candidate in the 2021 election, I find that younger and older candidates differed significantly in their stated policy priorities and preferences. Candidates under 40 were more likely to say that they would prioritize education, childcare, and employment if elected; more supportive of strengthening Japan's defense capabilities; and more positive toward enacting bills to recognize gay marriage and promote LGBT awareness. These patterns suggest that the greater presence of young people in Japan's House of Representatives could have significant consequences for the types of policies that get debated and ultimately implemented by the government.

Finally, I conclude by discussing the potential for reforms to increase youth representation. Before the pandemic, the LDP implemented a series of youth-related policies and there was talk of passing new laws aimed at increasing the number of young politicians. These discussions were largely sidelined as the government turned its focus to its COVID-19 response, leaving open the question of whether these reforms will be enacted in the future.

Too Young to Run?

The 2021 election witnessed the fewest candidates under 40 run for office or win a seat since the current electoral system was implemented in 1996 (Fig. 9.1). Just 99 of the 1,051 (9.4%) candidates who competed in the election were in their 20s or 30s, down more than half from 19.7% a decade earlier in 2012 and the lowest ratio since 1967 (9.2%). Even fewer young people secured a seat in the Diet, as only 23 of the 465 (4.9%) elected MPs were under 40. When the House of Representatives convened in November 2021 following the election, it did so with three times fewer young MPs than it did in 2009 (16.2%) and the lowest percentage of young MPs since 1990 (4.5%). While the relative number of young candidates and representatives began to increase in the early 1990s, and peaked in 2009 and 2012, this election marked a resumption of the status quo, with young people's representation returning to the low levels common during the years prior to electoral reform.

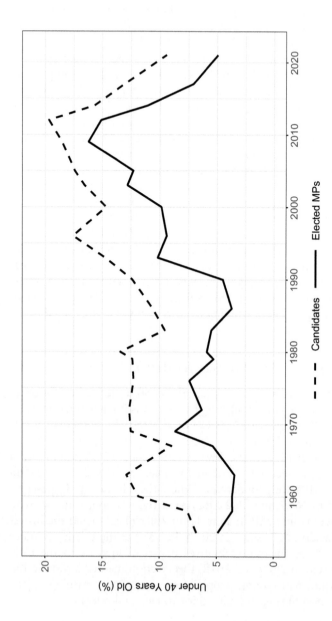

Fig. 9.1 Candidates and Elected MPs Under 40 (1955–2021) (*Notes* McClean [2020], Smith and Reed [2018], and Yanai [2021])

Japan's ruling coalition in particular fielded few young candidates (Table 9.1). The LDP's percentage of candidates under 40 (5.4%) trailed far behind that of main opposition and third force parties such as the CDP (9.2%), Japan Communist Party (JCP) (17.7%), and Japan Ishin no Kai (Ishin) (12.5%). The LDP's coalition partner Kōmeitō only fielded a single candidate under 40, Sone Shusaku (31), who ran as a pure PR candidate in the Tohoku bloc but failed to win a seat. Among the major parties, the LDP also had the highest average candidate age (56.6), oldest candidate (82), and highest percentage of candidates age 70 and over (12.8%). The LDP's elected MPs were likewise significantly older than those from the next two largest parties, the CDP and Ishin, the latter of which did not have an MP older than 65 (Table 9.2).

Table 9.1 Age of candidates by party

	Candidates	Age of candidates				
		Min	Mean	Max	Under 40	70 and over
Ruling coalition						
Liberal Democratic Party	336	25	56.6	82	18 (5.4%)	43 (12.8%)
Kōmeitō	53	31	53.3	69	1 (1.9%)	0 (0%)
Main opposition						
Constitutional Democratic Party of Japan	240	25	53.5	79	22 (9.2%)	16 (6.7%)
Japan Communist Party	130	26	52.6	74	23 (17.7%)	14 (10.8%)
Reiwa Shinsengumi	21	34	49.8	73	4 (19.0%)	1 (4.8%)
Social Democratic Party	15	48	64.0	76	0 (0%)	3 (20.0%)
Third force						
Japan Ishin no Kai	96	27	50.5	72	12 (12.5%)	2 (2.1%)
Others						
Independent	80	37	53.3	86	4 (5.0%)	13 (6.2%)
Democratic Party for the People	27	32	51.6	74	4 (14.8%)	2 (7.4%)
NHK Party	30	25	43.5	68	9 (30.0%)	0 (0%)
Other Parties	23	25	56.6	80	2 (8.7%)	3 (13.0%)
Total	1,051	25	54.2	86	99 (9.4%)	97 (9.2%)

Note Yanai (2021)

Table 9.2 Age of MPs by party

	MPs	Age of MPs				
		Min	Mean	Max	Under 40	70 and Over
Ruling coalition						
Liberal Democratic Party	259	31	57.0	82	11 (4.2%)	32 (12.4%)
Kōmeitō	32	42	56.4	69	0 (0%)	0 (0%)
Main opposition						
Constitutional Democratic Party of Japan	96	29	54.7	79	5 (5.2%)	8 (8.3%)
Japan Communist Party	10	49	62.3	74	0 (0%)	2 (20%)
Reiwa Shinsengumi	3	44	47.3	52	0 (0%)	0 (0%)
Social Democratic Party	1	65	65.0	65	0 (0%)	0 (0%)
Third force						
Japan Ishin no Kai	41	36	49.4	65	4 (9.8%)	0 (0%)
Others						
Independent	12	41	51.6	63	0 (0%)	0 (0%)
Democratic Party for the People	11	32	49.2	65	3 (27.3%)	0 (0%)
NHK Party	0	–	–	–	–	–
Other Parties	0	–	–	–	–	–
Total	465	29	55.5	82	23 (4.9%)	42 (9.0%)

Note Yanai (2021)

At the same time, it is worth noting that the LDP's young candidates outperformed their peers from other parties. Of the 18 LDP candidates in their 20s and 30s who ran for office, 11 (61.1%) secured a seat compared to 4 of 12 (33.3%) Ishin candidates, 5 of 22 (22.7%) CDP candidates, and a striking 0 of 23 (0%) JCP candidates. Thus, the gap in the percentage of candidates under 40 between ruling and opposition parties (Table 9.1) is much larger than the gap in the percentage of elected MPs under 40 (Table 9.2).

This discrepancy is likely due in part to the well-documented quality advantage that the LDP enjoys in candidate recruitment, with "quality" referring to traits that typically increase a candidate's likelihood of victory such as prior elected experience, financial resources, name recognition, and membership in a political dynasty (Smith 2018). For example, of the

18 young LDP candidates who ran in 2021, 7 (38.9%) were incumbents, all of whom won reelection. By contrast, just 5 of the 57 (8.7%) CDP, JCP, and Ishin young candidates were incumbents, of which only the 3 CDP incumbents held onto their seats.

Why did the number of young candidates and MPs fall so low in 2021, and why does Japan have so few young MPs relative to other OECD countries?

One possible answer to the first question is that the relative presence of young politicians in Japan appears to follow the trajectory of party competition and seat turnover in parliament (McClean 2020). The percentage of young candidates and MPs remained relatively low during the initial period of LDP dominance (1955–1990), began to increase with the LDP's brief loss of power (1993–1994) and the rise of the DPJ in the late 1990s and early 2000s, peaked with the alternations in power between the DPJ and LDP in 2009 and 2012, and then steeply declined with the return of LDP dominance from 2012 to 2021. The LDP's success in the last three elections has come in part thanks to many of the party's incumbents holding onto their seats, which in turn has created few opportunities for young candidates to gain a foothold in the House of Representatives. Thus, the return to single-party dominance has also brought a return to gerontocracy.

Turning to the second question, there are several possible explanations for Japan's comparatively low level of youth representation. First, Japan's electoral system advantages candidates who have significant name recognition, financial assets, and local ties. These resources are ones that individuals tend to accrue with age, making it difficult for young candidates to compete with more senior politicians (McClean 2020). Second, Japan's minimum age to run for national office (25) is tied for the highest in the OECD, and the country also had the highest minimum voting age (20) for years until lowering it to 18 in 2016. This delay in political socialization may discourage young people from seeking out political careers even after they reach the legal age of candidacy (Kamikubo 2019; Stockemer and Sundström 2018). Third, studies on the "vicious cycle" of youth political participation suggest that Japan's low level of youth representation may be related to its low level of youth turnout (see Steel 2022), with some finding evidence that an increase in youth turnout could benefit young candidates at the polls (McClean and Ono 2022).

Interestingly, two factors that do not appear to matter for youth representation are the age demographics of society and voter biases against young people serving in elected office. While Japan's low number of young lawmakers might seem natural given that it is the oldest country in the OECD (and world), the second-oldest OECD country is Italy, which has nearly nine times the percentage of representatives under 40 as Japan (42.7% vs. 4.9%). More broadly, there is no correlation between the age demographics of citizens and representatives among OECD nations (McClean 2020). Recent survey experiments also find that Japanese voters have generally positive views toward young candidates and instead strongly dislike elderly candidates (Eshima and Smith 2022; Horiuchi et al. 2020; McClean and Ono 2022).

Although few young people ran for office or won in 2021, there are still a few reasons to be optimistic about the next generation of leaders in Japan, at least within the LDP. This is because many young LDP members who first entered office in 2012 have since managed to hold onto their seats in the three subsequent elections (2014, 2017, 2021), giving them the track record needed to be assigned to party and government leadership positions at a relatively young age. This cohort includes the two youngest members of Prime Minister Kishida Fumio's cabinet: Makishima Karen (45), Minister in Charge of Administrative Reform and first female director of the LDP's youth division, and Kobayashi Takayuki (46), who holds the newly created post of Economic Security Minister. It also includes Murai Hideki (41), the youngest ever special adviser to an LDP prime minister, Fukuda Tatsuo (54), chair of the LDP General Council, and Kobayashi Fumiaki (38), deputy minister of the Digital Agency in the Cabinet Office.

These young LDP leaders are starting to make their voices heard within the party and government. For instance, in September 2021, Fukuda led a group of junior lawmakers in calling for a free and open vote to determine who should succeed Prime Minister Suga Yoshihide, rather than leaving the decision up to older faction bosses. Another example is Koizumi Shinjiro (40), who first won election in 2009 and is perhaps the best-known young politician in Japan as the son of a former prime minister. Koizumi served as Minister of the Environment (2019–2021) under Prime Minister Abe Shinzo, during which time he made waves by advocating for the right to take paternity leave and then becoming the first cabinet minister to do so in early 2020.

SURVEYING YOUNGER AND OLDER CANDIDATES

Why does the shortage of young candidates and MPs in the 2021 election matter? While this shortage may be worrying because of normative concerns about intergenerational equity (Bidadanure 2015) and its potential negative impact on broader youth political participation (see Steel 2022), in this chapter, I explore whether it may also have consequences for the types of policies that get promoted and implemented in the parliament.

To do so, I draw on data from the UTAS (2021) candidate surveys. While many elite surveys suffer from low response rates, the UTAS has managed to routinely achieve a response rate above 90% since its inception in 2003. The response rate in the 2021 election was 95.8%, with 95 of 99 (96.0%) candidates under 40 completing the survey.

In the statistical tests that follow, I use linear regression to estimate the effect of a candidate being under 40 years old on their policy priorities and preferences, with controls included for party and gender. The average candidate under 40 was 34.8 years old, while the average candidate 40 or older was 56.2. For policy priorities, I analyze replies to a series of questions that asked candidates to choose their top-three priorities from a list of 15 policy issues. The dependent variable is coded as 1 if a candidate chose a given policy as one of their top three, and 0 otherwise.[2]

For policy preferences, I evaluate responses to 17 survey questions that asked candidates whether they agree or disagree with a set of statements on foreign and security policy, economic policy, and social policy. Candidates answered each question using a 5-point Likert scale, which I have rescaled to make the results more intuitive for readers so that the dependent variable ranges from 1 (disagree) to 5 (agree).

Policy Priorities

Candidates under 40 identified a similar list of top government priorities as candidates 40 and over, although the two groups differed in their policy rankings and level of consensus. Among younger candidates, 59.1% selected education and childcare as a top priority, followed by 41.9% who listed pensions and healthcare and 37.6% who chose employment. For older candidates, the top selected policies were pensions and healthcare (48.6%), education and childcare (44.2%), and industrial policy (26.1%).

Adding controls for party and gender, the more formal tests in Table 9.3 show that candidates under 40 were significantly more likely than candidates 40 and above to say that they would prioritize education and childcare (14.7 percentage points) and employment (11.1 percentage points) if elected, and marginally less likely to say they would emphasize pensions and healthcare (10.1 percentage points). By comparison, differences between younger and older candidates were not statistically significant for the other 12 policy issues.

These results suggest that younger politicians may be more likely than their older colleagues to prioritize issues important to younger voters in office. While the voter survey portion of the UTAS (2021) is not available as of this writing, past studies have found that young Japanese voters care relatively more about education, childcare, and employment policies, as these are all issues that disproportionately affect younger members of society. By contrast, older voters tend to prefer that more government attention is paid to pensions and healthcare, as these are services that primarily benefit older citizens (McClean 2020; 2021).

Table 9.3 Policy priorities of candidates under 40

| Policy priority | Effect of candidate under 40 | | | |
	Estimate	SE	N	R^2
Foreign policy and security	−0.063	(0.042)	975	0.108
Finance	0.025	(0.036)	975	0.066
Industrial policy	0.002	(0.046)	975	0.103
Agriculture, forestry, and fisheries	−0.042	(0.039)	975	0.025
Education and childcare	0.147***	(0.053)	975	0.086
Pensions and healthcare	−0.101*	(0.052)	975	0.120
Employment	0.111**	(0.048)	975	0.053
Public safety	0.009	(0.010)	975	0.050
Environment	−0.004	(0.031)	975	0.083
Political and administrative reform	0.019	(0.030)	975	0.094
Decentralization	−0.020	(0.025)	975	0.028
Constitution	−0.011	(0.029)	975	0.133
Disaster prevention	0.020	(0.031)	975	0.070
Social capital	0.025	(0.023)	975	0.050
Nuclear power and energy policy	−0.037	(0.031)	975	0.049

Notes Controls for party and gender are included but not shown. UTAS (2021). *$p < 0.1$; **$p < 0.05$; ***$p < 0.01$

Policy Preferences

Table 9.4 shows the results for policy preferences. On foreign and security policy, candidates under 40 were significantly more supportive of Japan strengthening its defense capabilities and adhering to the three non-nuclear principles. While young candidates seem to favor an increase in defense spending, however, they were no more likely to say that Japan should acquire preemptive strike capability, emphasize pressure over dialogue with North Korea, or accept that the relocation of Marine Corps Air Station Futenma from Ginowan to Henoko is unavoidable.

There were fewer significant differences between candidate age groups in their stances on economic policies. Candidates under 40 were marginally less likely to favor raising taxes on the wealthy, but otherwise shared similar opinions as candidates 40 or older when it came to the size of government, public works spending, and consumption and corporate tax policies.

Finally, on social policy, young candidates were significantly more likely to support recognizing gay marriage by law and passing a bill to promote lesbian, gay, bisexual, and transgender (LGBT) awareness. By contrast, candidates in their 20s and 30s did not differ from candidates 40 or older in their views toward accepting foreign workers, releasing contaminated water from the crippled Fukushima Daiichi nuclear reactor into the ocean, or allowing women to keep their pre-marital surnames after getting married.

While it is challenging to estimate effects within parties given the limited number of young candidates, there do appear to be some significant differences across parties in the effect of candidate age. Most notably, there are substantially larger policy differences between younger and older members of the LDP than there are in other parties. Apart from the trends mentioned above, younger LDP candidates were also more likely than their older counterparts to view job security through public works as necessary and support married women keeping their surnames, but less likely to advocate for smaller government and restricting individual rights in the name of public safety. Interestingly, younger and older LDP candidates did not differ significantly in their views regarding strengthening Japan's defense capabilities—instead, much of the overall effect shown in Table 9.4 appears to be driven by younger CDP candidates favoring increases in defense spending more than their older party colleagues.

Table 9.4 Policy preferences of candidates under 40

	Effect of candidate under 40			
	Estimate	SE	N	R^2
Foreign and security policy				
Japan's defense capabilities should be strengthened	0.225**	(0.096)	999	0.651
Japan should have preemptive strike capability	−0.061	(0.099)	993	0.606
Japan should use pressure over dialogue with North Korea	−0.077	(0.101)	996	0.512
Japan should adhere to three non-nuclear principles	0.193**	(0.088)	998	0.356
The relocation of Futenma to Henoko is unavoidable	0.062	(0.084)	997	0.768
Economic policy				
Smaller government is better even if services suffer	−0.042	(0.083)	992	0.392
Job security through public works is necessary	0.003	(0.100)	996	0.211
Fiscal stimulus should be used to stimulate economy	−0.056	(0.088)	999	0.152
Consumption tax rate should be lowered	0.127	(0.104)	997	0.609
Taxes on wealthy people should be increased	−0.170*	(0.088)	995	0.405
Corporate tax rate should be raised	−0.094	(0.097)	992	0.535
Social policy				
Japan should promote acceptance of foreign workers	−0.114	(0.097)	994	0.112
It is ok to restrict individual rights for public safety	−0.083	(0.091)	993	0.502
Releasing Fukushima water in ocean is unavoidable	0.110	(0.096)	998	0.666
Married women should be able to keep surnames	0.120	(0.095)	991	0.519
Gay marriage should be recognized by law	0.255***	(0.098)	986	0.508
Japan should pass a bill promoting LGBT awareness	0.182**	(0.089)	986	0.389

Notes Answers range from 1 (disagree) to 5 (agree). Controls for party and gender are included but not shown. UTAS (2021). $^*p < 0.1$; $^{**}p < 0.05$; $^{***}p < 0.01$

POTENTIAL REFORMS TO INCREASE YOUTH REPRESENTATION

Fewer young people ran for the House of Representations in 2021 than in any election in the past 30 years, but those who did differed significantly from older candidates in their stated policy priorities and preferences. While this chapter only analyzes candidate survey responses from a single election, the findings suggest that political reforms aimed at increasing the number of younger representatives may also have implications for the types of policies that get incorporated into the policymaking process in Japan's parliament.

How likely, then, is the Kishida administration to enact new legislation that encourages more young people to pursue political careers?

Prior to the COVID-19 pandemic, the LDP, perhaps bolstered by its support from young voters, passed a series of bills focused (at least in part) on increasing youth participation in politics. These legislative initiatives included the legalization of Internet and social media use during election campaigns in 2013, the lowering of the voting age from 20 to 18 in 2016, and the lowering of the legal age of majority from 20 to 18, which takes effect in April 2022. In 2018, the LDP's Headquarters for Party and Political System Reform Implementation announced that it was also interested in increasing the number of young candidates by reducing the minimum age of candidacy to 20 for all elected offices.

Soon after the LDP's announcement, the Youth Policy Parliamentary Group, comprised at the time of 35 MPs in their 20s and 30s from six parties, came up with two proposals of their own to increase youth representation. The first was to lower the minimum age of candidacy for all elected offices even further to 18 to match the legal voting age. This proposal is in line with the recommendations of the UN's Not Too Young to Run campaign, which opposes laws that require young people to wait years between gaining the right to vote and being able to stand for office themselves. The group's second proposal was to make election campaigns less expensive by substantially reducing or eliminating the minimum deposit system, which requires candidates to put forward a large sum of money that they will forfeit if they are unable to receive a set share of the vote. While the stated intent of the minimum deposit is to prevent fringe candidates from running for office, the system also creates a high barrier to entry for younger political aspirants, who tend to have fewer financial assets than older people.

Since 2018, however, there has been little to no word from either the LDP or the Youth Policy Parliamentary Group as to the state of these policy proposals. Even if these reforms are enacted, it is difficult to predict how effective they will be at increasing youth representation in Japan. The LDP instituted a mandatory retirement age (73) for its candidates in the

PR tier but remains a relatively older party with few candidates or representatives under 40. Reforms to increase the number of female lawmakers have also proved ineffective thus far (see Kweon 2022). Thus, it remains to be seen whether the previously discussed institutional reforms can lead to a meaningful increase in the number of young politicians, or whether other types of efforts will be needed to encourage political ambition among younger generations.

NOTES

1. Different studies use different age cutoffs for young politicians depending on the institutional and cultural context. In this chapter, I adopt a commonly used cutoff of 40 for young legislative candidates and representatives, although the findings are similar if I use alternative age cutoffs.
2. I exclude candidates who did not select at least one policy priority as well as those who only selected "other" and wrote in their own policy priorities.

REFERENCES

Bidadanure, Juliana. 2015. "Better Procedures for Fairer Outcomes: Youth Quotas in Parliaments." *Intergenerational Justice Review* 2(15):40–46.

Eshima, Shusei and Daniel M. Smith. 2022. "Just a Number? Voter Evaluations of Age in Candidate Choice Experiments." *The Journal of Politics* https://doi.org/10.1086/719005.

Horiuchi, Yusaku, Daniel M. Smith and Teppei Yamamoto. 2020. "Identifying Voter Preferences for Politicians' Personal Attributes: A Conjoint Experiment in Japan." *Political Science Research and Methods* 8(1):75–91.

Inter-Parliamentary Union. 2021. "Parline Database." Accessed December 2021.

Kamikubo, Masato. 2019. "Age of Eligibility to Run for Election in Japan: A Barrier to Political Careers?" *Journal of Contemporary East Asia Studies* 8(1):14–29.

Kweon, Yesola. 2022. "Women's Representation and the Gendered Impact of COVID-19 in Japan." In Robert J. Pekkanen, Steven R. Reed, and Daniel M. Smith (eds.), *Japan Decides 2021: The Japanese General Election*. Palgrave Macmillan.

McClean, Charles T. 2020. *Silver Democracy: Youth Representation in an Aging Japan*. UC San Diego. PhD Dissertation.

McClean, Charles T. 2021. "Does the Underrepresentation of Young People in Political Institutions Matter for Social Spending?" Working Paper.

McClean, Charles T. and Yoshikuni Ono. 2022. "Too Young to Run? Voter Evaluations of the Age of Candidates." Working Paper.

Pomante, Michael J. and Scot Schraufnagel. 2015. "Candidate Age and Youth Voter Turnout." *American Politics Research* 43(3):479–503.

Rehmert, Jochen. 2022. "Candidate Selection for the 2021 General Election." In Robert J. Pekkanen, Steven R. Reed, and Daniel M. Smith (eds.), *Japan Decides 2021: The Japanese General Election*. Palgrave Macmillan.

Smith, Daniel M. 2018. *Dynasties and Democracy: The Inherited Incumbency Advantage in Japan*. Stanford, CA: Stanford University Press.

Smith, Daniel M. and Steven R. Reed. 2018. "The Reed-Smith Japanese House of Representatives Elections Dataset." https://doi.org/10.7910/DVN/QFEPXD, Harvard Dataverse, V1.

Steel, Gill. 2022. "Are the Kids Alright? Young People and Turnout in Japan." In Robert J. Pekkanen, Steven R. Reed, and Daniel M. Smith (eds.), *Japan Decides 2021: The Japanese General Election*. Palgrave Macmillan.

Stockemer, Daniel and Aksel Sundström. 2018. "Age Representation in Parliaments: Can Institutions Pave the Way for the Young?" *European Political Science Review* 10(3):467–490.

UTokyo-Asahi Survey, 2021 HoR Election. http://www.masaki.j.u-tokyo.ac.jp.

Wattenberg, Martin P. 2007. *Is Voting for Young People?* New York: Pearson Longman.

Yanai, Yuki. 2021. "Results of the 49th House of Representatives General Election." http://yukiyanai.github.io/jp/resources/.

CHAPTER 10

Should I Stay or Should I Go? Party Switching in Japan

Jordan Hamzawi

In the two decades since electoral reform, Japan's party system has been in constant flux. After a slow march toward a predominantly two-party system, government is currently dominated by the Liberal Democratic Party (LDP) and its coalition partner Kōmeitō, with an ever-changing roster of opposition parties vying for the spotlight. The 2021 election continued the recent state of political (non)competition in Japan as the Constitutional Democratic Party of Japan (CDP) and Nippon Ishin no Kai (henceforth, Ishin) were unable to make a dent in the LDP's sizeable majority. Japan's inability to break away from a party system dominated by the LDP is perhaps the most remarkable aspect of the country's politics and without question sets it apart from other democracies. While there are numerous contributing factors that explain Japan's anemic party

J. Hamzawi (✉)
Mount Holyoke College, South Hadley, MA, USA
e-mail: jhamzawi@mtholyoke.edu

© The Author(s), under exclusive license to Springer Nature
Switzerland AG 2023
R. J. Pekkanen et al. (eds.), *Japan Decides 2021*,
https://doi.org/10.1007/978-3-031-11324-6_10

competition, I focus here on how candidates navigate their partisan affiliation—which parties they run under, when they switch parties, and when they step away from politics altogether.

Candidate behavior says much about the state of politics in a country. In most cases, strong, well-established parties rarely experience party switching or have much turnover in their slate of candidates from election to election (Mershon 2014). Frequent party switching points to poor electoral performance, incohesive intraparty policy, ineffectual party leadership, and the general unpopularity of a party (Heller and Mershon 2009, Mershon 2014, O'Brien and Schomer 2013), all issues that many of Japan's opposition parties have suffered from—sometimes all at once (Kushida and Lipscy 2013, Scheiner and Thies 2021). Indeed, the simplest answer for the continued dominance of the LDP in Japan might be that the alternatives are just not that great. However, a deeper understanding of how Japanese politicians are navigating and shaping the party system may help explain why it is that Japan's opposition parties cannot seem to gain a foothold.

I analyze what candidates are choosing to do—staying with their parties, switching parties, or dropping out of politics—for all elections since the adoption of a mixed-member majoritarian (MMM) system in 1994. I find that Japan's opposition parties are sandwiched between two short term problems that ultimately hurt their ability to compete in the long term. The first problem is that candidates who cannot quite manage to win their seat are more likely to drop out of politics altogether, something that affects opposition parties more given that LDP candidates win about half of the single member district seats each election. Opposition parties must constantly recruit new candidates, hindering their ability to compete in districts while the LDP can rely on its relatively more experienced candidates and consistently contest every district. The second problem is that when opposition parties *do* manage to field strong candidates, the strongest candidates are more likely to switch parties if the party they run under has poor electoral performance. Instead of slowly building strength with a roster of seasoned candidates, Japan's opposition parties constantly collapse in on themselves because of candidate choices. I find that candidates, particularly candidates from the opposition, follow a pattern of switching from weak parties to new parties, preferring the potential of a new party over the issues with existing ones. This phenomenon helps explain the splintering of the Party of Hope (henceforth, Hope), one of the most consequential developments in the run-up to the 2021 election, as well as the constantly changing rightwing party that is currently Ishin. The 2021 election serves as the latest evidence that Japan's party system has yet to stabilize since the fall of the Democratic Party of Japan (DPJ) in 2012, and, given the lackluster performance of opposition parties in 2021, the party system will continue to be in flux.

The Who and Why of Party Switching

Candidates switch parties for a variety of reasons, though scholars focus primarily on office and policy considerations (O'Brien and Shomer 2013; Hix and Noury 2018). Whether candidates seek to simply hold on to their seat or wish to shape policy, all need to first win their election and party switching can serve as a means to that end (Aldrich and Bianco 1992; Heller and Mershon 2005, 2008; Thames 2007). However, switching parties is far from costless. Candidates need to worry about how voters will respond to them changing parties, how easily they can retain votes, and how much a new party affiliation is likely to benefit them compared with their current one (Klein 2021).

Given the inherent risk in changing parties, the likelihood of a candidate switching parties comes down to an interaction between the strength of candidates' individual appeal and the strength of those candidates' parties. Candidates with a reliable personal vote are more enabled to leave their current party than those who do not (Klein 2018), but if candidates already belong to a well-established party that is competitive, they have little incentive to switch. It is when parties exhibit weakness, typically through a combination of poor electoral performance and low policy cohesion, that some candidates start eyeing the exits (Heller and Mershon 2009).

Japan, with its MMM system mixing SMDs and proportional representation (PR), has many of the elements conducive to party switching that the literature emphasizes. SMDs allow candidates to cultivate a personal vote, giving them some flexibility in hopping to other parties. At the same time, these districts in combination with PR also allow party labels to have a strong influence on voters as well (Reed et al. 2012). On top of the basic institutional incentives inherent to MMM, Japanese parties use a "best-loser" process that makes the relationship between candidates and parties even more interdependent (Ariga et al. 2016). Under Japan's MMM system, voters cast one vote for their preferred candidate and one for their preferred party. Parties are awarded seats roughly equal to the percentage of votes they gain, and they award these based on how well their candidates performed. If candidates come close to winning their district, there is a good chance they can win a PR seat, making at least some candidates more reliant on parties than in a pure SMD system. These candidates are known as "zombies" since they are given a seat after having "died" in their election. All told, candidates must make a calculation between their personal appeal and their party's appeal when considering their options come election time.

As previously mentioned, the tug-of-war between personal appeal and party affiliation triggers party switching when parties have issues with electoral viability. If parties have anemic election results, candidates may start considering whether a different party might benefit them more. Policy congruence is another common issue that can motivate party switching. If candidates within a party have disparate policy preferences, either sincere or as part of their electoral appeal to their constituents, they will be quicker to consider switching. Japan has experienced party switching based on policy preference differences between candidates and parties in the past (Hamzawi 2020), and given the strong interconnection between candidate and party appeal in the MMM system, policy differences should characterize candidate choices in recent elections as well. Essentially, Japan is a country where under the right conditions—strong candidates running in a weak party—party switching is likely to occur.

Party Switching Under MMM

Party switching patterns since the adoption of MMM can be grouped into two periods—before 2012 and after 2012. Prior to 2012, party switching was on a steady decline as candidates joined either the LDP or the DPJ. With the collapse of the DPJ in 2012, candidates reversed this trend by drastically increasing the amount of party switching, and, as can be seen in Fig. 10.1, party switching in both periods is overwhelmingly driven by parties outside the LDP.

The collapse of the DPJ in 2012 is a surface-level explanation behind the inversion in the party switching trend. With the fall of a clear rival party to the LDP, candidates had numerous new parties to choose from and no indication as to which was the most viable (Nyblade 2013). However, it is not immediately clear why party switching has increased in frequency for opposition parties even after four elections. What is clear

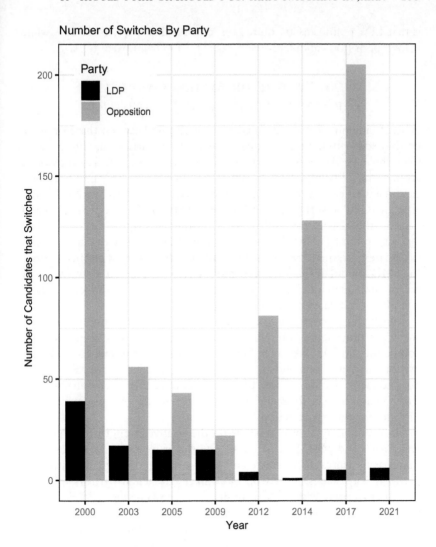

Fig. 10.1 Party switching over time

is that LDP politicians are quite satisfied with their party these days while many opposition candidates seem eager to hop from party to party.

Stay, Switch, or Retire? Candidate Choices in Democratic Competition

When facing an election, politicians must choose between three options: do they stay with their current party, switch their party affiliation, or retire from the race? Part of the story of electoral competition in Japan revolves around the difficulty the opposition parties have in recruiting enough candidates to contest every electoral district. For instance, in 2021, even after the CDP absorbed the Democratic Party for the People (DPP) and became the largest opposition party, it only managed to contest 217 districts to the LDP's 277 districts (Rehmert 2022). The disparate rate of candidate retirement between the LDP and the major opposition parties for SMD candidates can be seen more clearly in Fig. 10.2. In the most recent three elections, the opposition had between one third and nearly half of its candidates not contest the next election.

This high turnover rate in combination with the large amount of party switching underscores the chaotic environment that characterizes party competition in 2021. As such, I extend the theoretical framework scholars use for party switching and apply it to those politicians that do not contest a subsequent election. Thus, the dependent variable in my analysis is a trichotomous choice for each candidate: stay with the party, switch parties, or retire for the next election.

Since candidate choice depends on the relative strength of candidates and parties and MMM has separate vote shares for each, I use these vote shares as measures of candidate and party strength. Candidates with high personal vote shares should be more likely to switch parties *so long as* they are in a party with a low vote share. By the same logic, all else equal, parties with low vote share should experience more switching from strong candidates and more retirement from weaker candidates as these parties are less able to secure seats for those affiliated with them. I use candidate vote share, party vote share, and an interaction between the two to capture the dynamic between candidate and party strength.

I also add incumbency, age, and gender in my analysis to account for candidate specific attributes that are likely to influence a candidate's run choice. Whether a candidate is the challenger or an incumbent has a large influence on what a candidate will decide to do in the next election. If a

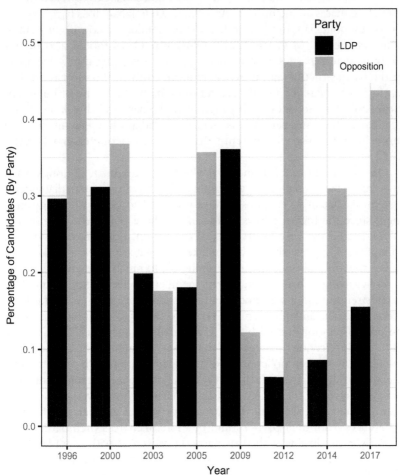

Fig. 10.2 Contesting elections over time

candidate lost their most recent election and would be a challenger in the next, it is more likely that he or she would switch parties or retire than a candidate that is an incumbent. As for age, while Japan does have some of the oldest politicians in the world, age should influence how likely a candidate is to retire (McClean 2022). Older candidates should also be less likely to switch parties as switching requires navigating a new hierarchy in the party structure and is generally more costly in the short term than staying with the party. Finally, gender disparity in the House of Representation continues to be extremely high, with women rarely breaking 10% of the seats. The many barriers that female candidates face may make them more likely to drop out or retire than their male counterparts (Kweon 2022).

On the party side, I include whether a candidate belongs to a governing party. Being in government—especially in a parliamentary system like Japan's—is almost always preferred to being out of government since the former allows politicians to shape policy, the distribution of funds, and the very institutions of the nation. Politicians that belong to a governing party should be less likely to switch parties or retire since doing so would likely forfeit their ability to do much of anything.

Policy congruence among party members is also a key element of party strength and a well-documented issue in the party switching literature (O'Brien and Shomer 2013). I use principal component analysis on policy questions posed by the UTokyo-Asahi Survey (UTAS) for the 2003–2017 elections to measure the policy preferences of candidates. I calculate the median policy score of candidates within each party to get a measure of the party's policy, then take the difference of each candidate's policy score from their party median to measure how divergent a candidate's preferences are from the party they are in. Candidates with larger differences from their party should be more likely to switch parties than those who are in line with their party. However, as with candidate vote share, the influence of a candidate's policy difference with their party on their choice of staying, switching, or retiring (henceforth, "run choice") depends on how strong their party is. Even if candidates have some policy disagreements with their party, if their party performs well, they should be less likely to switch or retire from it. Therefore, I include an interaction between party vote share and a candidate's policy difference.

While candidate strength and party strength should capture the primary influences on a candidate's run choice, these concepts do not operate in a vacuum. Candidates must consider the state of the district in which they would be competing, their status in that competition, and how much they would rely on the party. Competitive districts, where the margin of victory is small, should influence candidates' choices very differently than those districts where the outcome is all but already decided. Candidates should be more likely to recontest a competitive district even if they lost in the last election.

However, the competitiveness of the district has one other important implication for candidate choices. As previously mentioned, Japan's zombie candidates overwhelmingly come from competitive districts and are far more reliant on how well the party performs than those who are not. Potential zombies, therefore, are far less likely to switch parties or retire than those who have little chance of being resurrected through PR seats. I include an interaction between the competitiveness of a district and the party's PR vote share to account for this dynamic.

Putting these variables together, I form a model of a candidate's run choice that can be expressed as:

$$\text{Run Choice} = \alpha + \beta_1\text{Challenger} + \beta_2\text{Vote Share} + \beta_3\text{Age} + \beta_4\text{Female}$$
$$+ \beta_5\text{Governing Party} + \beta_6\text{Party Vote}$$
$$+ \beta_7\text{Policy Difference} + \beta_8\text{Competitive}$$
$$+ \beta_9\text{Competitive} * \text{Party Vote}$$
$$+ \beta_{10}\text{Policy Difference} * \text{Party Vote}$$
$$+ \beta_{11}\text{Vote Share} * \text{Party Vote} + \varepsilon$$

Given the trichotomous nature of the dependent variable and the model's emphasis on the electoral conditions candidates are facing when making their choice, I analyze this model using multinomial logit.

JAPAN'S OPPOSITION: STUCK BETWEEN A ROCK AND A HARD PLACE

The results of my model can be found in Table 10.1. The clear take-away from the model output is that candidates' run choices generally follow the theoretical expectations outlined in the party switching literature. Candidates with higher vote shares are less likely to retire, but as the interaction term between candidate and party vote indicates, candidates that outperform their parties are more likely to switch than to stay with their party. Policy differences also operate as expected, with greater policy differences between candidates and their party corresponding with a greater likelihood of them retiring or switching if their party has lower electoral performance.

Predicted probabilities help illustrate these results more intuitively. Figure 10.3 plots the predicted probability of a candidate's run choice based on candidate vote share and whether the candidate belongs to a party that performed poorly in the PR vote cast in the region where the SMD is (a party vote share of less than 15%) and a party that performed well (a party vote share of more than 30%).

Unsurprisingly, when a candidate's vote share is low, the most likely choice that he or she will make is to not contest the next election. However, as candidate strength increases, both candidates in weak and strong parties reach a point where they stick with the party. For candidates inside a strong party, there is a 0.5 probability that they will stay with the party with vote shares as low as 30%. Candidates in weak parties are far less likely to remain with their parties, peaking at a 0.47 probability of staying with their party with a vote share of 35%.

The real issue for opposition parties, which frequently have vote shares less than 20%, comes with the increasing likelihood of candidates switching parties as their vote share increases. For candidates in both strong and weak parties, the better they perform in the district, the more likely they are to switch parties. However, for strong parties the probability of switching parties never exceeds the probability of staying with the party. For weaker parties, the strongest candidates are *more* likely to switch parties than stay with their current party. Opposition parties in Japan therefore face the problem of having their strongest candidates leave, something that would certainly limit the long-term viability of the party.

Opposition parties face a similar problem with policy. Figure 10.4 plots the predicted probability of candidate run choice over policy differences between weak and strong parties. For candidates in strong parties, policy has minimal influence on their run choice, as the party switching literature expects. However, the story is quite different for candidates in weak parties. As candidates have greater policy differences with their parties, they become far less likely to stay with the party and more likely to switch parties.

In sum, Japan's opposition parties are between a rock and a hard place. Weaker parties hemorrhage both candidates that perform poorly and those that perform well and are more susceptible to party switching

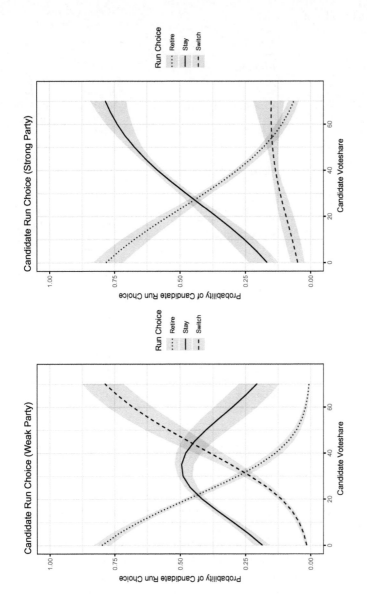

Fig. 10.3 Predicted probability of run choice (voteshare)

Table 10.1
Multinomial model of
run choice

Run choice	DV: Candidate run choice (Reference: retire)	
	Stay	Switch
Challenger	-0.96^{**}	— 0.77^{**}
	(0.09)	(0.14)
Candidate vote share	0.07^{**}	0.15^{**}
	(0.005)	(0.008)
Age	-0.03^{**}	— 0.04^{**}
	(0.002)	(0.004)
Governing party	0.37^{**}	— 0.59^{**}
	(0.12)	(0.17)
Party PR vote share	0.02^{**}	0.06^{**}
	(0.008)	(0.013)
Policy difference	-0.44^{**}	0.44^{**}
	(0.09)	(0.09)
Competitive	0.01^{*}	-0.01
	(0.004)	(0.008)
Policy diff*party vote	0.01^{**}	— 0.01^{**}
	(0.003)	(0.004)
Vote share*party vote	-0.02	— 0.02^{**}
	(0.001)	(0.001)
Competitive*party vote	-0.001^{**}	-0.001
	(0.001)	(0.001)
Constant	0.17	— 1.55^{**}
	(0.11)	(0.02)
N		5,508
Akaike Inf. Crit		7865.33

Note * $p < 0.05$, ** $p < 0.01$

in the face of policy differences. When the DPJ was the main rival to the LDP prior to 2012, it consistently performed well enough as a party that it could stem candidate incentives to switch parties. With the collapse of the DPJ, no other party has been able to adequately compete to a level that would prevent switching. As parties lose their strongest candidates, their ability to bolster their party vote share is also hindered, creating a negative feedback loop fostering the chaotic environment that defines

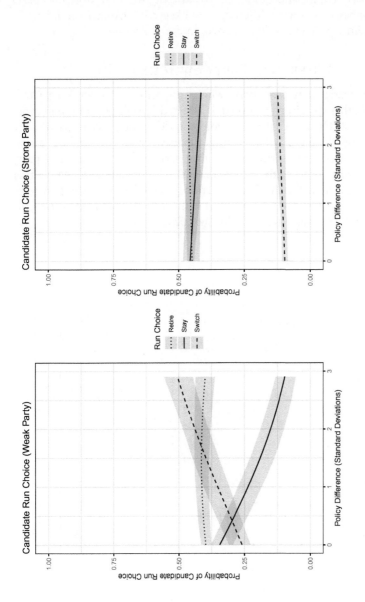

Fig. 10.4 Predicted probability of run choice (policy difference)

current party competition in Japan. Meanwhile, the LDP dissuades party switching based on policy differences and keeps its stronger candidates as it consistently performs well as a party in every election.

WHERE DO PARTY SWITCHERS GO?

The data clearly show that party switching is an issue for weaker parties, something that has disproportionately affected Japan's opposition in more recent years. However, when candidates do switch, what parties are they joining? Is the LDP poaching the best candidates or are candidates moving between various opposition parties? Fig. 10.5 displays party switching behavior since the adoption of MMM for candidates who either switched or retired for the 2021 election. The left side of the plot indicates the party these candidates stated with while the right side shows the party a candidate was affiliated with by 2021.

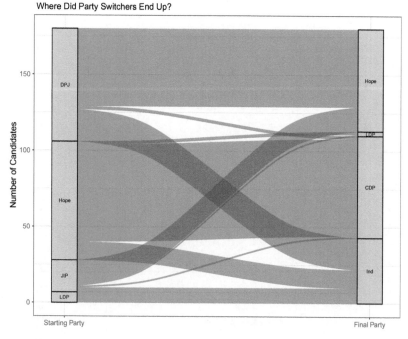

Fig. 10.5 Alluvial plot of party switching for 2021

A large number of switches unsurprisingly comes from DPJ politicians. DPJ members ended up primarily with Hope, where they retired in 2021, joined the CDP, or became independents. Only three switched to the LDP.

The next largest group of switchers came from Hope. The vast majority switched the CDP, a small handful became independents and just two switched to the LDP. Members of the Japan Innovation Party (JIP) had most of its politicians switch to Hope where they retired in 2021, some went to the CDP, and a few became independents. As for the LDP, almost all of its switchers became independents that continued to work closely with the LDP.

The flow of candidates between parties makes two things clear: candidates rarely switch to the LDP and DPJ politicians spread themselves across various opposition parties, many of which have since collapsed. Candidates are not moving from weak parties to strong ones, they are moving from weak parties to new parties. The problem of course is that new parties in Japan have not been able to perform well enough to discourage switching in subsequent elections, allowing the cycle to continue.

The 2021 election was a continuation of this trend. Nearly 150 candidates switched parties and most of that switching came from Hope candidates joining with the CDP. As a new party in 2017, Hope only managed to win 17% of the party vote and as 2021 approached, many of its candidates decided that it would be better to join with the CPD, the other new party in 2017 that performed slightly better at 19.8% of the party vote. While the CDP managed to double its seat share in 2021 relative to 2017 from 11 to 20% of Diet seats, the party itself had a nearly identical performance compared with 2017 at 20% of the party vote. All the gains the party had come from its candidates, not the party itself, putting the CDP in the same tenuous position as many of the other opposition parties that came before it. Whether the CDP manages to become a mainstay for future electoral competition will depend on how well the party label manages to increase its appeal with voters. Otherwise, many of its candidates may start looking for a new party to join.

For the time being, it seems that party competition in Japan will continue to be in flux, at least on the opposition side. However, if any party can manage to become strong enough that it can dissuade candidates from switching, the LDP will likely find itself facing a new rival as it did against the DPJ in the 2000s.

References

Aldrich, J. H. and Bianco, W. T., 1992. A game-theoretic model of party affiliation of candidates and office holders. *Mathematical and Computer Modelling*, 16(8–9), pp. 103–116.

Ariga, K., Horiuchi, Y., Mansilla, R. and Umeda, M., 2016. No sorting, no advantage: Regression discontinuity estimates of incumbency advantage in Japan. *Electoral Studies*, 43, pp. 21–31.

Hamzawi, J., 2020. Policy preferences and party switching: Evidence from the 2012 Japanese election. *Party Politics* 27(6), pp. 1268–1278

Heller, W. B. and Mershon, C. 2005. Party switching in the Italian Chamber of Deputies, 1996–2001. *The Journal of Politics*, 67(2), pp. 536–559.

Heller, W. B., and Mershon, C. 2008. Dealing in discipline: Party switching and legislative voting in the Italian Chamber of Deputies, 1988–2000. *American Journal of Political Science*, 52(4), pp. 910–925.

Heller, W. and Mershon, C. eds., 2009. *Political parties and legislative party switching*. Springer.

Hix, S. and Noury, A., 2018. Power versus ideology: Political group switching in the European Parliament. *Legislative Studies Quarterly*, 43(4), pp. 551–594.

Kato, J. and Yamamoto, K., 2009. Competition for power: Party switching and party system change in Japan. In *Political parties and legislative party switching* (pp. 233–263). Palgrave Macmillan, New York.

Klein, E., 2018. The personal vote and legislative party switching. *Party Politics*, 24(5), pp. 501–510.

Klein, E., 2021. Explaining legislative party switching in advanced and new democracies. *Party Politics*, 27(2), pp. 329–340.

Kushida, K. E., and Lipscy, PY., 2013. The rise and fall of the democratic party of Japan. In *Japan under the DPJ: The politics of transition and governance* (pp. 3–42). Shorenstein Asia-Pacific Research Center, Stanford, CA.

Kweon, Y., 2022. Women's representation and the gendered impact of COVID-19 in Japan. In Robert J. Pekkanen, Steven R. Reed, and Daniel M. Smith (eds.), *Japan decides 2021: The Japanese general election*. Palgrave Macmillan.

McClean, C., 2022. Generational change or continuity in Japan's leadership? In Robert J. Pekkanen, Steven R. Reed, and Daniel M. Smith (eds.), *Japan decides 2021: The Japanese general election*. Palgrave Macmillan.

Mershon, C., 2014. *Legislative party switching* (pp. 418–435). Oxford University Press, Oxford.

Nyblade, B., 2013. Keeping it together: Party unity and the 2012 election. In Robert J. Pekkanen, Steven R. Reed and Ethan Scheiner, (eds.), *Japan Decides 2012* (pp. 20–33). Palgrave Macmillan.

O'Brien, D. Z. and Shomer, Y., 2013. A cross-national analysis of party switching. *Legislative Studies Quarterly*, 38(1), pp. 111–141.

Reed, S. R., Scheiner, E. and Thies, M. F., 2012. The end of LDP dominance and the rise of party-oriented politics in Japan. *The Journal of Japanese Studies*, pp. 353–376.

Remhert, Jochen., 2022. Candidate selection for the 2021 general election. In Robert J. Pekkanen, Steven R. Reed, and Daniel M. Smith (eds). *Japan decides 2021: The Japanese general election*. Palgrave Macmillan.

Scheiner, E. and Thies, M. F., 2022. The political opposition in Japan. In Robert J. Pekkanen and Saadia M. Pekkanen, (eds.), *The Oxford handbook of Japanese politics* (p. 223). New York: Oxford University Press.

Thames, F. C., 2007. Searching for the electoral connection: parliamentary party Switching in the Ukrainian Rada, 1998–2002. *Legislative Studies Quarterly*, *32*(2), pp. 223–256.

UTokyo-Asahi Survey. http://www.masaki.j.u-tokyo.ac.jp.

Volpi, E., 2019. Ideology and party switching: A comparison of 12 West European countries. *Parliamentary Affairs*, *72*(1), pp. 1–20.

CHAPTER 11

Ministerial Selection Under Abe, Suga, and Kishida

Hiroki Kubo

How can we explain ministerial selection in Japan, particularly under the three cabinets of Abe Shinzō, Suga Yoshihide, and Kishida Fumio in the years after the 2017 general election? Moreover, how does the prime minister decide to take particular members of parliament (MPs) into the cabinet? The essence of parliamentary democracy is a single chain of delegation and executive accountability to the legislature (e.g., Strøm et al. 2003, 2008). In parliamentary democracies, ministerial selection is one of the most important aspects of the entire delegation–accountability relation, as it has a decisive influence on subsequent delegation processes, including cabinet governance, bureaucratic control, and policy implementation. Moreover, theoretically the post-allocation process is considered an effective tool of parliamentary control over cabinets (Bäck et al. 2011; Bäck and Carroll 2020). This leads to the question of what determines

H. Kubo (✉)
Department of Political Science, Meiji Gakuin University, Tokyo, Japan
e-mail: hkubo@law.meijigakuin.ac.jp

149

ministerial selection and what kinds of intra-party dynamics bring relative advantages for cabinet selection.

This chapter elucidates the ministerial elections under Abe, Suga, and Kishida between the 2017 and 2021 general elections. Since Japan's electoral reform in 1994, the political system has been restructured so that it is now characterized by weakened factional power politics and strengthened prime minister leadership. This chapter examines the relationship between the power of the prime minister and factions in the ministerial selection process.

After briefly reviewing the literature on minister selection in Japan, I analyze the outcomes of portfolio allocation from 2017 to the present. I compare LDP faction seat shares and the percentage of cabinet portfolios that each secured in the six cabinets formed since 2017. My analysis reveals that (1) there is overall proportionality between faction seat shares and number of cabinet portfolios, (2) there is nevertheless a relative advantage enjoyed by the prime minister's faction and the large main factions, and (3) independent LDP members are not disadvantaged in portfolio allocation.

Theory and Practice of Ministerial Selection in Japan

In representative democracies, politicians face the crucial problem of winning an election. After winning election, their problem is in forming the majority in the legislature and government formation, particularly in parliamentary democracies. The next stage is cabinet portfolio allocation, which indicates how majority parties share the spoils. The question of how and why parties divide the limited number of cabinet portfolios becomes pertinent.

Researchers have observed an empirical regularity in the proportionality of party seat shares and cabinet post shares (Gamson's Law: Gamson 1961; Browne and Franklin 1973). Although there is a theoretical challenge of the first-mover bargaining advantage of the formateur (Baron and Ferejohn 1989), this pattern is widely observed in large-N data analyses of Western democracies. Some theories (e.g., Carroll and Cox 2007) posit that pre-electoral coalitions can explain part of the empirical regularity between cabinet portfolios and party seat shares. In the field of coalition bargaining, numerous studies have focused on party-level analyses of relative bargaining power and cabinet portfolios (Bassi 2013; Strøm et al. 2008; Shugart et al. 2021). More recent research has paid attention to individual-level ministerial selection outcomes and the effect of intra-party politics on cabinet portfolio allocation (Dowding and Dumont 2008; Kam et al. 2010; Dowding and Lewis 2012; Dowding and Dumont 2014).

These questions are particularly salient in the context of Japanese politics. Since the 1950s, Japan has had one dominant political actor, the Liberal Democratic Party (LDP), the majority party in the National Diet. However, in tandem with the fact that Japan implemented electoral reform in 1994 from a single nontransferable vote (SNTV) system to a mixed-member majoritarian (MMM) system, the political system has seen large-scale shifts, including the internal structure of the LDP and the leadership of the prime minister (Reed 2005). The current political system is deemed more "centralized." That is, the change in Japan's electoral system has led to centralized party organization and strengthened leadership (Machidori 2012; Krauss and Pekkanen 2011). Some research suggests that the prime minister's popularity and the relationship with the prime minister relate to rank-and-file cabinet portfolio allocations (Ono 2012; Kubo 2019).

In sum, the relationship between the power of factions and cabinet portfolio allocations merits investigation, along with the effect of intra-party politics on cabinet portfolio allocation, specifically focusing on the role of the PM faction and intra-party politics.

CABINET PORTFOLIO ALLOCATION UNDER ABE, SUGA, AND KISHIDA

In this section, I consider the six cabinet portfolio allocation processes from the 2017 general election to the present: the Fourth Abe Cabinet (November 1, 2017–October 2, 2018), the First Reshuffle of the Fourth Abe Cabinet (October 2, 2018–September 11, 2019), the Second Reshuffle of the Fourth Abe Cabinet (September 11–16, 2020), the Suga Cabinet (September 16–October 4, 2021), the First Kishida Cabinet (October 4–November 10, 2021), and the Second Kishida Cabinet (November 10, 2021–the present). Prior to this period, the Democratic Party of Japan (DPJ) came into power in 2009 but shortly fell in 2012, when the LDP regained dominance and the Abe administration was established. This Abe administration won the three subsequent (2012, 2014, and 2017) general elections (Pekkanen et al. 2013, 2015, 2018). After the 2017 election, the government experienced six separate cabinet port-folio allocation events. After presenting a big picture of the six cabinets, I analyze in depth the first and second Kishida cabinets, formed shortly before and after the 2021 general election.

Table 11.1 shows the overall pattern of the six cabinets under Abe, Suga, and Kishida. The total number of portfolios (note that the PM is not counted as a cabinet minister) increased by one after the creation of the post of Minister of State for the Tokyo Olympic and Paralympic Games from 2020 to 2022. The mean age of cabinet members ranges from 60 to 63 (see also McClean 2022). The cabinet has always had one Kōmeitō cabinet member (Klein and McLaughlin 2022) and zero non-MPs. Female representation in recent Japanese cabinets ranges from one (about 5%) to three posts (15%). Among the recent three prime ministers, Kishida took a positive attitude toward cabinet female representation. In terms of the bicameral system, the upper house (the House of Council-lors) represents different aspects of Japanese society than the lower house does and is elected at different times. The ratio of cabinet members from the upper house members ranges from about 5% (2 posts) to 20% (4 posts). Rank-and-file MPs also have the opportunity to join the cabinet. Under three of the six cabinet portfolio allocation processes (the first and second reshuffles of the fourth term of the Abe government and the first term of Kishida), 13 members (about two-thirds) were replaced by new MPs. Although the LDP has continued to hold the majority for a long time, it has shown a high fluidity in terms of party organization and cabinet portfolio allocation.

Figure 11.1 illustrates the relation between the share of cabinet port-folios and LDP faction seats under the six cabinet portfolio allocation processes after the 2017 general election to the present. This discus-sion is anchored on the assumption that seat share is the only source of bargaining power in cabinet portfolio allocation. In the figures, the vertical axis indicates the seat share of each LDP factions. Kōmeitō is assumed to comprise one unitary faction. The horizontal axis indicates the share of cabinet portfolios. The 45-degree line indicates perfect equality between faction seat shares and cabinet portfolios; position in the upper left zone shows that the respective group holds an advantage in bargaining over cabinet portfolio allocation, while the lower right is the opposite, indicating a disadvantage in bargaining.

On the basis of the six graphs of cabinet portfolio allocations, the following can be concluded: (1) An overall proportionality between

Table 11.1   Backgrounds of Cabinet Ministers under Abe, Suga, and Kishida

cabinet	average age	upper house	female	non-MP	Kōmeitō	first-time minister	total portfolio
4th Abe cabinet	62.00	4	2	0	1	0	19
1st reshuffled of the 4th Abe cabinet	63.40	2	1	0	1	13	19
2nd reshuffled of the 4th Abe cabinet	61.55	2	2	0	1	13	19
Suga cabinet	60.38	2	2	0	1	5	20
1st Kishida cabinet	61.81	3	3	0	1	13	20
2nd Kishida cabinet	61.67	3	3	0	1	0	20

faction seat shares and number of cabinet portfolios is apparent, (2) the relative advantage of the PM's faction and large main factions can also be seen, and (3) independent LDP members are at no disadvantage.

First, regarding the overall proportionality between faction seat shares and cabinet portfolios, we find a strong empirical regularity of proportionality. Simple statistical analysis also shows a strong connection between values. The results of a regression analysis show that the coefficients of determination (R^2) of the six cabinet allocations range from 0.49 to 0.69 and the slope coefficient (beta) ranges from 0.99 to 1.26. These values also indicate a good degree of equality between cabinet portfolios and faction seat shares. Put simply, an increase in number of seats relates to more portfolios, regardless of faction.

Second, the PM's faction and other main factions have a relative advantage in cabinet portfolio allocation. Figures 11.1 shows that relatively large factions have advantages. For instance, the Hosoda–Abe (*Seiwaseisakukenkyu kai*), Aso (*Shiko kai*), and Kishida factions (*Kochi kai*) have relatively advantageous positions in cabinet portfolio allocation. Compared with their size (faction seat shares), they secured a large number of cabinet portfolios. In addition, the PM's faction has a relative advantage. During the Abe administration (2012–2020), the Hosoda faction had a relative advantage. In addition to the position of prime minister, a considerable number of cabinet positions was held by this faction, while Suga was an independent LDP member who did not belong

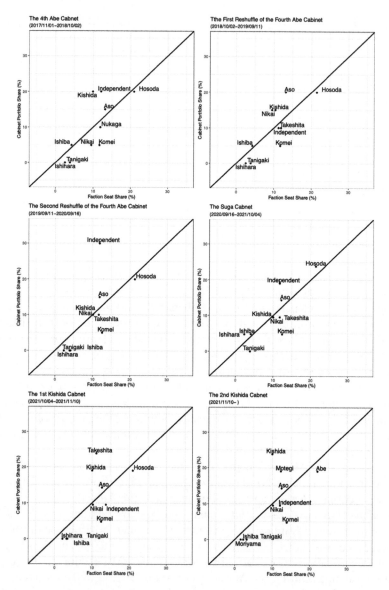

Fig. 11.1 Cabinet Portfolio Allocations under Abe, Suga, and Kishida

to any factions. Finally, during the Kishida administration, the Kishida faction took advantage of their position, similar to the trend in the Abe period.

Third, independent LDP members (i.e., those not belonging to any LDP factions) are not in a disadvantageous position, but rather are often selected as cabinet members. At first glance, this seems contradictory because without strong support from a strong faction, an independent LDP member has limited access to cabinet portfolios. This may be explained by the fact that the prime minister is strong enough to appoint any loyal independent members of the LDP regardless of the opinion of the LDP factions. This pattern is particularly obvious during the Abe and Suga periods.

Characteristics of Ministers under Kishida

Finally, I analyze the first and second Kishida cabinets. During the summer of 2021, the popularity of the Suga cabinet declined sharply, plunging the LDP into a state of disarray (Maeda 2022). Prime Minister Suga expressed his intention to resign from his post on September 3, after which the LDP elected a new president on September 29 (Nemoto 2022). Kishida was elected in the runoff voting. Both chambers of the National Diet appointed Kishida as the new prime minister, and the first Kishida cabinet was formed on October 4. Kishida dissolved the lower house on October 14. A general election was held on October 31, and the LDP retained its majority. On November 10, the second Kishida cabinet was formed.

Table 11.2 shows a list of the cabinet members of the first Kishida cabinet. The second Kishida cabinet was the same as the first except for two cases. In other words, the electoral result of LDP victory did not change the composition of the cabinet. However, the electoral result did exert a small influence on the cabinet, in that LDP Secretary General Amari Akira failed to be re-elected from his single-member district and won the seat from proportional representation. As a consequence, Foreign Minister Motegi Toshimitsu became the new LDP secretary general, which had two effects. First, as a result of the resignation of Minister Motegi shortly after the election, Prime Minister Kishida replaced him with Hayashi Yoshimasa on November 10. Second, although not related with the 2021 election, as the position of Minister of State for the Tokyo

Olympic and Paralympic Games was abolished, Horiuchi Noriko resigned on March 31, 2022.

In terms of its characteristics, the Kishida cabinet is similar to the previous four cabinets in terms of the regularity of the relationship between faction seats and cabinet portfolio shares. Moreover, large factions (Kishida, Motegi, Aso, and Abe factions) have continued to hold relatively advantageous positions in cabinet portfolio allocation. However, unlike the previous four cabinets, independent LDP members are under-represented in the Kishida cabinet. Another aspect of the Kishida cabinet is its notable freshness. Thirteen new MPs joined the first Kishida cabinet. In terms of seniority, relatively young MPs have been included in the cabinet. In addition, the cabinet has three female MPs, accounting for 15% of the cabinet members. Kishida is thus seen to have taken a positive attitude toward female representation in the cabinet. Finally, more than half of cabinet members are "second-generation" politicians.[1] On a super-ficial level, while first-time ministers and female MPs are highly likely to join the cabinet, factions and second-generation politicians dominate the LDP organizational structure and cabinet portfolio allocation.

Finally, I examine the relationship between electoral systems, electoral shock, and cabinet composition (Pekkanen et al. 2006, 2014; Shugart et al. 2021). While there is a fairly broad agreement on the theoretical framework regarding electoral incentives under a certain electoral system (single-member district or proportional representation system), the electoral shock of the 2021 LDP victory had almost no effect on cabinet composition except for the replacement of the minister of foreign affairs. In addition, in terms of electoral systems, all of the cabinet members from the lower house of the 1st Kishida cabinet hold single-member district seats. One exceptional case is Minister Wakatsuki Kenji, who failed to be re-elected in 2017 despite serving as minister. He retained his position after his failure of reelection. Except for this one case, all cabinet members come from single-member districts, and almost no members rose through proportional representation.

Conclusion

Cabinet portfolio allocation is a critical aspect of the democratic process. After an election, majority coalition groups divide the cabinet position in order to monitor each other, allocate benefits, and control the bureau-cracy. In this chapter, I analyzed the six recent cabinets from 2017 to

Table 11.2   Backgrounds of Cabinet Ministers in the First Kishida Cabinet

Position	Name	Faction	Seniority	Note
Prime Minister	Kishida Fumio	Kishida	9	
Minister for Internal Affairs and Communications	Kaneko Yasushi	Kishida	7	first-time minister
Minister of Justice	Furukawa Yoshihisa	Takeshita	6	first-time minister
Minister for Foreign Affairs	Motegi Toshimitsu	Takeshita	9	
Minister of Finance Minister of State for Financial Services Minister in charge of Overcoming Deflation	Suzuki Shun'ichi	Asō	9	
Minister of Education, Culture, Sports, Science and Technology Minister in charge of Education Rebuilding	Suematsu Shinsuke	Hosoda	3	upper house member first-time minister
Minister of Health, Labour and Welfare	Gotō Shigeyuki	Independent	6	first-time minister
Minister of Agriculture, Forestry and Fisheries	Kaneko Genjirō	Kishida	7	upper house member first-time minister
Minister of Economy, Trade and Industry Minister in charge of Industrial Competitiveness Minister for Economic Cooperation with Russia Minister in charge of the Response to the Economic Impact caused by the Nuclear Accident Minister of State for the Nuclear Damage Compensation	Hagiuda Kōichi	Hosoda	5	

(continued)

Table 11.2 (continued)

Position	Name	Faction	Seniority	Note
and Decommissioning Facilitation Corporation Minister of Land, Infrastructure, Transport and Tourism	Saitō Tetsuo	Kōmeitō	9	
Minister in charge of Water Cycle Policy				
Minister of the Environment	Yamaguchi Tsuyoshi	Nikai	6	first-time minister
Minister of State for Nuclear Emergency Preparedness				
Minister of Defense	Kishi Nobuo	Hosoda	5	
Chief Cabinet Secretary	Matsuno Hirokazu	Hosoda	7	
Minister in charge of Mitigating the Impact of U.S. Forces in Okinawa				
Minister in charge of the Abductions Issue				
Minister for Digital Agency	Makishima Karen	Asō	3	first-time minister female lawmaker
Minister in charge of Administrative Reform				
Minister of State for Regulatory Reform				
Minister of Reconstruction	Nishime Kōsaburō	Takeshita	5	first-time minister
Minister in charge of Comprehensive Policy Coordination for Revival from the Nuclear Accident at Fukushima				
Minister of State for Okinawa and Northern Territories Affairs				
Chairman of the National Public Safety Commission	Ninoyu Satoshi	Takeshita	3	upper house member

(continued)

Table 11.2 (continued)

Position	Name	Faction	Seniority	Note
Minister in charge of Building National Resilience				first-time minister
Minister in charge of Territorial Issues				
Minister in charge of Civil Service Reform				
Minister of State for Disaster Management and Ocean Policy				
Minister of State for Regional Revitalization	Noda Seiko	Independent	9	female lawmaker
Minister of State for Measures for Declining Birthrate				
Minister of State for Gender Equality				
Minister in charge of Women's Empowerment				
Minister in Charge of Policies Related to Children				
Minister in Charge of Measures for Loneliness and Isolation				
Minister in charge of Economic Revitalization	Yamagiwa Daishirō	Asō	5	first-time minister
Minister in charge of New Capitalism				
Minister in charge of Measures for Novel Coronavirus Disease and Health Crisis Management				
Minister in charge of Social Security Reform				
Minister of State for Economic and Fiscal Policy				

(continued)

Table 11.2   (continued)

Position	Name	Faction	Seniority	Note
Minister in charge of Economic Security	Kobayashi Takayuki	Nikai	3	first-time minister
Minister of State for Science and Technology Policy				
Minister of State for Space Policy				
Minister of State for the Tokyo Olympic and Paralympic Games	Horiuchi Noriko	Kishida	3	first-time minister
Minister in Charge of Promoting Vaccinations				female lawmaker
Minister for the World Expo 2025	Wakamiya Kenji	Takeshita	4	first-time minister
Minister in Charge of Cohesive Society				elected by PR in 2021
Minister in Charge of Overcoming Population Declinec and Health Crisis Management				
Minister of State for Consumer Affairs and Food Safety				
Minister of State for "Cool Japan" Strategy				
Minister of State for the Intellectual Property Strategy				

the present from the perspective of intra-party and factional politics. By comparing the LDP faction seat shares with cabinet portfolio shares, I adduce three characteristics. First is the overall proportional regularity between faction seat shares and number of cabinet portfolios. Second is the relative advantage of the PM and large main factions and the relative disadvantage of small factions. Third is that independent LDP members are not at a notable disadvantage.

The LDP won the 2021 general election, and as a result, the electoral change had no effect on cabinet composition except a couple of cases. However, if there is a major electoral change in future, the cabinet composition will be likely to change significantly.

NOTE

1. https://www.washingtonpost.com/politics/2021/10/06/japans-new-prime-minister-is-third-generation-politician-thats-more-common-than-you-might-think/.

REFERENCES

Bäck Hanna and Royce Carroll (2020). The Distribution of Ministerial Posts in Parliamentary Systems in Rudy B. Andeweg et al. eds. The Oxford Handbook of Political Executives. Oxford: Oxford University Press, pp. 314–335.

Bäck, Hanna, Marc Debus, and Patrick Dumont (2011). Who Gets What in Coalition Governments? Predictors of Portfolio Allocation in Parliamentary Democracies. *European Journal of Political Research* 50(4): 441–478.

Baron David P, and John A. Ferejohn (1989). Bargaining in Legislatures. *The American Political Science Review* 83(4): 1181–1206.

Bassi Anna (2013). A Model of Endogenous Government Formation. *American Journal of Political Science* 57(4): 777–793.

Browne Eric C, and Mark N. Franklin (1973). Aspects of Coalition Payoffs in European Parliamentary Democracies. *American Political Science Review* 67(2): 453–469.

Carroll Royce and Gary W. Cox (2007). The Logic of Gamson's Law: Pre-election Coalitions and Portfolio Allocations. *American Journal of Political Science* 51(2): 300–313.

Dowding Keith, and Chris Lewis (2012). *Ministerial Careers and Accountability in the Australian Commonwealth Government*. Canberra: ANU E Press.

Dowding Keith, and Patrick Dumont (eds.), (2008). *The Selection of Ministers in Europe: Hiring and Firing*. New York: Routledge.

Dowding Keith, and Patrick Dumont (eds.), (2014). *The Selection of Ministers Around the World*. New York: Routledge.

Gamson, William A. 1961 A theory of coalition formation. *American Sociological Review* 26(3): 373–382.

Kam Christopher, William T. Bianco, Itai Sened and Regina Smyth. (2010). "Ministerial selection and Intra-Party Organization in the Contemporary British Parliament." *American Political Science Review* 104(2): 289–306.

Klein, Axel and Levi McLaughlin. 2022. Kōmeitō in 2021: Strategizing between the LDP and Sōka Gakkai in Robert J. Pekkanen, Steven R. Reed and Daniel

M. Smith. (eds.), *Japan Decides 2021: The Japanese General Election*. Palgrave Macmillan.

Krauss Ellis S., and Robert J. Pekkanen (2011). *The rise and fall of Japan's LDP: Political Party Organizations as Historical Institutions*. Ithaca, NY: Cornell University Press.

Kubo Hiroki (2019). "The Logic of Delegation and Institutional Contexts: Ministerial Selection under Mixed-Member Systems in Japan." *Asian Journal of Comparative Politics* 4(4): 303–329.

Machidori Satoshi (2012). *Shusho Seiji no Seidobunseki: Gendai Nihonseiji no Kenryokukibankeiseii. [The Japanese Premiership: An Institutional Analysis of the Power Relationship]*. Tokyo: Chikura Shobo.

McClean Charles (2022). "Generational Change or Continuity in Japan's Leadership?" In Robert J. Pekkanen, Steven R. Reed and Daniel M. Smith (eds.), *Japan Decides 2021: The Japanese General Election*. New York: Palgrave Macmillan.

Maeda, Yukio (2022). "Public Opinion and COVID-19." In Robert J. Pekkanen, Steven R. Reed and Daniel M. Smith (eds.), *Japan Decides 2021: The Japanese General Election*. New York: Palgrave Macmillan.

Nemoto, Kuni (2022). "Party Politics: How the Liberal Democratic Party Avoided a Loss in 2021." In Robert J. Pekkanen, Steven R. Reed and Daniel M. Smith (eds.), *Japan Decides 2021: The Japanese General Election*. New York: Palgrave Macmillan.

Ono Yoshikuni (2012). Portfolio Allocation as Leadership Strategy: Intraparty Bargaining in Japan. *American Journal of Political Science* 56(3): 553–567.

Pekkanen, Robert J., Benjamin Nyblade, and Ellis S. Krauss (2006). Electoral Incentives in Mixed-Member Systems: Party, Posts, and Zombie Politicians in Japan. *American Political Science Review* 100(2): 183–193.

Pekkanen, Robert J., Benjamin Nyblade, and Ellis S. Krauss (2014). The Logic of Ministerial Selection: Electoral System and Cabinet Appointments in Japan. *Social Science Japan Journal* 17(1): 3–22.

Pekkanen, Robert J. Steven R. Reed, and Ethan Scheiner, (eds.), (2013). Japan Decides 2012: The Japanese General Election. New York: Palgrave Macmillan.

Pekkanen. Robert J., Ethan Scheiner, and Steven R. Reed. (eds.), (2015). *Japan Decides 2014: The Japanese General Election*. New York: Palgrave Macmillan.

Pekkanen, Robert J. Steven R. Reed, Ethan Scheiner, and Daniel M. Smith. (eds.), (2018). *Japan Decides 2017: The Japanese General Election*. New York: Palgrave Macmillan.

Reed, Steven R. (2005) "Japan: Haltingly toward a two-party system." In: Michael Gallagher and Paul Mitchell (eds.), *The Politics of Electoral Systems*, pp. 277–294. Oxford: Oxford University Press

Shugart, Matthew S., Matthew E Bergman, Cory L. Struthers, Ellis S Krauss, and Robert J Pekkanen (2021) *Party Personnel Strategies Electoral Systems and Parliamentary Committee Assignments* Oxford: Oxford University Press.

Strøm, Kaare, Wolfgang C. Müller, and Torbjörn Bergman (eds.), (2003) *Delegation and Accountability in Parliamentary Democracies*. Oxford: Oxford University Press.

Strøm, Kaare, Wolfgang C. Müller, and Torbjörn Bergman (eds.), (2008) *Cabinets and Coalition Bargaining: The Democractic Life Cycle in Western Europe*. Oxford: Oxford University Press.

PART II

The Campaign

CHAPTER 12

Public Opinion and COVID-19

Yukio Maeda

News media organizations in Japan publish election forecasts before every Diet election. Though some errors occurred in the past, the media forecasts for the October 31, 2021 general election were the most inaccurate in the past twenty years. On October 21, both *Yomiuri Shinbun* and *Nikkei Shinbun* reported that the Liberal Democratic Party (LDP) could fail to secure a simple majority because electoral cooperation among the opposition parties meant many districts had competitive two-person races. On October 26, *Sankei Shinbun* also predicted that the LDP could lose its simple majority in the lower house. In contrast, that same day *Asahi Shinbun* predicted that the LDP would win the majority of seats by a margin large enough to control the Diet committees.

In the end, the LDP won 261 seats, while the Constitutional Democratic Party (CDP) won only 96 seats. Clearly, *Asahi* won the contest for predictive accuracy among major news outlets. However, the conflicting media predictions show the difficulty of grasping how Japanese people understand political affairs and make voting decisions. With the benefit of

Y. Maeda (✉)
University of Tokyo, Tokyo, Japan
e-mail: q-ymaeda@g.ecc.u-tokyo.ac.jp

167

hindsight, this chapter analyzes Japanese public opinion leading up to the 2021 election.

CABINET APPROVAL RATINGS, 2017–2021

Cabinet approval ratings are the most important indicator of public opinion in contemporary Japanese politics (Krauss and Nyblade 2005; Takenaka 2006).[1] When approval ratings are high, prime ministers can pursue their own agenda high-handedly; low approval ratings fuel re-election anxieties among their Diet members, undermining the prime ministers' power. Thus, the key to understanding public opinion in any election cycle is to examine cabinet approval ratings after the previous general election. Figure 12.1 shows results for the Abe, Suga, and Kishida cabinets in Kyodo News polls from November 2017 to November 2021.[2]

While Abe Shinzō enjoyed high approval averaging 54.2% from December 2012, when his second premiership began, to October 2017 (Maeda 2018), his approval dropped to an average of 45.9% from November 2017 to August 2020.

His approval ratings deteriorated significantly twice during the latter period, first in the spring of 2018, roughly a year after the government was accused of providing special favors to close associates of the prime minister and his wife. The chief scandal, known as the Moritomo Gakuen affair, became public in February 2017 and had a large impact on political affairs leading up to the 2017 general election (Carlson and Reed 2018). The scandal entered a new phase in March 2018 when Akagi Toshio, a local Ministry of Finance (MOF) official, died by suicide after being ordered to alter the records of a sale of public land to Moritomo Gakuen. Akagi's death prompted a strong public reaction that lingered through the remainder of the Abe administration and thereafter.

Abe's approval rating improved in the spring of 2019 with the abdication of Emperor Akihito and the enthronement of his son, Naruhito. During this historic transition, news reports were saturated with celebratory coverage that crowded out other topics. The lack of negative stories about the government presumably contributed to the change in public opinion. The LDP handily won the House of Councillors (HC) election in July.

Abe enjoyed an approval rating in the mid-50 percent range in September 2019, but in November he was confronted with allegations of using publicly funded "cherry blossom viewing parties" to entertain

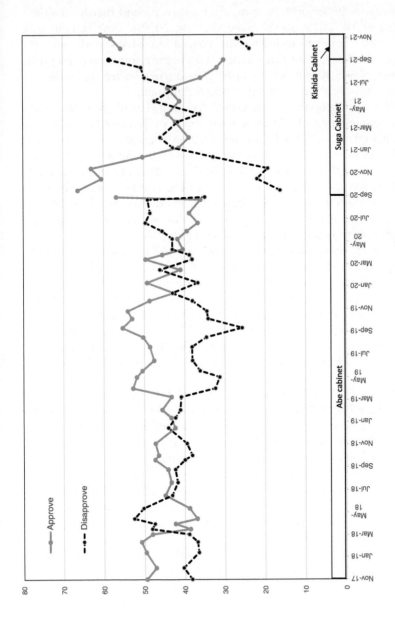

Fig. 12.1 Approval ratings of the Abe, Suga, and Kishida cabinets, November 2017–November 2021 (*Source* Kyodo News Poll)

hundreds of his supporters, many from his own constituency (*Yomiuri*, November 18, 2019; *Asahi*, November 19, 2019;). That autumn, Abe faced other scandals including the resignation of his trade minister, Sugawara Isshu, for violating election law and the resignation of his justice minister, Kawai Katsuyuki, for bribing local party leaders and others to support his wife's successful HC election campaign.

While Abe's popularity was slowly declining, Japan's first case of the novel coronavirus COVID-19 was confirmed on January 15, 2020. The first death from COVID-19 was reported on February 13. On February 27, Abe requested all schools in Japan to close until April. On March 24, he announced that the Tokyo Olympic Games would be postponed until 2021. Finally, Abe declared a state of emergency on April 7 for seven prefectures including Tokyo, expanded it nationwide on April 16, and then extended it on May 4. Throughout this period, the government's responses were widely criticized as slow and ineffective.

While the government was struggling with the pandemic and the Olympics, the Moritomo Gakuen scandal received renewed press attention in March 2020 when Akagi's widow sued the government and Sagawa Nobuhisa, former finance bureau chief of MOF. Akagi Masako disclosed her husband's suicide note, in which he accused Sagawa of forcing him to falsify official documents. The lawsuit again placed Abe's integrity at the top of the political agenda. All major polls found the public was demanding a reinvestigation of the affair (*Tokyo Shinbun*, March 29, 2020; *Asahi* April 21, 2020).

With all of these potential legal threats, Abe kept a close watch on who led the Public Prosecutors Office. Abe had long favored a prosecutor named Kurokawa Hiromu, who became chief of the Tokyo High Prosecutors Office in January 2019. Kurokawa was rumored to have weighed in on criminal cases on Abe's behalf, earning him the nickname of "Abe's guardian deity." Abe appeared ready to appoint Kurokawa as the next Prosecutor-General when he exempted Kurokawa from mandatory retirement at age 63 by overriding the previous interpretation of the related laws. This move invited strong criticism from the opposition parties in the Diet and the public.

Abe then attempted to revise the Law on the Public Prosecutor's Office to give the cabinet discretion to extend the mandatory retirement age for prosecutors. The submission of the bill for this revision sparked strong reactions on social media, especially on Twitter. The hashtag "I oppose the bill to amend the Public Prosecutor's Office Law" was first posted on May 9 and quickly spread very widely, far beyond the government's expectations (*Asahi*, May 19, 2020). Fearing further backlash, Abe gave up on getting the bill passed in the ongoing Diet session. On May 20, *Shūkan Bunshun*, a weekly magazine known for exposing political scandals, reported that Kurokawa violated the law on gambling by playing mahjong for money. Kurokawa promptly resigned, effectively terminating Abe's efforts to appoint him as Prosecutor-General.

The public's dissatisfaction caused the cabinet approval rating to fall to 29% in Asahi polls conducted on May 23–24. To make things worse, the former minister of justice and his wife were both arrested on June 18 for vote buying. All the media opinion polls indicated that Abe's approval ratings were close to his all-time low.[3] All these scandals and the prolonged impact of COVID-19 may have contributed to the deterioration of Abe's health problem, which triggered his first resignation in 2007. Abe abruptly announced his resignation on August 28, which was surprising not only to the general public but also to the most of the LDP Diet members (*Asahi*, August 29, 2020). The public viewed Abe more favorably after the announcement; his final approval rating surged to 56.9% in a Kyodo poll and 52% in a Yomiuri poll.[4]

Suga Yoshihide, chief cabinet secretary throughout Abe's second premiership, succeeded Abe. He received 66.4% approval ratings in Kyodo's September poll, which also asked respondents to select two issues, from a list of ten, they wanted Suga's cabinet to prioritize. 64.1% of respondents chose "measures against COVID-19" while only 35.2% chose "economy and employment." In Asahi's September poll, Suga's approval rating was 65%, and 63% responded affirmatively to the question, "Do you expect Prime Minister Suga's efforts regarding the novel coronavirus will be effective?" These results show that Suga's approval was closely tied to COVID-19 containment. The public's initial high expectations turned into a liability for Suga when coronavirus cases surged again.

After a few months of high support, Suga's approval ratings declined sharply from 63.0% in November 2020 to 38.8% in February 2021 in Kyodo polls. He was criticized for continuing a program encouraging domestic tourism through public subsidies despite the risks of COVID-19 transmission. The public had mixed views on the program since its launch (*Asahi*, October 19, 2020), and it became less popular when Japan entered its third COVID-19 wave in November. Suga ignored all of the criticism for weeks, including urgent recommendations from the

Subcommittee on the Novel Coronavirus, a group of experts selected by the government (*Asahi*, November 10, 2020). He finally announced the program would be suspended on December 14 (*Asahi*, December 21, 2020). In the December Yomiuri poll, 48% of the respondents agreed the program "should have been abandoned rather than suspended" while 42% endorsed the suspension (*Yomiuri*, December 28). Suga was again criticized for responding too late in public opinion polls after he declared a state of emergency in January (*Tokyo*, January 11, 2021; *Asahi*, January 25, 2021). Suga's approval rating slightly improved in March after the state of emergency was lifted, but voters remained equally divided between approval and disapproval.

Starting in May, Suga's disapproval level exceeded his approval simply because people were dissatisfied with his handling of the pandemic. Suga declared an emergency again on April 23 for three prefectures, and then repeatedly extended its geographical coverage and ending date. It was lifted on June 20 (except in Okinawa) but was reimposed on July 8. Throughout the summer he was criticized for weak leadership, ineffective responses to the pandemic, slow vaccination rollout, and his stubborn insistence on holding the Summer Olympics despite the state of emergency (for the Olympics and the 2021 election, see Leheny 2022). Facing the mounting criticisms within his own party as well as from the mass media, on September 3, he suddenly announced that he would not run for the LPD presidential election scheduled late in September (Nemoto 2022). Ironically, the state of emergency was finally lifted on September 30, a day after Kishida Fumio was elected as Suga's successor in the LDP presidential election.

How People Evaluated Abe, Suga, and Kishida

Media opinion polls usually ask respondents why they approve or disapprove of a cabinet. In Kyodo polls, respondents are asked to choose one out of six reasons for approving or disapproving. Multiplying approval ratings by the percentage of people who selected each reason for approval, and then dividing by 100 yields the percentages of those who approved of a prime minister for specific reasons in the entire sample, and the same applies to disapproval ratings. Comparing these percentages over time and across the premierships of Abe, Suga, and Kishida reveals shifts in how people understood political affairs. Figure 12.2 shows approval by specific reasons after the 2017 HR election.

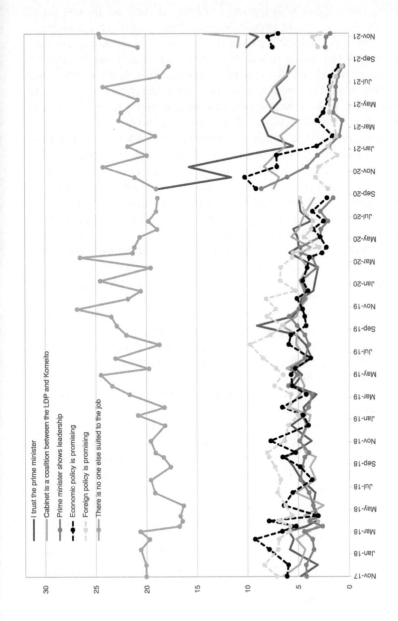

Fig. 12.2 Primary reason for cabinet approval, November 2017–November 2021 (*Source* Kyodo News poll)

Among respondents who approved of Abe, "there is no one else suited to the job" was the most popular reason. Early in his second premiership, people expected Abe to revive the Japanese economy through "Abenomics," but his approval after 2014 was based on his general performance (Maeda 2018). It is not surprising that Abe's approval was only weakly related to political issues because politically relevant personal attributes, such as leadership style and integrity, play a large role in how people view leaders (Miller et al. 1986; Kinder 1986).

The structure of Abe's approval becomes clear through comparison with Suga. First of all, 19% of the public supported Suga because they trusted him, while only 5% of the public cited trust as their reason for supporting Abe in his last month in office. People saw (or at least tried to see) Suga as trustworthy after the numerous scandals during Abe's administration. Suga did not impress the public with his own policies but rather by seeming different from Abe.

In the first three Kyodo polls of the Kishida administration, voters seemed to have a vague image of him. "No one else is suited to the job" was consistently the most popular reason among cabinet supporters. The second most popular reason for supporting Kishida was "because the cabinet is a coalition between the LDP and Kōmeitō," which on average was selected by 12% of respondents. In comparison, only 5.4% of respondents during Abe's tenure and 6.8% of respondents during Suga's tenure attributed their approval to the LDP-Kōmeitō coalition cabinet. Given that Kishida was still in his honeymoon period during these first few polls, it is surprising that so much of his approval rating had so little to do with him personally.

Figure 12.3 shows the distribution of reasons given by respondents who disapproved of a cabinet. In contrast to approval, which is typically based on general performance, disapproval is clearly a response to specific scandals or failures in policy implementation. People's responses to good news and bad news are asymmetric (e.g., Soroka 2006). In the case of Abe, people disapproved of him because they lacked trust in him. The Kyodo poll of April 2018, conducted after the death of the local MOF official was widely reported, found 30.7% of the entire public disapproved of Abe because of distrust (his overall disapproval rating was 52.6%). Even supporters of the Abe cabinet were not convinced by the explanation offered by the government (*Tokyo*, June 18, 2018; *Asahi*, June 18, 2018).

When people's attention turned elsewhere after Moritomo Gakuen and other scandals had receded, disapproval based on distrust declined.

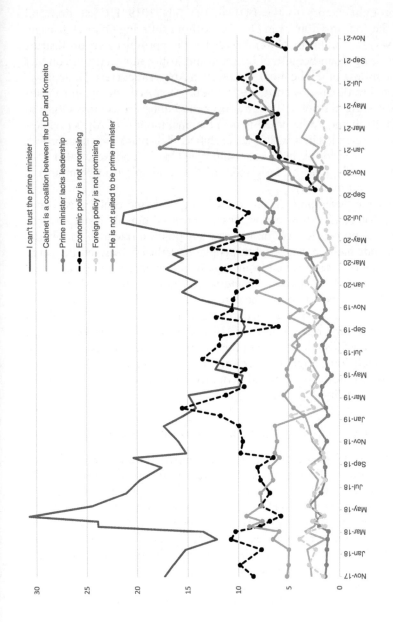

Fig. 12.3 Primary reason for disapproval, November 2017–November 2021 (*Source* Kyodo News poll)

Abe brought victory to the LDP in the July 2019 HC election and raised the consumption tax in October without suffering political damage. However, beginning in November 2019, disapproval based on distrust started rising again because of his trade and justice ministers' misconduct and the misuse of public funds to entertain Abe's supporters. Disapproval attributed to distrust reached another peak when Abe attempted to institutionalize greater political control over the Public Prosecutors Office in May 2020. It should be noted that in the final months of Abe's premiership, more people cited lack of leadership as their reason for disapproval. Abe was known for his bold leadership style (Maeda and Reed 2021) but his poor handling of the early stage of the pandemic made him appear indecisive and ineffective.

Pandemic developments also caused Suga's disapproval levels to rise sharply. Poll results show people clearly perceived him as lacking in leadership. It is unquestionably difficult for any political leader to handle the worst pandemic in a century, but people nevertheless believed the surge in COVID-19 cases resulted from Suga being indecisive and ineffective.

It is too early to draw meaningful conclusions from Kishida's poll results, but it is worth noting the percentage of people selecting the coalition cabinet as a reason for disapproving of Kishida is unusually high. In polls from his first three months in office, 7.3% of the public, on average, disapproved of Kishida because of the coalition cabinet, compared to 3.2% during Abe's long reign and 2.7% during Suga's year in office. Kishida seems to earn both approval and disapproval based on neither his policies nor his personality.

THE IMPACT OF THE CORONAVIRUS ON PUBLIC OPINION

The COVID-19 pandemic had a strong impact on the fate of all three prime ministers. To capture the impact of the pandemic on public opinion, many questions are asked in the media opinion polls. Here, I rely on the results from NHK opinion surveys because they consistently ask the same questions regarding the pandemic. Figure 12.4 shows the relationship between cabinet approval ratings and people's responses to the COVID-19 questions from February 2020 through September 2021.

The first question is, "How concerned are you that you or your family members will be infected by the novel coronavirus?" Respondents are asked to choose one of four answers. The percentages of people who

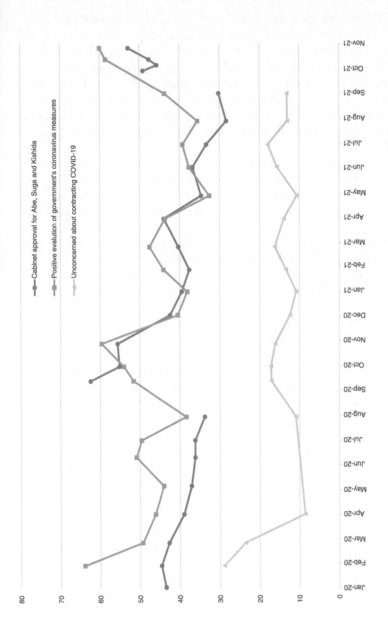

Fig. 12.4 Evaluations of government COVID-19 response and cabinet approval, January 2020–November 2021 (*Source* NHK Public Opinion Surveys)

chose either "not very concerned" or "not at all concerned" are repre-sented by triangles on the graph. The second question is, "How do you evaluate the government's efforts to prevent the spread of the novel coronavirus?" Respondents are again asked to choose from a list of four answers. For this question, the percentages of people who choose either "evaluate positively" or "evaluate somewhat positively" is represented with square symbols. Discontinuities in the line showing cabinet approval represent the transfers of power from Abe to Suga and from Suga to Kishida.

When the questions on COVID-19 were first polled in February 2020, 28.9% of respondents felt little or no concern about infection, but by April only 8.6% remained unconcerned. The coronavirus questions were not polled May–July, but the percentage of people who felt optimistic ranged between 10.6% and 17.9% from August 2020 to September 2021. The percentage feeling very or somewhat concerned about infection ranged from 76.0% to 87.1% during the same period.

In contrast, evaluations of the government's measures against coron-avirus fluctuated widely, with positive evaluation ranging from 32.6 and 63.9%. These fluctuations closely resembled shifts in cabinet approval in the same period (28.3 and 62.4%). It looks like they move in tandem. Initially, in February 2020, 63.9% of people positively evaluated the government's response, but that declined to 44.0% in May. In August, before Abe resigned, government response scored 38.4%. During the first few months of the Suga cabinet, when its approval rating exceeded 50%, those who evaluated the government's COVID-19 efforts positively also exceeded 50%. The timing and degree of the ups and downs in cabinet and pandemic response approval are very similar.

It is difficult to disentangle a causal relationship using these simple observational data, but it seems reasonable to argue that people's eval-uation of the pandemic response has driven cabinet approval, and not the other way around. Kishida had the good fortune to become prime minister in early October, when the number of infections was quickly declining and the government lifted many restrictions. In July, weeks before Suga announced his resignation, 35.5% of people positively evalu-ated the government's coronavirus policies and 28.3% approved of Suga. In contrast, in an NHK public opinion survey a week before the general election, 58.5% of people considered the government's measures effective and 47.6% approved of Kishida.

Rapid improvements in containing COVID-19 also influenced which issues people considered when deciding how to vote. The first poll on issues important to voters for the 2021 general election was NHK's October 8–10 poll. Out of list of six issues, COVID-19 ranked third (20.3%), trailing economic and fiscal policy (32.8%) and revising the social security system (22.6%). An NHK poll the following week had similar results. The Asahi poll of October 19–20 included an issues question with a slightly different list of policies, but coronavirus again ranked third (18%), behind social security (29%) and the economy and employment (27%). Clearly, the issues that voters are typically most concerned about were not overtaken by concern about COVID-19.

A series of three election-related polls conducted by Kyodo from October 16 to October 30 seems to have captured an important change during the last days of the campaign (*Chūgoku Shinbun*, November 2, 2021).[5] As shown in Table 12.1, economic policy continued to be the most important issue (35.6% on average), a result similar to the polling by NHK and Asahi. However, unlike these polls, the Kyodo polls found that the second most important issue for voters was COVID-19. 19.4% of respondents in Kyodo's October 16–17 poll indicated that coronavirus countermeasures were their primary concern. This percentage dropped to 16.1% in Kyodo's October 23–24 poll and then 13.7% in the October 29–30 poll. The declining number of infections and loosening of restrictions on daily life may have turned people's attention away from the coronavirus. This loss of interest may reflect a more positive evaluation of how the government was handling the pandemic. Though it was not a large shift, because cabinet approval during the COVID-19 era has fluctuated in sync with people's evaluation of the government's pandemic response, the shift must have worked in favor of Kishida and the governing LDP-Kōmeitō coalition.

CONCLUSION

The results of the 2021 election surprised many journalists and pollsters in Japan, as the majority of election forecasts signaled the wind of public opinion was blowing against the ruling parties. Media organizations made forecasting errors not only with pre-election surveys but also with exit polls (Murakami 2021). Immediately after the polling sites were closed, nationwide TV networks reported their forecasts using exit poll data. All agreed that the LDP would barely manage to hold a simple majority,

Table 12.1 What is most important for you in your voting decision for this election?

	October 16–17	October 23–24	October 29–30
Novel coronavirus countermeasures	19.4	16.1	13.7
Economic policy	34.7	36.7	35.3
Nuclear power and energy policy	2.9	3.3	3.7
Pensions, medical care, elder care	16.5	15.7	17.0
Child-rearing, measures against low birth rate	7.8	8.6	9.4
Diplomacy and security	4.2	5.0	4.9
Money in politics	6.5	5.5	6.2
Constitutional reform	1.5	2.6	2.4
Revitalizaing localities	3.3	3.7	4.8
Other	0.8	0.7	0.9
Don't know	2.4	2.1	1.7
	100.0	100.0	100.0

Source Kyodo News poll

though, in reality, the LDP won a solid majority of 261 seats. It is beyond the scope of this chapter to examine the causes of forecasting errors in pre- and post-election polls, but all of these errors indicate that many seasoned observers believed that the LDP would lose a good number of seats, if not its governing party status, to the CDP-led coalition of parties.

However, if one reads the results of opinion polls systematically, it is not too difficult to understand why the LDP did so well. An Asahi poll asked the following question about ten days before the election: "Do you think it would be good for LDP-centered government to continue in the future? Or do you think it would be better to replace it with a CDP-centered government?" The same question, with different opposition parties as the alternative, has been asked repeatedly. Table 12.2 shows people's responses before the general elections of 2003, 2005, 2009, 2017, and 2021.

Immediately before the 2003 and 2005 HR elections, about 30% of the public thought would be better to have a Democratic Party of Japan (DPJ) centered government. That number jumped to 49% before the 2009 HR election, which the DPJ won. Before the 2017 HR election,

Table 12.2 Preference for government led by the LDP or major opposition party in future

	2003	2005	2009	2017	2021
LDP-centered government	40	41	21	37	46
Non-LDP government	33	30	49	36	22

Source Asahi Shinbun opinion surveys

the public was evenly divided between wanting an LDP-centered or non-LDP government, but the LDP achieved a landslide victory because the opposition parties were badly fragmented. Before the 2021 HR election, 46% of the public preferred an LDP-centered government, a percentage higher than in any Asahi pre-election poll in the past twenty years. It is unclear why the public favored the LDP so strongly, but two factors—the replacement of the unpopular Suga with the unknown Kishida, and the rapid decline of COVID-19 infections—must have contributed to turning the tide of public opinion from the opposition parties to the LDP.

NOTES

1. The actual wording in polling questions is "approval of the cabinet," but this is commonly understood as approval of the prime minister.
2. Readers are warned that the scales of vertical axes and horizontal axes of the graphs in this chapter are not uniform. The consistency for comparison is sacrificed for the sake of visibility and readability of each figure.
3. The timing of Abe's lowest scores differed across the major polls. His low point in Asahi polls (29%) was May 2020; in NHK polls, Abe's lowest score (33.8%) was in August 2020. In Kyodo, Yomiuri, and Jiji polls Abe's nadir (35.8, 36, and 29.9%, respectively) was July 2017 after Moritomo Gakuen and another cronyism scandal had broken.
4. Media opinion polls do not always include questions on prime ministers after they announce they are leaving office. Asahi and NHK did poll on Abe's approval after his retirement announcement.
5. The author is grateful for Kyodo News for providing the numbers in Table 12.1, some of which are not published on the news report.

REFERENCES

Carlson, Matthew M., and Steven R. Reed. 2018. "Scandals During the Abe Administrations." In *Japan Decides 2017: The Japanese General Election*, edited by Robert J. Pekkanen, Steven R. Reed, Ethan Scheiner and Daniel M. Smith, 109–126. Cham: Springer International Publishing.

Kinder, Donald R. 1986. "Presidential Character Revisited." In *Political Cognition*, edited by Richard R. Lau and David O. Sears, 233–255. Hillsdale, N.J.: L. Erlbaum Associates.

Krauss, Ellis S., and Benjamin Nyblade. 2005. "'Presidentialization' in Japan? The Prime Minister, Media and Elections in Japan." *British Journal of Political Science* 35 (2): 357–368. https://doi.org/10.1017/S0007123405000190

Leheny, David. 2022. "The Olympics in the 2021 Election." In *Japan Decides 2021: The Japanese General Election*, edited by Robert J. Pekkanen, Steven R. Reed, and Daniel M. Smith, 375–386.

Maeda, Yukio. 2018. "Public Opinion and the Abe Cabinet: Alternating Valence and Position Issues." In *Japan Decides 2017: The Japanese General Election*, edited by Robert J. Pekkanen, Steven R. Reed, Ethan Scheiner and Daniel M. Smith, 127–147. Cham: Springer International Publishing.

Maeda, Yukio, and Steven R. Reed. 2021. "The LDP under Abe." In *The Political Economy of the Abe Government and Abenomics Reforms*, edited by Phillip Y. Lipscy and Takeo Hoshi, 87–108. Cambridge: Cambridge University Press.

Miller, Arthur H., Martin P. Wattenberg, and Oksana Malanchuk. 1986. "Schematic Assessments of Presidential Candidates." *American Political Science Review* 80 (2): 521-540.

Murakami, Kazuhiko. 2021 "'Jimin Kusen?' Terebi no Deguchi Chosa ga Ohazure datta Wake." Toyo Keizai Online Edition (https://toyokeizai.net/articles/-/466145, accessed on January 1, 2022).

Nemoto, Kuniaki. 2022. "How the Liberal Democratic Party Avoided a Loss in 2021." In *Japan Decides 2021: The Japanese General Election*, edited by Robert J. Pekkanen, Steven R. Reed, and Daniel M. Smith, 43–58.

Soroka, Stuart N. 2006. "Good News and Bad News: Asymmetric Responses to Economic Information." *The Journal of Politics* 68 (2): 372–385. https://doi.org/10.1111/j.1468-2508.2006.00413.x

Takenaka, Harukata. 2006. *Shushō shihai: Nihon seiji no henbō*. Chūkō shinsho Tōkyō: Chuo Koron Shinsha.

CHAPTER 13

Social Media in the 2021 Election Campaign

Robert A. Fahey

Japan's 2021 general election was the third lower house election to be conducted since the 2013 revision of the Public Offices Election Law removed the de-facto ban on Internet campaigning by electoral candidates. Including upper house elections, a total of six national elections have now been held under the new campaigning rules—but early enthusiasm for the potential effects of online campaigning rapidly waned after the first few elections under the new system showed little or no impact from the adoption of the new campaign medium (Williams and Miller 2016).[1] Activists and commentators who had hoped to see online grassroots campaign movements in the mold of the Obama 2008 United States presidential campaign arise in Japan were disappointed, but even if online campaigning has not been radically transformative, in subsequent years it has established itself as a key element of political campaigning in Japan. At the 2021 general election, almost 82% of candidates had an active Twitter account, and over 75% had a Facebook page. Between them, those candidates sent some 92,891 tweets over the course of the 12-day campaign

R. A. Fahey (✉)
Waseda University, Tokyo, Japan
e-mail: robfahey@aoni.waseda.jp

© The Author(s), under exclusive license to Springer Nature Switzerland AG 2023
R. J. Pekkanen et al. (eds.), *Japan Decides 2021*,
https://doi.org/10.1007/978-3-031-11324-6_13

period. The amount of effort that represents on the part of the candidates and their campaign teams speaks to their belief that there is value to online and social media campaigning efforts—which is unsurprising, as Japanese voters have been shown to be receptive to social media campaigning, just like their counterparts overseas (Kobayashi and Ichifuji 2015).

This chapter comprises a series of analyses outlining the online political landscape and showing how social media was used by candidates in the 2021 election. Social media data has significant limitations (especially in terms of how representative it may or may not be of the country as a whole) but is nonetheless an incredibly rich source of observations about the behavior of both candidates and voters around elections. Analysis of data including candidates' posts, their follower networks, and party and demographic differences in platform engagement can help us to further our understanding not only of the Internet as a political communication medium, but of the campaigning styles and issue engagement of parties and candidates, and of how their messaging is received by the broader public. In this chapter, we look first at the question of which kinds of candidates choose to engage with social media in their campaigns, then move on to a text analysis of their tweets and the policy-related keywords therein, before finally using candidates' network data to investigate the extent of online polarization at this election. The aim is to provide a broad overview of how social media was used in the election and what we might learn from it.

The use of online campaigning has grown gradually from election to election since 2013, supplementing rather than overturning existing modes of campaign activity and communication. It is worth bearing in mind that the revision to the law which permitted online campaigning was carried out by the Liberal Democratic Party (LDP)—in fact, it was one of the party's early priorities after its return to power under Abe Shinzō in 2012 (see Williams 2017 for a more in-depth discussion of this policy change), and it sits firmly within the party's tradition of making changes to Japan's electoral rules where it sees benefits for its own candidates (McElwain 2008). The actual impact of the rule change was more minor than it appeared on the surface; Japanese politicians had been using various online platforms for communication and outreach purposes since the 1990s (Tkach-Kawasaki 2003), with only the very short official campaign period before each election being legally off-limits for this activity. The LDP's decision to change the law thus marked less of a significant change to the strategies available to politicians (merely a shifting of the limitations regarding when they could be used), and more of a change in the LDP's own attitude to online campaigning. Following experiments with political engagement on social media during the LDP's time in opposition from 2009 to 2012, senior figures such as close Abe ally Sekō Hiroshige, who had held various leadership roles in the party's public relations and media strategy divisions, came to see social media and direct online communication with voters as a key component in a communications strategy that would tip the balance of the relationship between the government and Japan's increasingly fragmented media in the LDP's favor (Nishida 2015, pp. 143–144). Rather than being designed to spur radical transformation, the 2013 policy change was designed to preserve and cement the status quo by allowing the LDP to leverage what it perceived as its edge over its rivals in social media campaigning.

That the LDP has an edge in social media seems to be borne out by the ranking of candidates' Twitter accounts by followers seen in Table 13.1, with seven of the top ten accounts on election day (October 31) belonging to LDP candidates. Only two candidates had over a million followers—former LDP leadership hopeful Kōno Tarō had 2.4 million, and former prime minister Abe Shinzō had 2.3 million. The most-followed opposition figure was Reiwa Shinsengumi leader Yamamoto Tarō, with just over 450,000 followers; the only other opposition politicians in the top ten were Constitutional Democratic Party (CDP) members Haraguchi Kazuhiro and Ozawa Ichirō. The ranking makes clear that the LDP retains a significant advantage in the public reach of its high-profile members on social media—although it also hints at the fact that a popular Twitter account is no guarantee of electoral success. Ozawa ultimately lost his seat in the election despite having the CDP's second most popular Twitter account. Meanwhile, one of the LDP's most popular Twitter users is Sugita Mio, who has never won a single-member district (SMD) race and since 2017 has run only as a party-list proportional representation (PR) candidate—perhaps because of fears that her pastime of courting controversy on social media could backfire under the scrutiny of an SMD election.

Who Used Social Media in the 2021 Election?

The most successful social media accounts may be outliers—candidates in the 2021 election had just under 15,900 Twitter followers on average, but even this figure is significantly biased by the presence of hugely popular

Table 13.1 Top ten candidates by Twitter followers

	Name	Party	Twitter name	Followers
1	Kōno Tarō	LDP	@konotarogomame	2,403,322
2	Abe Shinzō	LDP	@abeshinzo	2,298,426
3	Suga Yoshihide	LDP	@sugawitter	488,772
4	Yamamoto Tarō	Reiwa	@yamamototaro0	453,946
5	Kishida Fumio	LDP	@kishida230	418,262
6	Takaichi Sanae	LDP	@takaichi_sanae	286,344
7	Haraguchi Kazuhiro	CDP	@kharaguchi	262,377
8	Sugita Mio	LDP	@miosugita	237,704
9	Ozawa Ichirō	CDP	@ozawa_jimusho	223,821
10	Ishiba Shigeru	LDP	@shigeruishiba	207,490

Twitter users like Kōno Tarō and Abe Shinzō, with half of the candidates having fewer than **2,100** followers; to place that in context, the average number of citizens in a lower house Single Member District is around **428,000** (Ministry of Internal Affairs and Communications 2021), making the potential direct impact of these candidates' Twitter usage marginal at best. Nonetheless, the usage of social media in some form has become commonplace among candidates from the major parties. Figure 13.1 shows the proportion of candidates from each party who had Facebook, Twitter, YouTube, or Instagram accounts during the 2021 election campaign, and shows that while there were some notable differences among the parties, a significant majority of candidates from every party operated at least a Twitter account, with most also having a Facebook page. YouTube and Instagram, while less commonplace, were also used by a sizeable minority of candidates.

A few interesting observations emerge from this graph. While opposition parties may lag the LDP in terms of followers, they have clearly embraced online campaigning, with around 90% of candidates for the main opposition parties having Twitter accounts. The LDP's candidates are a little less likely to use social media overall, though not by much; and uniquely among the parties, they prefer Facebook to Twitter (83% of LDP candidates used Facebook, while 77% used Twitter), though it is unclear whether this is due to a demographic difference among the platforms, a preference for Facebook's functionality, or some other factor. Among candidates of all other parties, Twitter is the most popularly used social media platform, likely reflecting its widespread popularity

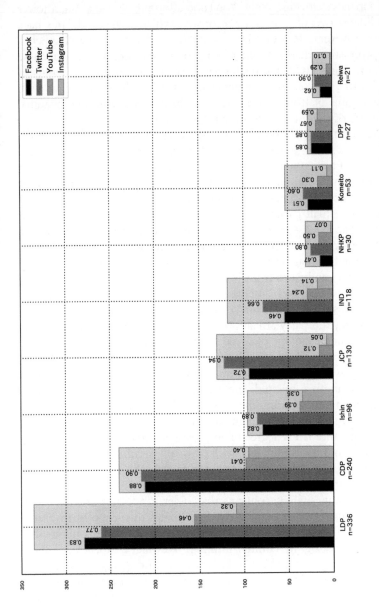

Fig. 13.1 Social media usage by candidates, per party *Notes* LDP = Liberal Democratic Party; CDP = Constitutional Democratic Party; JCP = Japanese Communist Party; IND = Independent and Unaffiliated Candidates; NHKP = Party to Protect the People from NHK; DPP = Democratic Party for the People. Data collected by the author; includes data sourced from the Yomiuri Shinbun, Asahi Shinbun and https://go2senkyo.com

among Japanese citizens. While YouTube adoption remains much lower for candidates overall, this is a platform in which LDP candidates have been early movers; 46% of LDP candidates had a YouTube channel, a higher proportion than any other major party. By contrast, the Japanese Communist Party (JCP) has been very successful in getting its candidates to use Twitter but seems to struggle with getting them to engage with other emerging platforms—only 12% of them had a YouTube channel, and only 5% of them used Instagram.

A counter-intuitive aspect of the distribution of social media usage among parties is that independents and smaller parties—who might have been expected to be the largest beneficiaries of online campaigning, given its low costs and potentially broad reach—are in fact very inconsistent in their use of social media platforms. Only two-thirds of independents and candidates for small parties had Twitter accounts, and less than half of them used Facebook—far lower than their rivals in large parties, and an unusual oversight given that setting up these accounts is effectively free. It is also notable that despite having an image as very online-oriented parties, several candidates from both new challenger parties—Reiwa and NHKP—did not use social media at all, and neither party was a notable outlier in terms of its candidates' online campaign activities.

Looking beyond party affiliation, we can also see certain demographic trends in candidates' usage of social media—specifically Twitter, the most popular platform used by candidates and the one for which usage data is most readily available to researchers. Figure 13.2 shows OLS regression results for a number of candidate factors (age, gender, party membership, and incumbency), using the number of Twitter posts sent during the campaign period as the dependent variable. The number of posts sent—a proxy for the candidate's degree of engagement with social media—varied significantly among candidates, with a small number of highly-active candidates sending over 1000 tweets during the 12-day campaign, while the median number was 48 tweets.

The regression analysis confirms that older candidates are somewhat less likely to use Twitter extensively—candidates in their 60s, in particular, were less frequent users of the platform than other age cohorts—but other results are slightly counter-intuitive. We might expect incumbent candidates, who generally benefit from strong existing support networks, to be less incentivized to spend time on social media campaigning, but the analysis shows the opposite to be true, with incumbents being more likely to tweet extensively—reinforcing the notion that online campaigning may favor the status quo rather than empowering challengers. Similarly, given the well-documented tendency for high-profile women to be harassed and abused online (Sobieraj 2020; Tonami et al. 2021), we might expect female candidates to be less likely to engage extensively on Twitter, but they were in fact more likely to do so than their male counterparts. There are a number of possible interpretations for this finding; one is that women continue to face significant stereotyping in their dealings with traditional media, such as finding it difficult to be taken seriously in more traditionally "masculine" areas of politics such as national security, and thus see more advantage to being able to directly shape their public profile over social media. Equally, it is also possible that women who choose to pursue political office—those undaunted by the perception of higher barriers to their success in this field—tend to be more media-savvy than their male counterparts (Fig. 13.2).

What Did the Parties' Social Media Campaigns Focus on?

The general pattern of adoption of social media campaigning by Japanese politicians has seen it used as a tool to supplement existing modes of campaigning—speeches, canvassing, engagement with traditional media, and so on. Consequently, many candidates use platforms like Twitter heavily to promote and publicize their traditional campaign activities, such as announcing their scheduled appearances at events, or the places they will be canvassing or making speeches on a given day. Far from disrupting this old-fashioned style of campaigning, in which candidates' main objective often seems to be establishing credentials as hard-working representatives by wearing out more shoe leather and tire rubber than their rivals, social media has often been used not as an arena for policy discussion or public engagement, but simply to document that traditional campaigning process. Regular social media updates often seem designed to impress upon followers just how hard the candidate is working and all the local areas they are visiting. This style of Twitter usage has, in previous elections, been especially prominent among LDP candidates. While opposition candidates have been more inclined to tweet about policy or national-level issues, LDP candidates' tweets are more likely to be locally focused, showcasing their connections to the local community and promoting their in-person canvassing activities. On social media, as in the election campaigns more broadly, it can sometimes feel like

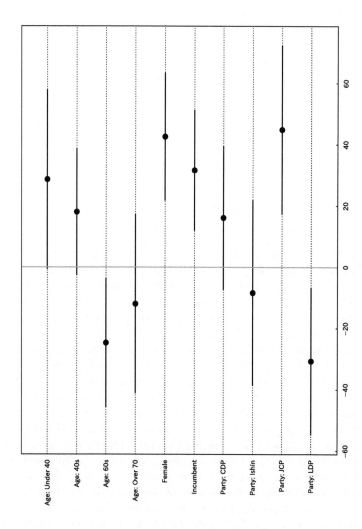

Fig. 13.2 Demographic correlates of Twitter usage by candidates *Notes* The dependent variable in this regression analysis (and thus the coefficient shown on the x-axis) is the number of Twitter posts sent by the candidate. The baseline age cohort is candidates in their 50 s, while the baseline for parties is all other candidates (including independents) besides those from the parties shown here

opposition parties are contesting a single national election, while the
LDP is contesting hundreds of individual local elections. This difference
reflects to some degree the fact that opposition parties are more reliant on
proportional representation votes (and thus on the strength of their party
brand), but also speaks to the campaign focus of many LDP candidates
who seek to emphasize above all their ability to provide goods to their
constituency and its interest groups.

In the 2021 election, this divide between the social media strategies of
the parties remained visible—but it was less clear than in past elections,
largely because of the engagement by candidates of all parties with the
debate around the government's handling of COVID-19. Figure 13.3
shows a correspondence analysis (see Greenacre, 2021) of the vocabulary
used in tweets by candidates of the six major parties. The party positions indicate a degree of relative similarity in their use of vocabulary,
and key vocabulary terms have been translated and marked on the graph,
showing how closely they are associated to tweets from each party. The
horizontal axis shows a clear divide between the language used by candidates of the ruling LDP-Kōmeitō coalition and those of the opposition
parties, while the vertical axis makes clear that candidates of the JCP were
notable outliers in their use of language, differing from both the ruling
and opposition mainstream parties.

As in prior elections, a number of terms generally found in social
media posts that are designed to support traditional campaign activities (as distinct from those promoting or discussing policy, track record,
etc.) are strongly associated with the LDP in this analysis. Among the
terms found close to the LDP's position (meaning that LDP candidates
were more likely than those from other parties to use these terms) are
"cheering" (*seien*), "support speech" (*ōen-enzetsu*)," canvassing" (*yūzei*),
"speech event" (*enzetsukai*), and "greetings" (*aisatsu*). However, even
more strongly associated with the LDP (and Kōmeitō) are a set of terms
with strong policy implications—"vaccination" (*sesshu*) and "vaccine"
(*wakuchin*) both appear here, along with "stability" (*antei*), "national
security" (*anzen-hoshō*), and "track record" (*jisseki*). This contrasts with
the policy-related terms found closer to the centrist and center-left opposition parties, such as "salary" (*kyūryō*), "livelihood" (*seikatsu*), "children"
(*kodomo*), "child-raising" (*kosodate*), "education" (*kyōiku*), and—especially close to Ishin's position—"free speech" (*hyōgen no jiyū*) and
"expansionary fiscal policy" (*sekkyoku zaisei*). The divide in vocabulary
between the parties reflects the drawing of battle lines over policy, in

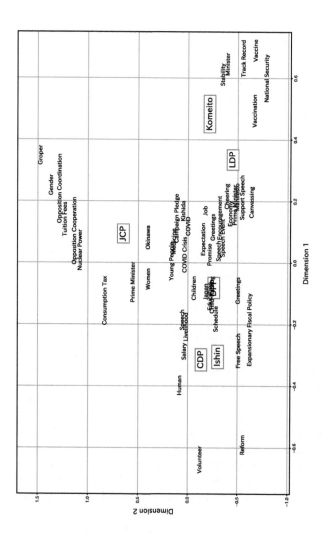

Fig. 13.3 Correspondence analysis of candidate tweets, by party *Notes* Correspondence Analysis (CA) is used here to uncover latent dimensions in the use of vocabulary across a set of texts. Tweets sent by candidates of each party are treated as a single large 'text' for this purpose. Dimension 1 can broadly be interpreted as showing the government / opposition divide in the use of language (see for example Curini et al. 2020), with policy terms seen here being mostly valence issues, while Dimension 2 shows a divide among the parties on more contentious social and cultural issues

line with the rise of policy-oriented campaigning documented in Catalinac 2016.[2] While there are no major surprises in the choice of topics by candidates of each party, it is clear that during the 2021 election social media was being used on both sides to directly address issues of policy and track record, not merely to reinforce traditional canvassing activities.

One party which stands out in this analysis is the JCP, whose distinct position in the graph sees it uniquely strongly associated with terms related to gender equality issues—including "gender" (*jendā*), "women" (*josei*), "gendered violence" (*seibōryoku*), and "groper" (*chikan*)—as well as to other key opposition focuses including "nuclear power" (*genpatsu*), "Okinawa", "consumption tax" (*shōhizei*), and "tuition fees" (*gakuhi*). One interpretation of this result is that while the mainstream opposition—notably the CDP—tried to focus on quality of life and pocketbook valence issues, mirroring the policy focus that had been so successful for the Democratic Party of Japan (DPJ) ahead of its landslide victory in 2009, JCP candidates continued to focus on more divisive issues like nuclear power, U.S. bases in Okinawa, and social justice, with the party effectively becoming a dominant voice on these issues during the election—at least on social media.

Is Japan Experiencing Online Political Polarization?

One significant opportunity that social media campaigning has opened up to researchers is the ability to observe not only politicians' campaigning activities, but also the engagement of ordinary social media users with those activities and with the accounts of political and media actors more generally. Observing the behaviors and interactions of ordinary users can give us significant insights into topical issues such as political, media and social polarization. Focusing on actions such as choosing to follow a politician or media outlet, or liking a given post, helps to bypass the problems caused by focusing on the text of users' posts, namely that only a small minority of vocal users ever actually write political posts compared to the large mass of users who (relatively) passively consume political content. Consequently, the large-scale network data created by the following relationships between politicians and regular social media users have been used to carry out various analyses, perhaps most notably estimating the Bayesian ideal points of political actors on a latent ideological scale—in other words, their political positions as measured through the perceptions revealed by the actions of many tens of thousands of ordinary social media users (Barberá 2015; Barberá et al. 2015).

This methodology has also been applied successfully to estimate the ideological positions of politicians and media organizations in Japan (Miwa 2017). Analysis of Twitter network data has also suggested that even though political polarization exists among Japanese social network users, they demonstrate relatively low levels of social polarization compared to those found in a sample of European nations (Fahey and Camatarri 2021).

Figure 13.4 applies this methodology (Barberá et al. 2015) to the full set of Twitter accounts used by candidates in the 2021 election. A random sample of 100,000 ordinary Twitter users who followed at least five political accounts was used to estimate ideal points for the candidates of seven major parties (excluding Kōmeitō, whose followers tend to follow few if any accounts from other parties, and vice versa, thus making the estimation of ideal points for their candidates unreliable) along with thirty of the most popular Twitter accounts operated by news media organizations. For each party, the distribution of its candidates' ideal points is plotted, while the positions of media accounts are indicated by vertical lines. The resulting positions for both parties and media organizations conform to known features of the Japanese political spectrum, although a number of interesting features emerge from the details, especially regarding challenger parties. Citizens on social media appear to perceive both Ishin and NHKP as sitting alongside the more centrist wing of the LDP, contrary to their often more extreme depiction in the media. Reiwa is similarly located on the left of the CDP's distribution, a position that's notably more centrist than the left-wing outlier JCP.

The positioning of parties' ideal point distributions on these graphs reinforces the existence of polarization in Japan's online political sphere, in that there is very little overlap between the distributions of the primary parties of the right (LDP, Ishin) and left (CDP, JCP), with only the relatively small Democratic Party for the People (DPP) filling the gap between them. Arguably of more interest, however, is the alignment of the parties' distributions to the positions of the media organizations shown in the chart. A large majority of media organizations (19 out of the 30 whose data were collected for this analysis) are spread around two points that lie in between the LDP and CDP distributions but have notably more overlap with the positions of opposition parties (both CDP and DPP) than with that of the LDP's very small left flank tail. Nikkei

Online, Yomiuri Shinbun, and Yahoo! News are all slightly to the right of this grouping, but the only media outlets which lie firmly within the LDP's distribution (and, consequently, the overlapping distribution of Ishin) are the far-right Sankei Shinbun and extreme-right blog site Hoshu Sokuhō. On the left side of the distributions, the main body of the CDP overlaps with Asahi Digital, the Chūnichi Shinbun, HuffPost Japan, Nikkan Gendai and the Tokyo Shinbun—all strongly left-wing publications—while the JCP's house newspaper, Akahata, lies in between the JCP and CDP on the spectrum.

A glass-half-full interpretation of the media positions would point to the large number of major organizations that the public seems to see as effectively maintaining a balance between government and opposition, occupying a space that may lean slightly toward the opposition's positions but is largely neutral ground between them and the LDP. A glass-half-empty perspective, however, would note that the bulk of the LDP's candidates occupy a space overlapping not with the traditional conservative media organizations like Nikkei and Yomiuri Shinbun, but with far- and extreme-right publications and blogs. It is important not to over-interpret this finding, and it should be emphasized that this is not an ideological assessment of the candidates themselves, but rather a position based on the media preferences of the ordinary Twitter users who follow them. The implication is that a significant proportion of LDP followers on Twitter prefer far-right media as their source of news over traditional center-right publications (the same being true, if not to quite the same extent, for CDP followers preferring more strongly left-wing publications like HuffPost Japan or the Tokyo Shinbun to more traditionally center-left media). This kind of evidence of media audience polarization has been a leading indicator of more widespread polarization in several other nations in recent years, including the United States (see for example Lelkes et al. 2017; Druckman et al. 2018; Wilson et al. 2020).

Conclusions

While the use of social media in political campaigning over the past eight years has not been the transformational force some commentators hoped for—and may even favor incumbents and the status quo in some regards—social media platforms have nonetheless become a standard part of political life in Japan and an important part of the country's broader media environment. In the 2021 election, most candidates from all parties

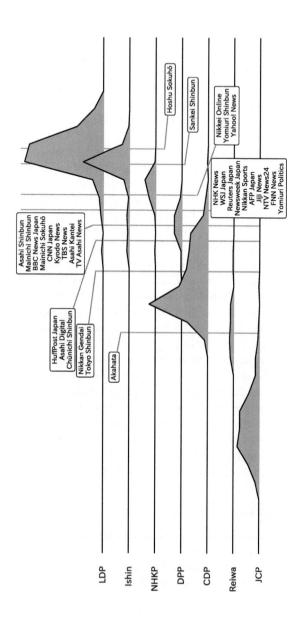

Fig. 13.4 Distribution of candidate and media positions, from Twitter network data *Notes* The horizontal axis in this figure is constructed from an ideal point estimation based on the following networks of 100,000 randomly sampled Twitter users who follow Japanese political and media accounts. Estimated points for parties' candidates are shown as a distribution, while estimated points for media accounts are shown as vertical lines. The dimension calculated from these points largely matches conventional understandings of the left–right axis of political competition among Japan's major parties. These positions reflect ordinary Twitter users' perception of actors' positions, rather than being based on actors' own statements or actions

were active on social media, but candidates from large, established parties dominated the online discourse, having a wider reach and tending to use social media more extensively. By contrast, many small challenger parties and independents, for whom social media should be a cost-effective tool, have struggled to adapt to this style of campaigning.

While using social media to support and promote more traditional campaign activities such as speech events and canvassing remains widespread, this election also saw significant engagement with policy issues and discussion of governing track records by candidates on Twitter—in line with both the longer-term general trend toward programmatic campaigning which has been documented since the 1990s, and the expectation that campaigning on social media would become more sophisticated as candidates become familiar and comfortable in engaging with the medium. In particular, candidates of the governing parties focused on messaging about the success of Japan's COVID-19 vaccination program and the need for ongoing stability, while mainstream opposition parties' candidates were more focused on quality-of-life issues such as employment, salaries, and childcare.

The study of social media data also provides insights into the question of polarization, not just among candidates but also among the ordinary social media users who follow them, and among media outlets. At this election, Japanese Twitter users showed some degree of political polarization online, but to a significantly lower degree than in other countries where online polarization has become a significant issue; crucially, they largely assessed major media organizations as somewhat neutral, lying in between the LDP and CDP's positions, which suggests that the narrative of media being biased or untrustworthy has not taken deep root. A note of caution, however, should be sounded over the tendency of many followers of LDP candidates to follow far-right media outlets; while social media users are not a representative sample of the population and it's entirely possible that politically engaged Twitter users are more extreme in their beliefs and preferences than the general public, the popularity of far-right media content among LDP supporters in this sphere demands further observation and research.

NOTES

1. For example, an Asahi Shinbun editorial headline on April 12, 2013 declared that "Internet election campaigns can change Japan's politics".

2. See also McKean and Scheiner (2000), Rosenbluth et al. (2011). Muraoka, 2018 shows that candidates who do not come from political dynasties are more likely to engage in policy-focused campaigning.

REFERENCES

Barberá, P. (2015). Birds of the Same Feather Tweet Together: Bayesian Ideal Point Estimation Using Twitter Data. *Political Analysis, 23*(1), 76–91.

Barberá, P., Jost, J. T., Nagler, J., Tucker, J. A., & Bonneau, R. (2015). Tweeting From Left to Right: Is Online Political Communication More Than an Echo Chamber? *Psychological Science, 26*(10), 1531–1542.

Catalinac, A. (2016). From Pork to Policy: The Rise of Programmatic Campaigning in Japanese Elections. *The Journal of Politics, 78*(1), 1–18.

Curini, L., Hino, A., & Osaka, A. (2020). The Intensity of Government–Opposition Divide as Measured through Legislative Speeches and What We Can Learn from It: Analyses of Japanese Parliamentary Debates, 1953–2013. *Government and Opposition, 55*(2).

Druckman, J. N., Levendusky, M. S., & McLain, A. (2018). No Need to Watch: How the Effects of Partisan Media Can Spread via Interpersonal Discussions. *American Journal of Political Science, 62*(1), 99–112.

Fahey, R. A., & Camatarri, S. (2021). From Filter Bubble to Social Cleavage: Social Polarisation in Europe and Japan. In A. Hino & F. Foret (Eds.), *Values in European and Japanese Politics*. Routledge.

Greenacre, M. (2021). *Correspondence Analysis in Practice*. CRC Press.

Kobayashi, T., & Ichifuji, Y. (2015). Tweets That Matter: Evidence From a Randomized Field Experiment in Japan. *Political Communication, 32*(4), 574–593.

Lelkes, Y., Sood, G., & Iyengar, S. (2017). The Hostile Audience: The Effect of Access to Broadband Internet on Partisan Affect. *American Journal of Political Science, 61*(1), 5–20.

McKean, M., & Scheiner, E. (2000). Japan's new electoral system: La plus ça change . . . *Electoral Studies, 19*(4), 447–477.

McElwain, K. M. (2008). Manipulating Electoral Rules to Manufacture Single-Party Dominance. *American Journal of Political Science, 52*(1), 32–47.

Ministry of Internal Affairs and Communications (2021). 令和2年国勢調査人口 (速報値) に基づく計算結果の概要 [Outline of Calculations Based on (Preliminary) Population Data from the 2020 National Census], Online: https://www.soumu.go.jp/main_content/000757018.pdf

Miwa, H. (2017). Twitterデータによる日本の政治家・言論人・政党・メディアのイデオロギー位置の推定 [Estimating the Ideology of Japanese Politicians, Political Commentators, Political Parties, and News Media Using Twitter Data]. *Japanese Journal of Electoral Studies, 33*(1), 41–56.

Nishida, R. (2015). メディアと自民党 [Media and the Liberal Democratic Party]. Kadokawa.

Rosenbluth, F., Saito, J., & Yamada, K. (2011). Electoral Adaptation in Japan: Party Strategy after Electoral Rule Change. *The Journal of Social Science*, *62*(1), 5–23.

Sobieraj, S. (2020). *Credible Threat: Attacks Against Women Online and the Future of Democracy* (1st ed.). Oxford University Press.

Tkach-Kawasaki, L. M. (2003). POLITICS@JAPAN—Party Competition on the Internet in Japan. *Party Politics*, *9*(1), 105–123.

Tonami, A., Yoshida, M., & Sano, Y. (2021). *Online harassment in Japan: Dissecting the targeting of a female journalist* (10:1164). F1000Research.

Williams, J. A. (2017). *Electoral Campaigning and the Internet in Japan in the 2010s* [Doctoral Dissertation, University of Washington], University of Washington ResearchWorks Archive, https://digital.lib.washington.edu/researchworks/handle/1773/39881.

Williams, J. A., & Miller, D. M. (2016). Netizens Decide 2014? A Look at Party Campaigning Online. In R. Pekkanen, S. Reed, & E. Scheiner (Eds.), *Japan Decides 2014: The Japanese General Election*. Palgrave Macmillan.

Wilson, A. E., Parker, V. A., & Feinberg, M. (2020). Polarization in the contemporary political and media landscape. *Current Opinion in Behavioral Sciences*, *34*, 223–228.

CHAPTER 14

Are the Kids Alright? Young People and Turnout in Japan

Gill Steel

Most young adults don't vote. Across the globe, analysts ask if anything can be done about this. In Japan, one response to persistent low turnout was to ramp up Get Out the Vote (GOTV) efforts that particularly targeted young adults: during the House of Representatives (HR) election campaign in 2021, celebrities, activists, and NPOs joined bureaucracies and political actors in these efforts. The state produced fliers and posters featuring celebrities, sent out sound cars, ran advertising campaigns in old and new media, produced an anime, and drafted in young people for street-based GOTV drives, to name but some of their efforts.[1] On the nongovernmental side, celebrities uploaded a video that went viral and artists designed downloadable posters. Activists ran online campaigns, including youth-led social media-based peer education campaigns, various websites offered to tell people which party they were closest to in response to a quiz on their own policy preferences, the Association for Promoting

G. Steel (✉)
The Institute for the Liberal Arts, Doshisha University, Kyoto, Japan
e-mail: gsteel@mail.doshisha.ac.jp

© The Author(s), under exclusive license to Springer Nature
Switzerland AG 2023
R. J. Pekkanen et al. (eds.), *Japan Decides 2021*,
https://doi.org/10.1007/978-3-031-11324-6_14

Fair Elections dispatched Election Meisui-kun (a winged yellow election mascot) on visits, and various companies offered discount shopping coupons to voters.[2]

The parties' responses were more mixed. If parties were trying to reach and mobilize young people, one way to do so would be to use or prioritize the platforms that skew young and design content that may appeal to a younger demographic. Instead, parties tended to concentrate on the platforms where they have most followers; in essence, concentrating on mobilizing supporters, rather than on independents or persuading weak identifiers. Most of the parties' and leaders' social media accounts posted a fairly limited range of content, even less of which seemed to target young people.[3] Graham et al. (2013) emphasize the interactive and participatory nature of social media and the potential to bridge the gap between politics and the public by developing a reciprocal relationship between politicians and citizens. However, that potential is only rarely realized in Japan and most political actors' social media content is a unidirectional form of communication and does not attempt engagement, dialogue, or interaction with young voters—or any voters—thus failing to exploit the potential that social media offers for facilitating a closer relationship with citizens. In descending order of popularity, the platforms of choice among the young are Line, Youtube, Twitter, Instagram, and TikTok (Sōmushō, 2022, p. 15) whereas Facebook is used more by the middle-aged. By 2021, most parties and party leaders had social media accounts and around 81 percent of candidates used Twitter and Facebook during the campaign (Corona ka no sentaku, 2021, see also Fahey, 2022). The party and leader accounts posted on Twitter the most, then Facebook, Instagram, and Youtube (in descending order) (Fig. 14.1). The comparatively few posts on Youtube demonstrate a failure to attempt to harness Youtube's potential reach among young people. The Japan Innovation Party (Nippon Ishin no Kai, known as Ishin), a small, right-wing party was an outlier in its Youtube use and also managed to garner youth votes (Sunahara, 2022). In its previous iteration, too, Ishin won votes from young people (Jou, 2015). Reiwa Shinsengumi (known as Reiwa), a small leftist party took out ads on Youtube and was the only party with a TikTok account.

The lack of engagement is surprising given the greater importance attached to digital campaigning during the COVID pandemic. The Liberal Democratic Party (LDP) and Kōmeitō were particularly concerned since their mobilization model relies on face-to-face contact,

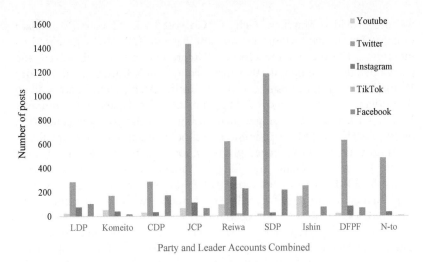

Fig. 14.1 The Digital Campaign (October 19–30, 2021) (*Source* Data compiled by author)

with LDP officials fretting, "You can't shake hands. It is difficult to hold rallies. Candidates who are proficient at digital campaigning are likely to win votes from independents." Yamaguchi Natsuo, Kōmeitō's leader, acknowledged this in his first live Instagram appearance, "I'm Nacchan! During the COVID pandemic, it has become difficult for Kōmeitō to broaden its support in person, which has been the forté of its supporters, the members of the Soka Gakkai" (Netto Senkyō, 2021). Yet they stuck to their standard campaign operating procedures (see Klein and McLaughlin, 2022), supplementing these with social media broadcasting, as had been the case in recent elections, even though the party made much of listening to citizens' voices through social media during the pandemic.

The social media content of the parties and leaders mainly consisted of "broadcasting" or spreading information (this is the case at the candidate level, too, as Fahey (2022) demonstrates, whose accounts do more broadcasting of their local activities than do the leader and party accounts). The LDP's Instagram posts, for example, explained its policies post by post (a few of which were about children and family policy) and government achievements and did not interact with supporters (although the LDP's website provided graphics, such as "Go vote" and "I voted," to share online). The Constitutional Democratic Party (CDP) also segmented its messaging. On the day the House of Representatives was dissolved, the party uploaded a deluge of 109 short videos, mainly featuring party leader Edano Yukio, to its website. According to the Asahi, young people liked the videos (Netto Senkyō, 2021). Similarly, the Japanese Communist Party (JCP), focused on single themes, but with the younger generation in mind, they created short anime on school rules and gender equality.

Almost all of the speeches given by some of the party leaders such as the JCP's Shii Kazuo and Reiwa's Yamamoto Tarō were uploaded (Senkyō, 2021). Parties uploaded videos of their rallies, Reiwa went a step further, creating a "viewable street rally" with a commentary on Yamamoto's activities: "On the train! Even before going to bed!" and transcribed and posted Yamamoto's speeches (see Netto Senkyō, 2021). The Social Democratic Party (SDP) engaged somewhat with supporters on Twitter, retweeting and acknowledging support but their Instagram posts relied on broadcasting information. Kōmeitō's Tokyo headquarters youth division promoted "#Tsugikome" to promote diversity and other policies that young people tend to support ("Kōmeitō will create the next generation"). Tsugikome combines *tsugi* (next) and *Kōme* (the abbreviation of Kōmeitō), also calling to mind *tsugikomu* (to invest in), implying that Kōmeitō is investing in the young for our futures. Yet they stuck to their standard campaign operating procedures (see Klein and McLaughlin, 2022), supplementing these with broadcasting information on social media, as had been the case in recent elections, even though the party had paid lip service to the importance of listening to citizens' voices through social media during the pandemic.

One other means to mobilize is through party platforms. Young adults tend to be progressive on social issues and the parties in the opposition electoral coalition pact (the CDP, JCP, SDP, and Reiwa) played to these policy preferences. In contrast to the LDP's anti-progressive stance, these opposition parties included pledges on gender equality, allowing different family names for married couples, and support for LGBT rights. The CDP had prominent pledges on gender equality and a photo of women politicians on their website (Rikken Women's Action), claiming that "Women's voices will change politics" but selected few women candidates (see Kweon, 2022). The JCP put gender at the center of its platform, vowing to eliminate wage gaps between men and women and highlighted this in its posters and pamphlets (Steel, 2022, chapter 6). Specific youth-oriented policies included pledges of funding for college.

Yet when all was said and done, the flurry of GOTV efforts led to very little. Electoral turnout overall is basically falling over time but the low turnout among young adults in particular has caused much hand-wringing about the future of democracy. Turnout in 2021 was 55.93%, slightly higher than in 2017, but still the third-lowest rate in the postwar era for a national election, as the press were fond of remarking. Turnout among teens, too, was slightly higher than it had been in the previous Lower House election. In the 2017 election, 40.49% of teenagers voted (Sōmushō, 2022) whereas in 2021, this amounted to 43.21% (Sōmushō, 2022).[4] Turnout thus fits with broader patterns in which Japanese young adults have been consistently underrepresented at the polls. Eighteen to twenty-nine years olds account for almost 12 percent of the voting age population but they made up a considerably smaller portion of the voting electorate (Fig. 14.2).[5] At every election, young people vote less than their older counterparts (the cohort with the highest turnout is included for comparison). Moreover, young people vote less than their same-age peers did in previous decades. The exception to the pattern is that teen voters, newly enfranchised in 2016 voted at higher rates than their 20-something counterparts in the Upper House Election.[6] The turnout gaps persist throughout the life cycle, implying that only some of mostly non-voting young adults mature into "habitual voters" later in life (Green and Shachar, 2000). And there are fewer habitual voters with each cohort. The political system will have to adapt, somehow, to a citizenry that is less engaged with politics.

Depoliticization, the Costs of Voting, and Campaign Context

Critics are quick to point the finger at young people for their suppos-edly apathetic, disinterested ways, but as I have argued elsewhere, the long-time ruling party, the LDP, has depressed young people's engage-ment with politics in the various ways it *depoliticizes* politics (this is combined with global trends that depress participation) (Steel, 2019). As part of this governing strategy of depoliticization, the state has limited citizens' opportunities for participation and has cultivated, or mandated, an atmosphere of depoliticization that discourages citizen interest and

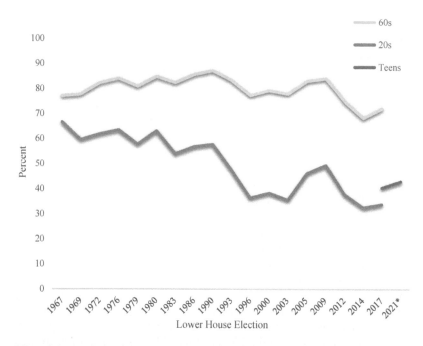

Fig. 14.2 Young Adults' Low Turnout (*Source* Sōmushō [Ministry of Internal Affairs and Communications] *Preliminary estimates)

engagement. The state does so through depoliticizing schools, broadcasting, restricting political activities in general (and specifically youth campaigning),[7] curtailing NPOs, and manipulating the electoral system (Ikeno, 2011; Krauss, 2000; Pekkanen, 2003, 2006; Reimann, 2009; McElwain, 2008). Depoliticization means that young people do not receive political information and cues from elites that impart a sense of the excitement of politics or the legitimacy of political conflict through mainstream channels. This is exacerbated by weakening potential countervailing forces such as unions or NPOs, making it hard for young citizens to connect their own preferences with politics and to begin participating (McClean [2022] suggests that the lack of young candidates may depress youth participation and the LDP has especially low numbers). Since research demonstrates that there is a strong habitual nature of political engagement, curtailing early integration into the political system may hamper engagement throughout the life cycle (Holbein and Hillygus, 2019; Fowler, 2006; Meredith, 2009; Plutzer, 2002).

The regulations that govern campaigning are part of this depoliticization and particularly affect young people. Minors are forbidden from campaigning and even when they turn eighteen, young people, who spend much of their lives online, are particularly restricted by the complex rules that govern internet campaigning. It is illegal, for example, for people under the age of eighteen to campaign off-line or to share partisan information on social media or retweet voting information shared by political accounts (Kōkōsei shinbun Online, 2021).[8] Moreover, the Public Offices Election Law mystifyingly divides the Internet into "e-mail" and "websites etc." The much-criticized stipulations allow the public to use "websites etc.," such as homepages and social media to campaign, but does not allow them to send e-mail or texts from cell phones (candidates and political parties can do so). In essence, party supporters cannot e-mail their friends asking them to vote for particular candidates nor can they forward e-mail vote requests from candidates. In contrast, LINE texts and Facebook are classified as "websites etc.," so the public can use those (Yuasa, 2014). The Law also forbids campaigning on election day; this includes sharing, commenting, or "liking" social e-mail posts, retweeting, or comment on vote requests. These convoluted rules may be daunting to citizens, since violators can face two years in prison or a fine of up to ¥500,000, while a "malicious offender" could be stripped of the right to run for public office or even to votes (Kiyohara, 2013; Mie, 2013).[9] Added to this, the dearth of young candidates, as outlined later, may make it more difficult for young people to connect with politics (McClean, 2022).

STRUCTURES, INSTITUTIONS, AND ELECTORAL TURNOUT

Reforms have limited effect, particularly against the long-term background of depoliticization. Lowering the voting age to eighteen, for example, may not raise turnout in the long term: the elevated turnout rates among teenagers may be due to the novelty of being among the first teen cohorts to be enfranchised (Horiuchi, Katsumata, and Woodard, 2021). Even if this were not the case, the teenage rate was only slightly higher than voters in their twenties, suggesting this will not fundamentally halt declining turnout.

Japanese citizens are automatically added to the electoral rolls when they reach eighteen, suggesting that turnout should be high as political scientists have long assumed that reducing the costs associated with registration increases turnout. Despite the ease of voting, turnout is basically decreasing over time because lowering the costs of voting only helps *some* people. Horiuchi, Katsumata, and Woodard (2021) argue that "the intensity of civic engagement under the automatic registration system is weak due to the lack of citizens' *self-initiated* actions for the registration itself" and that lowering the voting age in Japan did not enhance civic engagement among young people (Horiuchi, Katsumata, and Woodard, 2021). Although they suggest that self-initiated actions may be key, they, too, point to the importance of supporting institutions. In addition to this, campaign context is also important (Holbein and Hillygus, 2016, p. 364).[10] Institutions that might have contributed to a high-interest context such as unions, NPOs, broadcasting, and schools have been enfeebled.

Reforming institutions is no panacea for low turnout since reducing the costs of voting is not the only reason people stay home on election day. Research demonstrates that lowering the costs of voting does not automatically translate into massively higher turnout, especially among the resource-poor, the unmotivated, or the unengaged. In other words, the small increases in turnout do not make the voting public more descriptively representative of the voting-age population (Ansolabehere and Konisky, 2006; Berinksy, Burns, and Traugott, 2001; Burden, Canon, Mayer, and Moynihan, 2014; Burden and Neiheisel, 2013; Hanmer, 2009; Keele and Minozzi, 2013). If increasing youth turnout is a priority, reformers need to take a much broader approach.

Measures that have been introduced to stimulate turnout are not straightforward. Some polling stations allow early voting (fewer than 13%) (Haraguchi, 2021a), and some polling stations are located in high schools, universities and in commercial facilities (Haraguchi, 2021b). But as mentioned, context matters, particularly supporting institutions and social and familial networks. Early voting lowers the costs of voting but eliminates the potential learning role campaigns may have. It also makes voting a more individual, rather than social activity that dampens any build-up to a "frenzied Election Day in which media coverage and interpersonal conversations revolve around politics, early voting makes voting a more private and less intense process" (Burden et al., 2014, p. 98); this is particularly the case since campaigning is illegal before the official, short campaign period. Moreover, institutional reforms to lower the costs of voting would not increase engagement among the disinterested. Using results from a 2017 post-election survey as a guide, among the 20% of the sample who didn't vote, the top reason that those under 30 gave for not voting was that they had to work (Association for Promoting Fair Elections, 2017). The next most common reasons young people chose for not voting fit with my argument about the depoliticization of politics: lack of interest and "learned helplessness": they claimed not to understand the differences between the policies of the parties or the personalities of the candidates or they "thought it would be better for people like me who don't know anything about politics not to vote" (Association for the Promotion of Fair Elections, 2017).

RAISING THE COSTS OF VOTING

In direct contrast to reforms that lower the costs of voting, other specific institutional factors have the opposite effect, these include reducing the numbers of polling stations (Chunichi Shinbun, 2001) (which likely impacts rural, elderly voters) and excessive redistricting. Electoral redistricting had occurred in the previous two elections (McElwain, 2021), burdening voters with repeated information gathering since they could not rely on previously acquired knowledge and experience.[11] These circumstances also increase the information gathering costs, not only for young adults, but for the parental generation, adding to the difficulties of political socialization.

For some young adults, increased residential mobility may be a barrier to voting that they experience repeatedly and indeed, some previous work claims that mobility explains young people's low turnout (Maeda, 2019). Yet in 2017, only 6% of non-voting under 30s stated that it was because they were not eligible to vote where they live (whereas 9% of those 30 and over did) (Association for Promoting Fair Elections, 2017). Although the Absentee Voting system does allow people to vote where they live if they are registered elsewhere (Nakazono, 2017), the application process is cumbersome and cannot address the importance of social connections in shaping electoral behavior that some researchers suggest are particularly relevant for young adults (Franklin, 2008).

Given the long-term depoliticization of schools, it is doubtful that most schools are fulfilling their role as supporting institutions. The current citizenship education (*Shukensha Kyōiku*) teaching materials lack creativity and critics advocate for a more all-encompassing approach (Shiozawa, 2018; Maeda, 2019, pp. 65–66).[12] Moreover, research suggests that among high school students, discussion with friends had a stronger influence on political interest and voting intentions than lecturing about the election (Mimura and Fukaya, 2020). An NPO, the Network Association for Mock Election Japan assists schools in conducting mock elections but their reach is limited (http://www.mogisenkyo.com/).

Whereas Horiuchi et al. (2021) claim that young citizens who know that they can vote are more active in collecting information about politics and are more likely to have social interaction with other voters (Horiuchi et al., 2021), further research is needed into the contexts when this happens, when young people do so but still do not turn out, or do not do so at all. Demonstrating the importance of context and networks, Mimura and Fukaya (2020) argue that even leaflet and poster campaigns to publicize the election are important when they are mediated by parents and friends: political communication with parents (and personality traits) played a major role in this mechanism.

Voters do not choose candidates because of their age, but the age of candidates contributes to the context of the campaign. And when parties select few young candidates, this signals that younger voters' preferences are not prioritized since younger and middle-aged voters prefer candidates closer to their own age (McClean and Ono, 2021). The parties came up woefully short in descriptive representation of young citizens, instead of opting to prioritize incumbents. The average candidate age, at 54.2 years old, had increased since than the previous election; only 9.4% of the candidates were under 40 years old. 9.2% of the candidates were 70 or older ("A much smaller field," 2021; see also McClean, 2022). Some younger candidates used the hashtag #generationchangenotregimechange on Twitter to draw attention to their comparative youth, but this did not gain much traction.

CONCLUSION

In sum, reforms can increase turnout only a little and only among some subgroups. Without fundamental change, turnout is likely to remain low. Although young adults turn out to vote less than their older counterparts, exit polls confirmed that younger cohorts continue to be more likely to support the LDP and less likely to support the CDP (Ueki, 2021;

Nihon Keizai Shinbun 2021). Note that this tendency may have weakened slightly compared with 2017 (Ueki, 2021) and since the LDP's platform is more conservative than the median young adult on social issues, this value difference may loom larger in future elections. When 2021 resoundingly became a referendum on the LDP government's handling of the pandemic and the economy, however, this played to the LDP's strengths; when elections are about competence, the LDP carries the day among the young and old alike.

Acknowledgements I would like to thank Yoshitaka Masahiro for quick and careful research assistance. I also thank the editors for their comments.

Notes

1. See, for example, Wakamono no tōhyō-ritsu appu e senkan, anotekonote de PR shinbun, terebi rajio ya konkai hajimete SNS ni kōkoku/ Ōita (2021);

   Sōmushō [Ministry of Internal Affairs and Communications], (2021, p. 5);

   Kagoshima ken senkan wa 'Nihon kin mirai-banashi (2021);

   Sōmushō (2021).

2. These include No Youth No Japan (http://nynj2021.com/); the celebrity video https://www.youtube.com/watch?v=Ygtmbwj0sV4; posters (https://voteposter.cargo.site/), No Youth No Japan (http://nyn j2021.com/), and Go Vote Japan (https://govote.jp). Mielka, an NPO, for example, has an Election Navigator with sixteen questions (https://japanchoice.jp/vote-navi) and redesigned its website "Japan Choice" (https://japanchoice.jp/) to facilitate policy comparison between the parties (https://japanchoice.jp/policy-comparison). Similarly, Yahoo's Political Party Compatibility Diagnosis (https://news.yahoo.co.jp/sen kyo/match/party) does this in response to 10 questions. Jiji.com does this with their "vote matching" quiz (https://shugiin.go2senkyo.com/ votematches/). Meisui-kun can be viewed here.

3. Thus, Japanese candidates are similar to British candidates, in contrast to Dutch candidates who are more likely to embrace the interactive potential of Twitter (to which the public responds by engaging in further dialogue) (Graham, Jackson, and Broersma, 2014).

4. For a cross-national comparison, see John B. Holbein and Hillygus (2019, p. 4).

5. I include emerging adulthood and young adulthood in a broad "young adult" descriptor (Arnett, 2000; Ōtaka and Karasawa, 2014).

6. Hayashi (2016) claims that in the 1960s and 1970s, there was some discussion about lowering the voting age in Japan, but most of the public were opposed to this.

7. The law has 275 clauses that regulate virtually every aspect of campaigning ("Japan's election system choking on rules," 2017).

8. Minors have been given the right to vote in some regional referenda (Shiozawa, 2018).

9. Television advertising, too, is restricted: parties receive free media time, but the party election broadcasts are very restricted, even down to whether the candidate is allowed to sit or stand or use props (Curtis). Individual candidates and independents are even more restricted and are not allowed to buy advertising time or space (Krauss and Pekkanen, 2011; Lewis and Masshardt, 2002; Christensen, 2008, 230–231).

10. In lower-level elections, for example, turnout is higher when there is a lot at stake ("election significance") and when votes count ("vote significance") (Horiuchi, 2005).

11. This affected 34 percent of districts and just over a third of voters in 2017, for example. Kenneth Mori McElwain (2021) estimates that redistricting reduces turnout by 2–4%, particularly in urban districts.

12. See the supplementary materials on Sōmushō's (2019) website.

REFERENCES

A Much Smaller Field, Smallest Ratio of Young Candidates. (2021). *The Asahi Shinbun*. Retrieved from https://www.asahi.com/ajw/articles/14471542

Ansolabehere, Stephen, and Konisky, David M. (2006). The Introduction of Voter Registration and Its Effect on Turnout. *Political Analysis, 14*(1), 83–100.

Arnett, J. J. (2000). Emerging Adulthood: A Theory of Development from the Late Teens Through the Twenties. *American Psychologist, 55*(5), 469–480.

Berinksy, Adam J., Burns, Nancy, and Traugott, Michael W. (2001). Who Votes by Mail?: A Dynamic Model of the Individual-Level Consequences of Voting-by-Mail Systems. *Public Opinion Quarterly, 65*(2), 178–197. https://doi.org/10.1086/322196

Burden, Barry C., and Neiheisel, Jacob R. (2013). Election Administration and the Pure Effect of Voter Registration on Turnout. *Political Research Quarterly, 66*(1), 77–90. https://doi.org/10.1177/1065912911430671

Burden, Barry C., Canon, David T., Mayer, Kenneth R., and Moynihan, Donald P. (2014). Election Laws, Mobilization, and Turnout: The Unanticipated Consequences of Election Reform. *American Journal of Political Science, 58*(1), 95–109.

Christensen, Ray. (2008). Societal, electoral, and party explanations for the low representation of women in the House of Representatives. In M. Tremblay (Ed.), *Women and legislative representation: Electoral systems, political parties, and sex quotas.* Palgrave Macmillan.

Chūnichi Shinbun. (2001/10/28). Tōhyōsho, 20-nen de 7000-kasho-gen 36.5% de shimekiri jikan kiriage. Chūnichi Shinbun.

Fahey, Robert A. (2022). "Social Media in the 2021 Election Campaign." In Robert J. Pekkanen, Steven R. Reed, and Daniel M. Smith (eds), *Japan Decides 2021: The Japanese General Election.* Palgrave MacMillan.

Fowler, James. (2006). Habitual Voting and Behavioral Turnout. *Journal of Politics, 68,* 335–344. https://doi.org/10.1111/j.1468-2508.2006.00410.x

Franklin, Mark N. (2008). *You Want to Vote Where Everybody Knows Your Name: Anonymity, Expressive Engagement, and Turnout Among Young Adults.* Paper presented at the American Political Science Association, Washington D.C.

Graham, Todd, Broersma, Marcel, Hazelhoff, Karin, and van 't Haar, Guido. (2013). Between Broadcasting Political Messages and Interacting with Voters. *Information, Communication & Society, 16*(5), 692–716. https://doi.org/10.1080/1369118X.2013.785581

Graham, Todd, Jackson, Dan, and Broersma, Marcel. (2014). New Platform, Old Habits? Candidates' Use of Twitter During the 2010 British and Dutch General Election Campaigns. *New Media & Society, 18*(5), 765–783. https://doi.org/10.1177/1461444814546728

Green, Donald P., and Shachar, R. O. N. (2000). Habit Formation and Political Behaviour: Evidence of Consuetude in Voter Turnout. *British Journal of Political Science, 30*(4), 561–573. https://doi.org/10.1017/S0007123400000247

Hanmer, Michael J. (2009). *Discount Voting: Voter Registration Reforms and Their Effects.* Cambridge: Cambridge University Press.

Hayashi, Daisuke. (2016). '18-Sai senkyo-ken' de shakai wa dō kawaru ka. [How will society change with "18-yearold suffrage"?]. Tokyo: Shueisha Shinsho.

Haraguchi, Kazunori. (2021a, 2021/11/13). Shūin-sen 10-dai yūkensha no tōhyō-ritsu wa 1.5% no zōka. Wakamono no tōhyō o fuyasu tame ni motomerareru koto. Senkyo.com. Retrieved from https://go2senkyo.com/articles/2021a/11/13/64584.html

Haraguchi, Kazunori. (2021b, 2021/10/30). Shūin-sen 2021 wakamono no tōhyō jōkyō o takoku to hikaku shite miruto? Kiwadatsu Nihon no tei tōhyō-ritsu. Senkyo.com. Retrieved from https://go2senkyo.com/articles/2021b/10/30/64401.html

Holbein, J. B., and D. Sunshine Hillygus. (2016). Making Young Voters: The Impact of Preregistration on Youth Turnout. *American Journal of Political Science, 60.* https://doi.org/10.1111/ajps.12177

Holbein, John B., and D. Sunshine Hillygus. (2019). *Making Young Voters: Converting Civic Attitudes into Civic Action.*

Horiuchi, Yusaku, Katsumata, Hiroto, and Woodard, Ethan. (2021). Young Citizens' Civic Engagement and Civic Attitudes: A Regression Discontinuity Analysis. *Political Behavior.* https://doi.org/10.1007/s11109-021-09698-7

Horiuchi, Yusaku. (2005). *Institutions, Incentives and Electoral Participation in Japan Cross-Level and Cross-National Perspectives*: Routledge Taylor and Francis Group.

Ikeno, N. (2011). *Citizenship Education in Japan.* Bloomsbury Academic.

Japan's Election System Choking on Rules. (2017, January 23, 2017). *Nikkei Asian Review.* Retrieved from http://asia.nikkei.com/Politics-Economy/Policy-Politics/Japan-s-election-system-choking-on-rules?page=2

Jou, Willy. (2015). A Regional Party in a Centralized Country: The Case of One Osaka in Japan. *Regional & Federal Studies, 25*(2), 145–163. https://doi.org/10.1080/13597566.2014.1002834

Krauss, Ellis. S., and Pekkanen, Robert. J. (2011). *The Rise and Fall of Japan's LDP: Political Party Organizations as Historical Institutions.* Cornell University Press.

Keele, Luke, and Minozzi, William. (2013). How Much Is Minnesota Like Wisconsin? Assumptions and Counterfactuals in Causal Inference with Observational Data. *Political Analysis, 21*(2), 193–216.

Kiyohara, Shoko. (2013). Comparing Institutional Factors That Influence Internet Campaigning in the US, Japan, South Korea, and Taiwan. In Shoko Kiyohara, Kazuhiro Maeshima, & Diana Owen (Eds.), *Internet Election Campaigns in the United States, Japan, South Korea, and Taiwan* (pp. 55–78).

Klein, Axel and McLaughlin, Levi. (2022). Kōmeitō in 2021: Strategizing between the LDP and Sōka Gakkai. In Robert J. Pekkanen, Steven R. Reed, and Daniel M. Smith (eds), *Japan Decides 2021: The Japanese General Election.* Palgrave MacMillan.

Kōkōsei shinbun onrain. [Highschool Newspaper Online] (2021). Intānetto senkyo undō no chūi-ten 18-sai-miman wa ritsuīto mo shinaide [A note on Internet campaigning: Don't even retweet if you're under 18]. *Yahoo News.* Retrieved from https://news.yahoo.co.jp/articles/c0889f3cdcf4fb52a8bbccd41b57f71de5bd6418

Korona-ka no sentaku sonzai-kan masu 'netto senkyo'. (2021/10/21).

Krauss, E. S. (2000). *Broadcasting Politics in Japan: NHK and Television News.* Ithaca: Cornell University Press.

Kweon, Yesola. (2022). Women's Representation and the Gendered Impact of COVID-19 in Japan. In Robert J. Pekkanen, Steven R. Reed, and Daniel M. Smith (eds), *Japan Decides 2021: The Japanese General Election.* Palgrave MacMillan.

Lewis, Jonathan., & Masshardt, Brian. J. (2002). Election posters in Japan. *Japan Forum, 14*(3), 373–404. https://doi.org/10.1080/0955580022000008736

Maeda, Ryōta and Shiozawa, Ken'ichi. (2019). 18-Sai senkyo-ken o meguru kadai to wakamono no tōhyō-ritsu seiji ishiki — kokusei senkyo ni okeru todōfuken-betsu no tōhyō-ritsuoyobi seronchōsa dēta o moto ni —. Chiiki-gaku ronshū maki, dai 15.

Mimura, Norihiro and Fukaya, Ken. (2020). Atarashī yūkensha o kitei suru shakai-teki bunmyaku. [Social contexts that define new voters]. *Nenpō seiji-gaku [Annals of Political Science], 71*(1), 1, 341–341, 367.

McClean, Charles T. & Ono, Yoshikuni. (2021). Too Young to Run? Voter Evaluations of the Age of Candidates.

McClean, Charles T. (2021). Does the Underrepresentation of Young People in Political Institutions Matter for Social Spending? *Unpublished manuscript.*

McClean, Charles T. (2022). Generational Change or Continuity in Japan's Leadership? In Robert J. Pekkanen, Steven R. Reed, and Daniel M. Smith (eds), *Japan Decides 2021: The Japanese General Election.* Palgrave MacMillan.

McElwain, K. M. (2008). Manipulating Electoral Rules to Manufacture Single-Party Dominance. *American Journal of Political Science, 52*(1), 32–47. https://doi.org/10.1111/j.1540-5907.2007.00297.x

McElwain, Kenneth Mori. (2021). Paper Presented at the Press Conference: What Next for Japanese Politics? by Kenneth Mori McElwain, Kensuke Takayasu and Takuma Oohamazaki, Tokyo: Foreign Correspondents' Club of Japan.

Meredith, M. (2009). Persistence in Political Participation. *Quarterly Journal of Political Science, 4.* https://doi.org/10.1561/100.00009015

Mie, Ayako. (2013). Diet OKs Internet Election Campaigns. *The Japan Times.* Retrieved from https://www.japantimes.co.jp/news/2013/04/19/national/politics-diplomacy/diet-oks-internet-election-campaigns/#.Wb6NL9FrxXI

Nakazono, sumire. (2017/10/11. Hitorigurashi daigakusei no min'na 〜〜! Jūmin-hyō o utsushite nakute mo tōhyō dekiru tte shitteru ka 〜! Jūmin-hyō o utsushite nakute mo tōhyō dekiru yo! *Buzzfeed.* Retrieved from https://www.buzzfeed.com/jp/sumirenakazono/senkyo-hitorigurasi-touhyo

Netto senkyo, kakutō chūryoku tokusetsu saito ni kōyaku SNS, jakunen-sō ishiki Shūin-sen, korona de akushu ya shūkai kon'nan (2021, 2021-nen 10 tsuki 28-nichi 5-ji 00-bu). Asahi Shinbun. Retrieved from https://www.asahi.com/art icles/DA3S15091897.html

Nihon Keizai Shinbun. (2021/11/1). Hirei no deguchi chōsa, 18 〜 19-sai wa Jimin 36%. Jakunen-sō de yū. Retrieved from https://www.nikkei.com/art icle/DGKKZO77156800R01C21A1PE2000/

Otaka, Zui and Karasawa, Kaori. (2014/03/10). Chichioya to no seidjiteki kaiwa to kodomo no seiji kan'yo no kanren: Seijin keisei-ki no kodomo o taishō to shita kentō. [The Relationship between Political Conversation with

Fathers and Children's Political Involvement: A Study of Adult Children Hogakuronshu [The Yamanashigakuin Law Review] 72–73, 254–264.

Pekkanen, R. (2003). "Molding Japanese Civil Society: State-Structured Incentives and the Patterning of Civil Society." In S. J. Pharr (Ed.), *The State of Civil Society in Japan*. (New York: Cambridge University Press, 2003), pp. 116–134. Cambridge.

Pekkanen, R. (2006). *Japan's Dual Civil Society. Members Without Advocates*. Stanford: Stanford University Press.

Plutzer, Eric. (2002). Becoming a Habitual Voter: Inertia, Resources, and Growth in Young Adulthood. *American Political Science Review, 96*(1), 41–56. https://doi.org/10.1017/S0003055402004227

Reimann, K. D. (2009). *The Rise of Japanese NGOs: Activism from Above*: Taylor & Francis.

Shiozawa, Ken'ichi. (2018). "18-sai senkyō-ken" dōnyū no kōka to kongo — -chi-kata reberu ni okeru jūmin tōhyō no keiken o fumaete —'. In Mifune Takeshi (Ed.), Seidjiteki kūkan ni okeru yūkensha seitō seisaku (pp. 67–99): Chūō Daigaku Shuppan-bu.

Sōmushō. (2019). *Shukensha kyōiku no torikumi jōkyō-tō*. Retrieved from https://www.soumu.go.jp/senkyo/senkyo_s/news/senkyo/senkyo_nenrei/01.html

Sōmushō [Ministry of Internal Affairs and Communications]. 2021. Shūgiingiinsōsenkyo ni okeru nendai betsu tōhyō-ritsu no suii. [Trends in voter turnout by cohort in House of Representatives General Elections. Tokyo. Retrieved from https://www.soumu.go.jp/senkyo/senkyo_s/news/sonota/nendaibetu/

Steel, Gill. (2019). *Young People and Politics*. Paper Presented at the Japanese Politics Colloquium, The Nissan Institute of Japanese Studies, the University of Oxford.

Steel, Gill. (2022). *What Women Want. Gender and Voting Preferences in Britain, Japan, and the United States*. University of Michigan Press.

Sunahara, Yosuke & Zenkyo, Masahiro. (2022). Shokyokuteki shiji de yakushin shita Nippon Ishin no Kai. *Chuo Koron*, 130–137.

Ueki, Eiko. (2021). Jimin no wakamono ninki ni kageri? Rikken wa kōrei-sha tanomi tsudzuku Shūin senshutsu-guchi chōsa bunseki. *Asahi Shinbun*.

Wakamono no tōhyō-ritsu appu e senkan, anotekonote de PR shinbun, terebi rajio ya konkai hajimete SNS ni kōkoku/ Ōita (2021, 2021/10/29). Mainichi Shinbun. Retrieved from https://mainichi.jp/articles/20211029/ddl/k44/010/370000c

Yuasa, Harumichi. (2014). Intānetto senkyo undō to kōshoku senkyo-hō. Senkyo kenkyū *30*(2), 75–90. https://doi.org/10.14854/jaes.30.2_75

DATA

The Association For Promoting Fair Elections, Post-Election Survey for the 48th House of Representatives Election (2017).The data for this secondary analysis were provided by the Social Science Japan Data Archive, Center for Social Research and Data Archives, Institute of Social Science, The University of Tokyo.

CHAPTER 15

Did COVID-19 Impact Japan's 2021 General Election?

Michael F. Thies and Yuki Yanai

Liberal democracies have seen their commitment to supposedly inviolable rights tested during the COVID-19 pandemic. Public health policy responses including lockdowns, school closures, travel bans, mask-wearing mandates, and even vaccine mandates, may follow the best scientific advice about how to slow the spread of the disease and avoid overwhelming national healthcare systems. But they run up against the fundamental

Supplementary Information The online version contains supplementary material available at https://doi.org/10.1007/978-3-031-11324-6_15.

M. F. Thies (✉)
Department of Political Science, University of California, Los Angeles, CA, USA
e-mail: Thies@polisci.ucla.edu

Y. Yanai
School of Economics and Management, Kochi University of Technology, Kochi, Japan

liberal principle that citizens should be as free as possible from governmental controls over their behavior. The well-known trade-off between liberty and security has been at center stage in the age of COVID.[1]

One hallmark of liberal democracy has remained sacrosanct in the advanced democracies however: the continuation of free, fair, and frequent elections. With the pandemic now in its third year, all of the world's democracies have held general (and/or presidential) elections, or will have to do so soon. There have been scattered instances of short postponements (e.g., New Zealand), but the most important adaptations have been tweaks to the voting process such as the expansion of mail-in voting and early voting to minimize the need for citizens to assemble. Even those changes have been controversial in some of the more polarized political environments, but clearly the direction of travel in most countries has been to find ways to preserve democracy-as-usual despite the pandemic.

Naturally, citizens' feelings about the efficacy and methods of their governments' policy responses should be expected to affect the vote. The pandemic is clearly a high-salience issue, and governments have responded in a variety of ways, and with varied levels of success (or good or bad luck). Incumbents in those democracies have almost certainly kept an eye on trends in pandemic-related outcomes: infection rates, hospital capacity, deaths, and more optimistically, vaccination rates. They have also paid careful attention to the impact that their various policy responses have had on economic growth, employment, inequality, and debt, among other indicators. Just as political scientists have long discussed the "economic vote," the extent to which incumbents are rewarded or punished for the state of the economy (whatever their actual impact on the economy), so too can we think about the "COVID vote."

In this chapter, we will do two things. First, we will discuss the timing of the election. One distinction among democracies is whether a legislature can be dissolved and early elections called before the statutory end of the term. In nearly all parliamentary systems, governments have the luxury of choosing the most auspicious time for an election, or at least trying to do so.[2] Generally when a parliament serves its full term, it is because the incumbent government has been delaying until the last possible moment, hoping for a fortuitous event or economic upturn that will raise its support rate among voters. The 2021 Japanese general election was a case in point—the incumbent government gambled that delay would pay off and they seem to have won that gamble.

Second, although the overall impact of the pandemic on Japan had been mild relative to peer countries in terms of hospitalizations and deaths, outcomes did vary across the country. We study party vote shares at the prefectural level for heterogeneous effects on support for the incumbent government. We find that urban prefectures with higher death rates were less likely to support the Liberal Democratic Party (LDP), and interestingly, more likely to support *Ishin*, even controlling for proximity to that party's home in and around Osaka.

COVID-19 Performance, Changing Voter Priorities, and Election Timing

When the pandemic began in early 2020, Japan's parliament had passed the halfway point on its current four-year mandate; the next general election was due no later than autumn 2021.[3] But the then-Prime Minister Abe Shinzō had succeeded with snap elections in the past, having wrong-footed unprepared opposition parties in both 2014 and 2017 (Scheiner et al., 2016; Pekkanen and Reed, 2018), so the threat of a dissolution hung in the air. Autumn 2020 seemed the most likely target. Tokyo was set to host the Summer Olympic Games starting in late July. Abe himself had led Tokyo's bid for the Games and likely hoped that their success would provide a boost before a general election (but see Leheny, 2022, this volume).

The onset of the pandemic disrupted that plan. Suddenly, the prospect of welcoming delegations and spectators from around the world seemed like a terrible idea in a country that otherwise was doing its best to minimize foreign travel and to stamp out every small local outbreak of the coronavirus (Lukner, 2022, this volume). On March 24, the International Olympic Committee postponed the 2020 Olympics to late summer 2021.

This bought time, and hope that vaccines might arrive in time to allow a return to something like normalcy. It was too much time for Abe; when a recurrence of serious health concerns forced Abe to resign his post in September 2020, he was replaced by his long-time Chief Cabinet Secretary, Suga Yoshihide. As usually happens with a change in leadership in Japan, Suga began his term with much higher approval ratings that his predecessor had finished with. He might have dissolved the Diet right away and called an election to renew his coalition's mandate and cement his hold on the party leadership. Instead, he focused on the pandemic response and the question of how to hold the postponed Olympics safely.

In retrospect, perhaps Suga regretted his forbearance. As Fig. 15.1 shows, his cabinet's approval rating plummeted relentlessly throughout his single year in office.[4] Some of this was tied to public skepticism about the wisdom of going forward with the Games. Opponents expressed their discomfort with the idea of hosting the Olympics in the midst of the pandemic.[5] Meanwhile, Japan's own COVID-related numbers were worsening. A first peak in COVID-19 deaths occurred in January 2021, followed by an even higher one in early June (Fig. 15.2). Japan also started far behind its advanced-democracy peers in terms of its vaccine rollout (Fig. 15.3).[6]

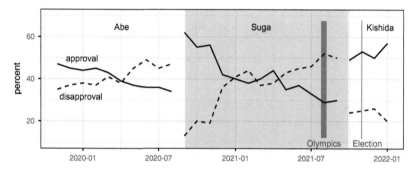

Fig. 15.1 Cabinet Approval and Disapproval Rates, December 2019–January 2022 (*Source* NHK)

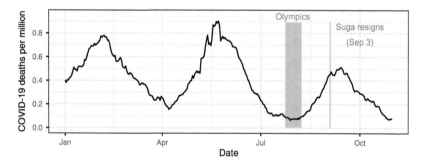

Fig. 15.2 Daily confirmed COVID-19 Deaths per Million People, January 1, 2021–October 31, 2021 (7-day rolling average) (*Source* Our World in Data)

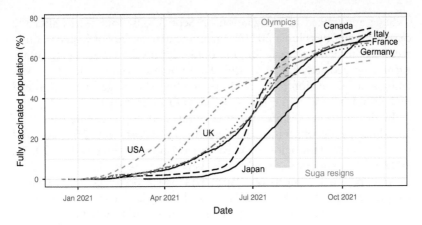

Fig. 15.3 Share of the population fully vaccinated against COVID-19, December 15, 2020–October 31, 2021 (*Source* Our World in Data)

The temptation of a snap election dwindled steadily. The LDP lost three Diet by-elections in April 2021 and then suffered a setback in the Tokyo Metropolitan Assembly election in July. The *Japan Times* opined that "[t]he result was likely attributed to voter dissatisfaction with Suga's response to the coronavirus pandemic and his stance on the Tokyo Olympics and Paralympics" (*Japan Times*, July 5, 2021, online edition). In the event, there were some positive tests among athletes and their reduced delegations, but no super-spreader surge ensued. Japan's own athletes were very successful, and while many citizens still disagreed with the decision to proceed, most were satisfied that the Games had gone about as well as could be expected in the circumstances (Leheny, 2022, this volume).

After the closing ceremony on August 8, the government had a three-month window in which to hold the election. Unfortunately for Suga, no post-Olympics boost materialized. On August 30, a poll by *Mainichi* showed Suga's approval rating at its lowest ebb, 26%, with a record-high 66% of respondents expressing disapproval. The most cited reason was a fear that the medical system would collapse (70%). According to *Mainichi*, only 14% of respondents "appreciated the Suga Cabinet's coronavirus countermeasures... well below the 70% who said they don't" (*Mainichi*, August 30, 2021). The same poll set the LDP's support rate at only 26%, even lower than in the prior poll, taken before the Olympics.

Suga announced his resignation on Sept 3, only four weeks after the closing ceremony (Gunia 2021). Again, the new cabinet of Kishida Fumio received the standard early jump in public approval.[7] Upon taking office, Kishida immediately called for the Diet to be dissolved on October 14th, and a general election to be held on October 31st. Suga's hesitation had tied Kishida's hands—the Diet Session had run its course.

In the election, despite dire predictions and unprecedented levels of coordination by opposition parties, the LDP lost only 25 seats, and romped home with a fourth consecutive landslide (Maeda Ko, 2022a, 2022b, this volume). Should this have been surprising? Looked at in cross-national comparison, Japan had had a pretty good pandemic. Despite the world's oldest population and a very late start on vaccinations (Lipscy, 2022, this volume), Japan has suffered remarkably few deaths or even severe hospitalizations in comparison with peer countries. Indeed, measured in terms of "excess deaths," Japan's total was in the negative: fewer people died in the period from January 2020 through October 2021 than would have been expected in the absence of a pandemic (see Fig. 15.4).

Figure 15.5, taken from our post-election survey,[8] shows that Japanese voters were quite dissatisfied with various aspects of the government's policy performance. The sole exception was approval of the recently

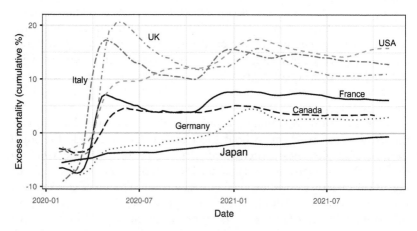

Fig. 15.4 Excess Mortality in G-7 Countries, January 2020–October 2021 (*Source* Our World in Data)

super-charged vaccine rollout. But voters may have appreciated that things were much worse in the United States and most of Europe, making most reluctant to gamble on government turnover.

Perhaps most importantly, the ruling coalition was fortunate that its gamble to run out the clock on the maximum time between elections paid off. Returning to Figs. 15.2 and 15.3 and focusing on the brief period between the end of the Olympics and the election, we can see that the election was timed very well for the incumbents. After a month of post-Olympics increase, COVID-related deaths peaked around the day of Suga's resignation, and plunged steadily through election day. Moreover, when Suga resigned, Japan still trailed its G-7 peers on vaccinations, but by election day it had shot up to second place, just behind Canada. Whether through good luck or good planning, the LDP had timed the election perfectly.

Data from opinion polls seem to track this narrative. Figure 15.6 shows data from a time series of *Nikkei* surveys asking respondents about their policy priorities. As we can see, COVID-19 countermeasures held top position in every survey between October 2020 and October 2021 but slipped to third place just before election day.

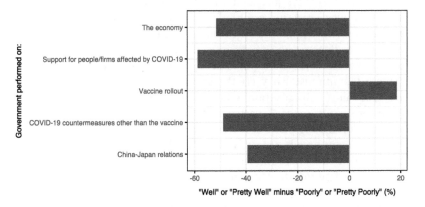

Fig. 15.5 Low Grades for Government Policy Responses to COVID-19 (*Source* Our own post-election survey [N = 3100, November 8, 2021]. *Note* "How well do you think the LDP-Kōmeitō government has managed each of these policy areas?" The figure shows net difference between the share of respondents answering "Well" or "Pretty Well" and the share answering "Poorly" or "Pretty Poorly")

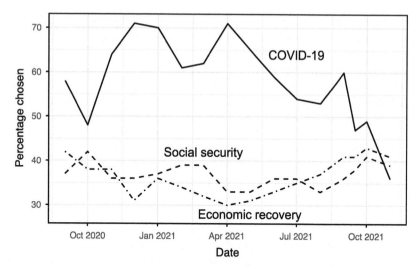

Fig. 15.6 Changes in Public Opinion about Policy Priorities, October 2020–October 2021 (*Source* Nihon Keizai Shinbun)

In our own surveys just after the election, we asked respondents to rank five policy areas in terms of the priority that they felt the post-election government should place on each. In Fig. 15.7, we display the results, according to the self-reported party identification of the respondent. We can see that economy took top priority for all voters other than Japanese Communist Party (JCP) supporters (for whom it was second after inequality). By contrast, COVID countermeasures came third or fourth for supporters of all parties and for non-partisans as well.[9]

To sum up the big picture, voters on election day renewed the mandate of a government on whose watch overall COVID-related health outcomes were excellent by international standards, and had even improved very rapidly in the last month. This wind in the government's sails was complemented by the timely installation of a fresh face as prime minister just before the election was called. Voters were not pleased with the government's performance, but considering the alternatives, most were content to stick with the devils they knew.

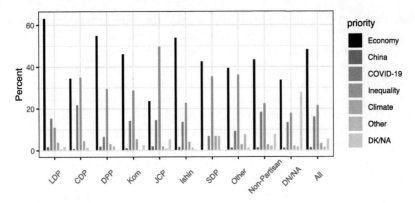

Fig. 15.7 Public Policy Priorities just after the Election, by Party Identification (*Source* Our own post-election survey [N = 3100, November 8, 2021]. *Notes* Party abbreviations: LDP – Liberal Democratic Party; CDP – Constitutional Democratic Party of Japan; DPP – Democratic Party for the People; Kom – Kōmeitō; JCP – Japanese Communist Party; Ishin – Japan Ishin no Kai; SDP – Social Democratic Party; DK/NA – "Don't Know" or No Answer)

LOCAL VARIATIONS IN THE "COVID VOTE"

National trends and national leaders certainly matter in general elections, but it is an aphorism of democracy that "all politics is local." In the remainder of this chapter, we search for heterogeneous effects across Japan's regions. Viruses tend to impact areas of higher population density more severely than areas of lower density. Metropolises are also the main travel and commercial gateways to the rest of the world and so a global pandemic is likely to spread more rapidly in more globalized areas. COVID-19 was no exception. Around the world, big cities were the early epicenters of transmission, hospitalizations, and deaths. Do Japan's relatively good national outcomes obscure important regional differences? Did the electoral ramifications of the pandemic vary accordingly?

Our central question is whether the incumbent government received less support in areas harder hit by COVID-19. To examine this, we regress the vote share of a political party on the cumulative number of deaths due to COVID-19. We use the *difference in a party's prefectural vote share in the PR tier between the 2017 and 2021* general elections as our response variable.[10] Because the prefecture is our unit of analysis, the number of observations is 47. Our primary explanatory variable is deaths due to the coronavirus. Specifically, we use the cumulative number of reported COVID-19 deaths per 1000 people in the prefecture from the beginning of the pandemic to the day before the election.[11]

We include several controls. First, we account for the urbanness of a prefecture, using two different measures. One is an indicator variable for whether prefecture is a part of any of the three largest urban employment areas (UEA) in Japan (Kanemoto and Tokuoka 2002).[12] The other is the percentage of the prefectural population that lives in a densely inhabited district (DID) within a prefecture.[13] We add one or the other of these urbanness measures as well as an interaction of urbanness with COVID-19 deaths.

Next, we control for both the cumulative number of COVID cases in the prefecture, and the percentage of people fully vaccinated before the election. We also include dummy variables indicating whether the Japan Innovation Party (Ishin) or Kōmeitō ran any SMD candidates in the prefecture. Ishin SMD candidates should mobilize the party's supporters, hence increasing its PR vote share. We expect a Kōmeitō district candidate to increase the *LDP's* PR-tier vote.[14] Next, we control for the number of SMDs in the prefecture, and the share of those SMDs that featured explicit electoral coordination among opposition parties. Finally, we add the change in turnout between the 2017 and 2021 elections and a measure of the prefecture's distance from Osaka because we expect that Ishin's appeal waned away from their home turf (Reed et al., 2013, 34).

Our complete model is thus:

$$\text{Vote swing}_{ip} = \beta_0 + \beta_1 \text{Deaths}_p + \beta_2 \text{DID}_p + \beta_3 \text{Deaths}_p \cdot \text{DID}_p + \sum_k \gamma_k X_{pk} + \varepsilon_{ip}$$

$$= \beta_0 + (\beta_1 + \beta_3 \text{DID}_p) \text{Deaths}_p + \beta_2 \text{DID}_p + \sum_k \gamma_k X_{pk} + \varepsilon_{ip}$$

where the subscripts i and p denote party and prefecture, respectively. The X_{pk} are the control variables. We estimate $\beta_1 + \beta_3 DID_p$ (replacing DID_p with UEA_p in the alternative model).

Figure 15.8 presents the main result.[15] The left column shows the results with the dummy variable UEA measuring urbanness; circles display the point estimates, and the line segments are 95-percent confidence intervals. The right column shows the results with the DID measure of urbanness; the solid lines represent the point estimates, and the shaded areas around the line mark 95-percent confidence intervals. The top row in the right column tells us that voters in more urban prefectures (DID > 60%) that suffered more deaths punished the LDP. In a prefecture with a 90-percent DID population, an additional ten deaths per thousand people decreased LDP's vote share by 4.6 percentage points. By contrast, the third plot on the right indicates that in more urban prefectures (DID > 50%), Ishin benefitted from higher death rates. In a prefecture with DID of 90, an additional ten deaths per thousand increased Ishin's vote share by 4.3 points. We cannot find a statistically significant effect of deaths on the vote shares of Kōmeitō, the CDP, or the JCP. The left column indicates a similar pattern; deaths decreased LDP's vote share and increased Ishin's in urban areas, but did not affect other parties' fortunes.

That the LDP's vote share suffered in harder-hit areas may not be surprising.[16] But why did Ishin, of all parties, seem to benefit from bad COVID news? In both our pre- and post-election surveys, we asked respondents how capable of governing they judged each party to be. Figure 15.9 shows the result. With the economy having risen to the top of voters' concerns just before the pre-election survey, it is not surprising that the LDP was seen by most as the most capable, and we can only speculate that its grade might have been lower had COVID-19 still been voters' top priority. A more interesting result is that Ishin out-polled all other opposition parties even before the election.[17] We surmise that Ishin's governance record in Osaka (city and prefecture) attracted more voters searching for a competent alternative to the LDP than did any other opposition party (or even Kōmeitō). It is also striking that perceptions of Ishin's competence jumped after the election—most likely an artifact of its surprisingly strong showing. Surely, Ishin hopes that this is the start of a virtuous cycle, whereby electoral success both results from and then further enhances the party's reputation for competence.

CONCLUSION

Around the democratic world, some countries experienced partisan turnover in government in their "pandemic elections" while others renewed incumbent governments for another term. Japan's ruling coalition had overseen a relatively mild pandemic in comparison with most of its rich-world peers. And in a parliamentary system with a statutorily brief pre-election campaign period (only 12 days), the incumbents had the luxury of choosing the timing of the election before the constitutional end of the term.

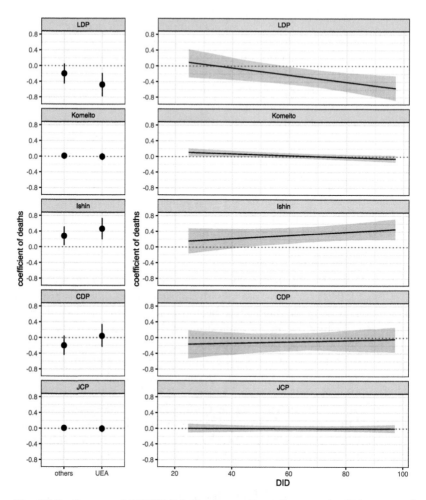

Fig. 15.8 Impact of COVID-19 Deaths on Party Support, by Urbanness of Prefecture (*Sources* For UEA: Kanemoto and Tokuoka 2002; For DID: s-Stat. *Population Census 2015*; For deaths, cases, and vaccine rollout: NHK. For electoral results: *The Asahi. Notes* The vertical axes show the regression coefficients for COVID-19 deaths per ten thousand population on the likelihood that a responded voted for a particular party, conditional on the urbanness of a respondent's home prefecture. The figures on the left measure urbanness as an indicator variable for location in one of the country's three largest "urban employment areas". The figures on the right measure urbanness as share of the prefectural population living in a Densely Inhabited District. Party abbreviations: LDP – Liberal Democratic Party; CDP – Constitutional Democratic Party of Japan; Kom – Kōmeitō; JCP – Japanese Communist Party; Ishin – Japan Ishin no Kai)

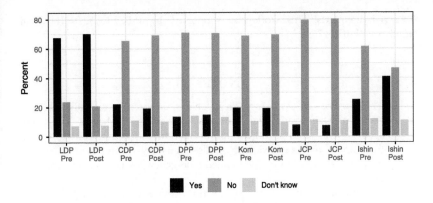

Fig. 15.9 Is Ishin the Most Credible Party after the LDP? (*Sources* Our own pre-election survey [N = 2025, October 20, 2021] and post-election survey [N = 3100, November 8, 2021] *Note* Percentage of respondents who answered "Yes" or "Somewhat" to the question "Is this party capable of governing?". Party abbreviations: LDP – Liberal Democratic Party; CDP – Constitutional Democratic Party of Japan; Kom – Kōmeitō; JCP – Japanese Communist Party; Ishin – Japan Ishin no Kai)

But the ruling coalition's best-laid plans for a post-Olympics election were pushed back by a full year—and a pandemic year at that. The Abe government's popularity had fallen by the time of his resignation in September 2020, and his successor Suga's approval ratings started high, but tumbled week after week. While the worries that the Olympics would become a super-spreader event proved too pessimistic, hopes of a polling boost were in vain.

The government postponed as long as they could, and their patience paid off. In the final few weeks before the election, COVID-19 deaths all but disappeared, vaccination rates finally caught up and surpassed those in other G-7 countries, and voters relegated the pandemic to third place among their priorities for government. COVID-19 wasn't irrelevant in Japan's election. Prefectures, particularly urban prefectures, that suffered higher death rates during the pandemic punished the LDP. But had the Diet's term expired a few months earlier, the outcome might have been quite different.

Acknowledgements This work was supported by JSPS KAKENHI Grant Number 19H01447.

NOTES

1. The *Varieties of Democracy Project* has monitored seven different categories of Democratic Violations since the pandemic began. They note such illiberal steps as official disinformation campaigns, restrictions on freedom of the press, violent or discriminatory enforcement of restrictions, the declaration of open-ended emergency powers. See Kolvani et al. 2021.
2. The literature on endogenous election timing sometimes refers to this game as "election surfing" (Kayser, 2005).
3. The 2017 General Election was held on October 22nd. Thus, the election should have been conducted before October 22, 2021. However, Article 31 of the Public Offices Election Act stipulates that an election can be postponed if the Diet session was opened within 31 days before the due date (31-(2)), and that the election must be held within 40 days after the Lower House is dissolved (31-(3)).
4. See Maeda Yukio, 2022, this volume for more on public opinion.
5. In one particularly poignant example of the trade-offs, the government recruited medical personnel to Tokyo to ensure the safety of the Olympic Village. This was not popular in those parts of the country obliged to donate their own local healthcare resources to protect foreign athletes in the metropolis (*The Asahi,* May 1, 2021, online edition).
6. Government decisions delayed the authorization of the various vaccines (Lipscy, 2022, this volume).
7. A *Nikkei*-TV Tokyo poll put his initial approval rating at 59% (Nikkei Asia 2021).
8. We conducted online surveys with respondents recruited by Yahoo! JAPAN Crowd Sourcing. The pre-election survey was conducted on Oct 20, and the post-election on Nov 8. The numbers of respondents were 2025 and 3100, respectively. Please note that these respondents participated in the survey to earn rewards (a small amount of cash points); the sample in each survey is not necessarily representative of the electorate.
9. Our pre-election survey shows the same pattern.
10. This is for two reasons. First, data related to COVID-19 are not available at the municipal or single-member-district level. Second, focusing on PR-tier contests provides more of an apples-to-apples comparison. All major parties nominate lists, and voters compare the same party platforms in all parts of the country. As seat allocation is proportional and lists are closed, voters have no reason not to vote sincerely. Single-member-district

elections, by contrast, vary more due to the characteristics of the individual candidates, strategic entry by parties, and strategic voting by voters (Cox 1997; Moser and Scheiner, 2012). PR vote shares are therefore a more reliable measure of party preferences in the electorate than SMD vote shares. Although the PR voting units are eleven regional blocks, we have access to prefectural-level party vote shares to match to our prefectural-level COVID-19 data.

11. Source: NHK. https://www3.nhk.or.jp/news/special/coronavirus/data/ (Last accessed: January 20, 2022). We also estimated all of the models below replacing COVID deaths with a measure of positive cases, but found no effects with the latter operationalization. We prefer deaths to cases as a measure tied to government performance for two reasons. First, it is probably a more accurate measure—deaths are much less likely to go un-reported than infections (which may be asymptomatic and hence go un-counted). Second, it seems plausible that citizens may not blame the government for the pandemic itself, but still hold it accountable for deaths—an indication of the efficacy of the healthcare system.

12. We also used a slightly different measure for the three largest *metropolitan areas* as defined by the Ministry of Internal Affairs and Communications. The results using this variable are similar to that with UEAs.

13. Source: s-Stat. *Population Census 2015.*

14. Kōmeitō and the LDP coordinated their district nominations, with Kōmeitō asking its supporters to vote for LDP in the PR tier in exchange for LDP voters supporting the Kōmeitō candidate in the district. We expect the *turnout* effect of a Kōmeitō SMD candidacy to be small, as the party is famous for its ability to mobilize its supporters no matter what (Klein and McLaughlin, 2022, this volume).

15. The full regression tables are available in the online appendix, where we show that our main result is robust to excluding some of the control variables.

16. While the inverse correlation between deaths and LDP vote share is probably not a coincidence, the causal mechanism linking the two is unclear. Was it simply that more voters in harder-hit areas turned against the LDP and voted for a different party or abstained? Or perhaps opposition parties were better able to recruit high-quality candidates in SMDs in such areas, which also boosted their PR vote shares? Interestingly, our surveys revealed no significant impact on vote choice of respondent's personal experience of COVID-19 or that of close family or friends, nor did those personal experiences significantly impact their policy priorities. See the online appendix for more detailed analysis.

17. All parties produced policy manifestos during the campaign, and could vary them by PR block. Notably, Ishin gave its COVID policies pride of place in its manifesto for the Kinki block (which includes Osaka),

but nowhere else. See the manifestos distributed by prefectural election boards. For instance, compare Tokyo (https://www.senkyo.metro.tokyo.lg.jp/uploads/R3syuin_hirei.pdf) and Osaka (https://www.pref.osaka.lg.jp/attach/42044/00409372/hirei_kouhou.pdf) [last accessed January 25, 2022].

REFERENCES

Asahi (The). 2021, May 1. "Medics Fuming at Request for 500 Nurses for Olympics" https://www.asahi.com/ajw/articles/14341415 (last accessed: January 25, 2022).

Cox, Gary W. 1997. *Making Votes Count; Strategic Coordination in the World's Electoral System*. New York: Cambridge University Press.

Gunia, Amy. 2021. "Japan's Prime Minister Yoshihide Suga Is Resigning. Here's What That Means." *Time*. 2021, September 3. https://time.com/6094995/japan-prime-minister-suga-resigns/ (last accessed: January 23, 2022.)

Japan Times (The). "LDP, Komeito Fail to Win Majority in Tokyo Assembly in Blow to Suga." *The Japan Times* July 5, 2021. https://www.japantimes.co.jp/news/2021/07/05/national/tokyo-assembly-election-2/ (last accessed: January 23, 2022).

Kanemoto, Yoshitsugu and Kazuyuki Tokuoka. 2002. "Proposal for the standards of metropolitan areas of Japan." *Journal of Applied Regional Science*, 7, 1–15.

Kayser, Mark A. 2005. "Who Surfs, Who Manipulates? The Determinants of Opportunistic Election Timing and Electorally Motivated Economic Intervention." *American Political Science Review*, 99(1), 17–27.

Klein, Axel, and Levi McLaughlin. 2022. "Kōmeitō in 2021: Strategizing between the LDP and Sōka Gakkai" In Pekkanen, Robert J., Steven R. Reed, and Daniel M. Smith, eds. *Japan Decides 2021: The Japanese General Election*.

Kolvani, Palina, Martin Lundstedt, Amanda B. Edgell, and Jean Lachapelle. 2021. "Pandemic Backsliding: A Year of Violations and Advances in Response to COVID-19. *V-Dem Institute* Policy Brief No 32, 6 July 2021. https://www.v-dem.net/media/publications/pb_32.pdf (last accessed: January 23, 2022).

Leheny, David. 2022. "The Olympics in the 2021 Election." In Pekkanen, Robert J., Steven R. Reed, and Daniel M. Smith, eds. *Japan Decides 2021: The Japanese General Election*.

Lipscy, Phillip Y. 2022. "Japan's Response to the COVID-19 Pandemic." In Pekkanen, Robert J., Steven R. Reed, and Daniel M. Smith, eds. *Japan Decides 2021: The Japanese General Election*.

Lukner, Kersten. 2022. "Covid-19: The International Dimension." In Pekkanen, Robert J., Steven R. Reed, and Daniel M. Smith, eds. *Japan Decides 2021: The Japanese General Election.*

Maeda, Ko. 2022a. "The 2021 Election Results: Continuity and Changes." In Pekkanen, Robert J., Steven R. Reed, and Daniel M. Smith, eds. *Japan Decides 2021: The Japanese General Election.*

Maeda, Yukio. 2022b. "Public Opinion and COVID-19." In Pekkanen, Robert J., Steven R. Reed, and Daniel M. Smith, eds. *Japan Decides 2021: The Japanese General Election.*

Mainichi (The). 2021, August 30. "Suga Cabinet's Support Rate Hits New Low of 26% as 70% Fear Medical Collapse: Poll." https://mainichi.jp/english/art icles/20210830/p2a/00m/0na/003000c (last accessed: January 25, 2022).

Moser, Robert G., and Ethan Scheiner. 2012. *Electoral Systems and Political Context: How the Effects of Rules Vary Across New and Established Democracies.* Cambridge University Press.

Nikkei Asia. 2021, October 5. "Kishida Approval Rating Starts at 59%, Below Abe and Suga: Nikkei Poll." *Nikkei Asia.* https://asia.nikkei.com/Politics/ Kishida-approval-rating-starts-at-59-below-Abe-and-Suga-Nikkei-poll (last accessed: January 25, 2022).

Pekkanen, Robert J. and Steven R. Reed. 2018. "Japanese Politics between 2014 and 2017: The Search for an Opposition Party in the Age of Abe." In Pekkanen, Robert, Steven R. Reed, Ethan Scheiner, and Daniel M. Smith, eds. *Japan Decides 2017: The Japanese General Election*, 15–28.

Reed, Steven R. Ethan Scheiner, Daniel M. Smith, and Michael F. Thies. 2013. "The 2012 Election Results: The LDP Wins Big by Default." In Pekkanen, Robert, Steven R. Reed, and Ethan Scheiner, eds. *Japan Decides 2012: The Japanese General Election*, 34–46.

Scheiner, Ethan, Daniel M. Smith, and Michael F. Thies. 2016 "The 2014 Japanese Election Results: The Opposition Cooperates but Fails to Inspire." In Pekkanen, Robert, Steven R. Reed, and Ethan Scheiner, eds. *Japan Decides 2014: The Japanese General Election*, 22–38.

DATA SOURCES

COVID deaths and cases - Source: NHK. https://www3.nhk.or.jp/news/spe cial/coronavirus/data/ (Last accessed: January 20, 2022)

Data for Figures 15.2, 15.3, 15.4: *Our World in Data* https://github. com/owid/covid-19-data/tree/master/public/data (last accessed: January 23, 2022).

DIDs: https://www.stat.go.jp/english/data/kokusei/index.html (last accessed: January 25, 2022).

Electoral results: *The Asahi*. https://www.asahi.com/senkyo/shuinsen/ (last accessed: January 25, 2022).

NHK cabinet support Polls: https://www.nhk.or.jp/senkyo/shijiritsu/ (last accessed: January 25, 2022).

Nikkei policy priorities: https://vdata.nikkei.com/newsgraphics/cabinet-approval-rating/ (last accessed: January 25, 2022).

PART III

The Issues: Domestic and International

CHAPTER 16

Japan's Response to the COVID-19 Pandemic

Phillip Y. Lipscy

I think the "Japan model" is about doing [COVID-19 response] in a democratic and liberal way.

—Nishimura Yasutoshi[1]

The coronavirus disease (COVID-19), caused by the severe acute respiratory syndrome coronavirus 2 (SARS-CoV-2), became a worldwide pandemic in 2019. The pandemic caused millions of tragic deaths worldwide, major economic and social disruptions, and calls for renewed cooperation to remedy shortcomings of global health governance.[2] Japan was affected relatively early on, attracting global media attention in February 2020 as the government of Abe Shinzō struggled to manage an outbreak on the Diamond Princess cruise ship. COVID-19 response

P. Y. Lipscy (✉)
Department of Political Science, Munk School of Global Affairs & Public Policy, University of Toronto, Toronto, ON, Canada
e-mail: phillip.lipscy@utoronto.ca

R. J. Pekkanen et al. (eds.), *Japan Decides 2021*, https://doi.org/10.1007/978-3-031-11324-6_16

239

dominated the remainder of Abe's tenure and that of his successor, Suga Yoshihide, who ruled from September 2020 to October 2021.

What features of Japan's COVID-19 response stand out, and how are they best explained? As illustrated by the opening quote, Japanese officials have promoted the "Japan model" as exemplary of how to manage the pandemic without sacrificing fundamental democratic values and civil liberties. Do these claims hold up to scrutiny? What impact did the pandemic and the government's response have on Japanese politics? How did the pandemic affect the outcome of the 2021 Lower House election, which saw the Liberal Democratic Party (LDP)-Kōmeitō coalition under the leadership of Prime Minister Kishida Fumio return to power, and did the Kishida government pursue a different approach?

This chapter proceeds as follows. First, I place Japan's COVID-19 response in cross-national context through comparison with other countries. Relative to other G7 countries, Japan stands out for relatively low cases and deaths per capita, but these numbers must be interpreted with caution due to residual uncertainties about factors such as the immunology of COVID-19. Next, I provide the political context for key characteristics of Japan's pandemic response, which generally avoided heavy-handed restrictions on civil liberties and emphasized technocratic measures designed by scientific experts. My central argument is that the Abe model of governance critically shaped both the strengths and weaknesses of the Japan model of COVID-19 response. Finally, I conclude with a discussion of Kishida's approach to COVID-19, which in its early months was suggestive of a somewhat different emphasis compared to Abe and Suga.

The Japanese COVID-19 Pandemic in Comparative Perspective

In this section, I present some basic data to place Japan's COVID-19 response in global, comparative perspective.[3] Figure 16.1 depicts cumulative confirmed COVID-19 deaths per million people for the G7 countries and several of Japan's regional peers. It is important to understand the limitations of COVID-19 statistics.[4] Autocratic countries like China have both the will and ability to manipulate these figures. Developing countries may lack the institutional capacity to accurately track cases and deaths. Figure 16.1 thus focuses on economically developed democracies (plus Singapore), which have both the capacity and levels of transparency that make it likely that the statistics reflect meaningful differences in outcomes albeit with some margin of uncertainty.

As the figure shows, Japan's low reported death count stands out compared to other G7 countries (Canada, France, Germany, Italy, the United Kingdom, the United States): Japan is the best performer according to this measure by a considerable margin. Although not depicted, the pattern is largely similar for reported cases. However, Japan's outcome measures are unexceptional compared to its regional peers, which have recorded comparable or lower cases and deaths. Japan had the highest level of reported deaths per capita among the depicted regional peers for much of 2021. The Omicron wave that started at the

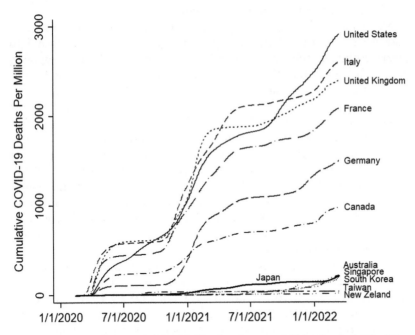

Fig. 16.1 Cumulative COVID-19 Deaths, January 2020–March 2022 (*Note* Compared to other G7 countries, Japan is characterized by an exceptionally low level of cumulative COVID-19 deaths per capita. However, Japan does not stand out compared to its regional peers. *Source* COVID-19 Data Repository, Center for Systems Science and Engineering [CSSE], Johns Hopkins University. Data as of March 13, 2022)

end of that year increased cumulative deaths in Australia, Singapore, and South Korea to a comparable level. This is useful context to consider when evaluating any merits of the Japanese approach to the pandemic.

Some scholars have argued that there are common themes that contributed to the favorable regional performance of East Asian countries, such as lessons learned from prior pandemics like SARS and MERS, effective institutional frameworks for pandemic response, social cohesion, and robust democratic institutions that allowed for proportional surveillance measures with transparency and accountability.[5] The validity of these claims will continue to be evaluated with greater nuance as new data and studies emerge—for example, strong social ties appear to be associated with low initial COVID-19 spread but higher case fatality rates once the disease is present within the community.[6]

Many variables that plausibly account for the strong performance of East Asian countries during the pandemic apply in equal measure to Japan. Although this chapter will focus primarily on Japan's response, it must be noted that the verdict remains out on whether it is best to speak of a unique "Japan model" or a broader "East Asian model" of COVID-19 response. Furthermore, it is possible that the virulence of the pandemic in the region was less severe due to yet unknown non-political and non-societal factors. For example, recent research suggests that there may be immunological differences between Japanese (and plausibly East Asian) populations and those in the West, which made it more difficult for SARS-CoV-2 to spread.[7] We cannot dismiss the possibility that better outcomes in Japan and among its neighbors—along with the option to manage the pandemic with relatively lax restrictions—will ultimately be attributed to confronting a less serious pandemic for reasons outside the realm of government policymaking.

One outcome measure that is less subject to such uncertainties is vaccinations, which can be measured directly with less concern about potential confounders. Figure 16.2 presents data on COVID-19 vaccine doses administered per capita. Japan was relatively late in getting its vaccination campaign off the ground, hindered by supply problems and bureaucratic hurdles: for example, the Ministry of Health, Labor and Welfare allegedly caused several months of delay by insisting on conducting randomized control trials not only on Japanese citizens, but also on Japanese soil.[8] This delay contributed to widespread concern over the Tokyo Olympics, which took place when only a small fraction of the Japanese public was immunized.[9] However, the pace of vaccinations picked up in the summer of 2021. By that fall, Japan's share of "fully vaccinated" people—defined as two doses at the time—climbed to the top of G7 countries and a level comparable to regional peers. This suggests Japan's vaccination challenges were more about procurement and distribution rather than vaccine-hesitancy among the population. Furthermore, Japan was late in rolling out booster shots, which meant the country remained a relative laggard in terms of total doses administered amidst the Omicron wave in late 2022, which highlighted the necessity of a third dose for adequate protection.

In terms of economic response, Japan appears to have been relatively successful in cushioning the short-term shock created by the pandemic.

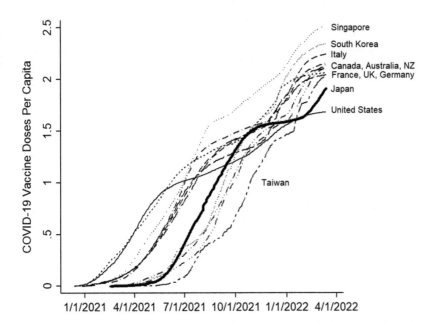

Fig. 16.2 COVID-19 Vaccine Doses Administered per Capita (*Note* Japan's vaccination campaign was slow in getting off the ground compared to other G7 countries, though it was ahead of some regional peers like Taiwan, which faced serious procurement challenges. The rollout of booster shots in Japan was also slow, leaving the country only ahead of the United States by early 2022 in doses administered per capita. *Source* Our World in Data [https://ourworldindata.org/explorers/coronavirus-data-explorer], accessed March 14, 2022)

The Japanese government responded to the pandemic with relatively large fiscal stimulus measures, and this was complemented by emergency monetary measures by the Bank of Japan, which had already adopted exceptionally loose policy under Abenomics.[10] The government explicitly prioritized the protection of employment and businesses in its economic response, and this objective was largely achieved.[11] Although Japanese GDP declined during the height of the pandemic, the recession was relatively mild compared to other major economies, and as Fig. 16.3 shows, the unemployment rate was maintained at an exceptionally low level. Corporate bankruptcies also held steady at pre-pandemic levels. The Japanese government thus saw its fiscal position deteriorate significantly during the pandemic, but domestic economic disruption was relatively modest in cross-national comparison.

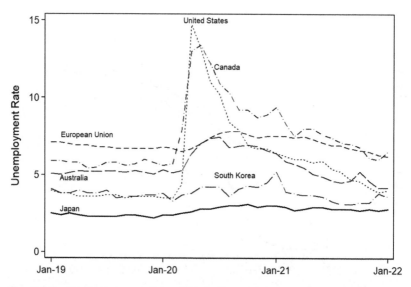

Fig. 16.3 Unemployment Rate (%), Before and During the Pandemic (*Note* Japan entered the pandemic with a relatively low unemployment rate, and the onset of the pandemic in January 2020 did not result in a noticeable increase. *Source* OECD [2022], Unemployment rate [indicator]. https://doi.org/10.1787/52570002-en [accessed March 14, 2022])

The Abe Model and the Japan Model of COVID-19 Response

As I have argued elsewhere, the second Abe Shinzō government (2012–2020) ruled Japan using a deliberate strategy that sought to take advantage of Japan's new electoral and administrative institutions.[12] His successor, Suga Yoshihide (2020–2021), was Chief Cabinet Secretary during the entire Abe government and one of the architects of this strategy. These two prime ministers oversaw Japan's COVID response from the beginning of the pandemic through October 2021, when Kishida Fumio replaced Suga as prime minister and led the LDP to a Lower House election victory. The Japan model of COVID response was thus critically shaped by the Abe model of governance.

The Abe model had three key components. First, Abe and Suga sought to manage public opinion and retain a high level of public support for the prime minister. The Abenomics reforms played a key role in this strategy—reformist economic messaging was seen as the key to maintaining broad public support, and the Abe government strategically pivoted to Abenomics growth themes when the prime minister's popularity began to wane. Public opinion was also managed through an aggressive media strategy, which restricted and controlled access to government officials, reduced opportunities for the prime minister to be questioned directly, shaped social media discourse through targeted activities by LDP supporters, and pressured critical voices by invoking the Broadcast Law and Radio Law.[13]

Second, the Abe model sought to maintain party discipline, an issue that had bedeviled both prior LDP and DPJ governments.[14] Discipline was promoted through practical reforms, such as appointments of the prime minister's close confidants to the Diet Affairs Committee and frequent coordination meetings. However, perhaps the most crucial element in maintaining party discipline under Abe was the credible threat of calling a snap Lower House election. The threat was made credible through two successful elections in 2014 and 2017. The former was particularly critical in silencing internal dissent over Abe's proposal to postpone a consumption tax hike, which Abe and Suga feared might precipitate an internal political contest and a direct challenge to the prime minister. The credible threat of snap elections was supported by the prime minister's relatively robust public support and a weak and divided opposition, which made an election loss relatively unlikely.

Third, the Abe government built on prior institutional reforms that had shifted power from the bureaucracy to the prime minister.[15] Through the creation of institutions like the Cabinet Bureau of Personnel Affairs and Japan's first National Security Council, and further expansion of the Cabinet Office, the Abe government further centralized power and solidified political control over the bureaucracy. Combined with various practical reforms and symbolic personnel decisions, this made it difficult for bureaucrats to resist or stymie policy priorities promoted by the prime minister.

It is a matter of debate whether the Abe model contributed to the longevity of the Abe government or whether other factors, like the relative absence of major crises or opposition weakness, were more important.[16] Nonetheless, the Abe Model is important context in understanding how Japan responded to COVID-19. The pandemic ultimately exposed important limitations of the Abe model and illustrated some distinctions between governing under normal circumstances and during a major crisis.[17]

The pandemic exposed the limitations of using Abenomics as a strategy to manage the prime minister's popularity. Before the pandemic, when faced with declining public approval, the Abe government had quickly pivoted to macroeconomic growth themes. Abe himself saw Abenomics as the key source of his popularity, which enabled the passage of controversial legislation in domains like security and secrecy.[18] However, the COVID-19 pandemic necessitated a trade-off between public health and macroeconomic performance that the government had not faced prior to 2020.

Both the Abe and Suga governments struggled to manage this transition. Implementing harsh lockdown measures or providing financial incentives to close businesses would have sacrificed the macroeconomic achievements of Abenomics, which the government routinely touted as core achievements.[19] As their public approval ratings declined amidst questions about their handling of the pandemic, both Abe and Suga stuck to their playbook by promoting macroeconomic measures like the "Go To" travel campaign, which subsidized domestic travel but likely contributed to a counterproductive increase in COVID-19 cases.[20] Although government officials publicly framed the Japan Model in normative terms, emphasizing universalistic values like civil liberties and democracy, the approach was also fundamentally aligned with the prioritization of macroeconomic growth under Abenomics.

The pandemic also diminished both prime ministers' authority vis-à-vis party backbenchers. As discussed above, the threat of calling a snap election was a key mechanism for maintaining party discipline under the Abe model. However, the credibility of this threat diminished as the virus spread and public approval of the government sagged. Suga perhaps had a brief window of opportunity to take advantage of high approval ratings after assuming power in the fall of 2020—circumstances that resembled those of Kishida's victory in 2021—but he chose not to call an election. The diminishing authority of the prime minister strengthened the role of alternative power brokers within the party like LDP Secretary General Nikai Toshihiro, and government decision-making increasingly became subject to internal contestation and perceived indecision. The "light touch" that characterized government intervention under the Japan model could be attributed in part to policy paralysis as the pandemic undermined one of the core pillars of the Abe model.

The pandemic also revealed a key shortcoming of the centralization of power that Abe and Suga had leveraged and deepened—it did not extend to the local level, which emerged as critical for pandemic response in areas like testing and the management of business closures.[21] Japanese local governments retain considerable autonomy in spite of increasing prime minister authority at the central level.[22] During the pandemic, this gave governors like Koike Yuriko (Tokyo) and Yoshimura Hirofumi (Osaka) an effective platform to challenge central government policy. The central government also struggled to coordinate and manage local responses, which magnified perceptions of incompetence.

Finally, Abe and Suga lost control of the media narrative, which they had carefully managed and cultivated through a variety of tactics prior to the pandemic. The Japan model placed scientific experts like Omi Shigeru and Oshitani Hitoshi front and center. These experts designed key elements that defined Japan's response, such as avoidance of the 3Cs (closed spaces, close-contact settings, and large crowds), emphasis on clusters, and retroactive contact tracing. The early emphasis on masks and risks of aerosol transmission appeared prescient in retrospect. Despite its virtues, this technocratic response—combined with the Abe model's emphasis on limiting media access to the prime minister—may have conveyed the impression that the nation's political leadership was aloof and absent during a major crisis.

The pandemic dominated the media and public discourse after March 2020, and coverage was often critical of the government's response.

Figure 16.4 compares COVID-19 deaths per capita and change in leader approval rating between January and June 2020 for several countries. The figure is suggestive of some relationship between early pandemic intensity and leader public approval—Scott Morrison of Australia enjoyed a large bump in approval as the pandemic was contained, while Boris Johnson of the UK saw his approval slide along with mounting deaths. However, it is striking that Abe's public approval declined during the pandemic despite cases and deaths in Japan remaining at a relatively low level. This was not due to a ceiling effect—the Morning Consult poll depicted in the figure put Abe's approval rating in January 2020 at 34%, a level almost identical to Scott Morrison, who enjoyed a large subsequent boost.

Figure 16.5 depicts search interest in the term コロナ (Corona) in Japan according to Google Trends since the beginning of the pandemic. The figure clearly captures the six COVID-19 waves Japan experienced, but it is also notable that interest was most intense in early 2020: this was

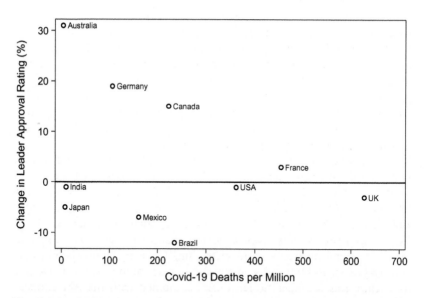

Fig. 16.4 COVID-19 Deaths and Change in Leader Approval, January–June 2020 (*Note* Limiting recorded COVID-19 deaths has not automatically translated into higher approval ratings for leaders. *Source* Morning Consult and European Centre for Disease Prevention and Control)

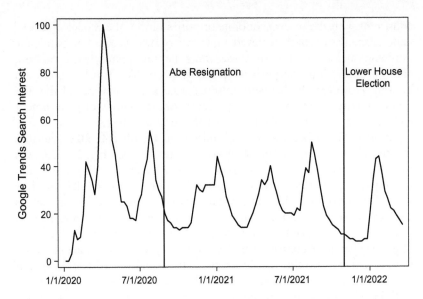

Fig. 16.5 Search Interest in コロナ (Corona) in Japan, Google Trends (*Note* The figure depicts search interest according to Google Trends for the term "コロナ" in Japan. The term is the conventional way COVID-19 has been described by the Japanese media and government [e.g., 新型コロナ・コロナウイルス]. The vertical lines indicate the dates of Abe's resignation announcement and 2021 Lower House Election)

a period in which Japan's case and death numbers remained low in international comparison and relative to subsequent waves. Abe's sharp and terminal decline in public approval thus coincided with a period of intense public scrutiny about the government's COVID-19 response. Concern about the pandemic declined from this peak but resurfaced during each wave under the Suga government.

THE 2021 ELECTION AND THE KISHIDA GOVERNMENT

The Japan model imposed relatively few restrictions on civil liberties and economic activity while seeking to control the COVID-19 pandemic through measures guided by scientific expertise. Its emphasis on maintaining economic activity by limiting government intervention was largely consistent with the macroeconomic priorities of the Abe model of governance. Japan's approach achieved a measure of success based on pandemic outcome measures, though these must be interpreted with caution, and Japan did not outperform regional peers like South Korea and Taiwan. However, the pandemic also exposed key weaknesses of the Abe model, contributing to real and perceived shortcomings of government leadership along with challenges from the local level.

Kishida Fumio became prime minister on October 4, 2021, and he secured a convincing victory only weeks later on October 31. There is thus little to examine specifically about Kishida's COVID-19 response and the impact it might have had on Japan's 49th Lower House election. It is notable, however, the election coincided with a trough in cases and deaths after the fifth wave and a decline in public interest to the lowest levels since the beginning of the pandemic, as illustrated in Fig. 16.5.[23] Kishida ultimately had little control over election timing, which was the first under the current constitution to occur after the expiration of the House of Representative's full four-year term. Thus, it stands to reason that the LDP benefited from remarkably good fortune when it mattered the most. Election exit polls generally suggested that the pandemic had receded in importance compared to economic and employment issues, where Japan's response had been relatively successful as discussed above.[24]

An interesting question is whether the ascendance of Kishida signaled a shift in Japan's approach to the pandemic. One of the first consequential acts of the Kishida government was the closure of Japanese borders to new foreign entrants in response to the Omicron variant, along with all classes of non-Japanese citizens from several African countries. Although the Abe and Suga governments had also imposed border restrictions, they had done so with considerable reluctance due to concerns about diplomatic relations, economic consequences, and the potential impact on the Olympics. Attracting high-skilled foreign talent and encouraging inbound tourism were important priorities under Abenomics, and border closures contradicted the principles of the Free and Open Indo-Pacific, Japan's signature foreign policy vision.

In contrast, Kishida's border closure was quick and decisive. The decision was supported by an extraordinarily large majority of the public and appeared to boost Kishida's public approval rating.[25] His government even briefly shut down reentry for Japanese citizens by requesting airlines to cease reservations, though this was quickly reversed and blamed on overzealous bureaucrats amidst widespread questions about constitutionality.[26] In its early months, Kishida's government thus appeared to represent a subtle shift away from the Japan model, placing greater emphasis on pandemic control relative to protection of civil liberties and economic activity, at least as it pertained to overseas travel and particularly by foreigners.

By early 2022, the Kishida government's border closure measures were met with significant pushback from stakeholders in the academic, policy, and the business community, including several public letters calling for relaxation.[27] Activism by these groups, as well as the plight of students who were denied entry despite being admitted to Japanese universities, received considerable attention in both mainstream and social media. This might have played some role in shifting public perception toward the measures: by March 2022, 62% of the public was in support of relaxing the border closure at least to some degree.[28] The Kishida government initiated a gradual reopening in February 2022, with an early prioritization of student entries.

It is notable that Kishida criticized Abenomics as he rose to power, arguing that the reforms had mostly benefited the privileged and failed to contribute to broad-based growth. Although Kishida's policy rhetoric was characteristically understated, this prioritization of "ordinary" citizens at the expense of foreigners and societal elites arguably represented a subtle shift in the direction of populism. The two prime ministers who previously achieved longevity under Japan's new political institutions—Koizumi and Abe—had sought popular appeal by emphasizing reformist themes. At the time of writing, it remained to be seen whether Kishida's early popularity signified the durable success of an alternative, quasi-populist strategy or a temporary bump often associated with the early months of a new Japanese prime minister.

NOTES

1. Nishimura was Minister in charge of economic revitalization and measures for the novel coronavirus pandemic during early phases of the pandemic. The quote is from The Independent Investigation Commission on the Japanese Government's Response to COVID-19 2020.
2. Takuma 2020, Johnson 2020, Fazal 2020. Also see the Lukner Chapter, this volume (Lukner, 2022).
3. An excellent and extensive overview on this topic is available in Asia Pacific Initiative 2020.

4. e.g., Lipscy 2020a, 2020b.
5. An and Tang 2020, Tiberghien 2021, Greitens 2020.
6. Fraser and Aldrich 2021.
7. Shimizu et al. 2021.
8. Kanako Takahara, "Japan prioritized domestic trials of Pfizer before rollout, vaccine czar says," *Japan Times*, 9/8/2021, https://www.japantimes.co.jp/news/2021/09/08/national/taro-kono-vaccine-domestic-trials/.
9. See Leheny chapter, this volume (Leheny, 2022).
10. IMF Fiscal Affairs Department 2021.
11. Asia Pacific Initiative 2020, 56.
12. Hoshi and Lipscy 2021.
13. Kingston 2016.
14. Reed, McElwain and Shimizu 2009, Kushida and Lipscy 2013.
15. Takenaka 2019.
16. Maeda and Reed 2021.
17. Lipscy 2020a, 2020b.
18. Interview of Abe in Oshita 2017, pp. 13–14.
19. For example, statistics on measures like GDP, unemployment, and corporate profits were updated regularly at government websites like https://www.kantei.go.jp/jp/headline/seichosenryaku/sanbonnoya.html and https://www.japan.go.jp/abenomics/index.html.
20. Anzai and Nishiura 2021.
21. Takenaka 2020.
22. Horiuchi 2009.
23. Also see the Thies and Yanai chapter in this volume for a detailed analysis (Thies and Yanai, 2022).
24. e.g.,　景気・雇用、コロナ対策を重視　　投票先の選択で—出口調査https://www.jiji.com/jc/article?k=2021103100830&g=pol.
25. オミクロン株の水際対策「評価」89%、スピード感に肯定的受け止め…読売世論調査　　https://www.yomiuri.co.jp/election/yoron-chosa/20211206-OYT1T50000/.
26. "国交省、独断で予約停止要請　　「スピード重視」も即撤回の背景は," *Mainichi*, 12/2/2021.　https://mainichi.jp/articles/20211202/k00/00m/010/407000c.
27. Among others, see "U.S.-Japan Community Urges Government of Japan to Relax Border Closure" by researchers, academics, government officials, and others involved in US-Japan relations (researchers, academics, government officials and others, accessed March 15, 2022); "Joint Statement on Entry Restrictions in Japan" by the American Chamber of Commerce in Japan, European Business Council in Japan, and International Bankers Association of Japan (https://accj.squarespace.com/s/220203-Joint-Statement-on-the-Entry-Restrictions.pdf; accessed March 15, 2022).

28. NHK, "内閣支持53%、不支持25%(NHK世論調査)," March 14, 2022, https://www.nhk.or.jp/senkyo/shijiritsu/ (accessed March 15, 2022).

REFERENCES

An, Brian Y. and Shui-Yan Tang. 2020. Lessons from Covid-19 Responses in East Asia: Institutional Infrastructure and Enduring Policy Instruments. *The American Review of Public Administration* 50(6–7): 790–800.

Anzai, Asami and Hiroshi Nishiura. 2021. "Go to Travel" Campaign and Travel-Associated Coronavirus Disease 2019 Cases: A Descriptive Analysis, July–August 2020. *Journal of Clinical Medicine* 10(3): 398.

Asia Pacific Initiative. 2020. *Shingata Corona Taio Minkan Rinji Chosakai.* Tokyo, Japan: Discover 21.

Fazal, Tanisha M. 2020. Health Diplomacy in Pandemical Times. *International Organization* 74(S1): E78–E97.

Fraser, Timothy and Daniel P. Aldrich. 2021. The Dual Effect of Social Ties on Covid-19 Spread in Japan. *Scientific Reports* 11(1): 1596.

Greitens, Sheena Chestnut. 2020. Surveillance, Security, and Liberal Democracy in the Post-Covid World. *International Organization* 74(S1): E169–E90.

Horiuchi, Yusaku. 2009. Understanding Japanese Politics from a Local Perspective. *International Political Science Review* 30(5): 565–573.

Hoshi, Takeo and Phillip Y. Lipscy, eds. 2021. *The Political Economy of the Abe Government and Abenomics Reforms.* New York: Cambridge University Press.

IMF Fiscal Affairs Department. 2021. Fiscal Monitor Database of Country Fiscal Measures in Response to the Covid-19 Pandemic. Available from https://www.imf.org/en/Topics/imf-and-covid19/Fiscal-Policies-Database-in-Response-to-COVID-19. (Accessed December 19, 2021).

Johnson, Tana. 2020. Ordinary Patterns in an Extraordinary Crisis: How International Relations Makes Sense of the Covid-19 Pandemic. *International Organization* 74(S1): E148–E68.

Kingston, Jeff. 2016. *Press Freedom in Contemporary Japan.* United Kingdom: Taylor & Francis.

Kushida, Kenji E. and Phillip Y. Lipscy. 2013. *Japan under the DPJ: The Politics of Transition and Governance.* Stanford, CA: Brookings Institution / Shorenstein APARC.

Leheny, David. 2022. "The Olympics in the 2021 Election." In Robert J. Pekkanen, Steven R. Reed and Daniel M. Smith, (Eds.), *Japan Decides 2021: The Japanese General Election.* New York: Palgrave Macmillan.

Lipscy, Phillip Y. 2020a. Covid-19 and the Politics of Crisis. *International Organization* 74(S1): E98–E127.

Lipscy, Phillip Y. 2020b. It's Too Soon to Call Coronavirus Winners and Losers: Given How Much Remains Unknown About the Virus, Talk of Success May Be Premature. *Foreign Policy* MAY 12.

Lukner, Kerstin. 2022. "COVID-19: The International Dimension." In Robert J. Pekkanen, Steven R. Reed and Daniel M. Smith, (Eds.), *Japan Decides 2021: The Japanese General Election.* New York: Palgrave Macmillan.

Maeda, Yukio and Steven R. Reed. 2021. The LDP under Abe. In *The Political Economy of the Abe Government and Abenomics Reforms,* edited by Phillip Y. Lipscy and Takeo Hoshi, 87–108. Cambridge: Cambridge University Press.

Oshita, Eiji. 2017. *Abe Kantei "Kenryoku" No Shotai.* Tokyo, Japan: Kadokawa.

Reed, Steven R., Kenneth Mori McElwain and Kay Shimizu. 2009. *Political Change in Japan: Electoral Behavior, Party Realignment, and the Koizumi Reforms.* Stanford: Shorenstein APARC.

Shimizu, Kanako, Tomonori Iyoda, An Sanpei, Hiroshi Nakazato, Masahiro Okada, Shogo Ueda, Miyuki Kato-Murayama, Kazutaka Murayama, Mikako Shirouzu, Naoko Harada, Michihiro Hidaka and Shin-ichiro Fujii. 2021. Identification of Tcr Repertoires in Functionally Competent Cytotoxic T Cells Cross-Reactive to Sars-Cov-2. *Communications Biology* 4(1): 1365.

Takenaka, Harukata. 2020. *Corona Kiki No Seiji - Abe Seiken Vs. Chiji.* Tokyo, Japan: Chuko Shinsho.

Takenaka, Harukata. 2019. Expansion of the Prime Minister's Power in the Japanese Parliamentary System: Transformation of Japanese Politics and Institutional Reforms. *Asian Survey* 59(5): 844–869.

Takuma, Kayo. 2020. Global Solidarity Is Necessary to End the Covid-19 Pandemic. *Asia-Pacific Review* 27(2): 46–56.

The Independent Investigation Commission on the Japanese Government's Response to COVID-19. 2020. Special Interview: Yasutoshi Nishimura Minister in Charge of the Response to Covid-19 (Economy Revitalization Minister). Tokyo, Japan: Asia Pacific Initiative.

Thies, Michael F. and Yuki Yanai. 2022. "Did COVID-19 Affect Japan's 2021 General Election?" In Robert J. Pekkanen, Steven R. Reed and Daniel M. Smith, (Eds.), *Japan Decides 2021: The Japanese General Election.* New York: Palgrave Macmillan.

Tiberghien, Yves. 2021. *The East Asian Covid-19 Paradox.* Cambridge: Cambridge University Press.

CHAPTER 17

Economic Policy Trilemma: Macroeconomic Politics in the 2021 Election

Kenya Amano⊙ *and Saori N. Katada*⊙

Japan's Lower House Election on October 31, 2021, came at the heels of 18-month massive COVID-19 stimulus measures where the Liberal Democratic Party (LDP) was judged based on the effectiveness of these measures and future economic plans. Opposition parties criticized the failures of the LDP economic policies, not only against the ongoing COVID responses but also the detrimental impacts of Abenomics of the last nine years. In the end, the LDP-Kōmeitō coalition won and kept the majority in the Lower House, but ongoing massive stimulus appeared to contribute little to the long-term growth of Japan's economy.

K. Amano (✉)
Department of Political Science, University of Washington, Seattle, Washington, USA
e-mail: kamano@uw.edu

S. N. Katada
Department of Political Science and International Relations, University of Southern California, Los Angeles, California, USA

© The Author(s), under exclusive license to Springer Nature Switzerland AG 2023
R. J. Pekkanen et al. (eds.), *Japan Decides 2021*,
https://doi.org/10.1007/978-3-031-11324-6_17

While Abenomics contributed to low unemployment, ascending stock prices, and relatively robust economic growth prior to the pandemic, its measures constrained the Japanese government facing the COVID-induced economic crisis. On the one hand, its signature first arrow known as "bold monetary policy" has exhausted monetary measures to stimulate the economy. On the other hand, despite Japan's prolonged primary balance deficit and significantly high level of public debt, low interest rate on government bonds maintained by the Bank of Japan (BOJ) has opened the possibility of fiscal expansion. Consequently, fiscal stimulus, the second arrow, has become the main measure in response to the COVID-19 pandemic during the fiscal year 2020 (April 2020–March 2021). As such, the Abe and Suga administrations implemented massive fiscal stimulus, totaling ¥76.8 trillion, as they promised to revitalize the Japan's post-pandemic economy.

How did the COVID-19 stimulus and economic challenges shape the LDP's economic policies and electoral strategy? There are two major revelations. First, while the size of the direct payments to households and small businesses was unprecedented, a closer examination of the fiscal packages suggests that the fiscal target shifted toward the end of the fiscal year to indirect subsidies to local governments and the LDP's client businesses such as construction and tourism. Second, despite Prime Minister Kishida Fumio's new economic plan under the slogan of "New Form of Capitalism," where economic growth and redistribution go hand-in-hand (on the selection of Kishida, see Nemoto, 2022, and Harris, 2022), its distributive tone had to be paired with the traditional growth strategy with the focus on supply-side at the time of the Lower House Election. Therefore, we argue that the LDP's economic policies have straddled between distribution and traditional supply-side growth strategies in the face of the 2021 Lower House Election without loosening the current fiscal discipline.[1]

How did such strategy, in turn, affect the opposition parties' strategic choice of the economic policy, and the election outcome? We claim that this straddling strategy pursued by the LDP-Kōmeitō coalition exploited the policy spaces for the opposition parties, which led to positive electoral outcome for the LDP. Given the condition where the LDP-Kōmeitō coalition has already encompassed the distributive policies and conventional growth strategy relying on existing industries, the only alternative way to calm people's distress and gain voter support was to conduct further fiscal stimulus in the form of hand-outs spending. Thus, the policy choice left for the opposition parties was either transferring resources from the rich and established industries to the poor by imposing progressive taxes—"redistributional (*saibunpai*)" policy—or compromising on the fiscal discipline by public debt expansion.

We call this struggle a trilemma of economic policy among Japan's conventional growth strategy, distribution, and fiscal discipline. The trilemma is more applicable when the monetary policy space is limited after the massive policy actions through Abenomics. This very monetary policy, nonetheless, paved the way for fiscal expansion, which was further stretched by the pandemic responses. The Constitutional Democratic Party (CDP) and the Japanese Communist Party (JCP) coalition pursued the fiscal discipline and distributive policy, whereas other parties including the Democratic Party for the People (DPP), Ishin, and Reiwa, promoted both distribution and growth strategies by loosening fiscal discipline through massive corporate tax cuts and issuance of new government bonds. As the 2021 election outcome would reveal, the strategic choice by the CDP-JCP coalition failed to gain support from a wide range of voters.

This chapter proceeds by first reviewing the Japanese government's economic policy responses to the COVID-19 pandemic. We then assess Prime Minister Kishida's New Form of Capitalism. Following the assessment, we examine the trilemma of economic policy that the opposition parties faced and how the trilemma helped the LDP-Kōmeitō coalition achieve their victory in the 2021 General Election and allowed a few smaller parties to gain grounds. The last section concludes with the implication of the LDP's winning economic strategy on Japan's long-term growth.

ECONOMIC POLICY RESPONSE
TO THE COVID-19 PANDEMIC

Prime Minister Abe Shinzō's economic growth strategy, dubbed as Abenomics implemented since late 2012, has shaped Japan's choice of economic policy response to the COVID-19 pandemic that started in early 2020. Abenomics' first arrow, massive monetary policy, was the most impactful macroeconomic policy (Park 2021; Park et al. 2018). This aggressive monetary policy under Governor Kuroda Haruhiko of the BOJ appointed by Prime Minister Abe in March 2013 has continued for eight years with the aim to reach the 2% inflation target. Since this target was never achieved, in the process, the BOJ has exhausted almost all the possible monetary policy options to stimulate the economy even before the COVID-19 struck Japan. The short-term call rate set by the BOJ was already in the negative territory from January 2016, and with the massive "qualitative and quantitative easing" (*ijigen no kinyū kanwa*), the BOJ held almost half of the outstanding Japanese Government Bonds (JGBs). The monetary policy had changed little since the introduction of the yield curve control policy (YCC) in September 2016, as the YCC allows the BOJ to focus on the long-term interest rate by maintaining the rate at around zero percent. Thus, the BOJ has not conducted the level of bond buying as their policy target, and the pace of buying bonds has slowed. Moreover, the level of asset purchase programs other than the JGB had already been high. For instance, the BOJ committed to purchasing Exchange Traded Funds (ETFs) at annual paces of about ¥6 trillion despite concerns that the ETF purchase deteriorates the corporate governance.[2]

Facing the pandemic, therefore, the BOJ's response has been limited to minor adjustments. In March and April 2020, under the stock market jitters and as the initial response to the pandemic, the BOJ increased the maximum amount of additional purchases of Commercial Papers, corporate bonds, ETFs, and Japan Real Estate Investment Trusts (J-REITs). The BOJ also facilitated new funds-supplying operations to support corporate financing through bank lending.[3] These measures were incremental compared to the policy actions that the BOJ had implemented in the last several years. Despite the limited monetary policy space, the BOJ's YCC with its large asset purchase has greatly contributed to widening fiscal space for the government by deliberately depressing the cost of government's borrowing (Buiter 2021).

As a result, the main task of stimulating the Japanese economy under the pandemic has fallen in the realm of fiscal policy, and the Japanese government implemented massive fiscal measures to respond to the crisis. The analysis of the budget and its implementation leads to three observations. First, there has been a massive demand for a fiscal stimulus under the pandemic despite Japan's dire fiscal health being exacerbated during the last 30 years under the country's stagnant economy. Second, there was a clear shift in the fiscal stimulus measures over the course of early 2020 to 2021 from direct payments toward households and small businesses to conventional supply-side growth strategy of industrial subsidies and public infrastructure investments. Third, despite massive budget commitment, the execution rate of these stimulus measures shows not only the concerns for absorption capacity of the Japanese economy but also electoral motivation behind such allocation.

The fiscal responses to the COVID-19 pandemic came in three stages (Table 17.1).[4] The initial response during fiscal year 2019 (February and March 2020) focused on infection control and healthcare provision. The initial policy action was quite urgent because of the outbreak of the COVID-19 on a cruise ship, Diamond Princess, in late January 2020, and the evacuation of Japanese nationals from Wuhan by the government-chartered aircrafts. Infectious controls, the PCR test, and healthcare system preparedness was urgently established (Takenaka 2020). Because there was no time to approve an additional budget at the Diet at that point, the amount of the expenditure was limited. On February 13, 2020, nonetheless, the Japanese government announced the Novel Coronavirus Disease (COVID-19) Emergency Response Package totaling ¥15.3 billion followed by the second package announced on March 10, which amounted to ¥430.8 billion. The second and third column of Table 17.1 shows the detailed expenditure by each category.[5]

Following the first stage, the government introduced two supplementary budgets to support households and businesses in the first quarter of the fiscal year 2020. In the first, supplementary budget passed the Diet in April 2020. The largest expenditure category, consisting of half of this first fiscal package, was "support for households" for ¥13 trillion, was mostly dedicated to the Special Cash Payments Program that credits ¥100,000 to each registered resident in Japan. The second largest category in the budget was "support for firms and workers" (35% of this supplementary budget). The largest expenditure item under this category was financial support for small and medium enterprises (SMEs). This category also included the expansion of the existing Employment Adjustment Subsidies and the Labor Insurance Special Account. Likewise, the second supplementary budget of approximately ¥32 trillion, larger than the first one, was passed on June 12. The largest component of this supplementary budget was "support for firms and workers," which was almost double the amount of the first supplementary budget. In this category, the budget was allocated to expand loan programs for firms, to establish a new rent support grant for SMEs, and to expand the Subsidy Program for Sustaining Businesses in support of SMEs established in the first supplementary budget. Overall, the economic packages doled out in the first quarter of the fiscal year 2020 aimed mainly at supporting

Table 17.1 Japanese Government's COVID-19 Fiscal Measures 2020–21 (billion yen)

Expenditure category	First Stage		Second Stage		Third Stage
	First EmergencyResponse FY 2019	Second Emergency Response FY 2019	First Supplementary Budget FY 2020	Second Supplementary Budget FY 2020	Third Supplementary Budget FY 2020
Infection control & Health and long-term care	7.8	46	758	2,784	2,519
	51.2%	10.6%	3.0%	8.7%	13.1%
RD for test kits, drugs, vaccines, etc	2.1	3	52	206	161
	13.5%	0.6%	0.2%	0.6%	0.8%
Support for households	–	21	13,046	341	434
		4.8%	50.8%	1.1%	2.3%
Support for workers and firms	0.6	276	8,981	16,231	7,769
	3.9%	64.1%	35.0%	50.9%	40.5%
Support for educational institutions	–	68	229	124	120
		15.8%	0.9%	0.4%	0.6%
Special grants to local governments	–	–	1,000	2,000	1,500
			3.9%	6.3%	7.8%
Others	4.8	17	126	226	6,674
	31.4%	4.0%	0.5%	0.7%	34.8%
Contingency funds	–	–	1,500	10,000	–
			5.8%	31.3%	

(continued)

Table 17.1   (continued)

Expenditure category	First Stage		Second Stage		Third Stage
	First Emergency Response FY 2019	Second Emergency Response FY 2019	First Supplementary Budget FY 2020	Second Supplementary Budget FY 2020	Third Supplementary Budget FY 2020
Total	15.3	431	25,691	31,911	19,176
	100.0%	*100.0%*	*100.0%*	*100.0%*	*100.0%*
Share of Annual Reg. Budget	0.0%	0.4%	25.5%	31.6%	19.0%
Date of Diet Approval	Feb 13, 2020	Mar 10, 2020	Apr 27, 2020	June 12, 2020	Jan 28, 2021

Notes Share of each policy package in italic. The numbers are aggregated by the authors following the categories by Ando et al. (2020)
Sources Ministry of Finance etc. The details of the data and documents referred to in the table are available at the author's GitHub repository (https://github.com/kenyamano/JapanDecides2021)

households and firms by directly and widely distributing funds, which accounted for 57.1% of the annual regular budget of the fiscal year 2020.

The third stage of the fiscal stimulus, whose supplementary budget was implemented in January 2021, the beginning of the last quarter of the fiscal year 2020, however, weakened the focus on direct supports toward households and firms. The components of this policy package were similar to the second supplementary budget (see the fifth and sixth column of Table 17.1). For instance, "support for firms and workers" still took the largest share of this supplementary budget package, and it allocated almost the same amount of budget to "infection control/health and long-term care" as the second supplementary budget.

What is notable, however, was a dramatic increase of the amount allocated to "other categories," which were not directly related to the imminent pandemic response. The policy statement indicated that the purpose of this finance was to realize the transformation of the economic structure and a virtuous economic cycle under the post-pandemic era. Despite such claim, this budget category offered only broad and vague expenditure plans such as "Digitalization and Green society," "Productivity improvement by structural reforms and innovation," and "Realization of the consumer-led virtuous economic cycle in the region, society, and employment."

Moreover, apart from the response to the COVID-19 pandemic, this third fiscal package included expenditure on infrastructures to enhance disaster prevention and national resilience. Therefore, while the third supplementary budget continued to support the health providers and firms, the main target has shifted toward the classic supply-side focus labeled a long-term growth strategy. In sum, this trend suggests that the governing coalition of LDP and Kōmeitō pursued the supports from the specific interest groups while appealing to the broad public by the straddling strategy that combined direct distributions, which parties on the left traditionally promote, and the conventional LDP-style infrastructure investments and public expenditure policy.

Finally, summing up all these fiscal stimulus packages, the total budgets were unprecedented: the size of these three supplementary budgets amounts to 76% of the initial regular budget of the fiscal year 2020. Vocal concerns presented by the Vice Minister of Finance Yano Kōji immediately before the Lower House Election sounded the alarm against lack of fiscal discipline and eminent fiscal disaster emerging in the horizon.[6] The economic impacts of these fiscal stimulus packages have also invited reservations as their execution rates are low. Comparing the actual expenditures to the aggregation of regular and supplementary budgets related to the policy response to COVID-19, the Board of Audit of Japan (BAJ) reported that only 65% were executed in the fiscal year 2019 and 2020.[7] Although it is true, as some argue, that the third supplementary budget was put in place in the last quarter of the fiscal year without enough time for implementation,[8] these lower execution trends are observed in many projects across all the supplementary budgets and in various categories of expenditure. For instance, the BAJ pointed out in its annual audit report that the subsidy to the local governments called Special Allocation for Revitalization to Cope with COVID-19 (*chihō sōsei kōfukin*), and the financial support for travel, culture, and arts industries executed only 33.1% and 35.0%, respectively.[9] Even for the core policies that help people and firms in need, the record showed low execution rates of 72.7% (help people) and 47.7% (help firms under financial duress). Moreover, the financial support for medical providers recorded 67.6%.

There was clear evidence of some projects having been executed inefficiently.[10] For instance, the BAJ identified the case in which a fair and competitive procurement process in the Subsidy Program for Sustaining

Businesses was stifled by the government not sufficiently disclosing information in the pre-bid contract when the project was outsourced. There is evidence of the contractor repeatedly subcontracted up to nine subcontractors generating a large amount of intermediate margins. The BAJ concluded that the project was outsourced in an inefficient manner demonstrated by the level of actual spending as a subsidy below the headline budget. Another example is the contract flaws in the "Go-To" travel campaign program, where the Ministry of Agriculture, Forestry and Fisheries contracted about half of the contractors without written contracts for outsourcing. The Japan Tourism Agency did not ensure how the contractors distributed the cancel fees paid by the government, either. Lastly, there were financial losses in the cloth mask distribution project, so-called "*Abe no masuku*" (Abe's masks), because millions of the masks have been damaged and gone unused, languishing in storage. These low execution rates as well as visible waste indicate how hyperbole the headline budget was and reveal strong electoral objectives in the face of imminent Lower House Election waiting in fall 2021.

Overall, despite the aggressive fiscal policy measures implemented by the Japanese government, which cushioned short-term shocks created by the pandemic (Lipscy 2022), the country's economic growth rate remained low among other major advanced economies.[11] In terms of the level of fiscal measures (as a percentage of GDP) among these economics, Japan's fiscal packages constitute the third largest after the United States and the United Kingdom (Gornostay and Sarsenbayev 2021). Nonetheless, according to the International Monetary Fund (IMF), Japan's average forecasted economic growth for the next five years (2022–2026) is 1.3%, lagging way behind others' average of 2.6%.[12]

KISHIDA'S NEW FORM OF CAPITALISM AND THE LDP'S MANIFESTO

Similar to the fiscal relief on the COVID-19, the LDP's policy stance in the face of the General Election shows the straddling strategy balancing a distribution and conventional supply-side growth strategy. The concept of New Form of Capitalism, according to Prime Minister Kishida, is based on a plan to revitalize the Japanese economy with "a virtuous cycle of growth and distribution."[13] Instead of "reform" that Abenomics had emphasized for the last nine years, "distribution" has become the key feature of Kishida's plan. At his administration's initial step in early

October, Kishida established New Capitalism Revitalization Headquarter and floated the idea of increasing the rate of taxation on financial and security transactions from the current flat rate of 20%. This was a strategy to increase Japan's fiscal revenue to the investment income that has risen among the wealthy Japanese.[14] Kishida also promoted a "stakeholder" economy, where firms distribute profits to workers, customers, and subcontractors, and not just to the "shareholders." He especially focused on the SMEs and proposed tax incentives for the companies that raise the wages for their workers.

Kishida's thinking on New Form of Capitalism derives its origin from the "National Income Doubling Plan (*shotoku baizō keikaku*)" of the 1960s led by the then-Prime Minister Ikeda Hayato, the founder of *Kōchikai*, a leading faction of the LDP that Kishida has headed since 2012.[15] Although the policy details of New Form of Capitalism are yet to fully emerge (at the time of the writing), the rise of this new strategy is in reaction to the decades of neoliberal policies in pursuit of economic efficiency following market fundamentalism and deregulation. Concomitantly, this was a way to deflect Abenomics' shortfalls in terms of the income distribution (Saiki and Frost 2020 inter alia) especially in the face of stagnating wage growth (Vogel 2021). The opinion polls taken just prior to the Lower House Election demonstrated such view as more than 60 percent of those polled responded that Abenomics has to be overhauled.[16] Furthermore, inequality for the first time became an important electoral issue as the country faced the pandemic (Lee 2022). In short, Kishida's strategy in the LDP presidential election was to emphasize distribution and address people's dissatisfaction with Abenomics and the government's COVID-19 responses.

Despite the progressive components of the New Form of Capitalism plan at the time of the LDP Party Presidential Election in September 2021, the LDP's party manifesto shelved such progressive ideas at the time of the October General Election campaign. One direct and obvious reason of this shift is the decline in stock prices in response to Kishida's capital gain tax increase idea, which was later withdrawn. But this shift was also in line with LDP's traditional clientelistic supply-side economic growth strategy taken since the rapid economic growth period of the late 1950s. The Japanese economy relied heavily on public investment not only to build necessary physical infrastructure devastated after World War II, but also to pump in pork-barrel projects to politically important rural areas and in support of construction contractors (Woodall

1996). Such heavy reliance on public works continued for Japan into the twenty-first century.[17] Despite the 1994 electoral reform that structurally reduced the political power of special interest by introducing single-member district votes, the local clientelism and attraction of public works has persisted particularly in the rural areas in Japan (Scheiner 2007). Thus, by dedicating 15 out of its 34-page manifesto to these issues,[18] the LDP's economic plans emphasized "strong economy" and the measures following the National Resilience Plan adopted in the aftermath of the 3/11 triple disaster of earthquake, tsunami, and nuclear plant meltdown of 2011, and laid out under National Land Resilience Basic Law that came into effect in 2013 under the LDP leadership.[19]

The rest of the LDP's manifesto included, in line with Kishida's initial vision, (re)building a robust middle-class economy with the wage increase, particularly in sectors such as nursing, home- or day-care, and by providing incentives for companies that raise workers' pay, which partly co-opting the opposition ideas. Meanwhile, the LDP was opposed to any sales tax cut, and in general in support of fiscal discipline. Therefore, Kishida and the LDP manifesto constituted the LDP's straddling strategy that, the internal politics in the LDP formed the policy agenda that perpetuated the conventional growth strategy through industrial policies, public expenditure, and infrastructure investments, yet it underscored the change from Abenomics by promoting the distributive policies.

Economic Policy Trilemma Facing the Political Parties During the Lower House Election

The LDP's straddling strategy exploits the policy space for the opposition parties, especially the CDP-JCP coalition. The distinct priorities taken by the parties demonstrated the trilemma among the three economic goals to demonstrate a credible commitment on their economic policies. The first goal is the economic growth capitalizing on the "old way of business" resorting to the supply-side of producers and large businesses, and catering to the vested economic interests and clientelism through measures such as infrastructure investment, be it green or traditional. The second goal is the emphasis on distribution with various types of hand-outs measures some targeted certain demography such as the poor or unemployed, as well as consumer-focused measures such as time-limited suspension (or reduction) of sales tax. The third and final goal is the fiscal discipline of the central government.

Taking the first two goals, the trade-off between supply-side focused growth strategy and distribution under neoliberalism has been the topic of extensive research in the fields of both economics and political science. In the late 1990s, "permanent austerity" (Pierson 2001), a precondition of policy credibility among the OECD countries, intensified the political conflict between the organized economic interests of businesses and mass public (especially in support of welfare state). Seminal work of Przeworski and Wallerstein (1988, p. 13) argues that "governments face a trade-off between distribution and growth, between equality and efficiency." That is particularly so when there is prominent structural dependence of the state on capitalists since the performance of the economy is the key for the legislators to achieve success in their re-election and maintain their popularity (Swank 1992). In such a context, however, the ideologies of the political parties play an important role in the choice within the trade-off. Generally, the conservative parties adopt supply-side growth strategy by increasing the productivity of capital, while socialist governments tend to depend on distribution to increase the productivity of workers (Boix 1998).

What is different in 2021 from the arguments seen in the existing literature, however, is the introduction of the third element, which is the prevailing acceptance from voters on the relaxation of fiscal austerity that used to be the pre-conditions of the trade-off. In the twenty-first century under the macroeconomic environment of "secular stagnation" (Summers 2016), and particularly in the aftermath of the 2008 global financial crisis and now the pandemic, the possibility of "helicopter money" (monetized fiscal stimuli) ushered in a new era of (potentially) governments' free spending without revenue constraints. Furthermore, the governments facing such environment, the challenge is to try to minimize the electoral costs associated with the state of crisis (Breunig and Busemeyer 2012, p. 924). While the traditional trade-off implies redistribution that transfers money from rich to poor, in the world under massive crisis-driven monetary and fiscal expansion, the trade-off between the two goals expands by adding the third dimension of fiscal discipline, leading to the economic policy trilemma.[20] Therefore, a strategic party could propose to fill in this new political space, by being a traditionally "irresponsible government" and neglecting fiscal discipline, and pursue both supply-side growth and distribution with the risk of inflation. Meanwhile, those parties that insist on fiscal discipline and stick to the two traditional policy dimensions continue to face the trade-off.

Based on this trilemma, we evaluate parties' manifestos to map their economic policies onto the three goals (Fig. 17.1). Specifically, we examine the parties' positions on public debt expansion, and introduction of progressive income tax, and corporate tax increases (fiscal discipline); distributive policies such as direct payments to households and sales and income tax reductions (distribution); and deregulation and public investment in a range of areas from renewable energy, digital economy, green innovation to supply chain and infrastructure resilience (supply-side growth strategy). As discussed above, after the Party Presidential Election, the LDP's manifesto tilted to the growth strategies compared to distributive policies. However, with support from the Kōmeitō, whose electoral campaign promise included direct payment to household, the LDP-Kōmeitō coalition cover wider areas of both growth and distribution policies that narrowed the choice for opposition parties. In addition, despite its emphasis on fiscal discipline, the LDP as the governing party has the power to set the budget ceiling in the face of pandemic. In contrast, the CDP-JCP coalition locates in the narrower area with low score in growth strategy, moderate score in distribution, and high fiscal discipline with progressive tax plan.

Moreover, opposition parties largely emphasized distribution in their electoral campaigns at the expense of fiscal discipline. The CDP, the DPP, and Ishin called for time-limited reduction of sales tax from 10 to 5%, while the JCP demanded its permanent reduction to 5%, and Reiwa called for its abolition. In addition, the JCP, the DPP, and Reiwa also supported issuing new bonds to finance national financial needs. When it comes to direct subsidies to households, all parties except for the LDP proposed these direct payments of hand-outs one way or another including even the LDP's coalition partner Kōmeitō. The DPP called for $1,000 (¥100,000)-allowance across the board and additional $1,000 for low-income population, and Ishin proposed introduction of the universal basic income.

When it comes to the balance between supply-side growth and distribution, in contrast to the LDP and Kōmeitō whose focus has been more on the producers, other parties have focused on the consumers. In addition to sales tax cuts and direct subsidies to individuals, the CDP, the JCP, the DPP emphasized support to households. Furthermore, Reiwa and the DFPF also demanded industrial policy and infrastructure investment via fiscal expansion. Meanwhile, most parties on the left of the LDP from the CDP, the JCP to the SDP emphasized the redistributive goal of

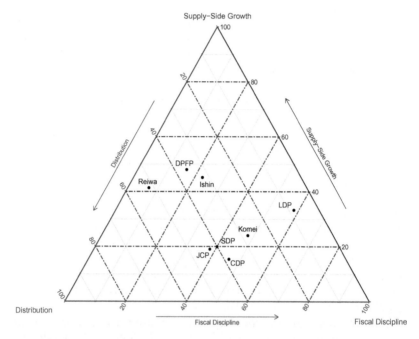

Fig. 17.1 Party positions in the trilemma: supply-side growth, distribution, and fiscal discipline at the 2021 Lower House Election (*Notes* Three dimensions of policy choice. We decompose the list of policies in parties' manifestos into three categories: "Supply-Side Growth" based on public infrastructure investments, and deregulation and tax cut on manufacturing and other suppliers; "Distribution" based on direct household subsidies, and income and consumption tax cut; "Fiscal Discipline" based on tax increases, and issue of government bonds. The components of policy categories must sum to 100. *Sources* The details of the data and scores referred to in this figure are available at the author's GitHub repository [https://github.com/kenyamano/JapanDecides2021]. Coded by the authors based on each party's manifesto)

fiscal policy by demanding more progressive income tax and supporting taxing the wealthy and capital gains more. In contrast, the DPP and Reiwa emphasized the new issuance of government bonds while Ishin mentioned nothing about fiscal management despite that they promote tax cut and fiscal expansion. We evaluate parties' position by scoring policies that are comparable across parties, then we aggregate these scores for three goals, even though some parties may have inconsistencies in their policies and goals, mapping onto the ternary plot in Fig. 17.1.

Although the economic policy was not the only issue of competition on which the 2021 Lower House Election was fought over, we see a pattern of favorable electoral outcome for the parties located on the top-left area in the ternary plot (Fig. 17.1), namely the DPP (the number of seats gained/lost: + 3), Ishin (+30), and Reiwa (+3). These were the parties that straddled between distribution and supply-side growth strategies at the expense of fiscal discipline. Meanwhile, those that neglected the growth strategy and positioned themselves in the bottom-middle between distribution and fiscal discipline such as the CDP (−13), the JCP (−2), and the SDP (0) did not do so well. Although the LDP (−13) and Kōmeitō (−2) lost some seats emphasizing growth with fiscal discipline (bottom right), the coalition was able to maintain the Lower House majority. The LDP's economic strategy in the middle of the pandemic led to its electoral success in 2021, but the visible electoral gains made by the parties that neglected fiscal discipline as in the case of Ishin foreshadows the future of economic policy priorities in Japan.

CONCLUSION

In this chapter, we examined the economic policies and strategies among the political parties in the face of 2021 Lower House Election as the Japanese economy faced the COVID-19 pandemic. Thanks to the macroeconomic actions taken under Abenomics and under the pandemic economic challenges, dramatic fiscal expansion was possible in 2020 and 2021. This shifted the conventional trade-off between production/supply-oriented and distribution-oriented economic policy to an economic policy trilemma including the third goal of a choice regarding fiscal discipline. In the context of the 2021 Lower House Election, the LDP-Kōmeitō coalition opted for straddling strategy to incorporate the supply-side growth policy but still with emphasis on distribution to households. This LDP economic strategy, in contrast to the opposition parties that emphasized either public debt expansion (DPP, Ishin, and Reiwa) or redistribution (CDP, JCP, and SDP), led to the LDP to win the majority in the election.

All in all, as mentioned above in the IMF's forecast, Japan's economic growth in the aftermath of the pandemic does not seem very likely. The third arrow of Abenomics, "the growth strategy through structural reform," aimed the Japanese economy to escape from the low growth equilibrium, but the progress was mixed: while the liberalization processes in the area of trade, agriculture, and corporate governance achieved significant progress, the reforms for the gender gap, stagnated wage growth and low productivity have fallen short (Lechevalier and Monfort 2017, Katada and Cheung 2018, Kushida 2018, Hoshi and Lipscy 2021).

Notwithstanding, the economic policies proposed by the LDP before the elections suggest continuity of such landscape. The concern is financial absorption capacity in the face of insufficient structural reform, which continues to loom large in the choice of LDP's economic policy focusing on the supply-side. When Japan's rigid economic structure limits profitable investment opportunities, pouring in massive funds does not lead to growth. In addition, bureaucracy's implementation capacity and lack of digitalization have exacerbated this challenge. Even on the consumer demand-side, the criticism was that a large portion of the direct handouts did not lead to consumption by the recipients as many opted to save the money for the rainier days. Hence, these institutional and structural hurdles have diminished the growth impact of the fiscal stimulus and the economic strategies, which underscores the continued need for structural reform and innovation to unleash Japan's growth potential. Meanwhile, the electoral support for the growth-oriented expansionary fiscal policy could shape the fiscal stance of the ruling coalition at the expense of fiscal discipline in the future.

Acknowledgements The authors would like to thank Christopher Adolph, Michihito Ando, Takeo Hoshi, Sebastien Lechevalier, Gene Park, and the editors of *Japan Decide 2021* for their helpful comments on our chapter.

NOTES

1. We define distributive economic policy as a resource allocation toward demand-side of the Japanese economy consisting of consumers and workers, where the typical policy menu is to implement series of direct payments or reductions on income and sales tax. On the other hand, the supply-side growth strategy focuses on the producers, industries, and businesses where the government executes public expenditure programs to stimulate private investments and exploit regulations.

2. Nomura Security reported that in December 2020, the BOJ became the largest shareholder of the Japanese stocks followed by Government

Pension Investment Fund. See *Nikkei*, "Nichigin, hajimete saidaino koku-naihoyushani," February 5, 2021, available at: https://www.nikkei.com/article/DGXZQODF057000V00C21A2000000.

3. See BOJ, "Enhancement of Monetary Easing in Light of the Impact of the Outbreak of the Novel Coronavirus (COVID-19)," available at: https://www.boj.or.jp/en/mopo/mpmdeci/state_2020/k200316b.htm/ , and "Enhancement of Monetary Easing," available at: https://www.boj.or.jp/en/mopo/mpmdeci/state_2020/k200427a.htm/ .

4. All data on the budget presented in this section are obtained from the Ministry of Finance and other sources and aggregated by the authors. The details of the data and documents referred to in the table are available at the author's GitHub repository: https://github.com/kenyamano/JapanDecides2021 .

5. These initial responses were covered by the contingency funds in the regular budget of the fiscal year 2019. The total amounts of the expenditures were 0.4% of the annual regular budget.

6. See Yano Kōji, "Konomama deha Kokka zaisei ha Hatansuru" November 2021, *Bungei shunju*, available at: https://bunshun.jp/articles/-/49082.

7. See BAJ, "Reiwa 2nendo kessan kensa houkoku no honbun," available at: https://www.jbaudit.go.jp/report/new/summary02/pdf/fy02_gaiyou_zenbun.pdf.

8. See *Nikkei*, "Seifu yosan no kurikoshi gaku, kako saikō no 30.7 choen," July 30, 2021, available at: https://www.nikkei.com/article/DGXZQOUA29DQP0Z20C21A7000000/.

9. See footnote 7.

10. All cases presented here are in the BAJ's annual audit report. See footnote 7.

11. Canada, France, Germany, Italy, Japan, the United Kingdom, and the United States.

12. IMF, October 2021, "World Economic Outlook Database."

13. Prime Minister Kishida's first policy speech at the Diet on October 8, 2021, available at: https://www.kantei.go.jp/jp/100_kishida/statement/2021/1008shoshinhyomei.html.

14. For "Ichioku-en-no kabe (The wall at the ¥100 million income)" discussion, see *Nikkei*, October 7, 2021, available at: https://www.nikkei.com/article/DGKKZO76408430X01C21A0EA2000/

15. For the summary, see Shimada Haruo "Atarashii shihon shugi no honrai no hōkō o tsuikyūseyo." Yomiuri Shinbun online, January 31, 2022, available at: https://www.yomiuri.co.jp/choken/kijironko/ckeconomy/20220128-OYT8T50087/.

16. Jiji reports 62 percent (https://www.jiji.com/jc/article?k=2021101500743&g=pol), Kyodo reports 68 percent (reported by Reuters: https://www.reuters.com/article/idJP2021101701000471).

17. Among most countries of the OECD, the ratio of public investment to GDP has slowly declined from 4 to 5 percent in the early 1970s to around 2 percent. Yet, Japan and South Korea have maintained a high ratio above 5 percent in the 2000s (Kohsaka 2007).
18. See LDP, "reiwa 3nen seiken kōyaku," available at: https://jimin.jp-east-2.storage.api.nifcloud.com/pdf/manifest/20211018_manifest.pdf.
19. At the time of the LDP Party Presidential Election, one of Kishida's opponents, Takaichi Sanae, promoted these ideas.
20. It may be true that three economic goals could be achieved at the same time when the economy is supported by the economic boom cycle (See Dore 1994). We consider, however, that the policy stance to pursue all three is impossible to realize and gain voters' support under the condition which Japanese economy faces persisting structural headwinds of low growth and the pandemic.

References

Ando, Michihito, Chishio Furukawa, Daigo Nakata, and Kazuhiko Sumiya (2020). "Fiscal Responses to the COVID-19 Crisis in Japan: The First Six Months," *National Tax Journal*, 73 (3), 901–926

Boix, Carles. (1998). *Political Parties, Growth and Equality: Conservative and Social Democratic Economic Strategies in the World Economy*. Cambridge: Cambridge University Press.

Breunig, Christian and Marius R. Busemeyer (2012). "Fiscal Austerity and the Trade-off between Public Investment and Social Spending," *Journal of European Public Policy*, 19:6, 921–938.

Buiter, Willem. (2021). *Central Banks as Fiscal Players: The Drivers of Fiscal and Monetary Policy Space*. Cambridge: Cambridge University Press.

Dore, Richard (1994). "Equality-efficiency Trade-offs: Japanese Perceptions and Choices." In: M. Aoki and R. Dore, (eds.), *The Japanese Firm. Sources of Competitive Strength*. Oxford: Oxford University Press, 379–392.

Gornostay, Egor and Madi Sarsenbayev (2021). "Overheating debate: Why not in Japan?", *Policy Briefs*, Peterson Institute for International Economics.

Harris, Tobias, 2022. "Abe's Legacy," In Robert Pekkanen, Steven Reed, and Daniel Smith (eds.), *Japan Decides 2021: The Japanese General Election*. Palgrave Macmillan.

Hoshi, Takeo and Phillip Y. Lipscy (2021). "The Political Economy of the Abe Government," in Hoshi, Takeo and Phillip Y. Lipscy, (eds.), *The Political Economy of the Abe Government and Abenomics Reforms*. Cambridge: Cambridge University Press.

Katada, Saori N. and Gabrielle Cheung. 2018. "The First Two Arrows of Abenomics: Monetary and Fiscal Politics in the 2017 Snap Election." In

Robert Pekkanen, Steven Reed, Ethan Scheiner and Daniel Smith (eds.), *Japan Decides 2017: The Japanese General Election*. Palgrave Macmillan; 243–259.

Kohsaka, Akira. 2007. *Infrastructure Development in the Pacific Region*. Routledge.

Kushida, Kenji E. 2018. "Abenomics' Third Arrow: Fostering Future Competitiveness?" In Robert Pekkanen, Steven Reed, Ethan Scheiner and Daniel Smith (eds.), *Japan Decides 2017: The Japanese General Election*. Palgrave Macmillan; 261–295.

Lechevalier, Sébastien and Brieuc Monfort (2017). "Abenomics: Has it worked? Will it Ultimately Fail?" *Japan Forum*. https://doi.org/10.1080/09555803.2017.1394352

Lee, Yeon Ju. 2022. "Does Income Inequality Matter in Japan?" In Robert Pekkanen, Steven Reed, and Daniel Smith (eds.), *Japan Decides 2021: The Japanese General Election*. Palgrave Macmillan.

Lipscy, Phillip Y. 2022. "Japan's Response to the COVID-19 Pandemic," In Robert Pekkanen, Steven Reed, and Daniel Smith (eds.), *Japan Decides 2021: The Japanese General Election*. Palgrave Macmillan.

Nemoto, Kuniaki. 2022. "How the Liberal Democratic Party Avoided a Loss in 2021." In Robert Pekkanen, Steven Reed, and Daniel Smith (eds.) *Japan Decides 2021: The Japanese General Election*. Palgrave Macmillan.

Park, Gene, Saori N. Katada, Giacomo Chiozza and Yoshiko Kojo (2018). *Taming Japan's Deflation: The Debate over Unconventional Monetary Policy*. Ithaca: Cornell University Press.

Park, Gene (2021). "The Bank of Japan: Central Bank Independence and the Politicization of Monetary Policy." Edited by Robert J. Pekkanen and Saadia M. Pekkanen, *The Oxford Handbook of Japanese Politics*. New York: Oxford University Press.

Pierson, Paul (2001). "Coping with Permanent Austerity Welfare State Restructuring in Affluent Democracies," in Pierson ed. *The New Politics of the Welfare State*. New York: Oxford University Press: 410–456.

Przeworski, Adam and Michael Wallerstein (1988), "Structural Dependence of the State on Capital." *American Political Science Review*, 1988, 82:1, 11–29.

Saiki, Ayako and Jon Frost (2020) "Unconventional Monetary Policy and Inequality: Is Japan Unique?" *Applied Economics*, 52:44, 4809-4821,

Scheiner, Ethan (2007). "Clientelism in Japan: The Importance and Limits of Institutional Explanations." In H. Kitschelt & S. Wilkinson (eds.), *Patrons, Clients and Policies: Patterns of Democratic Accountability and Political Competition*. Cambridge: Cambridge University Press: 276-297.

Summers, Lawrence (2016). "Secular Stagnation and Monetary Policy." *Federal Reserve Bank of St. Louis Review*, Second Quarter 2016, 98:2, 93–110. https://doi.org/10.20955/r.2016.93-110

Swank, Duane (1992). "Politics and the Structural Dependence of the State in Democratic Capitalist Nations." *American Political Science Review,* 1992, 86:1, 38–54.

Takenaka, Harukata (2020) *Korona kiki no seiji: Abe Seiken vs Chiji.* Chuo Koron shinsho.

Vogel, Steven K. (2021), "Abe's Slight Left Turn: How a Labor Shortage Transformed Politics and Policy." in Hoshi, Takeo and Phillip Y. Lipscy, (eds.), *The Political Economy of the Abe Government and Abenomics Reforms.* Cambridge: Cambridge University Press: 271–309.

Woodall, Brian (1996). *Japan Under Construction: Corruption, Politics, and Public Works.* Berkeley: University of California Press.

CHAPTER 18

Does Income Inequality Matter in Japan?

Yeon Ju Lee

Income inequality has dominated media headlines and the political agenda in numerous countries around the world. It has also shaped elections in many democracies. For example, income inequality is believed to be one of the factors that contributed to the rise of populist parties and candidates in a range of countries (e.g., Engler and Weisstanner 2021; Han 2016; Stoetzer et al. 2021).

Yet, there are countries in which income inequality has not been politically salient. For example, although India is one of the countries with the highest income inequality—the top 1% of earners make about 22% of total income (Bharti and Chancel 2019)—income inequality is largely absent from its political discourse. Given the high level of income inequality, we would expect it to be the top concern for voters and politicians in India. However, that has not been the case despite some discussions during the 2019 general election campaigns about addressing the issue through redistribution (*The Economic Times*, March 15, 2020). On the other

Y. J. Lee (✉)
Edmund A. Walsh School of Foreign Service, Georgetown University, Washington, D.C, USA
e-mail: yeonju.lee@georgetown.edu

R. J. Pekkanen et al. (eds.), *Japan Decides 2021*, https://doi.org/10.1007/978-3-031-11324-6_18

hand, there are countries (e.g., South Korea) where income inequality is low but is the key issue in elections and political debates.[1]

What about Japan, another country with relatively low levels of income inequality? Does income inequality matter in Japanese politics? If we were to answer this question regarding the House of Representatives (HR) elections in 2014 or 2017, the answer would probably be "no." Although inequality was an important issue during the 2009 general election, it has not been a main agenda item with a decisive impact on election outcomes since then, including the general elections in 2014 and 2017. Both voters and politicians paid more attention to Japan's economy, national security, and constitutional reform rather than to income inequality. Income inequality was invisible in media headlines covering the elections or pre-election public opinion polls. Even when inequality received some political attention, it was regional or social inequality rather than income inequality.[2]

However, the situation was different during the 2021 general election when the terms "income inequality" or "redistribution of wealth" appeared in media headlines, politicians' interviews, and party platforms. Does this change mean that income inequality mattered in the 2021 general election? Do politicians and voters now care about income inequality in Japan?

This chapter aims to address these questions by studying parties' election platforms, pre-election public opinion polls, and people's perceptions of income inequality. The key finding is that unlike in past elections, income inequality mattered for voters and parties in the 2021 election to some extent as the COVID-19 pandemic increased the political visibility of income inequality. People became aware of the problems of Abenomics, including a rising income gap, as the pandemic further strained the economy and directly impacted people's well-being. Both ruling and opposition parties responded to the increased awareness of income inequality by introducing various measures to address the issue in their election manifestos, including Prime Minister Kishida's vision of "new capitalism," to promote growth and distribution simultaneously. This chapter will also discuss why the 2021 election differed from previous ones and examine how income inequality has evolved in Japan.

A Brief Overview: Income Inequality in Japan

Income inequality may not have been politically salient in Japan because it has remained low compared to other advanced economies, such as the United States. In 2020, Japan ranked 43rd in the global ranking for income inequality based on the Gini index, while the United States ranked 112th (Ipsos 2021).

Japan's income inequality has been relatively low even when we look at trends over time. Figure 18.1 shows how income inequality has evolved in Japan and two other advanced democracies with economies of a comparable size—the United Kingdom and the United States[3]—since 1970. Although Japan's pre-tax and transfer income inequality (panel a) has been rising since the end of the 1970s, it has been significantly lower than that of the United Kingdom or the United States. A similar pattern holds for post-tax and transfer income inequality (panel b) except that income inequality decreased dramatically in the United Kingdom in 2000 before rising again around 2013. Due to this decline from 2000 to 2013, the post-tax and transfer income inequality in the United Kingdom has been lower than that of Japan since about 2010 to date.

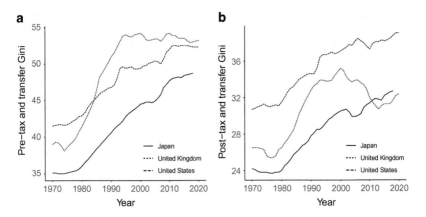

Fig. 18.1 Income Inequality in Japan, the United Kingdom, and the United States (*Data Source* The Standardized World Income Inequality Dataset. **a** Income Inequality Before Taxes and Transfers **b** Income Inequality After Taxes and Transfers)

Although Japan's income inequality has been low from a comparative perspective, it has changed significantly over time. Throughout the 1970s, income inequality remained very low and almost constant. Income inequality after taxes and transfers even decreased slightly during this period. The average pre-tax and transfer and post-tax and transfer Gini coefficients for the 1970s were 35.1 and 23.8, respectively (Standardized World Income Inequality Database). Since 1980, income inequality increased dramatically until it became stagnant (pre-tax and transfer income inequality) or fell (post-tax and transfer income inequality) between 2002 and 2005. It rose significantly again and then slowed down in 2010 with a small decrease between 2012 and 2014. Income inequality has been increasing in Japan since then.

Panels (a) and (b) of Fig. 18.2 suggest that this pattern of the evolution of income inequality in Japan and the economy are correlated. In the 1970s, when income inequality was low and steady, GDP growth was slow with a gentle slope. Relative redistribution,[4] which is the percentage by which the pre-tax and transfer Gini is reduced, increased throughout the 1970s as shown in panel (c) of Fig. 18.2. When the Japanese economy grew exponentially in the 1980s and the beginning of the 1990s, income inequality also rose sharply. Redistribution decreased greatly during this time as the government focused on increasing productivity and growth rather than redistribution through taxes and welfare policies. In the early 1990s, Japan's "lost twenty years" of economic stagnation began with the end of the "bubble economy" in which financial and real estate asset prices increased dramatically.[5] Market income inequality also became stagnant and disposable income inequality dropped significantly in the early and mid-2000s. Due to the economic constraint, redistribution also remained low. In the later 2000s, GDP, income inequality, and redistribution began to rise.

It is notable that income inequality and GDP have decoupled since the early 2010s. In the very beginning of the 2010s, GDP and income inequality appeared to move in tandem; GDP plummeted around 2012 and income inequality decreased slightly. However, while GDP continued to fall, income inequality started to rise in the mid-2010s. This gap between GDP and income inequality grew larger as income inequality continued to increase and GDP continued to fall. The increasing gap implies that the distribution of incomes became more unequal while the Japanese economy could not recover from stagnation.

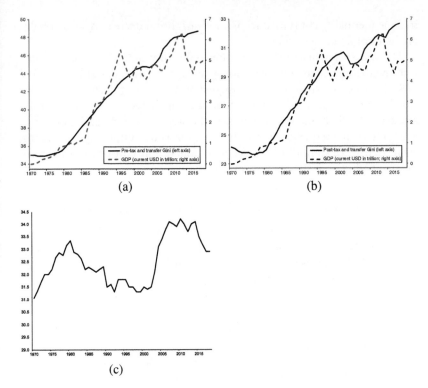

Fig. 18.2 GDP and Income Inequality (*Data Source* The Standardized World Income Inequality Dataset; the World Bank. **a** GDP and Income Inequality Before Taxes and Transfers **b** GDP and Income Inequality After Taxes and Transfers **c** Relative redistribution)

This period of divergence between income inequality and GDP overlaps with Prime Minister Abe Shinzō's second term (2012–2020) during which "Abenomics" came into being. Abenomics is an economic program that Prime Minister Abe and his government launched in 2012 to revive the Japanese economy after more than two decades of deflation.[6] They prioritized growth and efficiency over redistribution through increasing the money supply and government spending, and enacting structural reforms. The program appeared to have some positive effect as GDP rebounded from 4.4 trillion USD to 5.0 trillion USD in 2016. However, income inequality continued to rise, redistribution decreased substantially, and economic growth stalled again.

Despite this worsening of income inequality and shrinking redistribution, income inequality was not a main issue in the 2014 and 2017 HR elections. Inequality was construed as an issue of "regional vitalization" reflecting the social and economic gap between urban and rural areas rather than income differences between the rich and poor. But even regional inequality was only a minor issue. Other agenda items, such as the consumption tax, security policy, and constitutional reform determined people's votes in those elections.

INCOME INEQUALITY AND THE 2021 ELECTION

Without a clear demand from the public to address economic disparities, there have been no notable changes in the government's economic policy since the 2017 HR election. Income inequality continued to grow as the incomes of the poor and middle classes, as well as the economy, remained static. Was income inequality largely invisible in the 2021 HR election, as it was in the previous elections, or did it gain some political salience? To answer this question, it is crucial to understand whether voters cared about income inequality.

Although income inequality has been rising since the 1980s, the public has not perceived this. For example, Fig. 18.3 illustrates the distribution of responses to whether people agreed or disagreed with the statement "differences in incomes in Japan are too large" in 2009 and 2019. Income inequality after taxes and transfers increased by 4.81% from 2009 to 2019. Yet, as the figure shows, on average, fewer people perceived that income differences were larger in 2019 than 2009: 43.15% of the respondents strongly agreed that differences in incomes in Japan are too large in 2009, whereas only 36.5% strongly agreed with the statement in 2019—a decrease of 15.4%. On the other hand, people who did not think there were large income differences increased from 7.18% in 2009 to 9.5% in 2019—an increase of 32.3%.

However, evidence suggests that people started to become aware of income inequality as an important issue during the 2021 election season. For instance, a public opinion survey conducted in October 2021 asked a representative sample of 222,695 eligible voters about which issue areas they wanted the Lower House members to prioritize.[7] Seven percent

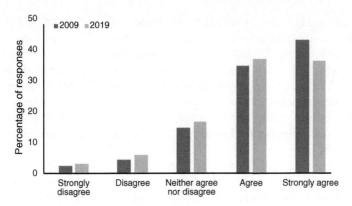

Fig. 18.3 Perceptions of income inequality in Japan: "Income differences in your country are too large." (*Data Source* International Social Survey Programme)

of respondents chose income disparity, which was the fifth most important issue after economic policy, COVID-19, pensions and social welfare, and diplomacy and security.[8] This is a notable change since income inequality was not even included in most polls in the 2014 and 2017 elections. It is also significant that income inequality received more than twice the number of votes as constitutional reform (3%), which was of "uncommonly high" salience in the 2017 election (McElwain 2018).

Moreover, when another pre-election poll asked eligible voters to choose which of two issues—economic growth or economic inequality— should be the next prime minister's focus, 41% chose economic inequality while 43% chose economic growth.[9] Considering that economic growth was the most pressing issue in almost all the polls and surveys, the fact that economic inequality was only two percentage points lower in respondents' preferences is a strong indicator that income inequality arose as a politically salient issue for voters in 2021.

Parties' election manifestos also reflected increased public attention to income inequality. Japan's largest opposition party, the Constitutional Democratic Party (CDP), emphasized reducing income inequality. It aimed to achieve an "all-middle-class society" through redistribution. Specific measures included increasing income taxes on the rich and setting higher corporate tax rates on large businesses. The party also proposed to exempt people who earned 10 million yen or less from income taxes and temporarily lower the consumption tax to 5%. The CDP also signed a joint policy pact with three other opposition parties—the Social Democratic Party, the Japanese Communist Party, and Reiwa Shinsengumi—which included addressing income inequality as one of six policy areas.[10] These opposition parties vowed to make a fairer tax system and strengthen its redistributive function by placing higher tax rates on the wealthy, raising the minimum wage, and expanding welfare provisions, such as public support for housing, education, health care, nurseries, and elderly care.

The ruling Liberal Democratic Party (LDP) also regarded alleviating income disparities as a key issue. Candidates for the LDP leadership election declared the importance of addressing income inequality in their campaigns. In his policy speech to the 205th Session of the Diet in October 2021, Prime Minister Kishida Fumio stressed that there could be "no growth without redistribution." He put forward his vision of a "new capitalism (新しい資本主義)," which promotes a "virtuous cycle of growth and distribution," rather than choosing between "growth or distribution."

However, the specific measures that he presented during the election campaign, such as decreasing the tax burden on companies that raise wages, were not very different from those of the Abe administration. The higher income tax rate that Prime Minister Kishida proposed in the LDP presidential election was missing from the LDP platform for the 2021 HR election. In fact, the LDP policies to alleviate economic disparities and empower the middle class focused on economic growth rather than redistribution, which differs from the opposition parties. This approach also seems to differ from Prime Minister Kishida's own stance of "no growth without redistribution." How he planned to implement his vision of "new capitalism" to achieve both economic growth *and* redistribution was unclear.[11]

WHY DID INCOME INEQUALITY MATTER IN THE 2021 ELECTION?

Unlike previous elections in which income inequality was not important to voters and parties, income inequality emerged as a politically salient issue in the 2021 election. Terms such as "income inequality" or "redistribution of wealth" appeared in media headlines, editorials, and party platforms frequently during the election season reflecting people's increased awareness of income inequality. What led to this change?

First, the negative consequences of Abenomics played a significant role in raising people's awareness of income inequality in the country. Although Abenomics received some positive assessments—that it brought a marginal increase in the inflation rate, stock market growth, and a decrease in unemployment—many criticized the program for widening the income and wealth gaps without generating a structural change for continued economic growth (e.g., Ito 2021; *Time*, October 13, 2021). Increased stock and corporate profits only benefitted the rich and large companies without "trickling down" to enhance the well-being of the majority of people. Wages and household incomes remained stagnant. According to government data, nominal wages rose only by 1.2% from 2012 to 2020. The average wealth of households decreased by 3.5% while the wealth of the top 10% increased from 2014 to 2019 (*Financial Times*, November 21, 2021; *Japan Times*, October 12, 2021). Increases in the consumption tax added a burden on regular households and dampened people's consumption.

However, these factors alone cannot explain why income inequality mattered to people in the 2021 election. The negative consequences of Abenomics already existed in 2017, but income inequality was not a salient issue in the 2017 general election. No dramatic changes in the levels of income inequality, economic growth, and redistribution occurred in 2020 or 2021. Although the downsides of Abenomics may have been necessary conditions, they were not sufficient enough to change the perceptions of voters and parties.

The critical factor that triggered the public's change of attitude during the 2021 election was COVID-19. This unexpected pandemic hit the world severely toward the end of 2019 and the beginning of 2020 with a total of 281,808,270 confirmed cases and 5,411,759 deaths as of December 29, 2021.[12] Since its first confirmed case of the disease on January 16, 2020,[13] Japan has suffered from the pandemic, and COVID-19 has had a detrimental effect on the Japanese economy. The spread of the disease halted economic activities at all levels, including domestic consumption and exports, which are key drivers of the Japanese economy. The economy shrank 4.8% in 2020. A year-long delay of the Tokyo 2020 Summer Olympics, which took place in the summer of 2021, brought a large deficit instead of expected economic gains. Japan's economy contracted by an annualized 3.6% in the third quarter (July–September) of 2021. The pandemic further increased Japanese households' economic and financial burdens.[14]

With the strained economy and their well-being directly affected by COVID-19, people began to perceive the existing problems of Abenomics, including rising income inequality. Although everyone experienced the consequences of the pandemic, those who were less well-off were hit more severely. People became increasingly dissatisfied with the government and its economic policies. More than a majority of those responding to a survey conducted shortly after the 2021 HR election articulated their discontent with Abenomics.[15] Responding to an open-ended write-in question about the economic policy, many expressed explicit frustration with the income disparities in Japan. Following are some of those responses:

> The government said wealth will 'trickle down.' But do we see that now? No. The rich are getting richer, and we are all getting poorer.
> The economy is still bad. I think it's worse. The economic gap is becoming larger. The government is not doing anything right about the economy or COVID-19.
> Large companies and the wealthy never suffer. It's always the ordinary people. We pay so much tax but that money is never used for us.
> Abenomics is useless. Politicians and the government should abandon this policy and really do something about the economy and inequality.

Voters wanted the new cabinet to depart from Abenomics and take a different route from previous governments. For example, in a survey conducted in September 2021, 58% responded that the next Prime Minister should not continue the policies of Prime Ministers Abe and Suga (*Asahi*, September 13, 2021). Only 28% said that the incoming Prime Minister should maintain the policies of the past administrations. Another pre-election poll conducted just before the Lower House election in October 2021 showed a similar result; 57% of the respondents claimed that the new Kishida cabinet should not comply with Abe and Suga's policy stance (*NHK Seiji ishiki getsurei chōsa*, October 11, 2021).

In response to these preferences, political parties—including the ruling LDP—acknowledged the negative aspects of Abenomics, such as stagnant wages and an increasing income gap between the haves and have-nots. They framed their economic policies with an emphasis on addressing income inequality and distribution of wealth, departing from Abenomics which had focused on growth and efficiency. Prime Minister Kishida promised to implement an economic regime of growth and redistribution as a form of "New Capitalism." Opposition parties (i.e., the CDP, SDP, JCP, and Reiwa) sought to reform the tax system by levying heavier taxes on the incomes of the rich and the profits of large corporations to redistribute wealth. As COVID-19 aggravated and exposed economic disparities in the country, reducing income inequality became an important political issue for parties and voters along with managing and ending the pandemic and rebuilding the economy.

CONCLUSION

Does income inequality matter in Japan? Although income inequality has been rising in Japan since the 1980s, it did not matter much in Japanese politics. Perhaps because income inequality in Japan is still relatively low compared to other advanced economies, most Japanese were unaware that the income gap between the rich and poor has been increasing due to static wages and household incomes, as well as shrinking financial redistribution. When income inequality garnered some public attention, it was seen as an issue of regional inequality or economic and social gaps between urban and rural areas, not as an income gap between the rich and poor.

Income inequality began to matter when COVID-19 hit Japan at the beginning of 2020. The pandemic had a detrimental effect on the already stagnant economy, which had a direct impact on people, especially those who were less well-off. It made the growing income gap visible to people. Surveys and polls prior to the 2021 election showed that people were frustrated with the government and its economic policy; they wanted a change. Political parties were aware of the public dissatisfaction and put forward various measures to revive the economy, address income inequality, and re-build the middle class before the election. Although the parties had similar goals, their approaches differed; the united opposition—the CDP, JCP, SDP, and Reiwa—focused on redistribution while the ruling LDP put more emphasis on growth.

Why did the LDP win the election and secure a sole majority if voters were discontented with the existing economic policies that led to increasing income inequality and if they wanted a new policy? There are many possible factors that led to the victory of the LDP despite public dissatisfaction with the party and its handling of the economy and the pandemic. Although income inequality emerged as a visible issue in

Japanese politics, it was not one of the most important issues that had a decisive impact on voters' choices in the 2021 HR election.

In addition, the LDP and opposition parties used similar framings for their policies to address economic inequality. Although specific plans did not differ greatly from those tried under the Abe and Suga administrations, Prime Minister Kishida suggested his vision of a "new capitalism" using growth through redistribution to address rising income gaps and stalled wages and household incomes, which was similar to the opposition parties' stance. The difference between the ruling and opposition parties' relevant policies was too marginal for voters—even those for whom income inequality was a primary concern—to shift their votes to the opposition.

Now that the Japanese public has become conscious of economic inequality in their country, it will remain a salient issue unless people's economic conditions significantly improve through substantial increase in wages and household incomes or through redistribution. For example, in South Korea, income gap between the haves and have-nots has been one of the critical issues in general and presidential elections since people's perceptions of income inequality became acute in late 2000s. Although the parties stated before the 2021 election that they will address the income gap through redistribution to spark economic growth, their election platforms lacked specific and differentiated measures and strategies to bring tangible results. Whether Prime Minister Kishida and his newly created New Capitalism Realization Headquarters can implement a new form of capitalism through concrete and innovative action plans, and which party will dominate by demonstrating an effective and distinctive set of policies to address the issues of income and wealth inequality, will have significant implications for future elections in Japan.

NOTES

1. South Korea ranked 32nd in the global ranking for income inequality based on the Gini index (Ipsos, "Inequalities around the globe: What the world sees as most serious," March 19, 2021). Its wealth inequality is also low with a wealth Gini coefficient of 67.6 on a scale where 70 indicates low wealth inequality and 80 or higher means high wealth inequality (Credit Suisse Global Wealth Report 2021).
2. See Hijino (2016) and Chiavacci (2018) for analyses of regional inequality in the 2014 and 2017 elections respectively. See also Chiavacci (2022) for the role of social inequality in Japanese democracy and politics.

3. The United States is the world's largest economy by nominal GDP. Japan and the United Kingdom mark the third and the fifth largest, respectively.

4. Relative redistribution is calculated as the difference between pre-tax and transfer Gini and post-tax and transfer Gini divided by pre-tax and transfer Gini and then multiplied by 100.

5. See Chapter 14 in Ito and Hoshi (2020) for more information about Japan's two Lost Decades and the lessons learned from this period of economic stagnation.

6. For more details about Abenomics and its limits, read Chiavacci (2018), Katada and Cheung (2018), and Kushida (2018).

7. The survey was conducted by the research company Green Ship. The results were posted on *Kyodo News* on October 13.

8. See Chapter 11 in this volume for an in-depth analysis of public opinion including issues that mattered in people's voting decisions in the 2021 election.

9. *Asahi*, September 13, 2021. The remaining 16% consisted of no response or "I do not know.".

10. The other five issues were constitutionalism, COVID-19, a decarbonized society, gender equality, and government transparency.

11. The Prime Minister provided more detailed explanations regarding implementing "new capitalism" in his policy speech to the 208th Session of the Diet on January 17, 2022. The implementation strategies comprise two parts: Growth Strategy and Distribution Strategy. Growth Strategy includes digitalization, climate change, economic security, and science and technology and innovation. Distribution Strategy focuses on wage increases, investment in human capital, and building the middle class of the next generation by raising household incomes of families with children and youths. Both strategies emphasize close cooperation between the public and private sectors. His full speech is available at https://japan.kantei.go.jp/101_kishida/statement/202201/_00009.html.

12. These numbers are reported cases to the World Health Organization (WHO) as of 4:14 pm CET, December 29, 2021. https://covid19.who.int/

13. Ministry of Health, Labour, and Welfare, Japan.

14. Also, see Chapters 16 and 17 in this volume for further discussion of consequences from the pandemic.

15. Author's original survey.

REFERENCES

Bharti, Nitin and Lucas Chancel. 2019. "Tackling inequality in India: Is the 2019 election campaign up to the challenge?" *WID World Issue Brief* 2019/2.

Chiavacci, David. 2018. "Inequality and the 2017 Election: Decreasing Dominance of Abenomics and Regional Revitalization" in *Japan Decides 2017: The*

Japanese General Election, ed. Robert J. Pekkanen, Steven R. Reed, Ethan Scheiner, and Daniel M. Smith, 219–242. Palgrave Macmillan.

Chiavacci, David. 2022. "Social Inequality in Japan" in *The Oxford Handbook of Japanese Politics*, ed. Robert J. Pekkanen and Saadia M. Pekkanen, 451–470. Oxford University Press.

Engler, Sarah and David Weisstanner. 2021. "The threat of social decline: Income inequality and radical right support." *Journal of European Public Policy* 28(2): 153–173.

Han, Kyung Joon. 2016. "Income inequality and voting for radical right-wing parties." *Electoral Studies* 42: 54-64.

Hijino, Ken V.L. 2016. "Regional Inequality in 2014: Urgent Issue, Tepid Election." In *Japan Decides 2014: The Japanese General Election*, ed. Robert J. Pekkanen, Steven R. Reed, and Ethan Scheiner, 183–198. Palgrave Macmillan.

Ipsos. 2021. "Inequalities Around the Globe": What the world sees as most serious.

Ito, Takatoshi. 2021. "An Assessment of Abenomics: Evolution and Achievements." *Asian Economic Policy Review* 16(2): 190-219.

Ito, Takatoshi and Takeo Hoshi. 2020. *The Japanese Economy, Second Edition*. MIT Press.

Katada, Saori N. and Gabrielle Cheung. 2018. "The First Two Arrows of Abenomics: Monetary and Fiscal Politics in the 2017 Snap Election." In *Japan Decides 2017: The Japanese General Election*, ed. Robert J. Pekkanen, Steven R. Reed, Ethan Scheiner and Daniel M. smith, 243–259. Palgrave Macmillan.

Krauss, Ellis S. and Robert J. Pekkanen. 2010. "The Rise and Fall of Japan's Liberal Democratic Party." *The Journal of Asian Studies* 61(1): 5-15.

Kushida, Kenji E. 2018. "Abenomics' Third Arrow: Fostering Future Competitiveness?" In *Japan Decides 2017: The Japanese General Election*, ed. Robert J. Pekkanen, Steven R. Reed, Ethan Scheiner and Daniel. M. Smith, 261–295. Palgrave Macmillan.

Maeda, Ko. 2010. "Factors behind the Historic Defeat of Japan's Liberal Democratic Party in 2009." *Asian Survey* 5(5): 888-907.

McElwain, Kenneth Mori. 2018. "Constitutional Revision in the 2018 Election." In *Japan Decides 2017: The Japanese General Election*, ed. Robert J. Pekkanen, Steven R. Reed, Ethan Scheiner and Daniel M. Smith. Palgrave Macmillan.

Solt, Frederick. 2020. "Measuring Income Inequality Across Countries and Over Time: The Standardized World Income Inequality Database." *Social Science Quarterly* 101(3):1183–1199. SWIID Version 9.2, December 2021.

Stoetzer, Lukas F., Johannes Giesecke and Heike Klüver. 2021. "How does income inequality affect the support for populist parties?" *Journal of European Public Policy*. https://doi.org/10.1080/13501763.2021.1981981.

Women's Representation and the Gendered Impact of COVID-19 in Japan

Yesola Kweon⊙

According to the World Economic Forum, as of March 2021, Japan placed 120th out of 156 countries in the gender gap ranking, placing last among other major advanced economies.[1] Since the start of the tenure of former Prime Minister Abe Shinzō (2012–2020), the Japanese government has made various policy attempts to enhance women's participation in both the public and private sectors. After almost 10 years, however, these initiatives have yielded mixed results.

This chapter examines the current status of women's representation in the Japanese economy and politics. First, I evaluate the impact of Womenomics, a set of policy initiatives implemented under the Abe regime to increase women's workforce participation. Next, by analyzing recent survey data, I assess the implications of existing gender disparities in the context of the ongoing COVID-19 pandemic. The latter half of the chapter considers gender representation in the political realm,

Y. Kweon (✉)
Sungkyunkwan University, Seoul, South Korea
e-mail: yesola.kweon@skku.edu

including parties' gender-related pledges, the share of women candidates, and the electoral outcomes in the 2021 general election. Finally, this chapter concludes by surveying factors that contribute to the long-term underrepresentation of women in politics.

WOMEN'S ECONOMIC REPRESENTATION

Womenomics: Progress and Challenges

Upon former Prime Minister Abe's return to power in 2012, he pledged to create a society where "all women can shine." Abe's policy priority focused primarily on the revitalization of Japan's economy, with women's advancement being seen as a central tool to fight the country's labor shortage and declining birthrate. Both formal and informal policies were adopted to this end. Table 19.1 lists Womenomics initiatives implemented by the government between 2013 and 2020. These initiatives mostly focused on labor market and social investment policies. They include equal pay for equal work, improved training for women, increased flexibility in work styles, and family policies aimed at helping women balance professional and domestic demands (Vogel 2021). In 2015, the Abe government announced the Fourth Basic Plan for Gender Equality (BPGE), which was later modified under the administration of Prime Minister Suga Yoshihide (2020–2021). This initiative set goals for the realization of balanced gender ratios in multiple areas by 2025. The BPGE is different from other policies in that it sought to go beyond workforce participation. More specifically, the plan emphasized enhancing women's leadership in public and private sectors and expanding women's participation in decision-making processes.

Policy efforts by the government to enhance gender equality yielded improvements in several areas. The largest was in the realm of women's employment. Female labor participation increased from 62.6% in 2012 to 72.77 in 2019.[2] More importantly, the employment rate of women with children (aged 25 to 44), a group often disadvantaged in the labor market, increased from 67.7% in 2021 to 76.5 in 2018. The rate of women who continue working after their first child also increased from 40.4% in 2009 to 53.1% around 2014 (GEBCO 2020).

Despite this progress, challenges remain. The gender wage gap has seen little improvement. The average wage of university-educated females has only slightly increased between 1988 and 2017, hovering around 70%

Table 19.1 Womenomics Initiatives (2013–2020)

Dates	Policies
June, 2013	Japan Revitalization Strategy- JAPAN is back: specified women's empowerment at the center of economic growth strategy
April, 2014	Raise of childcare leave benefits
June, 2014	Declaration on Action by Male Leaders Coalition for Empowerment of Women
March, 2015	The Cabinet Office order on disclosure of corporate affairs
December, 2015	The Forth Basic Plan for Gender Equality
May, 2015—(Annual)	The Intensive Policy to Accelerate the Empowerment of Women
March, 2016	Guidelines for Utilization of Public Procurement and Subsidies Toward the Promotion of Women's Advancement
April, 2016	The Act on the Promotion of Female Participation and Career Advancement in the Workplace
June, 2017	Plan for Raising Children in a Peaceful Environment
May, 2018	Act on Promotion of Gender Equality in the Political Field
June, 2018	Workstyle Reform Act
June, 2018	Revision of Corporate Governance Code
May, 2019	Revision of the Equal Opportunity Employment Act
December, 2020	The Fifth Basic Plan for Gender Equality

Note The Workstyle Reform Act does not exclusively focus on gender equality. Nevertheless, many policies promoted by this act such as equal pay equal work or flexible work styles are seen as vital for increasing women's workforce participation

of the male counterparts' average wage. Similarly, for people with low levels of education, though the wage gap has shrank during this same time period, the wage ratio still remains around 70% (Nagase 2021). In addition, relatively little progress has been made in increasing women's access to leadership roles and improving the quality of their employment. The growth in women's employment has been driven by positions in pink-collar sectors, mostly in health and welfare industries, which are often low-skill and low-paid jobs (Kawaguchi et al. 2021). A significant gender gap in high-ranking work also prevails, with men dominating almost 90% of such positions (Nagase 2021; GEBCO 2020). Figure 19.1 shows that over half of female employees have precarious irregular employment such as part-time and temporary jobs (about 56% as of 2020), whereas the

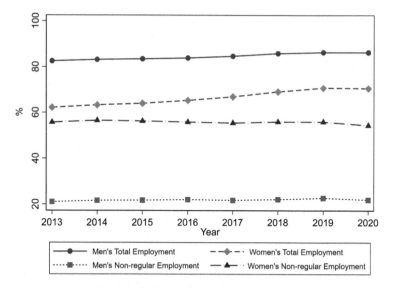

Fig. 19.1 Share of Employment and Non-regular Employment by Gender (*Source* Statistics Bureau of Japan)

share of non-regular employment occupied by men is significantly lower (22.2%).[3] This indicates that while the rate of women's employment has improved since the Abe regime, the quality of their jobs has not.

The Gendered Impact of the COVID-19 Pandemic
Women's overrepresentation in non-regular and low-skill low-paid jobs brings with it greater economic vulnerability in times of crises like the COVID-19 pandemic. Given that non-regular employees have greater exposure to furloughs and layoffs, the pandemic has had a distinctly gendered impact. According to a survey by the Ministry of Internal Affairs and Communications, the number of employees on furlough in May 2021 was 5.97 million, the largest figure since December 1967. Among these, females were three to four times more likely to be on furlough than their male counterparts (Zhou 2021). Women's economic and occupational insecurity was further exacerbated during the pandemic, due to the temporary closure of nurseries, kindergartens and schools. During the first three months of the pandemic, when school closures first began, the average working hours and income for women with underage children

dropped by 15.5 and 8.8%, respectively, as opposed to 7.1 and 3.9% for men (Zhou 2021) (Figs. 19.2 and 19.3).

Using YouGov Covid Data Hub v1.0. (Jones 2020), I further examined the gendered impacts of COVID-19 on public perceptions and political attitudes.[6] The cross-sectional data are based on the surveys of public attitudes and health behavior in relation to COVID-19 collected from 29 countries. In this chapter, I only focus on the Japanese data that are pooled over 39 waves starting from the first week of April 2020 to the first week of November, 2021. The top left graph in Fig. 19.2 shows the impact of various demographic factors on the likelihood of people believing that COVID-19 has had a large influence on their life. Not surprisingly, women are more likely than men to believe that their lives are heavily affected. In addition to gender, having children leads to even more significance being attached to the pandemic. In fact, the impact of this trait is even greater than gender. Further, the top-right graph shows that for women, up to 3 children, the perception that one's life is heavily

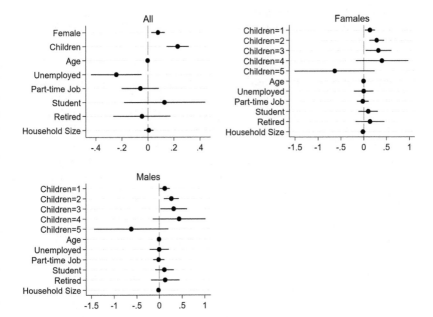

Fig. 19.2 Effects on Perceptions that One's Life is Heavily Influenced by COVID-19[4]

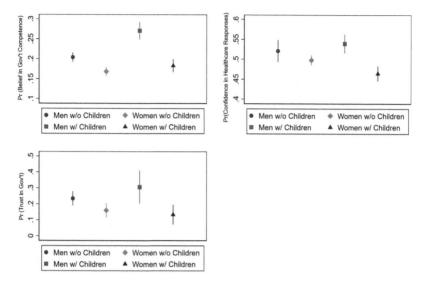

Fig. 19.3 Belief in Government Competence, Confidence in Healthcare Responses, and Trust in Government by Gender and Those with/without Children[5]

affected by COVID-19 strengthens as the number of children increases. Similarly, as presented in the bottom-left graph in Fig. 19.2, men with children are more likely to feel the effect of COVID-19 on their lives.

The pandemic has also imposed gendered implications for political attitudes. Figure 19.3 shows predicted probabilities of belief in government competence, confidence in healthcare responses, and trust in government for men and women with and without children.[7] It demonstrates that women, particularly those with children, on average have lower levels of confidence in the healthcare response to COVID-19, belief in government competence, and trust in government. By contrast, men with children exhibit the strongest levels of belief in those categories. The gendered difference between those with children is statistically significant across all three categories. While this subject warrants more in-depth examination, the different perceptions of COVID-19 and its impact between males and females can have important electoral effects. In fact, recent exit polls show that if only women had voted in this election, the LDP would have lost more seats, indicating that Japanese women tend to be more left-leaning than male voters.[8] However, the negative economic impacts connected to COVID-19 for women, if not resolved, may result in lower rate of voter turnout in the long term. Female vote turnout in this election (55.80%) was comparable to the male turnout (56.06%) in this election. However, as many studies show (Emmenegger et al. 2015; Kweon 2018), economic insecurity can increase vote abstention if voters do not see any party that can represent their interests.

WOMEN'S POLITICAL REPRESENTATION

Women's underrepresentation is an issue not only in the economy, but also in the political realm. Nevertheless, several indicators preceding the 2021 general election hinted that the future might bring a positive change. It was the first general election since the enactment of the Act on Promotion of Gender Equality in the Political Field. Though not mandated, this 2018 law encouraged parties to balance the number of male and female candidates. The BPGE also aimed to raise the ratio of female candidates in national elections to 35% by 2025. Finally, in the Liberal Democratic Party (LDP)'s presidential election, two women, Takaichi Sanae and Noda Seiko, competed against other two male candidates as the first women in 13 years seeking leadership in the ruling party. This encouragement, however, did not lead to an increase in female parliamentarians in the election (See Nemoto 2022 and Smith 2013 on candidate nomination processes).

Party Pledges on Gender Equity Issues in the 2021 General Election

All major parties had pledges devoted to gender-related issues, many of which were similar across the ideological spectrum. Major parties demonstrated their commitment to labor market and domestic policies by emphasizing support for non-regular employment, fertility treatment, and childbirth and child-rearing. Nevertheless, noticeable differences between the LDP and other opposition parties did exist. While all other parties listed these policy pledges on their platforms under a separate section of diversity and/or gender equality, the LDP included their initiatives for women-related issues as a part of their "new capitalism" economic agenda. The LDP framed women's employment and family support as a part of economic strategy rather than as a rights issues. In that sense, the LDP's approach to women's issues under the Kishida regime resonates the Abe regime's Womenomics. The LDP's junior coalition partner, Kōmeitō's women-related policies also mostly focused on child-rearing and childbirth and labor market policies for women's employment. The only noticeable difference between the two parties was that Kōmeitō supported selective surnames for married couples while the LDP did not.

By contrast, opposition parties, particularly left-leaning ones, pledged policies that were directly related to women's social rights. The Constitutional Democratic Party of Japan (CDP) advocated anti-discrimination measures and gender mainstreaming of government budget and policies. The CDP, SDP (Social Democratic Party), and Japanese Communist Party (JCP) all emphasized gender quotas or affirmative action for women in politics. Another area where opposition parties differ from the LDP was issues related to LGBTQ rights and separate surnames for married couples. With only the exception of the LDP, all other parties supported same sex marriage and selective surnames for married couples.

Female Candidates and Elected Members

While often halting and diluted, the past decade has witnessed an array of government efforts to enhance gender equality. However, the results of these interventions on the role of women in electoral politics has been disappointing (See Miura 2017). Table 19.2 presents the number and share of women among candidates and elected MPs. Out of 1051 contenders, there were only 186 women, making up 17.7% of candidates. This rate is comparable to the rate in the 2017 general election. Among the nine parties participating in the election, the ruling coalition had the lowest share of women candidates with the LDP slating 9.8% and Kōmeitō having 7.5%. The SDP had the highest female share with 60%. The largest opposition party, the CDP, had 18.3%.

With respect to the number of women elected, out of 465 seats, female candidates were selected for 45 seats, making up 9.76% of Diet members. This is down two seats from the 2017 election. Again, the ruling LDP has the lowest share of women MPs, 7.7%. Among parties that had more than 10 elected candidates, the JCP has the highest ratio of women, 20%.

WHY SO FEW WOMEN IN JAPANESE POLITICS?

In the aftermath of this election, one could easily ask why there have been so few women in Japanese politics for so long. The enhancement of

Table 19.2 % of women among candidates and elected MPs by parties

	Women Candidates		Elected Women	
	Number	Ratio (%)	Number	Ratio (%)
Liberal Democratic Party	33	9.8	20	7.7
Kōmeitō	4	7.5	4	12.5
Constitutional Democratic Party	44	18.3	13	13.54
Japan Ishin no Kai	14	14.6	4	9.76
Democratic Party for the People	8	29.6	1	9.09
Japanese Communist Party	46	35.4	2	20
Social Democratic Party	9	60	0	0
Reiwa Shinsengumi	5	23.8	1	33
NHK Party	10	33.3	-*	-

Note *NHK Party Did not Win Any Seat in This Election

women's representation in politics requires a multidimensional effort. In order to explain the lack of women in Japan's political sphere, we need to consider both supply-side and demand-side factors.

Supply-Side Factors

On the supply-side, the lack of women can be explained largely by four factors: (1) the absence of institutional mandates, (2) the best-loser rule, (3) LDP dominance, and 4) double binds for females.

First, despite continuous effort by some progressives to create a mandated gender quota, Japan failed to do so because of strong pushback, mostly from the conservative ruling party. However, gender quotas are one of most the effective and widely used ways to enhance descriptive women's political representation (Krook 2009). Today, more than 130 countries employ some form of electoral gender quotas. In both Taiwan and South Korea, mandatory gender quotas have contributed significantly to the increased number of elected women (Shin 2014; Huang 2015).

Besides a gender quota, the best-loser rule disincentivizes women's representation in Japan. Japan has a mixed electoral system that combines SMD and PR tiers, and it allows dual candidacy, enabling one candidate to simultaneously run in both tiers. Parties often use the best-loser rule to populate the PR lists, nominating multiple candidates at the same rank. Under this rule, dual-listed candidates who lose their SMD contests are reranked on the PR list according to how closely they came to winning the SMD. As a result, those who lose in SMD contests by a small margin are the most likely to win PR seats.

PR systems tend to be more effective than SMD models at enhancing both the descriptive and substantive representation of women (Schwindt-Bayer and Mishler 2005; Kweon and Ryan 2021). However, best-loser rules undermine these beneficial features of PR by favoring those who are competitive in district elections. First-time politicians and women who tend to have a weak base in their constituencies have a lower chance of winning seats in both electoral tiers (Kerevel et al. 2019). Further, there is strong preference for incumbent candidates by parties, (See Rehmert 2022 in this volume), reducing women's chances for nomination.

LDP dominance also presents a high barrier to women's entry into politics. The average winning rate of the LDP's female candidates is much higher compared to that of opposition parties. More than 50% of LDP candidates who are women win their seats (Lin and Yang 2021). This means that if the LDP is willing to support more female candidates, the impact will be substantial. Nevertheless, the 2021 election demonstrates that the party has little willingness to actively promote women politicians.

Lastly, running for office requires enormous commitment of time and lifestyle. However, women are more likely to be expected to commit to familial care and housework responsibilities. Such social and cultural demands cut against the requirements of a full-time political career, undermining women's representation in politics. This is particularly a problem in politics as voters tend to prefer candidates with traditional profiles such as being married and having children (Iversen and Rosenbluth 2010; Teele et al. 2018).

Demand-Side Factors

Even when institutional reforms favorable to women's representation are made, without strong public support, a substantive alteration to the gender disparity still may not occur. On the demand-side, this section focuses specifically on two elements: (1) civil society and social movements and (2) public opinion. First, Japan has a long history of women's movements beginning with the suffragette and labor movements of the early twentieth century. Nevertheless, women's movements have remained fragmented and decentralized. In addition, women's organizations have tended to emphasize the role of women as wives and mothers and focus on non-political issues such as consumer rights or environmental protection (Shin 2011). Women's groups played a crucial role in the creation of the Equal Employment Opportunity Law and the legislative process related to domestic violence. Nevertheless, the small and dispersed nature of women's organizations resulted in the absence of a unified voice for political reforms to enhance women's visibility in politics (Gaunder 2015).

The fragmented nature of feminist social movements continues to be reflected in recent #MeToo and Flower Demo movements. Both campaigns called for action against sexual violence and harassment as well as against widespread gendered practices within companies. While these movements helped create an accessible space for women to share their experience with sexism (Miura 2021), it had a limited impact on the political realm. This result comes in contrast to the impact of similar feminist movements in South Korea, which led to both legislative and political changes (See Hasunuma and Shin 2019). There, over 100 pieces of legislation related to sexual violence and gender discrimination were proposed and several policy proposals and the revision of laws on sexual harassment and gender-based violence were made.

With respect to public opinion, interest in gender issues has been growing in Japan. According to a Kyodo News Survey, more than 60% of the respondents believe gender equality is not realized in the country. The figure increases to 70% when limited to only female respondents.[9] Yet, the salience of gender issues is weaker compared to other electoral issues and demand for political reform is limited. Similarly, while NHK survey shows that about 60% of respondents, particularly women and the young, indicated that child-rearing issues were their policy priorities,[10] such interest was subordinated to economic concerns and policies related to the COVID-19 pandemic.

Studies on voters' preference for female politicians also provide mixed results. Some find that voters do not punish women candidates electorally nor are they are less likely to approve of policy statements by female politicians (Miwa et al. 2020). By contrast, others find that female politicians experience greater disadvantages than their male counterparts in garnering voter support (Ono and Yamada 2020), or while there is no penalty for women, they receive less of a boost from experience than male counterparts (Horiuchi et al. 2020).

CONCLUSION

This chapter has considered women's representation in the economic and political realms of Japan. With respect to the economy, despite various Womenomics initiatives by the government, a considerable gender disparity in labor markets prevails. Though women's employment has significantly increased since 2012, women remain economically vulnerable as they are overrepresented in precarious jobs and sectors. Additionally, my findings suggest that women with children are most likely to believe that the pandemic has had a heavy impact on their lives, and they have the lowest confidence in healthcare responses and government counter measures. This means that the pandemic has not only resulted in an economic impact, but more importantly, it also has gendered political consequences.

In the political realm, despite considerable similarities in policy pledges related to women's issues across parties, there exists a key difference between the LDP and other left-leaning opposition parties. In particular, the LDP's women-related initiatives in 2021 were heavily oriented toward labor market policies. By contrast, other left-leaning parties' gender equality initiatives included those directly related to women's social rights and political representation. The LDP's disinterest in women's representation is reflected in its lowest share of women candidates and elected lawmakers, and overall the number of women elected to the Diet declined relative to the previous election.

With respect to public opinion and attitudes toward women's issues and gender representation, various surveys show that there has been growing interest in both topics. However, the key questions here are whether voters, particularly female voters, see the need for female representation in politics and whether growing public interest in gender issues will translate into greater political reform for women. The answer to these questions depends on whether the public can discern a connection between women's descriptive and substantive representation. Given the current political environment in Japan, however, this connection may not be abundantly clear. Though there certainly are female representatives who have progressive views on gender issues, the low visibility of these individuals in politics means that the presence of a few conservative women who explicitly embrace patriarchal norms, such as Sugita Mio, Marukawa Tamayo, or Takaichi Sanae, can significantly weaken the connection between descriptive and substantive representation, muffling a public sense of urgency for greater representation of women in parliament.

Notes

1. https://www.weforum.org/reports/global-gender-gap-report-2021.
2. Source: World Bank https://data.worldbank.org/indicator/SL.TLF. ACTI.FE.ZS?locations=JP (accessed November 2nd, 2021).
3. Data are from Statistics Bureau of Japan.
4. Coefficient plots based on ordinary least squares regressions using data from the Imperial College London YouGov Covid Data Hub v1.0. (Jones 2020). A coefficient (indicated by a circle marker) indicates a change in the dependent variable (the belief that one's life is heavily influenced by Covid-19) resulted by one unit increase in a given independent variable.
5. Predicted probabilities based on logistic regressions using data from the Imperial College London YouGov Covid Data Hub v1.0. (Jones 2020).
6. Perception of the impact if Covid-19 on one's life (on a 7-point scale) was regressed on female, children, age, unemployment status, part-time job status, student, retirement status and household size using OLS. Robust standard errors were clustered by regions and fixed effects for survey waves (total 39 waves) were included.
7. Figures are based on logit regressions. Robust standard errors were clustered by regions, and fixed effects for survey waves were included. Other demographic attributes such as age, employment and job status, and household size were controlled for.
8. See   https://www.nikkei.com/article/DGXZQOUA02D9R0S1A101C 2000000/
9. Source: Kyodo News https://english.kyodonews.net/news/2021/05/ 2f10c466c375-over-60-say-gender-equality-not-realized-in-japan-kyodo-poll.html?phrase=gender%20&words=gender.
10. Source: NHK News https://www3.nhk.or.jp/news/html/20210924/ k10013275421000.html (accessed November 1st, 2021).

References

Emmenegger, Patrick, Paul Marx, and Dominik Schraff. 2015. "Labour Market Disadvantage, Political Orientations and Voting." *Socio-economic Review* 13(2): 189–213.

Gaunder, Alisa. 2015. "Quota Nonadoption in Japan: The Role of the Women's Movement and the Opposition." *Politics & Gender* 11(1): 176-186.

Gender Equality Bureau Cabinet Office (GEBCO). 2020. "II. Progress and Achievements." in *Women and Men in Japan 2020*.

Hasunuma, Linda and Ki-young Shin. 2019. "#MeToo in Japan and South Korea: #WeToo and #WithYou." *Journal of Women, Politics, and Policy* 40(1): 97–111.

Horiuchi, Yusaku, Daniel M. Smith, and Teppei Yamamoto. 2020. "Identifying Voter Preferences for Politicians' Personal Attributes: A Conjoint Experiment in Japan." *Political Science Research and Methods* 8(1): 75–91.

Huang, Chang-Ling. 2015. "Gender Quotas in Taiwan: The Impact of Global Diffusion." *Politics & Gender* 11(1): 207–217.

Iversen, Torben, and Frances Rosenbluth. 2010. *Women, Work, and Politics: The Political Economy of Gender Inequality.* New Haven, NJ: Yale University Press.

Jones, Sarah P., Imperial College London Big Data Analytical Unit and YouGov Plc. 2020. *Imperial College London YouGov Covid Data Hub*, v1.0. YouGov Plc. April 2020.

Kawaguchi, Daiji, Keisuke Kawata, and Takahiro Toriyabe. 2021. "An Assessment of Abenomics from the Labor Market Perspective." *Asian Economic Policy Review* 16: 247–278.

Kerevel, Yann P., Austin S. Matthews, and Katsunori Seki. 2019. "Mixed-member Electoral Systems, Best Loser Rules, and the Descriptive Representation of Women." *Electoral Studies* 57: 153–162.

Krook, Mona Lena. 2009. *Quotas for Women in Politics: Gender and Candidate Selection Reform Worldwide.* New York: Oxford University Press.

Kweon, Yesola. 2018. "Types of Labor Market Policy and the Electoral Behavior of Insecure Workers." *Electoral Studies* 55: 1–10.

Kweon, Yesola and Josh M. Ryan. 2021. "Electoral Systems and the Substantive Representation of Marginalized Groups." *Political Research Quarterly.* Online first version.

Lin, Chao-Chi and Wan-Ying Yang. 2021. "Electoral Rules, Nomination Strategies, and Women's Representation in Japan and Taiwan." *Social Science Japan Journal.* Online first version.

Miura, Mari. 2017. "Persistent Women's Under-Representation in Japan." In *Japan Decides 2017: The Japanese General Election,* (eds.), Robert J. Pekkanen, Steven R. Reed, Ethan Scheiner, and Daniel M. Smith. New York, NY: Palgrave Macmillan.

Miura, Mari. 2021. "Flowers for Sexual Assault Victims: Collective Empowerment through Empathy in Japan's #MeToo Movement." *Politics & Gender.* Online first version.

Miwa, Hirofumi, Musashi Happo and Kaho Odaka. 2020. "Are Voters Less Persuaded by Female than by Male Politicians' Statements?" *Journal of Elections, Public Opinion and Parties.* Online first version.

Nagase, Nobuko. 2021. "Abe's Womenomics Policy: Did It Reduce the Gender Gap in Management?" In *The Political Economy of the Abe Government and*

Abenomics Reforms, (eds.), Hoshi, Takeo and Philip Y. Lipscy. New York, NY: Cambridge University Press.

Nemoto, Kuniaki. 2022. "How the Liberal Democratic Party Avoided a Loss in 2021." In *Japan Decides 2021: The Japanese General Election*, (eds.), Robert J. Pekkanen, Steven R. Reed, Daniel M. Smith. Palgrave Macmillan.

Ono, Yoshikuni, and Masahiro Yamada. 2020. "Do voters prefer gender stereotypic candidates?" *Political Science Research and Methods* 8(3): 477–492.

Rehmert, Jochen. 2022. "Candidate Selection for the 2021 General Election." In *Japan Decides 2021: The Japanese General Election*, (eds.), Robert J. Pekkanen, Steven R. Reed, Daniel M. Smith. Palgrave Macmillan.

Schwindt-Bayer, Leslie A. and William Mishler. 2005. "An Integrated Model of Women's Representation." *Journal of Politics* 67(2): 407–428.

Shin, Ki-young. 2014. "Women's sustainable representation and the spillover effect of electoral gender quotas in South Korea." *International Political Science Review.* 35(1): 80–92.

Shin, Ki-young. 2011. "The Women's Movements." In *The Routledge Handbook of Japanese Politics*, (ed.) Gaunder, Alisa, London, UK: Routledge, 175–186.

Smith, Daniel M. 2013. "Candidate Recruitment for the 2012 Election: New Parties, New Methods ... Same Old Pool of Candidates?" In *Japan Decides 2012: The Japanese General Election*, (eds.), Robert J. Pekkanen, Steven R. Reed and Ethan Scheiner. London: Palgrave Macmillan, 101–122.

Teele, Dawn, Joshua Kalla, and Frances Rosenbluth. 2018. "The Ties That Double Bind: Social Roles and Women's Underrepresentation in Politics." *American Political Science Review* 112(3): 525–541.

Vogel, Steven K. 2021. "Abe's Slight Left Turn: How a Labor Shortage Transformed Politics and Policy." In *The Political Economy of the Abe Government and Abenomics Reforms*, (eds.), Hoshi, Takeo and Philip Y. Lipscy. New York, NY: Cambridge University Press.

Zhou, Yanfei. 2021. "How Women Bear the Brunt of Covid-19's Damages on Work." *Japan Labor Issues* 5 (28): 2–8.

CHAPTER 20

Black Lives Matter in Japan: The Specter of Race and Racism Haunting Japan

Michael Orlando Sharpe

Although Black Lives Matter (BLM) impacted the US 2020 election, it was more background in Japan's 2021 polls but brought important issues of race and racism into the national conversation. This chapter argues that BLM in Japan follows a long pattern of ambivalence around race as the world's first non-white modern power. As such, claims making has revolved around historically marginalized groups' specific interests that strategically access transnational social justice movements and international and human rights machinery. The Buraku movement's 1924 Declaration of the National Levelers Association, known as Japan's first human rights declaration, drew inspiration from the 1917 Russian Revolution, the League of Nations, and Taisho democracy. Buraku advocacy produced Dowa and human rights education about Buraku issues since the 1960s. Inspired by the US Civil Rights movement, the non-citizen

M. O. Sharpe (✉)
York College and the Graduate Center of the City University of New York, New York, NY, USA
e-mail: msharpe@york.cuny.edu

Zainichi Korean minority won many welfare benefits and legal protections. Consequentially, by the mid-1980s Japan's welfare benefits for settled foreign residents were among the world's most generous but somewhat inadequate for newer migrant noncitizens (Chung 2014, 401; 2020, 8). Through transnational native movements and human right pressures, the indigenous Ainu were officially recognized by the Japanese government in 2008 (Tsutsui 2018).

BLM in Japan has been successful in highlighting the notions and attitudes that perpetuate antiblack racism but has fallen short in joining concerted action among newer and older excluded groups under an antiracist banner. This chapter will first discuss BLM Japan's immediate impact, second Japan's racial gymnastics, third the complexities of black admiration and antiblack racism, and finally what BLM tells us about race, racism, and coalition building possibilities. As Japan opens to immigration (Sharpe 2014; Hollifield and Sharpe 2017; Strauz 2019; Liu-Farrer 2020), the realities of old and new racisms will increasingly become center stage with antiracist collective action and policy innovation critical to Japan's future development as a liberal democracy.

Background: Older and Newer "Races"

The media coverage of the June 2020 Black Lives Matter (BLM) protests in Tokyo and Osaka raises two contradictory discourses. One narrative declares the protests as pivotal and the largest in Tokyo history (some 3,000 participants) with parallel Osaka demonstrations.[1] Another describes the protests as "falling flat," with little impact.[2] The specter of race and racism haunts Japan as it is both conspicuously absent and omnipresent in its modern history. This stands alongside Japan's postwar master narrative of uniquely exclusive homogeneity (*tan'itsu minzoku*) or near synonymity of nation, language, race, and culture. Embedded is a dismissal of diversity as virtually and hence racism as not a Japanese problem.

Official rhetoric and commonsense notions of homogeneity obstruct Japan's historic minorities. These "invisible" minorities include indigenous Ainu (24,000) and Okinawans (1 million), Burakumin (outcastes) (3 million), and *Zainichi* Korean (colonial descendants[3]) (600,000) or 4–6% of Japan's population (Lam 2005, 225; Siddle 1996, 6). As post Meiji Japanese intellectuals and policymakers were influenced by Western race pseudoscience, these groups have been historically deemed "inferior races" with descent based assigned traits in immutable, biological, and hierarchical terms (Takezawa 2011: 9). Until 2019, Japan officially prohibited unskilled foreign labor (Kashiwazaki 2000; Sharpe 2014). Facing demographic and labor shortages, post 1990 reforms created immigration "side doors" that have added diversity with "new races" of visible "newcomers." They include often exploited "trainee" laborers, co-ethnics, asylum seekers, and undocumented mostly from Asia but also Latin America and Africa. In 2018, Prime Minister Abe Shinzō paradoxically announced a measure to dramatically increase unskilled foreign workers while stating that it is not an immigration policy (Chung 2020: Strauz 2022). The foreign resident population was 2.32%[4] in 2019 with 21,919 international marriages and growing numbers of mixed-race (*hāfu/double*) Japanese children.[5] Japan's policy trajectory suggests Prime Minister Kishida Fumio will continue expansion of the immigration regime to include permanency for immigrants and their families.[6]

Despite old and new heterogeneity, it is not uncommon to encounter "Japanese Only" signs in public places in major Japanese cities. Article 14 of the Japanese constitution prohibits discrimination based on race, creed, sex, social status, or family origin, but nothing in Japanese law makes discrimination illegal (Ardou 2015). Japan has avoided implementation of a national law on the basis that discrimination itself is not a serious problem. Since the mid-2000s contentious demonstrations occur between far-right anti-Korean and antiracist pro-Korean movements. Hate speech has been prominent on social media with *Zaitokukai* (Civil Association Against Privileges for Resident Koreans) and other groups calling *Zainichi* Koreans "criminals," "cockroaches," for their murder, as well as targeting new migrants (Park 2017, 66). This incendiary speech includes that aimed at Burakumin and racist tropes against blacks, and mixed-race Japanese luminaries as not representative of Japan.[7] Ultranationalist cybercommunity *Netto-uyoku* and others propagate conspiracy theories that claim BLM as Chinese government propaganda. Some older Japanese activists problematize racism in Japan as only anti-Korean with antiblack racism a minor problem due to small black population (50,000) (Capobianco 2015, 190). This characterization, however, is contradicted by Japanese entertainers' widespread practice of using blackface, akin to minstrelsy.

In 2017, Japan's first national survey of foreign residents' human rights reported discrimination in employment and housing, racist taunts, hate speech, and Japanese-only recruitment.[8] On its Tokyo website,

BLM states: "Our mission is to strengthen our ties with the Japanese community through anti-racist action, community outreach efforts, and education of black history and the history of racism in order to move towards a more culturally diverse and understanding environment for all."[9] BLM has sparked a national conversation about antiblack racism, racism against mixed-race Japanese and visible foreigners, but less so about invisible minorities.

BRINGING RACE AND RACISM
INTO JAPAN'S NATIONAL CONVERSATION

BLM impacted Japan by speaking a national discourse about race and racism through protest, social media, television, and the 2021 Tokyo Olympics. Thousands marched in the 2020 Blacks Lives Matter demonstrations in solidarity with the struggle against antiblack racism and police brutality in the United States and internationally. This intensified discussion about Japan's related issues including an earlier alleged police mistreatment of a Kurdish resident.[10] Tennis phenom Naomi Osaka promoted joining the protests, wore BLM merchandise, and even had a temporary tournament withdrawal over another US police killing of a black man.[11] In an effort to possibly claim the brown-skinned Osaka, Nissin foods distributed a "white-washed" cartoon of her with white skin and light brown hair for which they ultimately apologized.[12]

NHK, Japan's public broadcaster, also came under fire for releasing an animated video that attempted to explain the BLM protests after the murder of George Floyd. The NHK video portrayed stereotypical caricatures of African Americans looting with a narrator speaking in crude and vulgar Japanese about inequality and the Coronavirus as the protests' sources. The NHK piece did not address the roots of systemic racism in the United States namely 400 years of enslavement of black people, Jim Crow, and racial segregation. The video failed to acknowledge BLM's priority issues, e.g., the systemic police killings of unarmed blacks, racial profiling, police brutality, and the US justice system. The video was decried internationally and in Japan for its stereotypical and racist images and contemptable historical and contextual omissions.[13] The US Embassy in Tokyo condemned the video. NHK apologized and launched an initiative to retrain its staff on human rights.

Alternatively, the Tokyo 2021 Summer Olympics opening ceremonies shocked the world with biracial Japanese and black world class athletes leading Japan's Olympic delegation, including tennis icon Osaka (Japanese/Haitian) lighting the Olympic cauldron and basketball star Rui Hachimura (Japanese/Beninese) as Japan's flag bearer. In partial violation of article 50 of the IOC charter's political speech prohibition, the Japanese Olympic women's soccer team uncharacteristically breached etiquette and protested in solidarity against racial discrimination of black players on England's national team (see also Leheny 2022).[14]

Additional tragedies further contributed to the national conversation on race. A Nigerian man died by suicide while in immigration detention in 2019 and a Sri Lankan woman died in a similar facility in 2021 drawing protests to reveal what happened. BLM in Japan drew both pride and ire on social media but its most far-reaching impact is its bringing of antiblack racism and racism in general into Japan's national conversation. All of this speaks to a powerful ambivalence about race and racism that has its roots in Japan's modern political development.

Japan's Racial Gymnastics as World's First Non-White Power

Race and racism have been central in modern Japan. Encounters with Western powers made for racial gymnastics over less than 200 years from invented monoethnicity, multiethnic empire, to postwar homogeneous reembrace. Modern Japan came of age during the rise of Western racial pseudoscience and notions of inherent white racial supremacy and non-white inferiority. The Meiji Restoration of 1868 and its need to establish a united and "prosperous county and a strong army" (*fukoku kyohei*) was epitomized in Japan's policy objectives which included equivalency in treaty revision, international recognition, and ultimately colonial expansion to be on par with Western counterparts (Kawai 2015, 29; 2020, 7; Siddle 1996, 10; Hane 1992, 85).

Like Germany, Japan is a "late developer" its modern state formed with the late nineteenth-century Meiji Restoration from a disparate populace and promotion of a common ethnically homogenous nationalism. It can be said that the Japanese learned from Otto von Bismarck (Prussia/Germany) and his notion of "blood and iron" about an ethnic conception of nationhood. The official end of feudalism in 1871 coincides with the Edict of Emancipation's superficial abolishment of Buraku caste discrimination and their ordering along with the internal colonialism and

homogenization of the Ainu and Okinawan indigenous minorities constituted as "alien races," primitive, or racially immature. It is notable that
the colonial administration of Hokkaido was later similarly employed in
the colonization of Taiwan in 1895 and annexation of Korea in 1910 (De
Vos and Wagatsuma 1966; Siddle 1996; Park 2017; Weiner 1995, 450;
Takezawa 2011, 9; De Vos and Lee 1981).

As "non-white," Japanese theoretically constituted an "inferior"
people. Fukuzawa Yukichi, a preeminent Meiji intellectual, popularized
Blumenbach's taxonomy of the five races and the idea of racial classi-
fication but replaced geography with color situating the yellow race in
between white and black (Kawai 2015, 28). He ranked the world's countries as civilized and semi-civilized and noted Japan as semi-civilized on
the way to being civilized (Weiner 2009, 7). For Fukuzawa and other
intellectuals, Japan must achieve the same level civilizational status as the
West to not face potential Western domination like China and other non-
Western countries. Hence, Japan followed the Meiji slogan of "Leave
Asia and Enter Europe" (*datsu-a nyu-o*) (Takezawa 2015, 5, 11). In
an example of racial positioning, Taguchi Ukichi justified this "on the
claim that the Japanese were Aryans and Caucasians" (Oguma 2002,
144–145, 147). Meiji period political elites did not simply import but
rather adapted Western racial ideologies—such as Social Darwinism and
eugenics to suit Japan's policy objectives. In Japan's first work on "race
betterment" Takahashi Yoshio's 1884 *A Treatise on the on Improving the
Japanese Race*, advocated intermarriage between the white and yellow
races as well as physical fitness, clothing, education, diet and better living
and moral standards to "improve the Japanese race" (Otsubo 2005, 63;
Kawai 2015).

Japan's 1908 defeat of Russia and the "racial equality bill" proposal at
the 1919 Paris Peace Conference challenged white supremacy and precipi-
tated Afro-Asian transnational solidarities to unite colored peoples against
white supremacy (Shimazu 1998; Koshiro 2003; Araki 2014; Horne
2018). Some in and out of Japan saw the country as the "champion of
the darker races" (Allen 1994). Japan used Pan-Asianism "Same Origin,
Same Race" (*dō-so dō-shu*) with itself as Asia's unifier to justify colonialism
and racism (Shin 2010, 33; Weiner 1995, 443).

This was a multiethnic empire that strived to colonize with the
Japanese at the top of the hierarchy and the denigration of other Asians
peoples as backwards and inferior. The contemporary *Zainichi* Korean
and Chinese minorities originate in this colonial expansion and subjected

to forced labor, assimilation, and sexual exploitation establishing today's discriminatory patterns. African American intellectual W. E. B. Dubois was a supporter of Japan's empire until he became disillusioned in viewing militarism in Manchuria (Kearney 1995). Japan's imperial exploits include horrific incidences of racially motivated violence. In the pandemonium around the 1923 Great Kanto Earthquake, some six thousand Koreans were killed by vigilantes because of groundless rumors they poisoned the water supply to murder Japanese and commit crimes. Another example is the mass murder of some 200,000–300,000 Chinese people in the 1937 Nanjing Massacre. With Japan's defeat in WWII and the 1954 San Francisco Peace Treaty, there is the sole option of Japanese nationality deprivation for former colonial subjects, the "unmixing of Japan" (Lie 2001) and the reembrace of Japanese homogeneity. Strict border controls were promoted by both Japanese and US authorities to control the perceived communist threat, and their foreign residents from nearby Korea and China. This provides a background for understanding BLM, racism, and immigration in Japan.

THE COMPLEXITIES OF BLACK ADMIRATION AND ANTIBLACK RACISM IN JAPAN

Antiblack racism in Japan follows the lineage of modernity and pseudo-science that influenced Japanese racial perceptions. Naiveté is an argument often made by some to disavow antiblack racism on the claim that they never had slaves on their territory or a significant black population. For example, the comic Hamada appeared in minstrel-like blackface to impersonate Eddie Murphy in the movie Beverly Hills Cop. While the criticism of this and others is racial insensitivity because the butt of the joke is black people, the defense is often Japanese naiveté or paying homage.

The historical record is a bit more complicated. Some ancient Japanese art reveals a preference for pale skin as darker skin was likely associated with field labor. Wagatsuma (1967, 407) argues that lighter skin in Japan has always been associated with "spiritual refinement" and "feminine beauty" and darker skin regarded as "ugly" long before its Western interactions. However, Russell (2009, 84–85) contends Japan had contact with Africans from the sixteenth century with no existent antiblack skin color bias but rather admiration prior to contact with the West. He notes the example of the African man, *Yasuke*, who achieved samurai status after having been brought to Japan by the Europeans as a servant.

The Iwakura Mission of 1871–1873 to Europe and the United States had the goal to acquire Western knowledge but also impacted Japanese intellectuals own "race thinking" about inferior and superior races (Yoshino 1992, 23; Weiner 1995, 43). Koshiro (2003, 185) argues the Iwakura Mission members were initially impressed with African Americans as "colored *yet* modern and Westernized" people and a model for Japan that pushed education to catch up with the "superior white race." As Japanese ideas about African Americans were influenced by Western antiblack racism and skin color correlates, they extricated themselves and aspired to be accepted as "honorary whites" due to military and industrial triumphs and colonial endeavors (Koshiro 2003, 186).

The mission members drew parallels between Native Americans and Ainu becoming extinct as well as African Americans and Burakumin as lower-class people with inherent weaker intellectual ability and inferiority and "conflations of physiological and cultural characteristics" (Weiner 1995, 439; 2009, 5–6). Notions of white supremacy and non-white, particularly black, inferiority is best illustrated in Fukuzawa's race descriptions, "The white race is beautiful in their facial and physical features. They are bright and civilized. They are the most superior race... [The yellow race has short noses and slanted eyes. Although they are resilient and diligent, they are less talented and progressed. [The black race] have a flat nose and unusually large eyes. They are physically very strong but are lazy and least progressed" (Kawai 2015, 29). African American writer Langston Hughes compared the racialization of Koreans in Japan's empire to blacks in the United States (Huh 2017). Reminiscent of the 1923 Great Kanto Earthquake that targeted Koreans, in the midst of the 2011 Great East Japan earthquake, internet rumors alleged that Koreans and blacks were "throwing poison into wells."[15] Kadia (2020, 104–105) cites a Japanese attitudinal survey during allied occupation reflected positive views of (white) Americans and other Westerners and negative perceptions of blacks, likely exacerbated by SCAP segregation policies, as well as East and Southeast Asians, particularly Koreans.

The doctrine of antiblack racism exists in Japan as it does elsewhere but the ways in which race and racism live have important similarities and differences dependent on context. Alleged traditional preferences for pale skin converge with white supremacy and reflected in skin lightening and pop culture. Racism in Japan is a complex mosaic that often reflects country of origin, associated somatic norm and level of development. For these reasons, some argue that white Americans and white

Europeans are at the top of the food chain of visible foreigners with Africans and South Asians toward the bottom. The UN Special Rapporteur Doudou Diene's scathing 2006 UN special report on racism in Japan was largely ignored by the Japanese media.[16] The UN Human Rights Commission recommended Japan prohibit hate speech, citing increasingly serious vitriol particularly against ethnic Koreans. However, there is an interesting fascination with African Americans renowned and mimicked for cultural, athletic, and musical innovation in popular culture. One can witness Africans perform what seems like hip hop inspired impersonations of African Americans in the trendy Tokyo neighborhoods of Roppongi and Harajuku in what they probably envision as more acceptable to some Japanese unable to distinguish English accents. Additionally, reflected in social media is the noteworthy fact that some African Americans living in Japan feel much freer and empowered than in the United States or Europe with little threat of police murder. Black public intellectuals like John Russell and Baye McNeil and young people on social media have brought to light issues of antiblack racism and helped Japanese realize connections to other racisms in Japan. Japan offers a rare non-Western, advanced, and liberal democratic opportunity to understand how antiblack racism and racism in general works.

Conclusion: What Does Black Lives Matter Tell Us About Japan?

BLM is a foreshadowing of race as a major issue in Japan's future elections. Already racist scapegoating has been used against Koreans and others to mobilize Japanese voters in local elections. BLM tells much about the unresolved racial dilemmas of Japanese non-white power and the coalition building possibilities for old and new excluded groups in Japan. The official denial of racism belies and reinforces the practice of everyday racism (Essed 1990). This has facilitated specific organized group interests that access transnational social movements and international and human rights mechanisms but has not yet facilitated antiracist collective action.

For example, *Zainichi* Koreans movements have converged with international conventions and removal of exclusionary clauses against foreigners (Milly 2014, 63). In the single most successful postwar Korean resident mass mobilization, the finger printing law, once required of all foreigners, was abolished for the benefit of special permanent residents, i.e., *Zainichi* Koreans in 1993 and for all residents in 1999. Notably, this was reinstated in 2007 for all noncitizens due to concerns about terrorism, but not for the majority Korean special permanent residents (Chung 2010, 107, 109).[17] The post 2000's antiracist actions against *Zaitokukai* and other ultranationalists focus on *Zainichi* Koreans and Chinese. The many bills introduced by Kōmeitō for permanent resident voting rights reflects the interests of *Zainichi* Korean noncitizens with membership in *Sōka Gakkai*, Kōmeitō's partner Buddhist religious organization (Sharpe 2014; McLaughlin 2019). In July 2014 the Osaka High Court upheld a ruling that found *Zaitokukai* guilty of racial discrimination and ordered it pay ¥12 million. Since 1993, the Buraku liberation movement maintains the International Movement Against All Forms of Discrimination and Racism (IMADR) that lobbies with other groups around caste based and racial discrimination issues at the United Nations level (Tsutsui 2018). Japan's Diet passed anti-hate speech legislation and an Act on the Promotion of the Elimination of Buraku Discrimination in 2016 but the laws lack penalties and rather ineffectual. 2012 saw the birth of an Ainu political party. A 2019 law was passed to protect and promote Ainu culture but Okinawans are still not recognized as an indigenous people. Japanese foreigner support groups such as Solidarity with Migrants Japan (SMJ) advocate for foreign residents rights. IMADR comes the closest to addressing racism across groups but its efforts remain focused on descent based discrimination.

BLM in Japan has helped to bring race, racism, and diversity into Japan's national conversation. It can assist in providing an opportunity to address and expose antiblack racism, the similarities and differences in racisms against visible and invisible marginalized groups and facilitate antiracist coalition building. The presence of biracial black Japanese athletes and celebrities Miss Universe Japan Ariana Miyamoto (Japanese/African American) and Miss Japan Priyanka Yoshikawa (Japanese/Indian) representing Japan, despite backlash, speak to changing self-perceptions. Dr. Ossouby Sacko, a naturalized Japanese citizen (Mali), became the first African to become president of an accredited Japanese university Kyoto Seika University in 2018.[18] In politics, Marutei Tsurunen (Finland), Japan's first foreign-born naturalized politician, Shikun Haku (Japanese/Korean), as well as Renho Murata (Japanese/Taiwanese) have served in Japan's Diet (Sharpe 2014). Two foreign-born naturalized politicians, Puranik Yogendra from India and Noemi Inoue of Bolivia, won seats in the April 2019 Tokyo local assembly elections. The evidence presented thus far suggests a complicated picture of Black admiration, antiblack racism, and the ways in which racism works but must be contextualized.

As Japan's population diversifies, the specter of race and racism looms until it is acknowledged. Japan's elections will undoubtedly be impacted by recognition or denial of old and new heterogeneity. Coalition building across groups under antiracism and policy innovation is critical to Japan's inclusive development and liberal democracy.

NOTES

1. https://theworld.org/stories/2020-09-16/blm-tokyo-tackles-japan-s-own-issues-anti-black-racism (accessed January 6, 2022).
2. https://www.vice.com/en/article/y3gq3g/why-the-black-lives-matter-movement-fell-flat-in-japan (January 6, 2022).
3. In 2019 there were 281,266 special permanent residents with ROK nationality (*Zainichi* Koreans) They along with Taiwanese former imperial subjects and descendants were deprived of Japanese citizenship. http://www.moj.go.jp/isa/content/001335873.pdf (January 11, 2022).
4. http://www.moj.go.jp/isa/content/001335873.pdf (January 11, 2022).
5. https://www.e-stat.go.jp/dbview (accessed June 25, 2021).
6. https://www.japantimes.co.jp/news/2021/11/18/national/japan-indefinite-visas/ (accessed January 11, 2022).
7. https://www.japantimes.co.jp/community/2021/05/24/voices/online-harassment-part-japans-post-racism/ (accessed June 21, 2021).
8. Analytical Report of the Foreign Residents Survey—Revised Edition—Center for Human Rights Education and Training June 2017. https://www.moj.go.jp/content/001249011.pdf (accessed January 28, 2022).
9. https://www.blacklivesmattertokyo.org/ (accessed January 6, 2022).
10. https://www.japantimes.co.jp/news/2020/06/14/national/black-lives-matter-spreads-tokyo-2000-people-march-protest-racism/ (accessed June 15, 2021).
11. https://time.com/5888583/naomi-osaka-masks-black-lives-matter-us-open/; https://www.washingtonpost.com/world/asia_pacific/japanese-tennis-player-naomi-osaka-speaks-out-for-black-lives-matter-faces-bac klash/2020/06/08/f8432ca0-a92f-11ea-a43b-be9f6494a87d_story.html (accessed January 11, 2022).
12. https://mainichi.jp/english/articles/20200918/p2a/00m/0na/020 000c (accessed January 11, 2022).
13. https://www.washingtonpost.com/world/asia_pacific/japan-cartoon-about-black-lives-matter-protests-racist-offensive/2020/06/09/32d 4226c-a9f7-11ea-a43b-be9f6494a87d_story.html (accessed January 11, 2022).

14. https://www.bloomberg.com/news/articles/2021-07-29/black-lives-matter-racial-justice-protests-take-stage-at-tokyo-olympics-2021 (accessed January 11, 2022).
15. https://www.japantimes.co.jp/community/2021/05/24/voices/online-harassment-part-japans-post-racism/ (accessed January 8, 2022).
16. https://digitallibrary.un.org/record/566139?ln=en (accessed June 28, 2021).
17. https://www.moj.go.jp/ENGLISH/IB/ip.html (accessed January 11, 2022).
18. https://www.kyoto-seika.ac.jp/eng/about/overview/greeting.html (accessed January 12, 2021).

REFERENCES

Allen, Ernest. 1994. "When Japan Was "Champion of the Darker Races": Satokata Takahashi and the Flowering of Black Messianic Nationalism", *The Black Scholar*, Vol. 24, No. 1, pp. 23–46.

Araki, Keiko. 2014. "Africa for Africans and Asia for Asians: Japanese Pan-Asianism and Its Impact in the Post-World War I Era", in Kendahl Radcliffe, Jennifer Scott, and Anja Werner (eds.), *Anywhere But Here: Black Intellectuals in the Atlantic World and Beyond*. University Press of Mississippi.

Ardou, Debito. 2015. *Embedded Racism: Japan's Visible Minorities and Racial Discrimination*. Lanham: Lexington Books.

Capobianco, Paul. 2015. "Confronting Diversity: Africans Challenging Japanese Societal Convictions", *Contemporary Japan*, Vol. 27, No. 1, pp. 189–212.

Chung, Erin. A. 2010. *Immigration and Citizenship in Japan*. New York: Cambridge University Press.

Chung, Erin. A. 2014. "Japan and Korea: Immigration Control and Immigrant Incorporation", in James F. Hollifield, Philip L. Martin, and Pia Orrenius (eds.), *Controlling Immigration: A Global Perspective*. 3rd Edition. Stanford University Press.

Chung, Erin. A. 2020. *Immigrant Incorporation in East Asian Democracies*. Cambridge: Cambridge University Press.

De Vos, George and Changsoo Lee. 1981. "The Colonial Experience, 1910–1945", in Changsoo Lee and George De Vos (eds.), *Koreans in Japan: Ethnic Conflict and Accommodation*. Berkeley and Los Angeles: University of California Press.

De Vos, George and Hiroshi Wagatsuma. 1966. *Japan's Invisible Race: Caste in Culture and Personality*. Berkeley: University of California Press.

Essed, Philomena.1990. *Everyday Racism: Reports from Women of Two Cultures*. Hunter House.

Hane, Mikiso. 1992. *Modern Japan: A Historical Survey*. 2nd Edition. Boulder: Westview Press.

Hollifield, James F. and Michael O. Sharpe. 2017. "Japan as an Emerging Migration State", *International Relations of the Asia-Pacific*, September, Vol. 17, No. 3, pp. 371–400.

Horne, Gerald. 2018. *Facing the Rising Sun: African Americans, Japan, and the Rise of Afro-Asian Solidarity*. New York: NYU Press.

Huh, Jang Wook. June 2017. "Beyond Afro-Orientalism: Langston Hughes, Koreans, and the Poetics of Overlapping Dispossessions", *Comparative Literature*, 1 June, Vol. 69, No. 2, pp. 201–221.

Kadia, Mariam Kingsberg. 2020. *Into the Field: Human Scientists of Transwar Japan*. Stanford: Stanford University Press.

Kashiwazaki, Chikako. 2000. "Citizenship in Japan: Legal Practice and Contemporary Development", in T. Alexander Aleinikoff and Douglas Klusmeyer (eds.), *From Migrants to Citizens: Membership in a Changing World*. Washington, DC: Carnegie Endowment for International Peace.

Kawai, Yuko. 2015. "Deracialized Race, Obscured Racism: Japaneseness, Western and Japanese Concepts of Race, Modalities of Racism", *Japanese Studies*, Vol. 35, No. 1, pp. 23–47.

Kawai, Yuko. 2020. *A Transnational Critique of Japaneseness: Cultural Nationalism, Racism, and Multiculturalism in Japan*. Lamhan: Lexington Books.

Kearney, Reginald. 1995. "The Pro-Japanese Utterances of W.E.B. Du Bois", *Contributions in Black Studies*, Vol. 13, Article 7.

Koshiro, Yukiko. 2003. "Beyond an Alliance of Color: The African American Impact on Modern Japan", *Positions: East Asia Cultures Critique*, Vol. 11, pp. 183–215.

Lam, Peng-Er. 2005. "At the Margins of a Liberal-Democratic State: Ethnic Minorities in Japan", in Will Kymlicka and Baogang He (eds.), *Multiculturalism in Asia*. Oxford: Oxford University Press.

Leheny, David. 2022. "The Olympics in the 2021 Election", in Robert J. Pekkanen, Steven R. Reed, and Daniel M. Smith (eds.), *Japan Decides 2021: The Japanese General Election*. Palgrave Macmillan.

Lie, John. 2001. *Multiethnic Japan*. Cambridge: Harvard University Press.

Liu-Farrer, Gracia. 2020. *Immigrant Japan: Mobility and Belonging in an Ethno-Nationalist Society*. Ithaca: Cornell University Press.

McLaughlin, Levi. 2019. *Sokka Gakkai's Human Revolution: The Rise of a Mimetic Nation in Modern Japan*. Honolulu: University of Hawaii Press.

Milly, Deborah J. 2014. *New Policies for New Residents: Immigrants, Advocacy, and Governance in Japan and Beyond*. Ithaca and London: Cornell University Press.

Oguma, Eiji. 2002. *A Genealogy of 'Japanese' Self-Images*. Melbourne: Trans-Pacific Press.

Otsubo, Sumiko. 2005. "The Female Body and Eugenic Thought in Meiji Japan", in Morris Low (ed.), *Building a Modern Japan: Science, Technology, and Medicine in the Meiji Era and Beyond*. New York: Palgrave Macmillan.

Park, Sara. 2017. "Inventing Aliens: Immigration Control, 'Xenophobia' and Racism in Japan", *Race and Class*, Vol. 58, No. 3, pp. 64–80.

Russell, John G. 2009. "The Other: The Black Presence in the Japanese Experience", in Michael Weiner (ed.), *Japan's Minorities: The Illusion of Homogeneity*. 2nd Edition. Abington: Routledge.

Sharpe, Michael O. 2014. *Postcolonial Citizens and Ethnic Migration: The Netherlands and Japan in the Age of Globalization*. Houndmills, Basingstoke: Palgrave Macmillan.

Shimazu, Naoko. 1998. *Japan, Race, and Equality: The Racial Equality Proposal of 1919*. London and New York: Routledge.

Shin, Hwaji. 2010. "Colonial Legacy of Ethno-Racial Inequality in Japan", *Theory and Society*, May, Vol. 39, No. 3/4, pp. 327–342.

Siddle, Richard. 1996. *Race, Resistance, and the Ainu of Japan*. London: Routledge.

Strauz, Michael. 2019. *Help (Not) Wanted: Immigrant Politics in Japan*. Albany: SUNY Press.

Strauz, Michael. 2022. "Immigration and Democracy in Japan", in Robert Pekkanen and Saadia Pekkanen (eds.), *The Oxford Handbook of Japanese Politics*. New York: Oxford University Press.

Takahashi, Yoshio. 1961 [1884]. "Nippon jinshu kairyō ron", in *Meiji bunka shiryō sōsho*. 1. Tokyo: Meiji Bunka Shiryō Sōsho Kankōkai, Vol. 6, pp. 19–55.

Takezawa, Yasuko (ed.). 2011. *Racial Representations in Asia*. Kyoto: Kyoto University Press and Melbourne: Trans Pacific Press.

Takezawa, Yasuko. 2015. "Translating and Transforming 'Race': Early Meiji Period Textbooks", *Japanese Studies*, Vol. 35, No. 1, pp. 5–21.

Tsutsui, Kiyoteru. 2018. *Rights Make Might: Global Human Rights and Minority Social Movement in Japan*. Oxford: Oxford University Press.

Yoshino, Kosaku. 1992. *Cultural Nationalism in Contemporary Japan: A Sociological Enquiry*. London and New York: Routledge.

Wagatsuma, Hiroshi. 1967. "The Social Perception of Skin Color in Japan", *Daedalus*, Spring, Vol. 96, No 2, pp. 407–443.

Weiner, Michael. July 1995. "Discourses of Race, Nation, and Empire in Pre-1945 Japan", *Ethnic and Racial Studies*, Vol. 18, No. 3, pp. 433–456.

Weiner, Michael (ed.). 2009. *Japan's Minorites: The Illusion of Homogeneity*. 2nd Edition. Abington: Routledge.

CHAPTER 21

Constitutional Revision in the 2021 Election

Kenneth Mori McElwain⊙

Despite seeming momentum for constitutional change following the 2017 House of Representatives (HR) election, the ruling Liberal Democratic Party (LDP) failed to amend the supreme law over the following four years. Three factors were at play. First, there was significant disagreement among pro-amendment parties on constitutional priorities, notably between the LDP and its coalition partner, the Kōmeitō. Second, the resignation of Abe Shinzō, an ardent proponent of constitutional change, in September 2020 weakened political will at the top levels of government to push this contentious issue forward. Third, the COVID-19 pandemic dominated the government's attention, both in terms of domestic (Lipscy 2022, this volume) and international (Lukner 2022, this volume) affairs, and left little time for parliamentary deliberation (Thies and Yanai 2022, this volume).

These constraints also manifested in the muted role that constitutional revision played in the 2021 HR election. On the one hand, the LDP, reiterating its 2017 election manifesto (McElwain 2018), continued to call

K. M. McElwain (✉)
Institute of Social Science, University of Tokyo, Tokyo, Japan
e-mail: mcelwain@iss.u-tokyo.ac.jp

R. J. Pekkanen et al. (eds.), *Japan Decides 2021*,
https://doi.org/10.1007/978-3-031-11324-6_21

for amendments relating to Article 9, education rights, the allocation of House of Councillors (HC) seats, and "state of emergency" (SOE) provisions. Of these, emergency powers gained significant attention. The LDP argued that responses to Covid had been hampered by restrictions on the government's ability to implement strong lockdown measures. As will be discussed in greater detail later, the addition of emergency provisions was backed by most winning candidates, as well as by a majority of voters.

On the other hand, constitutionalism did not become an electoral cleavage, because opposition parties did not make it a focal point in their criticism of the LDP government. First, Abe's replacements, Suga Yoshihide and Kishida Fumio, did not share his passion for amendments, and thus did not provide an effective foil against whom the opposition could marshal. Second, numerous centrist and right-wing opposition parties, including the Democratic Party for the People (DPP) and Nippon Ishin no Kai (Ishin), made clear they were willing to deliberate constitutional revisions after the election. Even the Constitutional Democratic Party (CDP), while not in favor of the LDP's priorities, stated their willingness to discuss possible revisions. With no coordinated pushback against the LDP's amendment goals, the issue did not become a priority for most voters.

This chapter begins with a brief review of postwar constitutional politics, with particular attention on events since the 2017 HR election. I will then discuss how the COVID-19 pandemic shifted attention on constitutionalism from Article 9 to SOE powers. An analysis of party manifestos shows that most parties refrained from taking strong positions on constitutional change. However, elite surveys indicate that support for SOE measures now outstrips that for amending Article 9. Data from post-election voter surveys also suggests that pro-amendment sentiment is growing. That said, the issue took low priority among most voters, making the future fate of constitutional revision murky.

CONSTITUTIONAL POLITICS

Ratified in November 1946 and promulgated in May 1947, the Constitution of Japan (COJ hereafter) is the oldest unamended constitution in the world today. That said, its origin and contents have long been controversial. The COJ was drafted by officers of the post-WWII Allied Occupation, during when Japanese sovereignty was limited.[1] Despite undergoing substantial revisions during Diet deliberations, critics have decried the constitution as an imposed document that lacked democratic legitimacy. The COJ's contents have also been described as excessively "Western," particularly in its elevation of individual rights over collective duties (Winkler 2011).

The heart of national debate has centered on the Article 9 "Peace Clause," which prohibits Japan from using military force (Article 9.1) or possessing "war potential" (Article 9.2). For much of the postwar period, the Cabinet Legislation Bureau, which acts as legal counsel to the Cabinet, interpreted Article 9 to mean that Japan can only possess military capabilities that are designed exclusively for national defense (Samuels 2007). Conservative critics have argued that Article 9 limits Japan's collective self-defense options, including its alliance obligations to the United States, whose troops have been stationed in Japan since WWII, in the event of attacks on American troops outside of Japanese borders.

To that end, the Abe Cabinet formally reinterpreted Article 9 in July 2014, stating that the Self-Defense Forces (SDF) could use minimally necessary force when a Japanese ally was under attack from other nations or when there were threats to Japanese citizens (Liff 2017). These were codified into two new laws, dubbed *Heiwa Anzen Hōsei*, in September 2015, allowing the SDF to engage in collective self-defense and deploy overseas to protect Japanese allies and the lives of overseas nationals (Green 2022, this volume).

While this weakened the urgency of amending Article 9, Abe still saw constitutional change as a cornerstone of his legacy. In May 2017, *Yomiuri Shimbun* published an interview with Abe on the 70th anniversary of the COJ's promulgation, wherein he stated his desire to amend the constitution by 2020. Leading up to the 2017 HR election, Abe and the LDP sharpened their attention on four amendment topics (McElwain 2018). The first was the addition of a third paragraph to Article 9 that explicitly acknowledged the existence of the SDF. While this change would not materially change the SDF's functions, it would obviate criticism from some constitutional scholars that the SDF was inherently unconstitutional under Article 9.2. The second was to expand the right to free education to include secondary and tertiary education. This had long been demanded by Ishin, a possible partner in constitutional amendment. The third was to guarantee each prefecture at least one seat in the House of Councillors (HC). While this had been the de facto practice in the past, four rural prefectures were merged into two districts for the

2016 HC election to reduce rising malapportionment. The final proposal was to add a new chapter on "state of emergency" provisions to expand executive branch powers and allow the postponement of HR elections during natural disasters, foreign attacks, or domestic disorder. This topic has long been a conservative fixation, and its popularity rose after the political uncertainties following the 2011 Great East Japan Earthquake.

The LDP continued to push these issues after the 2017 HR contest, but it needed to navigate the procedural rules for amendment, as stipulated in Article 96. Each proposed amendment requires two-thirds concurrence in the lower and upper houses, followed by a simple majority in a voter referendum. While the two-thirds parliamentary hurdle is quite common globally (McElwain and Winkler 2015), it has created strategic complications for the LDP, which has never won the requisite seats alone. As such, it has proposed topics that are seen positively by other pro- (or at least, not anti-) amendment parties, such as Kōmeitō and Ishin. At the same time, Japan has never held a national referendum, making it difficult to form educated guesses about their outcome. Since 2017, public opinion polls indicate that support for constitutional change is roughly 50–50, but few specific amendment proposals garner stable majority support. One reason is citizens' concerns that the LDP is pushing forward amendments for partisan goals (McElwain et al. 2021). Because voters prefer amendments that receive broad elite support, the LDP needs buy-in from other political parties, ideally from one of the main center-left parties such as the CDP.

However, Abe ultimately failed to amend the constitution during his tenure. The party publicized concrete amendment wording for its four priorities in March 2018, and in a May 2019 address, Abe declared that he still sought to make 2020 the year of a new constitution. However, three problems remained (cf. McElwain 2022). First, most opposition parties refused to deliberate constitutional revision under Abe, claiming that his push for collective self-defense legislation in 2015 violated the spirit of Article 9. Second, Abe's implication in the Moritomo Gakuen and Kake Gakuen scandals, which involved accusations of favoritism toward his supporters and friends, raised public mistrust and stripped him of needed political capital (Maeda 2022, this volume). Third, the tail end of Abe's tenure in 2019 was filled with delicate political events that required dedicated attention, including local elections, imperial transition, the G20 Summit, and Upper House elections.

The biggest wildcard of all was the COVID-19 pandemic, which dominated the political agenda in 2020 and 2021 (Lipscy 2022; Lukner 2022; Thies and Yanai 2022, all this volume). The Japanese government's response was passive by international standards. In stark contrast to countries that closed public transportation and workplaces, limitations on business and personal behavior lacked legal enforcement, due to constitutional protections of civil liberties such as the freedom of movement. Instead, the government could only issue requests or "soft directives" that relied on voluntary compliance with social distancing guidelines (Cato et al. 2020).

COVID raised the salience of amending one specific element of the COJ: adding state of emergency provisions that would allow the state to override certain individual rights during crises. The LDP claimed that the constitution hamstrung the government's ability to take decisive actions to halt the pandemic, including legally enforced stay-at-home and business closure orders. Abe and his successors, Suga and Kishida, argued that the COJ needed to add SOE measures, so that the national government could better coordinate and enforce pandemic responses.

Of course, questions remain about how exactly SOEs should be designed, including who has the authority to declare SOEs and what extraordinary powers should be given to national or local governments.[2] However, public sentiment has become more favorable since the Covid pandemic. Table 21.1 compares the results of public opinion polls on constitutional amendment by the *Yomiuri Shimbun* in April 2017 and May 2021. Overall approval of constitutional change (Q1) rose from 49 to 56%, theoretically pushing the issue above the majority threshold necessary to ratify an amendment. This was not driven by changes in attitudes toward Article 9 (Q2): those who agree that the SDF's constitutionality should be explicitly enumerated only rose marginally from 52 to 55%. Instead, the key driver appears to be the perceived necessity of enumerating SOE provisions (Q3). Despite some differences in question wording, support for clarifying the obligations and powers of the government during emergencies almost doubled, from 31 to 59%.

CONSTITUTIONAL AMENDMENTS IN THE 2021 ELECTION

Despite seeming public enthusiasm, political parties in the 2021 HR contest took relatively muted stances on constitutional revision. Table 21.2 summarizes the position of each party on different amendment

Table 21.1 Yomiuri survey on constitutional amendment: 2017 vs. 2021

Q1: Do you think that the current constitution should be amended?	
Yes	49% → 56%
No	49% → 40%
Q2: The LDP is considering amending Article 9 to specify the constitutionality of the Self Defense Forces, while keeping Article 9's proscription of maintaining war potential as is. Do you agree or disagree with this proposal?	
Agree	52% → 55%
Disagree	43% → 38%
Q3: The Constitution does not specify the obligations and powers of the Government during national emergencies, such as natural disasters and the spread of infectious diseases, and so these rules are currently established by law. Which response is closest to your view?	
Amend COJ to enumerate gov't obligations and powers	31% → 59%
Do not amend the constitution and continue statutorily	65%[a] → 37%

[a] 2017 survey separated the "Do not amend" option into pass new laws (49%) and keep as is (16%)

Note 2021 survey responses published in Yomiuri, May 3, 2021. 2017 responses were published on April 29, 2017. Questions and answers were translated by the author

topics, taken from their party manifestos and supplemented with analyses by the *Asahi Shimbun* (October 19, 2021). Circles denote explicit support for revision; triangles denote issues that parties stated they were willing to consider. Only two parties openly declared their support for specific amendments. The LDP's manifesto included their four priorities from 2017: (1) enumerating the SDF; (2) establishing state of emergency provisions; (3) guaranteeing educational access; (4) reforming the apportionment of HC seats. Ishin similarly backed educational access, but also noted the need to establish a Constitutional Court that would take a more active role in checking the government, as well as the establishment of a system of states (*dōshūsei*) with greater regional autonomy. Ishin's positions are essentially identical to their 2017 manifesto.

By contrast, other parties were less clear on their constitutional vision. The LDP's coalition partner, Kōmeitō, only announced a willingness to deliberate SOE provisions and the establishment of environment rights,

Table 21.2   Party manifesto positions on constitutional amendment

	LDP	CDP	Ishin	Kōmei	DPP	JCP	Reiwa	SDP
Self Defense Forces	○							
National emergency	○			△				
Education	○		○					
HC Districts	○							
Decentralization			○					
Constitutional courts			○		△			
Environment			△					
HR dissolution		△			△			

○ denotes explicit support for amendment. △ denotes willingness to deliberate issue in the Diet
Party positions taken from each party's manifesto, supplemented with analysis by Asahi (October 19, 2021)

but did not call for these outright. The main opposition party, CDP, only noted that they would consider constraints on government authority, notable restrictions on the PM's power to dissolve the Diet and call snap elections. This latter point was backed by DPP, which—like Ishin—also proposed the creation of an autonomous constitutional court. The clearest opposition to the LDP was stated in the manifestos of the JCP, SDP, and Reiwa, all of whom considered amendments to be unnecessary at best and dangerous at worst.

Two reasons can be deduced for the less hostile position of CDP and DPP toward amendment. First, because the CDP had coordinated candidate nominations with the JCP, SDP, and Reiwa, they could not explicitly back specific amendments without turning off left-wing voters. At the same time, the CDP had been accused by conservatives of knee-jerk opposition to LDP policies without offering alternative solutions. To be seen as a viable governing party, it needed to maintain an openness to at least deliberating constitutional change. As for the DPP, being more positive on constitutional amendment was a strategic maneuver to differentiate itself from the CDP and sell its bona fides as a true centrist party. Second, there was arguably little incentive for CDP and DPP to take strident positions on constitutionalism because the issue itself had muted salience in the 2021 contest. While a multi-party anti-amendment alliance was viable in 2017 with the pro-revisionist Abe in government, his departure had robbed opposition parties of a bogeyman around whom they could justify electoral partnership.

Of course, opposition parties may have been more vocal if voters saw constitutionalism as a central focus of the election. However, there is mixed evidence on this point. The ISS COVID Panel Survey (ISS Survey, hereafter) conducted an online post-election survey on November 1–10, 2021, following up on previous survey waves in December 2020 and March 2021. The top panel of Table 21.3 (Amendment Topic) shows the percentage of voters who supported six different amendment topics, separated by the party that they voted for in the PR tier of the 2021 HR election.[3] Three points are worth noting. First, support for each of the individual amendment topics exceeds fifty percent, except for limitations on the PM's ability to dissolve the lower house (48.5%). This suggests a general openness to, or at least an interest in, constitutional amendment among voters. Second, support for different amendment topics generally follows elite priorities. LDP voters supported the enumeration of the SDF and emergency provisions at higher rates than those of other parties. JCP supporters, by contrast, opposed most LDP priorities, except for broadening education access. Third, the most popular topic was adding a right to a clean environment, which was backed by three-quarters of respondents across party lines. This has long been popular but has received less attention in elite discourse, in large part because the LDP has raised concerns about its potential negative consequences for industrial development (McElwain et al. 2021).

Table 21.3 Voter preferences on constitutional revision

Amendment topic	LDP	CDP	Ishin	Kōmei	DPP	JCP	Total
Self Defense Forces	74.1	41.1	70.0	59.9	63.5	33.6	59.7
National emergency	75.5	48.5	67.6	72.6	67.3	33.2	61.3
Education	54.8	60.2	54.4	60.7	59.1	58.0	56.1
Constitutional courts	55.4	60.4	59.0	50.7	58.0	54.5	57.0
Environment	73.1	74.2	76.3	81.0	76.7	69.6	73.3
HR dissolution	45.7	51.6	48.2	54.9	55.6	45.4	48.5
COJ as top 3 priority	9.8	8.4	8.2	4.0	8.8	15.9	8.6

Note Data taken from ISS COVID Panel Survey, Wave 3 (2021). Cells in the top row (Amendment topic) show percentages of support for different amendment topics, dichotomized from a six-point Likert scale. The bottom row (COJ as top 3 priority) shows the percentage of respondents who selected "Constitutionalism" as a Top 3 policy priority in their vote choice. Both rows show averages by PR vote destination (party). Total percentages are shown in the furthest right column

Despite broad popular support for a wide range of amendment topics, it is also true that constitutionalism had low salience. The ISS Survey asked respondents to select the Top 3 policy issues that influenced their vote choice from a list of seventeen topics. The bottom row of Table 21.3 shows the percentage of respondents who selected constitutionalism (either pro- or anti-amendment) as a top-three concern. Overall, only 8.6% of respondents chose this issue, ranking it eleventh, far below other priorities such as COVID-19 (45%), fiscal and monetary policy (39.3%), and pensions and healthcare (33.9%). The highest interest was among JCP supporters (15.9%), who in general are anti-amendment. Among ostensibly pro-amendment parties such as the LDP and Ishin, its prioritization failed to exceed ten percent. Among Kōmeitō backers, it rated just 4%, denoting significant differences within the governing coalition that may complicate future attempts at constitutional amendment.

AFTER THE ELECTION: WHITHER CONSTITUTIONAL REVISION?

Pro-amendment parties either held their ground (as in the case of the LDP) or made major strides (Ishin) in the 2021 HR election. According to data from UTAS 2021, 78.8% of SMD candidates who won outright or were resurrected in the PR tier support constitutional change, including every member from Ishin and DPP, 96% from the LDP, and 89% from Kōmeitō. This is roughly consistent with the results of the 2017 election, when 82% of victors backed revision (McElwain 2018). On paper, then, it appears that constitutional change may finally be attainable.

However, collective parliamentary enthusiasm for revising the COJ may conflict with disagreements over revision priorities. As shown in Table 21.2, no amendment topic had explicit support in the manifestos of more than two parties. At the same time, there remain significant intra-party disputes, including within the LDP on its four amendment goals (McElwain 2022). While amending Article 9 has been the party's goal since its founding in 1955, some senior LDP legislators have argued that simply enumerating the SDF is insufficient, pushing instead to revise Article 9.2's proscription against military forces altogether. The expansion of education rights is also divisive. Making educational expenses from kindergarten to university free, as desired by Ishin, is expected to cost four trillion yen (thirty-four billion USD, in January 5, 2022 exchange rates), making it prohibitively expensive for fiscal conservatives.

That said, the landscape after the 2021 election looks more promising for pro-revision groups. Figure 21.1 shows the proportion of election SMD winners and PR zombies who support COJ amendments to enumerate the SDF, states of emergency, expanded education rights, HC districting, decentralization, a constitutional court, and environmental rights. Unlike in 2017, two issues—the SDF (56%) and emergency provisions (54%)—exceed majority support within the Diet, although both fall short of the necessary two-thirds. These numbers are inflated by the strong performance of the LDP, which backs these two topics at exceedingly high rates (87% and 84%, respectively).

The topic with the greatest odds of amendment is likely the specification of national emergency provisions. It is popular among voters, as shown in Table 21.3, and its salience has risen with the ongoing COVID-19 pandemic, as shown in Table 21.1. It is also not opposed by Kōmeitō, which generally backs additions of new topics to COJ (*kaken*), but is less enthused about changes to Article 9 (Klein and McLaughlin 2022, this volume). While the LDP's 2018 proposal did not anticipate COVID, it would give the Cabinet the power to (1) issue necessary directives

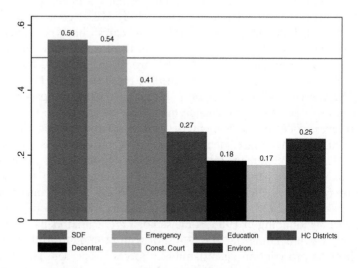

Fig. 21.1 Support for constitutional revision among election winners (*Note* Data on candidate positions from UTAS 2021)

to protect human life and assets; (2) postpone HR elections with the agreement of 2/3 of the affected chamber.

That said there are two limitations. First, while SOE measures are popular, their salience grows and ebbs with natural disasters. McElwain and Winkler (2015) note that support for SOEs rose after the 3.11 Triple Disaster, but gradually waned after a few years. The same may be true for Covid, assuming that its centrality in political discourse subsides in the future. Second, it is not clear if the national emergency powers envisioned by the LDP are what are relevant to COVID-19. The LDP's goal is to strengthen the powers of the central government, including its ability to override civil liberties such as freedoms of movement and assembly. However, countries that have implemented enforced lockdowns, such as the United States and Western Europe, have not fared as well as Japan in terms of case counts or mortality rates. Indeed, in the Japanese case, it appears that "soft mandates" worked, because citizens are highly sensitive to news about rising case counts (Shoji et al. 2021). As discussed in the Lipscy chapter (2022), governors have been front and center in Covid communication; while they are not uniformly popular, they are seen as more "present" than the central government, at least pre-Kishida.

PM Kishida has continued to call for constitutional amendment, in part to mollify concerns from conservatives about his ideological bona fides (Harris 2022, this volume). He does not have Abe's reputation as an amendment diehard, which makes it difficult for leftist parties to cast him as a villain against whom their supporters should mobilize. However, there are no signs that Kishida will utilize political capital, including precious deliberation time in the Diet, on constitutional change over pandemic responses. Even if he does, LDP candidates in competitive districts may be less enthused: constitutionalism tends to energize leftist voters more than right-wingers or centrists (McElwain 2020). Indeed, while COVID-19 has strengthened support for enumerating state of emergency clauses, interest in SOEs may evaporate once Covid subsides, as it did after the 2011 Great East Japan Earthquake. As such, it remains uncertain whether the LDP will see strategic merit in pushing constitutional change forward in the foreseeable future.

NOTES

1. For a fuller discussion of the COJ's ratification and promulgation, see Hellegers (2001) and Hahm and Kim (2015).

2. For a comparative analysis of the LDP's state of emergency proposal, see McElwain (2017).
3. These percentages omit survey respondents who did not vote. Parties that received less than 4% of the PR vote in the ISS Survey are omitted for presentation purposes. Further details on the ISS COVID Project can be found at: https://web.iss.u-tokyo.ac.jp/methodology/en/subprojects/covid-19.html.

References

Cato, Susumu, Takashi Iida, Kenji Ishida, Asei Ito, Kenneth Mori McElwain, and Masahiro Shoji. 2020. "Social Distancing as a Public Good Under the COVID-19 Pandemic." *Public Health* 188: 51–53.

Green, Michael Jonathan. 2022. "Foreign Policy and Defense." In *Japan Decides 2021: The Japanese General Election*, edited by Robert J. Pekkanen, Steven R. Reed, and Daniel M. Smith, 347–359. Palgrave Macmillan.

Hahm, Chaihark, and Sung Ho Kim. 2015. *Making We the People: Democratic Constitutional Founding in Postwar Japan and South Korea, Comparative Constitutional Law and Policy*. Cambridge: Cambridge University Press.

Harris, Tobias. 2022. "Abe's Legacy." In *Japan Decides 2021: The Japanese General Election*, edited by Robert J. Pekkanen, Steven R. Reed, and Daniel M. Smith, 87–102. Palgrave Macmillan.

Hellegers, Dale M. 2001. *We the People: World War II and the Origins of the Japanese Constitution*. Vol. 2. Stanford, CA: Stanford University Press.

Klein, Axel and Levi McLaughlin. 2022. "Kōmeitō in 2021: Strategizing Between the LDP and Sōka Gakkai." In *Japan Decides 2021: The Japanese General Election*, edited by Robert J. Pekkanen, Steven R. Reed, and Daniel M. Smith, 71–86. Palgrave Macmillan.

Liff, Adam P. 2017. "Policy by Other Means: Collective Self-Defense and the Politics of Japan's Postwar Constitutional Reinterpretations." *Asia Policy* 24: 139–172.

Lipscy, Phillip Y. 2022. "Japan's Response to the COVID-19 Pandemic." In *Japan Decides 2021: The Japanese General Election*, edited by Robert J. Pekkanen, Steven R. Reed, and Daniel M. Smith, 239-254. Palgrave Macmillan.

Lukner, Kerstin. 2022. "Covid-19: The International Dimension." In *Japan Decides 2021: The Japanese General Election*, edited by Robert J. Pekkanen, Steven R. Reed, and Daniel M. Smith, 333–346. Palgrave Macmillan.

Maeda, Yukio. 2022. "Public Opinion and Covid-19." In *Japan Decides 2021: The Japanese General Election*, edited by Robert J. Pekkanen, Steven R. Reed, and Daniel M. Smith, 167–182. Palgrave Macmillan.

McElwain, Kenneth Mori. 2017. "Using Constitutional Data to Understand "State of Emergency" Provisions." In *Social Sciences of Crisis Thinking*. Tokyo: Institute of Social Science, University of Tokyo.

McElwain, Kenneth Mori. 2018. "Constitutional Revision in the 2017 Election." In *Japan Decides 2017: The Japanese General Election*, edited by Robert J. Pekkanen, Steven R. Reed, Ethan Scheiner, and Daniel M. Smith, 297–312. Palgrave Macmillan.

McElwain, Kenneth Mori. 2020. "When Candidates Are More Polarised Than Voters: Constitutional Revision in Japan." *European Political Science* 19: 528–539.

McElwain, Kenneth Mori. 2022. "Naze Abe wa Kenpō wo Kaisei Dekinakatta ka." In *Kenshō Abe Seiken: Hoshu to Realism no Seiji*, edited by Asia Pacific Initiative, 41–78. Tokyo: Bunshun Shinsho.

McElwain, Kenneth Mori, Shusei Eshima, and Christian G. Winkler. 2021. "The Proposer or the Proposal? An Experimental Analysis of Constitutional Beliefs." *Japanese Journal of Political Science* 22 (1): 15–39.

McElwain, Kenneth Mori and Christian G. Winkler. 2015. "What's Unique About Japan's Constitution? A Comparative and Historical Analysis." *Journal of Japanese Studies* 41 (2): 249–280.

Samuels, Richard J. 2007. *Securing Japan: Tokyo's Grand Strategy and the Future of East Asia*. Ithaca: Cornell University Press.

Shoji, Masahiro, Susumu Cato, Takashi Iida, Kenji Ishida, Asei Ito, and Kenneth Mori McElwain. 2021. "Variations in Early-Stage Responses to Pandemics: Survey Evidence from the COVID-19 Pandemic in Japan." *Economics of Disasters and Climate Change* 6 (2): 235–258.

Thies, Mike and Yuki Yanai. 2022. "Did COVID-19 Impact Japan's 2021 General Election?" In *Japan Decides 2021: The Japanese General Election*, edited by Robert J. Pekkanen, Steven R. Reed, and Daniel M. Smith, 219–237. Palgrave Macmillan.

Winkler, Christian G. 2011. *The Quest for Japan's New Constitution: An Analysis of Visions and Constitutional Reform Proposals (1980–2009)*. Routledge Contemporary Japan Series. Routledge.

CHAPTER 22

COVID-19: The International Dimension

Kerstin Lukner

In the 2021 general election, tackling the COVID-19 pandemic domestically as well as dealing with foreign and security policy challenges were both important campaign topics. In a Nippon Television exit poll, "anti-corona measures" (*shingata korona taisaku*) (15%) and "foreign and security policy" (14%) were ranked as second and third most important issues for voters, exceeded only by economic stimulus measures (22%) (see also Thies and Yanai 2022).[1] However, political parties largely ignored the combination of both aspects in their election campaigns, i.e., addressing the fight against the novel coronavirus as a global issue that needed coordinated answers at the international level and thus required an explicit "COVID-19 foreign policy."[2]

This is surprising for at least two reasons. First, Japan has a track record as a global health advocate that set priorities on global health issues in its foreign policy and official development assistance (ODA) long before COVID-19 emerged. Second, the LDP-Kōmeitō coalition has certainly been following specific foreign policy goals when it comes to supporting

K. Lukner (✉)
University of Duisburg-Essen, Duisburg, Germany
e-mail: kerstin.lukner@uni-due.de

other countries in their fight against COVID-19, e.g., by means of distributing medical equipment and vaccines, especially to countries in the Southeast Asian and Info-Pacific (SEA-IP) region. Against this backdrop, this chapter scrutinizes the way Japan has been coping with the COVID-19 crisis beyond its own national borders at the bilateral, regional, and multilateral level and the rationale behind it. It shows that apart from backing the fight against the pandemic specifically in the SEA-IP region, Japan's actions have been primarily guided by its strategic competition with China, i.e., the intention to increase its regional influence by means of COVID-19 related health diplomacy.

Ordinary Diplomacy No More

The outbreak and spread of COVID-19 have severely constrained Japan's diplomatic activities since spring 2020. Corona-induced travel bans resulted in the cancellation of important diplomatic meetings at all levels (MOFA 2021, 3) such as the long-awaited state visit by Xi Jingping to Japan in April 2020. It would have been the first visit of a Chinese president for ten years (Kevasan 2020, 68) and a welcome chance to address persistent bilateral tensions. The 2020 Tokyo Olympic Games were first postponed and eventually conducted in 2021 without foreign spectators, depriving the governing elite of the chance to use the extraordinary sports event to stage-manage Japan as an influential player in the global arena (Leheny 2022). Especially in 2020, officials at Japan's foreign ministry were busy issuing travel alerts and organizing the return of about 12.000 nationals from all over the world (MOFA 2021, 6), including many experts working in ODA projects. As a result, not only diplomatic meetings, but also ODA-related work, such as trainings for the local staff in the recipient countries, had to be conducted online as video conferences (Yoshikawa 2020). In short, Japan's ordinary diplomacy and foreign policy routines were for most parts severely interrupted in 2020 and continue to be heavily disrupted by the corona crisis.

Lack of Leadership

Especially during the first year of the pandemic, powerful countries with strong health expertise such as the United States did not seek an active leadership role to cope with the global health emergency (Patrick 2020). Rather, most governments took an inward-turn, attempting to cope with the pandemic domestically, rather than globally—a move criticized as "crisis nationalism" (Hanrieder 2020, 536). Japan had long claimed that it was a leader in global health, also with regard to the fight against infectious diseases, as demonstrated by past diplomatic initiatives. Negotiations at the G8 Kyushu-Okinawa Summit (2000) resulted in the decision to establish the Global Fund to Fight AIDS, Tuberculosis, and Malaria in 2002; at the G8 Hokkaido-Toyako Summit (2008) Japan set a focus on global health issues and announced to act as co-organizer of the first Global Health Summit in Berlin one year later (Takuma 2020a); at the G7 Ise-Shima Summit (2016) a "Vision for Global Health" was adopted. Moreover, recent Japanese initiatives have aimed at strengthening health systems and introducing universal health coverage worldwide (Toda 2020, 38), a focus that is also reflected in Japan's ODA policy. In 2015, then-Prime Minister Abe Shinzō published an article entitled "Japan's Vision for a Peaceful Healthier World" in the esteemed medical journal *The Lancet*, arguing that "health [was] fundamentally a global issue" that "[required] collective action" (Abe 2015, 2367). Yet, the China-U.S. competition paralyzed the global response to the COVID-19 crisis at first. Particularly under the presidency of Donald Trump, Japan could not rely on its close ally for orientation and coordination, but it had to define its own foreign policy reaction to the pandemic, utilizing its ODA and health diplomacy on the one hand and concentrating on its stance toward China in the context of the World Health Organization (WHO) on the other.

COVID-19, THE WHO, AND JAPAN

As the key international organization responsible for expert guidance during health emergencies, the WHO has been severely criticized for lacking speed and resoluteness in its response when first reports about a novel respiratory disease in Wuhan emerged. While the International Health Regulations oblige WHO member states to provide the relevant data in a timely manner when they suspect or discover a novel infectious disease and to work closely with the organization, the WHO does not have any compulsory power to enforce such cooperation (Lukner 2014). As with the outbreaks of Sars-Cov-1 in 2003, China was reluctant to share information when the Sars-CoV-2 virus first emerged, markedly limiting the WHO's ability to offer informed advice. This notwithstanding, many observers accused the organization of being too close to China, most notably former U.S. President Trump. In a similar vein, Asō Tarō, Japan's

Deputy Prime and Finance Minister at the time, critiqued the WHO as the "Chinese Health Organization."[3] International polls indicate that the Japanese population also viewed the WHO's dealing with the COVID-19 crisis skeptically. In late September 2020, 67% of the Japanese respondents thought that the WHO had done a "very bad" or "somewhat bad" job during the crisis; among the 14 advanced economies chosen for the comparative poll this negative assessment was only topped by respondents from South Korea (80%).[4] However, in contrast to Trump, former Prime Minister Abe never considered leaving the WHO but argued in favor of reforms.[5]

The following pattern has emerged when it comes to Japan's response: The government criticizes different aspects of China's way of dealing with COVID-19 on the one hand and supports WHO reforms on the other. For instance, when the second part of the "WHO-convened Global Study of the Origins of SARS-Cov-2"[6] was published in March 2021, Japan, under Prime Minister Suga Yoshihide, was among the 14 states worldwide that officially voiced concern over the report. In their joint statement, the group questioned whether the WHO had been able to conduct its work "free from interference and undue influence" in China and whether it had been able to gain "access to complete, original data and samples."[7] Moreover, Japan co-sponsored and successfully campaigned for a resolution that aimed at strengthening the WHO's preparedness and response efforts to health emergencies.[8] In order to additionally improve the level of preparedness and response capacity at the regional level (a request the WHO has been making for a long time) and to intensify health cooperation with ASEAN (Association for Southeast Asian Nations) states, Japan has been supporting the plan to set up an ASEAN Centre for Public Health Emergencies and Emerging Diseases (Takuma 2020b, 53). In fact, this dichotomy of cooperating with countries in the SEA-IP region in the fight against SARS-Cov-2 and of intensifying the competition with China in the health sector seems to be at the core of Japan's implicit "COVID-19 foreign policy."

COVID-19-Related Health Diplomacy

While the nature of pandemics appears to necessitate a coordinated international reaction, via the WHO and regional groupings such as ASEAN, it offers individual states ample room to realize their own national interests when formulating their foreign policy response at the same time

(Fazal 2020, E78–E79). From the Japanese perspective, China is the actor that has most noticeably been using the pandemic to create good-will and appreciation in countries heavily affected by Sars-CoV-2, by first providing much needed medical supplies such as masks, gloves, and protective equipment and then by offering its domestically produced vaccine (Sinovac). Japanese observers and government representatives perceive those acts as Chinese attempts to expand its strategic influence in Asia (and beyond) by capitalizing on the coronavirus pandemic in the context of its health diplomacy. In 2020, President Xi already declared a future vaccine made in China would be a global public good. In Japan, this Chinese soft power approach has been watched with great concern.

At the diplomatic level, Tokyo attempted early on to counter Beijing's activities with own initiatives. In April 2020, the government announced it would offer the Japanese anti-flu drug Avigan to about 50 countries free of charge to support the treatment of COVID-19 patients.[9] Four months later, it intensified efforts to distribute medical equipment such as ambulance beds, CT scanners and further medical gear to numerous countries. In the extra budget for fiscal year 2020, the government earmarked Yen 48 billion for corona-related support for developing countries. Then-Foreign Minister Motegi Toshimitsu emphasized the difference to China's approach, saying that Japan's aid not only focused on delivering single medical items such as masks once, but also was envisaged to support the improvement of the health care systems in the recipient countries in a sustainable fashion (on top of providing emergency support).[10] In mid-2020, Motegi went on a rare diplomatic trip to visit Southeast Asian countries, advertising Japan's aid approach and explaining its assistance plans.[11] Yet, it remains debatable in how far Japan's approach to catch up with front-runner China was successful at that time. In the "State of Southeast Asia: 2021 Survey Report," which is based on 2020 data, ASEAN countries clearly assess China as having provided most COVID-19 support to the region, Japan ranks only second (44.2% and 18.2% respectively) (ISEAS Yusof Ishak Institute 2021, 13).

Tokyo's concern that China could be able to increase its political-strategic influence in the SEA-IP region by complementing its medical diplomacy of 2020 with an additional layer of vaccine diplomacy was realized in early 2021. Kitaoka Shin'ichi, a political scientist by training and at that time head of Japan's International Cooperation Agency, which is responsible for the implementation of many ODA projects on-site, commented that Beijing was expanding its power with a "new weapon," i.e., China-made vaccination supplies.[12] From the Japanese perspective, the main concern was that Beijing's vaccination diplomacy, i.e., offering its Sinovac inoculant at a low price and prior to any other country, could lead to increasing levels of sympathy in the recipient countries when it came to otherwise controversial Chinese foreign policy moves (see also Vekasi 2022). By mid-2021, Tokyo came up with its own version of a somewhat comprehensive vaccination approach in its health diplomacy, consisting of three layers, i.e., bilateral, regional, and multilateral support. It included vaccine donations to individual countries, commitments to finance the regional production and distribution based on QUAD (Quadrilateral Security Dialogue) agreements, and assistances to international organizations such as the WHO-related COVAX (COVID-19 Vaccines Global Access) program.

Bilateral

At the bilateral level, Tokyo started to send domestically produced AstraZeneca vaccines to Taiwan and various ASEAN countries in June 2021. Japan delivered several million doses to Taiwan free of charge when the country was facing a severe COVID-19 crisis but rejected mainland China's Sinovac inoculant for political reasons. Beijing criticized Japan's support as political misuse of vaccines and as bold interference in China's domestic affairs.[13] Next, Tokyo offered larger quantities of AstraZeneca vaccines to Vietnam and later to Indonesia, Thailand, the Philippines, and Malaysia. Foreign Minister Motegi claimed that the severity of the COVID-19 crisis in the recipient country played a crucial role for choosing the bilateral provision of vaccines as way of support because it could be organized faster than through multilateral programs. Yet, he admitted that the nature of the bilateral relationship with the recipient countries and Japan's strategic considerations such as in the context of the Free and Open Indo-Pacific (FOIP) vision were also important.[14] According to an Asahi Shimbun report of early August 2021 Japan ranked third after the United States and China in the free provision of bilateral vaccination support.[15] Of the 24.65 million doses it shipped to other countries by early 2022 the largest amount went to Vietnam (7.35 million doses), followed by Indonesia (6.88 million), Taiwan (4.2 million), the Philippines (3.08 million), Thailand (2.04 million), and Malaysia (1 million). To additionally support the distribution system for vaccines, Japan has been engaged in facilitating bilateral "Last One Mile

Support" to ensure that vaccines are delivered to their final destination via an effective cold chain. By the end of June 2021, the government provided 13.7 billion Yen for cooling infrastructure (cooling refrigerators, transport vehicles, etc.) to 59 countries, many of them in the SEA-IP region.[16] In short, while the Japanese government—very much like the Chinese one—claims that its vaccination distribution is primarily guided by humanitarian principles and should not be mixed up with diplomatic objectives, it in fact appears highly politicized. In the SEA-IP region, the vaccination campaigns of China and Japan essentially focus on the same countries, reinforcing their strategic rivalry for power and influence.[17] The fact that the Sinovac vaccine has proven to be largely without effect is certainly to Japan's advantage, offering Tokyo the chance to solidify its role as health leader and humanitarian aid donor vis-à-vis other countries in the neighborhood.[18]

Regional

Looking at the minilateral level of regionally coordinated support, Japan teamed up with its QUAD partners to jointly counter the pandemic in the Indo-Pacific region. In March 2021, COVID-19 prompted QUAD members, i.e., Australia, India, Japan, and the United States, to convene their first-ever summit in a virtual format; the grouping was originally instigated by then-Prime Minister Abe in 2007. At the summit, then-Prime Minister Suga and his counterparts pledged to deliver 1 billion doses of COVID-19 vaccines to countries in the Indo-Pacific by the end of 2022. Initially, QUAD intended to produce U.S. licensed vaccines in India and subsequently distribute them across the region by Australia and Japan.[19] While India played a central role in the plan due to its manufacturing capabilities, it stopped the export of vaccines to meet its own demand when the country experienced stark increases in COVID-19 cases due to the emergence of the novel Delta variant in spring and summer 2021. Still, when QUAD leaders met for a second time in Washington D.C. six months later, their countries had delivered close to 79 million of the promised doses.[20] While the collaboration on COVID-19 countermeasures set a new focus for QUAD and served as an important impetus for the two summit meetings, most observers agree that security concerns related to China and the tacit understanding about the need to counter Beijing's moves are the QUAD's key motive to cooperate.[21] For Japan, the provision of vaccines across the Indo-Pacific region in the QUAD context is strongly connected to its FOIP strategy with Southeast Asian countries at the center.

Multilateral

When it comes to a comparatively fair distribution of vaccines across the globe that is not based on strategic calculations of single countries or the geopolitical competition between different powers, COVAX stands out as the main international mechanism. Organized by the WHO, the Global Alliance for Vaccines and Immunizations and other partners under the COVAX ACT (COVID-19 Tools) Accelerator framework initiated in April 2020, it aims at offering a fair and equitable global access to COVID-19 vaccines (and support their development beforehand), regardless of a country's wealth.[22] Richer countries can support COVAX by either donating money for the purchase of vaccines or contributing them directly. Japan joined the program in late summer 2020, offering 172 billion Yen in prepayments for vaccine development.[23] In early 2022, it had donated 17.63 million vaccine doses through the COVAX program with Bangladesh (4.55 million), Iran (3.61 million), Nepal (1.61 million), and Sri Lanka (1.46 million) as main recipient countries.[24] In international comparison, Japan (60 million) ranked sixth as key donor after the United States (857.5 million), the European Union (471.5 million), Germany (175 million), France (120 million), and the United Kingdom (100 million), if both, the doses already donated and the doses announced to be donated to COVAX, are considered.[25] In the case of Japan, there is thus a stark discrepancy amounting to 42.37 million doses the country promised to contribute to COVAX, but has not donated yet (early 2022).[26] Besides, the amount of vaccines Tokyo did in fact supply through bilateral channels pursuant to its strategic choice is about 40% higher than the one provided via COVAX.[27] Most strikingly, in both cases the target countries of Japan's donations show a strong focus on the SEA-IP region. In sum, Japan has so far sought to realize two goals in its multilateral aid strategy at the same time: serving global vaccination campaign while simultaneously enforcing Japan's national interests vis-à-vis China.

COVID-19 BEFORE AND AFTER THE 2021 ELECTION

The LDP-Kōmeitō government pursued an active "COVID-19 foreign policy" prior to the 2021 general election that was tightly connected to its strategic rivalry with China. However, neither the two ruling parties nor the opposition referred to this particular facet of Japan's COVID-19 crisis management in their election campaigns, but rather focused on related domestic aspects such as testing and vaccination strategies, border control measures, or the founding of a Japanese Center for Disease Prevention and Control. The international dimension of Japan's response to COVID-19 described in this chapter notwithstanding, the government's counter-pandemic policies have emphasized virus control at home so far (Lipscy 2022), reflecting the global trend of a rather inward-looking crisis nationalism. This is most clearly revealed by the country's strict border control regime that has been implemented at the beginning of and during different peaks of the ongoing COVID-19 pandemic. At such points in time, border control protocols allow Japanese nationals to reenter Japan, but they deny the same to most permanent residents and anyone else. Likewise, such national self-centrism is expressed in what has been dubbed "vaccine nationalism," i.e., the fixation on vaccination campaigns at the domestic level without paying due attention to the low vaccination rates in poorer countries. In early February 2022, 68.718% of the population had been inoculated in high-income countries, but only 12.11% in low-income countries.[28] Given such disparities, the risk that new virus variants might emerge in places with low vaccination rates continues to exist. Both, the Delta and Omicron variants, first emerged in countries with low vaccination rates and then quickly spread around the globe, challenging the effectiveness of the available vaccines and thus the ability to cope with Sars-CoV-2 in advanced countries as well.

To fully realize its position as global leader during health emergencies, Japan's international engagement to fight COVID-19 would have to go beyond calculations that seem to center on its strategic rivalry with China. For instance, Tokyo could act more energetically when it comes to its support for the global vaccination campaign, donating larger funds and vaccines to the COVAX itself while urging others to do the same. It could encourage discussions about patent protection wavers or alternative ways to accelerate the production and distribution of vaccines at the global level. If the strong linkages between the pandemic situation at the domestic and the global level were addressed more openly, a "COVID-19 foreign policy" could possibly be suitable to serve as election campaign issue as well, prompting political parties to present their ideas on the subject. However, in Japan's 2021 general election this was not the case.

NOTES

1. Nippon Television, 31 October 2021, Deguchi Chōsa, Q2, https://www.ntv.co.jp/election2021/exitpoll/?target=all (accessed 20 November 2021).
2. E.g., see NHK, 2021, Shingata korona taisaku – kakutō no kōyaku, https://www.nhk.or.jp/senkyo/database/shugiin/2021/pledge/policy/01/ (accessed 20 November 2021).
3. *New York Times*, 29 May 2020, Trump Slammed the W.H.O. over Virus. He's Not Alone, https://www.nytimes.com/2020/04/08/world/asia/trump-who-coronavirus-china.html (accessed 14 November 2021).
4. Pew Research Center, 2020, International Cooperation Welcomed Across 14 Advanced Economies, https://www.pewresearch.org/global/2020/09/21/international-cooperation-welcomed-across-14-advanced-economies/ (accessed 14 December 2021).
5. Kyodo News, 18 April 2020, WHO Reform Needed, but Japan Has No Plan to Cut Funding: Abe, https://english.kyodonews.net/news/2020/04/2a997200cf27-who-reform-needed-but-japan-has-no-plan-to-cut-funding-abe.html (accessed 14 December 2021).
6. World Health Organization, 2021, WHO-Convened Global Study of the Origins of SARS-Cov-2: China Part, https://www.who.int/publications/i/item/who-convened-global-study-of-origins-of-sars-cov-2-china-part (accessed 17 December 2021).
7. U.S. Department of State, 30 March 2021, Joint Statement on the WHO Convened Covid-19 Origins Study, https://www.state.gov/joint-statement-on-the-who-convened-covid-19-origins-study/ (accessed 17 December 2021). The full list of states includes Australia, Canada, Czech Republic, Denmark, Estonia, Israel, Japan, Latvia, Lithuania, Norway, the Republic of Korea, Slovenia, the United Kingdom, and the United States.
8. MOFA Japan, 02 June 2021, Seventy Fourth World Health Assembly, https://www.mofa.go.jp/ic/ghp/page23e_000611.html (accessed 17 December 2021).
9. *Asahi Shimbun*, 10 April 2020, As Pandemic Strains Usual Diplomacy Route, Strategies Change.
10. *Japan Times*, 28 August 2020, Japan Accelerates Medical Aid Diplomacy amid China's Rising Clout, https://www.japantimes.co.jp/news/2020/08/28/national/medical-aid-diplomacy-china/ (accessed 25 November 2021).

11. *Nikkei Asia*, 18 August 2020, Japan's "Medical Diplomacy" in ASEAN Aims to Sap China Clout, https://asia.nikkei.com/Spotlight/Corona virus/Japan-s-medical-diplomacy-in-ASEAN-aims-to-sap-China-clout (accessed 08 December 2021).
12. Kitaoka, Shinichi, 2 August 2021, The World and Japan after Covid-19—Japan Should Lead the Free World With ODA, JICA News, https://www.jica.go.jp/english/news/field/2021/20210802.html (accessed 4 October 2021).
13. *Asahi Shimbun*, 4 June 2021, Japan Sending Taiwan 1.24 Million Doses of AstraZeneca, https://www.asahi.com/ajw/articles/14365375 (accessed 13 November 2021).
14. Press Conference by Foreign Minister Motegi Toshimitsu, 15 June 2021, https://www.mofa.go.jp/mofaj/press/kaiken/kaiken22_000023.html (accessed 13 November 2021).
15. *Asahi Shimbun*, 08 August 2021, Nihon wa sekai san'i „wakuchin gaikō" koku – sesshu okure demo naze?, https://asahi.com/articles/ASP876 5DDP7PULFA01N.HTML (accessed 13 November 2021).
16. MOFA, Japan's COVID-19 Vaccine-Related Support (January 2022), https://www.mofa.go.jp/files/100226669.pdf (accessed 15 February 2022).
17. *Foreign Policy* (Ramani Samuel), 23 July 2021, Vaccines Are Japan's New Tool to Counter China, https://foreignpolicy.com/2021/07/23/vaccine-diplomacy-covid-japan-china-competition/ (accessed 28 October 2021).
18. Coleman, Beaty, 09 August 2021, Japan and Vaccine Diplomacy. Blog Post—New Perspectives on Asia, https://www.csis.org/blogs/new-perspectives-asia/japan-and-vaccine-diplomacy (accessed 22 December 2021).
19. *The Diplomat* (Kei Hataka, Brendon J. Cannon), 27 September 2021, Why the Quad Is Crucial, https://thediplomat.com/2021/09/why-the-quad-is-crucial/ (accessed 10 November 2021).
20. MOFA, 24 September 2021, Joint Statement from Quad Leaders, https://www.mofa.go.jp/files/100238179.pdf (accessed 22 December 2021).
21. *The Diplomat*, 27 September 2021.
22. GAVI—The Vaccine Alliance, COVAX Explained, https://www.gavi.org/vaccineswork/covax-explained (accessed 10 December 2021).
23. *Asahi Shimbun*, 15 September 2020, Wakushin kokusai kyōdō kōnyū ni seishiki sanka – maebaraikin 172 oku en, https://www.asahi.com/articles/ASN9H66FLN9HULBJ00X.html (accessed 10 December 2021).
24. MOFA, Japan's Covid-19 Vaccine-Related Support (January 2022).
25. Our World in Data, Covid-19 Vaccine Doses Donated to Covax, https://ourworldindata.org/grapher/covax-donations (accessed 15 February 2022).

26. Most donors have donated far less than promised so far.
27. To be fair, it needs to be added that Tokyo transferred USD 200 million to COVAX AMC (Advanced Market Mechanism), a funding pool to support the acquisition of inoculants as well as the buildup of infrastructure for vaccination campaigns in low- and middle-income countries, in 2021. See footnote 16.
28. UNDP Data Futures, Global Dashboard for Vaccine Equity, https://data.undp.org/vaccine-equity (accessed 15 February 2022).

REFERENCES

Abe, Shinzo. 2015. Japan's Vision for a Peaceful and Healthier World. *The Lancet* 386 (12 December): 2367–2369.

Fazal, Tanisha. 2020. Health Diplomacy in Pandemical Times. *International Organization* 74 (1): E78–E97.

Hanrieder, Tine. 2020. Priorities, Partners, Politics. The WHO's Mandate Beyond the Crisis. *Global Governance* 26: 534–543.

ISEAS Yusof Ishak Institute. 2021. *State of Southeast Asia: 2021 Survey Report*. Singapore: ASEAN Studies Centre at ISEAS-Yusof Ishak Institute.

Kevasan, K.V. 2020. Japan's China Dilemma in the COVID-19 Pandemic Situation. In *China's Strategic Ambitions in the Age of COVID-19*, ed. Kartik Bommakanti, 68–72. New Delhi: ORF and Global Policy Journal.

Leheny, David. 2022. The Olympics in the 2021 Election. In *Japan Decides 2021: The Japanese General Election*, ed. Robert J. Pekkanen, Steven R. Reed, and Daniel M. Smith. New York: Palgrave Macmillan.

Lipscy, Phillip Y. 2022. Japan's Response to the COVID-19 Pandemic. In *Japan Decides 2021: The Japanese General Election*, ed. Robert J. Pekkanen, Steven R. Reed, and Daniel M. Smith. New York: Palgrave Macmillan.

Lukner, Kerstin. 2014. Health Risks and Responses in Asia. In *The Oxford Handbook of the International Relations of Asia*, ed. Rosemary Foot, Saadia Pekkanen, and John Ravenhill, 606–621. Oxford: Oxford University Press.

MOFA—Ministry of Foreign Affairs Japan. 2021. *Diplomatic Bluebook 2020*. Tokyo.

Patrick, Stewart. 2020. When the System Fails. *Foreign Affairs* 99 (4): 40–50.

Takuma, Kayo. 2020a. Global Solidarity Is Necessary to End the COVID-19 Pandemic. *Asia-Pacific Review* 27 (2): 46–56.

Takuma, Kayo. 2020b. Japan Leading Global Health Governance. *East Asia Forum*, 30 September.

Thies, Michael F. and Yuki Yanai. 2022. Did COVID-19 Impact Japan's 2021 General Election? In *Japan Decides 2021: The Japanese General Election*, ed. Robert J. Pekkanen, Steven R. Reed, and Daniel M. Smith. New York: Palgrave Macmillan.

Toda, Takao. 2020. Japan's Leadership in Human Security During and After the COVID-19 Pandemic. *Asia-Pacific Review* 27 (2): 26–45.

Vekasi, Kristin. 2022. China in Japan's 2021 Elections. In *Japan Decides 2021: The Japanese General Election*, ed. Robert J. Pekkanen, Steven R. Reed, and Daniel M. Smith. New York: Palgrave Macmillan.

Yoshikawa, Yusaku. 2020. How COVID-19 Has Affected Japan's Official Development Assistance. *East Asia Forum*, 2 December.

CHAPTER 23

Foreign Policy and Defense

Michael J. Green

Japan's October 2021 Lower House election was the first national referendum on the future of the country after eight years under Prime Minister
Abe Shinzō. In terms of foreign policy and defense, the most striking
result was how little change in direction voters seemed to want. The
four contenders to lead the ruling Liberal Democratic Party (LDP)—
former Foreign Ministers Kishida Fumio and Kōno Tarō, and former
Interior Ministers Takaichi Sanae and Noda Seiko—varied somewhat in
tone on China, values diplomacy, and Kōno defense spending, but none
ran against Abe's basic national security strategy (Kishida and Kōno
largely stuck with current policy while Takaichi ran from the right and
Noda slightly from the left) [for details, see Nemoto 2022, this volume].
Even in the October general election, only the small Japanese Communist
Party (JCP) stuck with its time worn opposition to Japan's remilitariza-
tion but ramped-up its split with the Chinese Communist Party, while
the Nippon Ishin no Kai (Ishin) promised a more muscular version of
Abe's strategy and the Constitutional Democratic Party (CDP) offered a

M. J. Green (✉)
United States Studies Centre, University of Sydney, Sydney, NSW, Australia
e-mail: michael.green@sydney.edu.au

R. J. Pekkanen et al. (eds.), *Japan Decides 2021*,
https://doi.org/10.1007/978-3-031-11324-6_23

vaguely more multilateralized version of the same. On the whole, the opposition parties chose to challenge the ruling coalition's credibility on COVID and domestic policy rather than foreign affairs and defense, despite the enormous challenges confronting Japan in its near abroad.

The 2021 election offers further confirmation that Abe's foreign policy legacy will be the most significant since Prime Minister Yoshida Shigeru, whose post-war doctrine of economic recovery, alliance with the United States, and low-risk international posture dominated Japanese foreign policy formation throughout the Cold War. Not only did Abe's policies remain largely unchanged, his advisors and allies continued to control the ruling party as Tobias Harris notes in his chapter (Harris, 2022, this volume). Indeed, Yoshida's foreign policy vision was far more contested in the early post-war period than Abe's proactive national security policy today. As I noted in *Japan's Reluctant Realism*, a new consensus began emerging in the 1990s on the need for a more proactive Japanese foreign policy to counterbalance a rising China in Asia (Green 2000). By the time Abe returned to power in 2012 on a promise to restore alliance solidarity with the United States and Japanese diplomatic initiative in Asia, he found few dissenters within the LDP and deep support for his balance-of-power strategy from pockets of the outgoing Democratic Party of Japan (DPJ), including its last prime minister, Noda Yoshihiko.

Abe's grand strategy was codified in Japan's first published *National Security Strategy* in 2013 and largely conformed with realist logic in international relations theory.[1] Realists posit that a nation facing a deteriorating balance of power has three options: *bandwagoning* with the rising power through accommodation; *internal balancing* against the rising power by developing new sources of indigenous power; or *external balancing* by aligning with other states also threatened by the rising power (Waltz 1979). Abe explicitly rejected *bandwagoning* when he declared emphatically at the Center for Strategic and International Studies in February 2012 that "Japan is not now and will never be a tier two power."[2] Abe pursued *quantitative internal balancing* through incremental increases in defense spending and modest economic growth fueled by quantitative easing, stimulus spending, and some sectoral reforms under his "Abenomics" program. He achieved greater *qualitative internal balancing* through the most sweeping reforms of Japan's national security institutions since the 1950s, particularly with the creation of a new National Security Council system that would direct decision-making and resource allocation from the top. Abe embraced the third of the realists' options, *external balancing*, by revising the interpretation of Japan's Constitution to allow collective self-defense with the United States and other allies; massive infrastructure financing for Asia under the Free and Open Indo-Pacific framework; and closer alignment with other maritime democracies, particularly through the U.S.-Japan-India-Australia "Quad" (Green 2022).

Japan is expected to update the first *National Security Strategy* in 2022 and the LDP presidential race and lower house election spotlighted the issues that will likely feature in the new strategy: modernizing the U.S.-Japan alliance; developing new defense capabilities to keep pace with China's military expansion; managing intensified competition with Beijing around Taiwan, human rights, and technology; and shoring up Japan's position in Asia against continued Chinese revisionist ambitions. For though Abe's overall strategy was deemed a success at home and abroad—the Australian Lowy Institute concluded in its survey of regional power in 2019, that Japan had become "the leader of the liberal order in Asia"—the fact is that the overall balance-of-power dynamics continue to slip away from Japan in important areas.[3] The trajectory of Japanese foreign policy strategy may not have changed with the 2021 election, in other words, but the success of that strategy still depends on the ability of the Kishida administration to address the questions the media and other candidates raised during the campaign.

BETTING ON THE U.S.-JAPAN ALLIANCE

If Abe's expansion of defense cooperation with the United States under the 2015 bilateral Defense Guidelines and recognition of the right of collective self-defense was too much for the Japanese public, it certainly did not show in the 2021 election. Kishida vowed throughout the campaign to work closely with President Joe Biden to "develop resolute diplomacy based on the Japan-U.S. alliance" and the other LDP contenders largely did the same.[4] The CDP also called the alliance "the cornerstone of Japan's foreign policy" and in outreach to Washington-based experts, including this author, party leader Edano Yukio sought to reassure that the party's earlier flirtations with distancing from the United States were now over. Though the CDP used "multilateral diplomacy" to give a liberal institutionalist flavor to cooperation with like-minded states and continued to oppose relocation of U.S. Marine Corps Air Station from Futenma to Henoko in Okinawa, these were questions of degree rather than direction when it came to strengthening the alliance.[5] The only substantive opposition to the alliance, as was noted, came from the JCP.

Yet despite the broad consensus on strengthening the U.S.-Japan alliance to counter China, two possible areas of friction with Washington did emerge. The first was evident in Tokyo's growing frustration with Washington over the Biden administration's unwillingness to work with Japan on regional economic statecraft in the wake of the Trump administration's unilateral withdrawal from the Trans-Pacific Partnership (TPP—now called the Comprehensive and Progressive Trans-Pacific Partnership or CPTPP). During the campaign, a number of prominent cabinet members called on Washington to change course and join CPTPP now that China has made a bid to join the pact and further displace U.S. regional economic leadership and by extension Japan's. Washington's vague promises of a forthcoming Indo-Pacific economic strategy did little to reassure.

The second area of potential divergence is over nuclear weapons strategy. In mid-2021 the Biden administration began its official Nuclear Posture Review (NPR) with prominent progressives and arms control advocates in Congress and the administration calling for adoption of "No First Use" (a pledge not to be the first to use nuclear weapons) and "sole purpose" (a pledge only to use nuclear weapons in retaliation for an adversaries use of nuclear weapons). Given China's rapidly expanding strategic nuclear arsenal and North Korea's sizable chemical and biological stockpiles, Japan's national security experts are close to unanimous in their opposition to any such declaratory changes by the United States that might weaken the credibility of extended deterrence. However, Kishida campaigned on a pledge to increase nuclear disarmament efforts based on his own upbringing in Hiroshima. The Prime Minister has not tipped his hand on which way he will go in this debate, but if either the Biden administration or Kishida change course on extended deterrence policy, the criticism of the Prime Minister and possibly the alliance could mount within the LDP.[6]

DEFENSE CAPABILITIES: AN UNPRECEDENTED ENTHUSIASM FOR FIREPOWER

The 2021 LDP presidential race also featured the most extensive debate on Japanese offensive firepower in post-war history. This debate was understandable in the context of China's military expansion in the East and South China Seas and North Korea's continuous testing of missile systems that target Japan, but politics were also at play. Abe's protégé, Takaichi Sanae, took the most hawkish stance, advocating that Japan double defense spending to 2% of GDP to come into line with NATO commitments. Her position resonated with Ishin and conservatives within the LDP, securing her the position of the party's Policy Research Council (*Seichōkai*) which she used to ensure that the LDP platform for the election included the 2% of GDP defense spending pledge. Kishida looked moderate by comparison when he used modest increases in the JFY 2022 defense budget proposal to break a de facto 1% of GDP cap on defense spending without going up to 2% of GDP in his first year in power.[7]

Two of Kishida's challengers in the LDP presidential contest endorsed in some form the idea that Japan also needed more weapons capable of striking enemy targets at distance. Though this topic was labeled "enemy base strike capability" (*tekki kichi kōgeki nōryoku*) by the media and many in politics, only Takaichi proposed what experts would call "deterrence by punishment"—or the ability to hold targets deep within China or North Korea at risk. Kōno noted the importance of integrating potential "second strike" capabilities in a comprehensive strategy for improved intelligence and operational coordination with the United States and enhanced missile defense capabilities at home. Noda took a position on the relative left, calling for more discussion and raising questions about the need for intelligence, implications for the alliance, and her preference for diplomacy as the first resort, but she avoided claims that strike capability was somehow unconstitutional or counterproductive (in general Noda avoided specifics on foreign policy and defense issues, which are not her strong suite compared with the other candidates).

Kishida, meanwhile, cruised down the middle, expressing support for enemy strike capability as a "viable option" that he would "definitely consider."[8] Kishida's first defense budget included tactical stand-off strike—what experts call "deterrence by denial" against invading armadas rather than targeting of home bases. But the debate continued within Takaichi's Policy Research Council and remains an unresolved issue for the 2022 *National Security Strategy*.

China: Managing Intensifying Competition

As Kristin Vekasi notes in her chapter (Vekasi, 2022, this volume), "the 2021 elections produced few voices within the electorate or political candidates who would argue for deeper engagement or conciliatory policy toward China." A clear majority of candidates polled by *Mainichi* during the 2021 election favored either continuing Japan's confrontational stance toward China or even strengthening it. (36% of LDP candidates wanted a stronger stance and 85% of the JRP; while 81% of Kōmeitō candidates stated that the current policy was fine and the CDP was divided, with 29% wanting a stronger stance and 34% a softer stance.)[9] Within the LDP ranks there was intense mudslinging against candidates seen as too soft on China, with Kishida coming under suspicion because his *Kōchikai* faction once had a history of advocating friendship with China and the faction's former leader, Katō Kōichi, had led opposition to Abe's emergence as leader in 2006.[10]

Kishida's choice of Foreign Minister, Hayashi Yoshimasa, and Kōno also came under intense attack from hawks in weekly magazines for being sleeper agents for Beijing, in Hayashi's case because he had led the honorific China-Japan Parliamentary Friendship League and Kōno because his father was a famous dove in the 1990s. Yet both Kōno and Hayashi were former Defense Ministers, trained in politics working for conservative members of the U.S. Congress, and were well within the mainstream thinking in the LDP. In fact, the stances Kōno and Hayashi held were little different from the position on China that Abe had taken by 2018 as he sought to maintain credibility with coalition-partner Kōmeitō and with the business federation *Keidanren,* which despite growing alarm at Beijing's predatory economic policy, still wants to do business in China. The real fight was political: Kōno only came under attack for being soft on China when it looked like he might win the LDP race in the summer of 2021 and Hayashi only after he moved from the Upper to the Lower House thus positioning himself as a contender for the prime minister's job (neither faced criticism for being soft on China when they were nominated as Defense Ministers). One might consider the mudslinging over China the opening round of the next leadership fight between the relatively younger Takaichi, Hayashi, and Kōno.[11] The utility of the China card in that debate will depend on Beijing's actions over the coming years.

In at least three areas Kishida appeared ready to escalate confrontation with China—but out of principle rather than ideological fervor. The first was Taiwan. *Nikkei* polls showed before the election that 74% of Japanese believe their country should help with the defense of Taiwan. The loss of

Taiwan's de facto autonomy would be a blow for Japan: weakening confidence in U.S. security commitments; putting the critical high-end supplier Taiwan Semiconductor Manufacturing Company (TSMC) under Chinese control; and potentially putting the PLA right off Japan's southern flank in the First Island Chain (Tokuchi 2021). Abe made headlines in the first months of the new Kishida administration by stating that Japan would have no option but to help defend Taiwan, effectively boxing in the new Kishida government.[12] But if the Kishida government disagreed, it was not evident, as the government appointed a senior official to focus on Taiwan and leaked in December that the Defense and Foreign Ministries were preparing contingency plans with the United States for the Taiwan scenarios based on the more permissive rules allowed under the right of collective self-defense.[13] Kishida himself has strong family ties to Taiwan, going back to great grandparents who ran a kimono shop on the island at the turn of the century and was prominently featured earlier in his career meeting with Taiwan's anti-Beijing President Lee Teng-hui.

Kishida has also been outspoken about China's human rights violations, as a candidate endorsing a resolution before the Diet condemning China, which Noda, Takaichi, and Kōno also endorsed.[14] Kishida also pledged to appoint a special advisor on human rights and chose for that post former Defense Minister Nakatani Gen.[15] But Kishida's approach to democracy support had a more pragmatic than ideological bent compared with Abe's. Kishida led a parliamentary group sponsored by the Japan Center for International Exchange (JCIE) that examined improvements in Japan's aid for democracy and governance, for example, and he sent an offering rather than worshiping in person at the Yasukuni Shrine for the Autumn Festival just before the general election. Takaichi, in contrast, emphasized rectification of Japan's wartime image rather than support for democratic governance and she did make an in-person offering at the Autumn Festival.

Finally, Kishida geared up for increased technology competition with China—as did all the LDP candidates in one form or another. Despite significant dependence on China's market, Japan's technology companies were steadily tapering their export or transfer of high-end semiconductor equipment to China throughout the Abe years.[16] As Prime Minister, Kishida appointed Japan's first Economic Security Minister, the well-regarded former bureaucrat Kobayashi Takayuki, to continue to strengthen export control and investment screening policies vis-à-vis China.[17] The technology strategy had already worked its way through the LDP under the guidance of Kobayashi's mentor, former Economic Minister Amari Akira and neither the opposition parties on the left tied to labor unions nor the more hawkish Ishin on the right opposed strategies aimed at reshoring hi-tech supply chains back to Japan. Still, Beijing threatened retaliation against any economic sanctions imposed and continued pressuring Japan to accept China's accession to the CPTPP. Kishida argued China did not meet the standards, but in Washington Japanese diplomats pleaded for help from the Biden administration.[18]

Candidates from all parties in the *Mainichi* policy survey before the election argued that dealing with China's rise is the most important issue for Japanese diplomacy. It could also be one of the most important variables in Japanese domestic politics.

Shoring Up a Free and Open Indo-Pacific

Abe's diplomacy in Southeast Asia proved a particular success and a surprise for critics who thought a right-wing leader would frighten former victims of Japan's empire. Yet while opinion polls consistently indicated that Japan is the most trusted nation in Southeast Asia today, the same polls also reveal that Southeast Asians see China continuing to displace the United States and Japan as the most powerful actor in their sub-region.[19] In response, all the LDP candidates endorsed Abe's Free and Open Indo-Pacific strategy, which was promulgated by the Foreign Ministry in 2015 when Kishida was in charge. While the opposition leaders did not always refer to FOIP by name, they agreed on the importance of relations with the Association of Southeast Asian Nations (ASEAN) as the epicenter of geopolitical competition with China in Asia. Kishida promised to do more, announcing U.S. $1.8 billion in new aid to combat COVID and climate change, a careful reading of what will continue winning Japan influence as China creates both inroads and resentment with more massive ports, railroads, and debt traps under the Belt and Road Initiative.[20]

The weak point in Japan's diplomatic position in Asia remains the Korean peninsula (Glosserman and Snyder 2018). Kishida promised to meet with Kim Jong Un face-to-face to resolve the fate of Japanese citizens abducted decades ago by the North, but Pyongyang was disdainful in response.[21] Meanwhile, Kishida and the other LDP candidates were hesitant to offer any such olive branch to democratic U.S. ally South Korea, nor did the opposition parties push for reconciliation.[22] Kishida is said to be particularly distrustful of Seoul after President Moon Jae-in reversed his predecessor's commitment on a resolution of the comfort women issue which Kishida had personally convinced Abe to accept in the first place. Kishida continued emphasizing during the election that Japan has done its part and "the ball is in South Korea's court."[23] Mindful of the Upper House election in July 2022 and hopeful perhaps that Korea's March 2022 presidential election might yield a more flexible leader in the Blue House, Kishida gave no ground. Indeed, he retreated compared with Suga, who had declared Korea a "most important neighbor" in his first Diet speech as prime minister, while Kishida chose in his December 2021 speech to simply call Korea "an important neighbor."[24] Kōno and Noda did not push for reconciliation either, Kōno because his father had negotiated the first agreement with Seoul on comfort women that was now deeply unpopular in the LDP, and Noda because of her husband's family ties to Korea. Takaichi took no position on the diplomacy but characteristically urged correction of Seoul's criticism of Japan's past.[25] In the end, this Achilles Heel in Japanese grand strategy showed no signs of improvement during the 2021 election.

Strategically Political Stability Is the Key

In the end, the variation on relations with South Korea, defense spending, human rights, or nuclear weapons represent debates over the ways and means of Japan's grand strategy rather than the ends. And to the extent candidates argued for new tools in the tool kit, they did so after generally endorsing what Abe put there first. It is also worth noting that one of the most important tools a nation can bring to international affairs is internal solidarity, where Japan's 2021 election revealed far more consensus on foreign policy than the United States, Korea, Taiwan, or many other democracies under pressure from China could claim. As Mireya Solis of the Brookings Institution has observed, Japan is almost unique among major democracies in not being distracted by a major populist backlash and internal divisions over globalization (Solis 2021). This itself is an underappreciated source of national strength.

But if Japan has a potential weakness in the execution of its grand strategy, it may be about the stability of leadership at the top rather than the choices made on specific tools in the foreign policy toolkit. The historical pattern has been for strong prime ministers (such as Koizumi Junichirō or Nakasone Yasuhiro) to be followed by a string of weak leaders who struggle to stay in office—unable to cultivate effective relationships with other world leaders or a mandate to pass necessary budgets and implement legislation in the Diet. Kishida's moderation may disappoint those on the right but might prove the most important strategic consideration of all if it leads to strong coalition ties with Kōmeitō, success in the Upper House election, and a long-term stable government. Unless, of course, his lack of risk-taking and his careful calibration end up looking feckless and ineffective in the face of new challenges from China or crises at home. Such is politics in Japan.

Notes

1. Kantei National Security Council, *National Security Strategy*, December 17, 2013, http://japan.kantei.go.jp/96_abe/documents/2013/__ics Files/afieldfile/2013/12/17/NSS.pdf.
2. Shinzo Abe, "'Japan is Back', Policy Speech by Prime Minister Shinzo Abe" (speech, Center for Strategic and International Studies (CSIS), Washington D.C., United States, February 22, 2013).
3. The Lowy Institute cautioned that Japan's overall power was still slipping relative to China. See: "Asia Power Index 2019 Key Findings," Lowy Institute, https://power.lowyinstitute.org/downloads/Lowy-Institute-Asia-Power-Index-2019-Key-Findings.pdf
4. "Mt. Fuji Meeting | Prime Minister: 'Resolute Diplomacy based on the Japan-U.S. Alliance' || Foreign Minister Motegi: 'The United States should return to the TPP'." *Nikkei Keizai Shimbun*, October 23, 2021. https://www.nikkei.com/article/DGXZQOUA2284J0S1A0 21C2000000. (Accessed December 20, 2021).
5. "Realistic Diplomacy to Protect Peace" Constitutional Democratic Party of Japan (CDP). https://cdp-japan.jp/news/20210924_2169. (Accessed December 20, 2021).
6. Kishida's website notes that he is the first foreign minister from Hiroshima which suffered nuclear attack and would therefore be "the most resolute politician on nuclear disarmament and non-proliferation," See: https://kishida.gr.jp/wp-content/uploads/2018/03/shou062.pdf.
7. "Mid-term Defense Build Up Plan Submitted," *Nikkei Shimbun*, December 16, 2021. https://www.nikkei.com/article/DGXZQOUA1 44710U1A211C2000000/ (Accessed December 20, 2021).
8. Nippon TV, "The LDP Presidential Election: Will the LDP possess capabilities for enemy base attacks? What do you think about the pension system? What about post-election matters? The four candidates discuss these topics in-depth on 'Shinsou News!'," YouTube Video, 50:11, September 24, 2021. https://www.youtube.com/watch?v=g2XGPcnsajA.

9. "2021 Lower House Election: Candidate Survey No. 1," *Mainichi*, October 27, 2021. https://mainichi.jp/english/articles/20211026/p2a/00m/0na/026000c.
10. "The 'Kishida Shock' returns as the Nikkei 225 drops to 300 yen... A look behind the prime minister's 'gaffe'," *Gendai Business*, December 17, 2021. https://gendai.ismedia.jp/articles/-/90486.
11. Okada Jyun. "China is Wary of Prime Minister Kishida Fumio's Taiwan Policy," Toyo Keizai Online, November 26, 2021. https://toyokeizai.net/articles/-/471549.
12. "Former Prime Minister Abe Says Japan and U.S. Could Not Stand By If China Attacked Taiwan," *Reuters*, November 30, 2021. https://www.reuters.com/world/asia-pacific/former-pm-abe-says-japan-us-could-not-stand-by-if-china-attacked-taiwan-2021-12-01/.
13. "Japan creates new post to handle Taiwan affairs, as tensions rise with Beijing," *South Morning China Post*, December 17, 2021. https://www.scmp.com/news/china/diplomacy/article/3160168/japan-creates-new-post-handle-taiwan-affairs-tensions-rise.; "Japan, U.S. Draft Operation Plan for Taiwan Contingency: Sources," *Kyodo*, December 23, 2021. https://english.kyodonews.net/news/2021/12/f5ed60ab6502-japan-us-draft-operation-plan-for-taiwan-contingency-sources.html.
14. "On the resolution to condemn China, the three presidential candidates say that it "should be adopted"; meanwhile, Kono does not respond." Sankei News, Sankei Shimbun. September 22, 2021. Accessed December 20, 2021. https://www.sankei.com/article/20210922-RGIGUBUPL.
   "Leadership Race Document: Mr. Kono finally responds; China Resolution should be 'issued'." Sankei News, September 24, 2021. Accessed January 30, 2022. https://www.sankei.com/article/20210924-Z7R6B35APBJETMW4YGGWRYGJKU/.
15. The Asahi Shimbun Digital. (Editorial) "Japan's Human Rights Diplomacy: Commitment to Universal Values," *The Asahi Shimbun Digital*. (Accessed December 22, 2021). https://www.asahi.com/articles/DA3S15114701.html.
   "Former Defense Minister Nakatani to serve as Special Advisor to the Prime Minister on human rights," The Asahi Shimbun Digital, November 8, 2021. https://www.asahi.com/articles/ASPC841N6PC8UTFK003.html.

16. "Japanese Business Rethinks Hi-Tech Deals with China," *Nikkei Asia*, September 3, 2020, https://asia.nikkei.com/Politics/International-rel ations/US-China-tensions/Japanese-business-rethinks-high-tech-deals-with-China; Akira Amari, *"Amari Akira no Kokkai Repōto Sōran* [Amari Akira's Diet Report Overview]," Amari Akira Official Blog, August 6, 2020, https://amari-akira.com/01_parliament/2020/410.html

17. "Kobayashi Named to New Post of Economic Security Minister," *Kyodo*, October 4, 2021, https://www.nippon.com/en/news/kd8177094896 96948224/

18. "Prime Minister Kishida Says He Will Say to China What Must Be Said," [*Kishida Shusho, Tai-Chukoku 'Iu beki koto ha shikari Iu'*] *Yomiuri*, October 5, 2021. https://www.yomiuri.co.jp/politics/20211005-OYT 1T50067/ (Accessed December 20, 2021).

19. See, for example: Tang Siew Mun et al., The State of Southeast Asia: 2020 (Singapore: ISEAS-Yusof Ishak Institute, 2020), https://www.iseas. edu.sg/images/pdf/TheStateofSEASurveyReport_2020.pdf .

20. Asahi Shimbun. "Joint Communique of the 50th ASEAN Foreign Ministers' Meeting on August 4th." August 2, 2017. Accessed December 22, 2021. https://mainichi.jp/articles/20170802/ddm/007/030/098 000c.

21. "North Korea – Suga and Abe's Hostile Policy, People's Eternal Curse? | Joongang Ilbo." n.d. https://japanese.joins.com/JArticle/ 283241 (Accessed December 21, 2021).

22. SankeiNews. "[Uncut] Japan National Press Club Organizes LDP presidential election; candidate debate." YouTube video, 2:20:36. September 18, 2021. https://www.youtube.com/watch?v=T-WlgyNpx_Y (Accessed December 21, 2021).

23. "Friction with South Korea on Reversing the Comfort Women Agreement: 'Kishida will show his true colors next July'" *JoongAng Ilbo (Japanese vr.)*, https://japanese.joins.com/JArticle/283405(Accessed December 22, 2021); "Abe, alarmed over the Comfort Women Agreement, reminded him once more the night before the signing, 'are you sure?'": Asahi Shimbun, https://www.asahi.com/articles/ASP5M4Q0J P4NUTFK00F.html (Accessed December 22, 2021); "The ball is in their court" SankeiNews. 2021. "[Uncut] Japan National Press Club Organizes LDP presidential election; candidate debate," https://www.youtube. com/watch?v=T-WlgyNpx_Y.

24. "Policy Speech by Prime Minister KISHIDA Fumio to the 205th Session of the Diet (Speeches and statements by the Prime Minister) | Prime Minister of Japan and His Cabinet." October 8, 2021. https://japan. kantei.go.jp/100_kishida/statement/202110/_00005.html.

25. "Bipartisan movement to enact a law sanctioning human rights abuses in China." Sankei News. December 27, 2020. https://www.sankei.com/art icle/20201227-OL6NLFGGLRMYVIGNGLKMORGGVM/.

REFERENCES

Glosserman, Brad and Scott A. Snyder. 2015. *The Japan-South Korea Identity Clash: East Asian Security and the United States*. New York: Columbia University Press.

Green, Michael. 2000. *Japan's Reluctant Realism: Foreign Policy in an Era of Uncertain Power*. New York: Columbia University Press.

Green, Michael 2022. *Line of Advantage: Japan's Grand Strategy in the Era of Abe Shinzō*. New York: Columbia University Press.

Harris, Tobias. 2022. "Abe's Legacy." In Robert J. Pekkanen, Steven R. Reed, and Daniel M. Smith (eds.), *Japan Decides 2021: The Japanese General Election*. Palgrave Macmillan.

Nemoto, Kuniaki. 2022. "How the Liberal Democratic Party Avoided a Loss in 2021." In Robert J. Pekkanen, Steven R. Reed, and Daniel M. Smith (eds.), *Japan Decides 2021: The Japanese General Election*. Palgrave Macmillan.

Smith, Sheila. 2014. *Intimate Rivals: Japanese Domestic Politics and a Rising China*. New York: Columbia University Press.

Solis, Mireya. 2021. "The Underappreciated Power: Japan after Abe," *Foreign Affairs*, No. 99:6, November/December.

Tokuchi Hideshi, "Will Japan Fight in a Taiwan Contingency: An Analysis of the 2021 Japan Defense White Paper," *Prospects and Perspectives*, No. 42 (August 2021), https://www.pf.org.tw/article-pfen-2089-7283. (Accessed January 2, 2022).

Vekasi, Kristin. 2022. "China in Japan's 2021 Elections." In Robert J. Pekkanen, Steven R. Reed, and Daniel M. Smith (eds.), *Japan Decides 2021: The Japanese General Election*. Palgrave Macmillan.

Waltz, Kenneth. 1979. *Theory of International Politics*. Reading, MA: Addison-Wesley pp. 168–170.

CHAPTER 24

China in Japan's 2021 Elections

Kristin Vekasi

Japan had two big elections in the fall of 2021: first for the president of the Liberal Democratic Party (LDP) on September 29, and then the Lower House general elections on October 31. Campaign rhetoric in both of these elections was quite critical towards China, both in campaign speeches from candidates and in the party manifestos that stake out policy positions. The 2021 elections provide one more sign that Japan is formulating more assertive national security and economic policies, some of which are already being implemented.

In the race for LDP president, Takaichi Sanae, a lower-house member further on the right-wing of the LDP, along with claiming on an election poster that she was the "only man" running for the post claimed she would "defend Japan against the China menace." Kishida Fumio, the winner, avoided that harsher language but laid out security, economic, and human rights threats from China (Nikkei, 2021). While the LDP backed off on the most hawkish rhetoric in the general election, voters were still

K. Vekasi (✉)
Department of Political Science and School of Policy and International Affairs, University of Maine, Orono, ME, USA
e-mail: kristin.vekasi@maine.edu

R. J. Pekkanen et al. (eds.), *Japan Decides 2021*,
https://doi.org/10.1007/978-3-031-11324-6_24

warned that voting for opposition candidates was equivalent to a "pro-China" vote, equating the left-wing Japanese Communist Party (JCP) with the Chinese Communist Party despite deep ideological distance (Dooley and Ueno, 2021).

The 2021 elections produced few voices within the electorate or political candidates who would argue for deeper engagement or conciliatory policy towards China. The LDP electoral victory may presage a more hawkish China policy, particularly if parties on the right such as Nippon Ishin no Kai (Ishin) or other likeminded politicians manage to broaden their electoral appeal. However, this prediction must be tempered with the moderating influence of the LDP's long-time, stable coalition partner Kōmeitō. While not shying away from critique of China, Kōmeitō alone put forward a more positive vision for the future of Japan–China relations.

POLITICS AND ECONOMICS IN THE JAPAN–CHINA RELATIONSHIP

Japan has long maintained a delicate balance with China, trying to nurture and value the economic relationship amid increasing security and human rights concerns at both elite and popular levels. As relations between the United States and China have grown increasingly frosty, Japan's security relationship with the United States has made this diplomacy all the more difficult (Green, 2022). The security and economic issues are increasingly intertwined, much to the chagrin of business stakeholders.

At the popular level, conciliatory or friendly political ties towards China do not have a large constituency in Japan. Japanese see China as a threat because of their large and growing military, concerns about territorial disputes, and violations of Japan's maritime territories. China enjoyed friendly popular sentiment within Japan from normalization in the 1970s to Tiananmen in 1989, and again in the early 2000s. However, since the souring of relations in 2012, an annual survey done by Genron NPO has found that over 80% of the Japanese public consistently report a negative impression of China (Genron NPO, 2020), and that figure topped 90% in 2021 (Kudo, 2021). Negative impressions of China among Japanese were primarily derived from concerns about the Senkaku Islands territorial dispute (57%) and a lack of trust at the individual (33%) and official political levels (40%). Japanese respondents also view China as a security threat, close behind North Korea. In 2021, 71% of Japanese respondents reported that they saw China as a security threat to Japan, an increase from 58% in 2019 and 63% in 2020. The numbers for North Korea were 85% in 2019 and 77% in 2021, demonstrating the growing primacy of China as national security threat in Japanese public opinion. The initial months of the coronavirus pandemic only exacerbated issues of distrust and lack of transparency (Lukner, 2022).

Economic ties with China are key to Japan's prosperity, and Japanese businesses have by and large been able to navigate the sometimes tense diplomatic relationship and popular animosity on both sides (Vekasi, 2019). To some extent, this difference is reflected in popular opinion: only 13% of Japanese respondents to the Genron NPO poll reported that "economic friction" was causing tense Sino-Japanese relations (Kudo, 2021). China has been Japan's largest import source since 2002 and competed with the United States as the most important export destination since 2008: in 2020, 26% of Japan's exports and 22% of its imports were with China (UN Comtrade). China plays a pivotal role in Japan's international supply chains and is an important export market for direct-to-consumer goods as well as precision components for final assembly and re-export or sale. Business people in Japan are more bullish on China than are the general public. The 2020 survey on overseas manufacturing from Japan Bank for International Cooperation—conducted under the shadow of the US-China trade conflict *and* the global pandemic—placed China as the most promising destination for overseas investment for ease of manufacturing and satisfaction with profitability (JBIC, 2021). Japanese companies largely have no desire to disengage with the China market. On the contrary, many are pursuing new investments and even cooperative ventures with Chinese enterprises throughout Asia (Ministry of Economy, Trade, and Industry, 2021).

As a close and "intimate" rival, China has been a useful bogeyman in Japanese political discourse and clear target in Japan's increased securitization (S. Smith, 2015). Harsh criticism for China's human rights record and actions in the East China Sea have broad appeal across the ideological spectrum within parties as well as the general public. Even given this broad agreement, however, there is divergence on the focus of complaints and potential remedies.

Foreign Policy in Japanese Elections

Foreign policy, or for that matter domestic policy, is not typically the critical factor shaping electoral results in Japan. Voter choice in 2021 was driven more by party than policy (Horiuchi et al., 2018; Maeda,

2022). Nevertheless, foreign policy debates play an important role in electoral campaigns, public opinion can shape the direction of foreign policy, and most importantly campaigns and electoral discourse do shape the direction of foreign policy after the election.

Foreign policy has become increasingly important in Japanese elections over the past decades, with an arguable shift from particularism to nationalized elections, and a "rightward" trend in foreign policy appeals. The electoral reforms of the 1990s marked a notable increase in political attention and campaigning on national security and foreign policy issues (Catalinac, 2016; Estevez-Abe et al., 2008), and facilitated "Japanese voter support for an active security policy" that had not been seen since the opposition to the US-Japan Security Treaty in the 1970s (Rosenbluth, Kohno, et al., 2008: 232). The 2017 general election could notably be interpreted as a foreign policy referendum due to Abe's bold changes to the foreign policy status quo (S. Smith, 2018).

Campaign statements, party manifestos, and media surveys help unpack party policies towards Japan's two core relationships with China, national security and economics, as well as human rights issues. Manifestos are not firm promises, but are important indications of party priorities and the direction of policy and provide a snapshot of political communication and party priorities (Catalinac, 2016; Winkler, 2017). The bulk of the analysis here focuses on how the different parties discuss policy towards China, with a focus on the policies of the ruling LDP. Some of the smaller parties are excluded from the analysis, but the major parties as well as a broad range of ideological viewpoints are included.

The core foreign policy issue in Japanese politics and elections has typically been the US-Japan alliance, but China now plays an equally important role, a shift shown by Smith in discussions of the 2017 election and highlighted by Green in this volume (Green, 2022; S. Smith, 2018). With respect to the alliance, the parties have a traditional right-left split: the LDP, and parties on the right are typically more supportive of the alliance and the parties on the left less supportive (McElwain, 2014). As we will see in the analysis of campaign manifestos, the parties' China policies are aligned to a certain extent with perspectives on the alliance: parties on the right tend to favor more defense spending and a securitized response to the China challenge, and the parties on the left an approach that centers diplomacy and institutions. The Kōmeitō position, however, leans to the left on China (Klein and McLaughlin, 2022).

Security

Before the election, the NHK polled candidates on key issues, including security. Table 24.1 shows the percent of party candidates that agreed or partially agreed with statements promoting increased defense spending and reform of Article 9 to specify a role for the Japanese Self Defense Force in the constitution. While neither of these questions directly address China, they are indicators of candidate orientations towards the two key security dimensions that are increasingly aimed at China and provide evidence of how individual candidates align with their party manifestos. There is strong support on the right for increased defense spending: the LDP and Ishin are almost unanimous in their support for increased defense spending, as are a surprising almost 80% of Kōmeitō respondents. On the left, support is far more limited: 40% of CDP respondents and none of the JCP respondents agree with the proposal. There is more heterogeneity for Article 9 revision: while 95% of LDP respondents say yes, only a third of Kōmeitō and two-thirds of Ishin politicians agree. The parties on the left are essentially united in opposition, with only 10 CDP politicians out of a total of 317 candidates from the parties on the left.

Japan's security relationship with China plays an explicit and implicit role in multiple sections of the LDP's policy statements before the election including the framing of "economic security" in the manifesto (and the drafting of a new Economic Security Law) and the increased scope of

Table 24.1 NHK candidate survey by party

Party (number of candidate respondents)	Percent supporting increased defense spending (%)	Percent supporting clarification of the JSDF role in Article 9 of the constitution (%)
Liberal democratic party (267)	93	95
Kōmeitō (9)	78	33
Constitutional democratic party (212)	39	5
Japanese communist party (105)	0	0
Nippon Ishin no Kai (91)	95	64
Total (834)	60	47

Source NHK candidate survey by party (NHK, 2021)

China-related security issues. After her failed bid for the LDP presidency, noted China hardliner Takaichi Sanae was placed on the team responsible for the LDP manifesto. While Kishida does not share her more bombastic views towards China, there are indications in manifesto of a more assertive stance.

The LDP manifesto includes language that explicitly identifies Chinese actions and policies as threats to national security. This posture is not entirely new. The LDP's 2019 House of Councillors election manifesto referred to China's "drastic increase of arms and maritime advances" alongside the threat of North Korea's nuclear program, clearly identifying China as a military threat. The 2021 manifesto contains similar language, in addition to expressing concern about "China's unilateral efforts to change the status quo around the Senkaku Islands and Taiwan through force." Including Taiwan alongside Japanese specific territorial claims is an escalation of rhetoric (LDP, 2021). Although China elevated the foreign policy importance of the Diaoyu Islands in 2012 when they named them a "core national interest," bringing Taiwan into the PRC has been a primary foreign policy goal of the CCP since 1949.[1] The LDP inclusion of PRC threats to Taiwanese de facto sovereignty as a Japanese national security concern in the election manifesto publicly clarifies how LDP leadership views the linkages between Taiwanese and Japanese national security, and perhaps makes ambiguity more difficult (Green, 2022; Liff, 2021).

The manifesto also includes language on defense spending, specifically advocating raising Japan's military budget to at least 2% of GDP, again reflecting talking points that Takaichi raised on the campaign trail. Japan has long held a norm of military spending at 1% of GDP, which makes Japanese military spending quite high given the country's status as the world's third-largest economy (Lind, 2004; Miyashita, 2007). The manifesto frames the possible defense spending increase as moving Japan in line with NATO countries. While doubling defense spending would be a dramatic change from the status quo, it is notable that this point was not included in the shorter pamphlet sent to voters, but only in the longer document, signaling a weaker public commitment.

Ishin had a far less detailed manifesto than the other parties, and did not include specific criticism (or praise) of China. Raising the 1% cap is one of their core "realist" foreign policy ideas along with strengthening the US-Japan alliance (Nippon Ishin no Kai, 2021b). On its website, Ishin writes that Japan has a "mutually beneficial relationship based on common strategic interests" with China and that it is necessary to enter into deeper conversation with them, policy in line with Japan's 2019 National Security Strategy. The party also raises the possibility of working with China, the United States, and South Korea on North Korea issues (Nippon Ishin no Kai, 2021a).

The Kōmeitō has historically held much more conciliatory views towards China, and continues to do so today. Kōmeitō has a long-term and stable coalition with the LDP, maintained by mutual dependence, which constrains the LDP on foreign policy and security issues while providing them Kōmeitō's votes (Liff and Maeda, 2019). As Harris and McLaughlin (2021) explain, Kōmeitō "enjoys the strongest and most stable relationship with China, and Kōmeitō and Sōka Gakkai leaders have forged intimate connections with senior Chinese leaders" and are likely to moderate the LDP's stance (Harris and McLaughlin, 2021; see also Klein and McLaughlin, 2022). In their manifesto, Kōmeitō overlaps with the LDP's critique of China's human rights record and territorial issues. However, they emphasize the long relationship, history of solving problems, and say that "Japan–China relations are not only important for the two countries, but also for regional and even global peace and stability." Kōmeitō's position is for more official diplomacy and person-to-person informal diplomacy as soon as the pandemic situation allows (Kōmeitō, 2021). If any Japanese political party can be labeled "pro-China," it is Kōmeitō.

The Constitutional Democratic Party (CDP) strikes a balance between critiques of China while pushing for diplomatic solutions, somewhat like Kōmeitō. Using language similar to the LDP, they criticize China on human rights issues such as Hong Kong and the Uyghurs, as well as territorial issues in the East China Sea, and express concern about China's rapid military buildup. The CDP advocates working with allies on these foreign policy issues, particularly within a strong US-Japan alliance. While 40% of CDP candidates did support increased defense spending, no such language was included in the manifesto, and they clearly state any clarifying addition to the constitution for the JSDF (CDP, 2021).

The JCP embraces principles of pacifism and rejects the more hawkish approach of the ruling parties. It is also quite critical of the Chinese Communist Party, with which it formally broke ties in 1967 (Berton and Atherton, 2018; Chapter 7; Kim, 1976). On the 100th anniversary of the CCP's founding, the head of the JCP Shii Kazuo wrote, "China's hegemonic acts in the East China Sea and South China Sea as well as its human-rights suppression in Hong Kong and the Xinjiang Uyghur Autonomous Region are alien to socialism. The Chinese party conducting such acts is not worthy of calling itself as a 'communist party'" (quoted in *Japan Press Weekly*, 2021). In its campaign manifesto, the JCP uses very similar language, expressing concern about human rights and territorial issues. However, the JCP clearly differentiates its policy from the LDP through a rejection of increased defense spending and militaristic solutions. instead advocating "measured diplomacy" and a rules-based order, preferably without the US-Japan military alliance (JCP, 2021).

Economy

Beyond security, the key policy issue related to China is economic security. Economic security includes the protection of sensitive and strategic technologies, building secure and resilient supply chains, and bolstering cybersecurity and anti-espionage efforts. After establishing an economic section at the National Security Secretariat in 2019, the Japanese government began working on a more comprehensive economic security bill in 2021 (Igata and Glosserman, 2021), which became law in 2022. There are some similarities to the position of the United States that "economic security is national security," and one of the aims of the law is to facilitate US-Japan national security-related economic cooperation.

Much of the economic security discourse has been focused on China (Igata and Glosserman, 2021). Existent policies to build supply-chain resilience, for example, target sectors where Japan is heavily dependent on China (Solis, 2021) or extra monitoring and possible exclusion of investments from Chinese state-owned enterprises (Takahashi, 2021). At the same time, the new economic security minister Kobayashi Takayuki "denied Japan's economic security measures were specifically targeted at China, saying the government had no intention to intervene in the private sector's deep business ties with the world's second-largest economy," showing the delicate balance between politics and business (Inagaki and Lewis, 2021).

Only the LDP directly addresses economic security directly in their manifesto. As existing policies are both recent and originated from prior LDP-led governments and the bureaucracies it is perhaps unsurprising that the opposition parties do not yet have formally expressed policy statements. Other manifestos, such as Ishin's, do express support for building free trade ties with other "liberal" countries. While the LDP's lengthy discussion of economic security is not *only* implying China, many of the sectors included are those where Japan is highly dependent on or competing with China such as artificial intelligence or semiconductors. Closer economic security cooperation with the United States, could also further entangle Japan more deeply in US-China competition and complicate the business-politics tightrope.

IMPLICATIONS OF THE 2021 ELECTIONS
FOR JAPAN–CHINA RELATIONS

The 2021 elections illuminated how the political winds suggest a more assertive security and human rights posture towards China. The critical language in most party manifestos and campaign rhetoric are leading indicators of some actual political changes occurring post-election about economic security and Taiwan issues.

A month after the election, former Prime Minister and LDP powerhouse Abe Shinzō gave a virtual speech at the Taiwanese Institute for National Policy Research said that "a Taiwan emergency is a Japanese emergency, and therefore an emergency for the Japan-U.S. alliance" (quoted in Blanchard, 2021). The Kishida government is creating a new diplomatic position with responsibilities over the East China Sea, a portfolio that will include the disputed Senkaku/Diaoyu Islands as well as Taiwan (Chen, 2021). In response to Abe's speech, Beijing summoned the Japanese ambassador for an emergency meeting (*Japan Times*, 2021).

Economic policy is increasingly reflecting a more securitized orientation. Economic ties between Japan and China have long been, and do still remain, a stabilizing element of the relationship. While Japanese businesses have been diversifying from the China market, there remains great interest in maintaining market presence and deepening institutional ties such as the recently signed Regional Comprehensive Economic Partnership. China and Taiwan have both recently requested membership in the Comprehensive and Progressive Trans-Pacific Partnership trade agreement. There is reportedly interest from the business community in admitting both China and Taiwan, but even if both meet the qualifications to the satisfaction of members, the entry process will be a diplomatic tightrope. Abe himself stated support for Taiwan's entry to the CPTPP as an indication of broad support for the Taiwanese regime.

Prime Minister Kishida created a new cabinet-level position for economic security issues, headed by Kobayashi Takayuki, a former vice-minister for defense. Kobayashi's new position will seek to deepen economic ties with Taiwan, particularly in the semiconductor sector, but he is also a member of the more pro-China Nikai faction (Inagaki, 2021; Tachikawa, 2021). This new position elevates the supply-chain security-national security connection to the highest levels of government. This position will be instrumental in trying to guide new economic security legislation through the Diet in 2022, much of which will be focused on investment screening mechanisms, and protecting sensitive and crucial technologies from rivals, particularly China. While private businesses will remain the primary driver of the economic relationship, the potential for securitization could threaten to undermine any commercial peace. While there has not been overt retaliation against Japan for its increased security posture since the 2012–2014 Senkaku dispute, China has not been shy about using economic coercion against other states such as South Korea or Australia. For now, Beijing is remaining largely silent on the political rhetoric from Tokyo, but more the more concrete policy changes on the horizon could trigger retaliatory economic measures.

While these changes do indicate more hawkish Chinese policy in Japan, the more pacifist and pro-China Kōmeitō will ease dramatic policy changes. Kōmeitō's tempering hand evident in post-election events. Both Kōmeitō and the LDP have opposed a human rights resolution in the current extraordinary session, and Japan has not joined its allies in a diplomatic boycott of the 2022 Beijing Olympics, both indicators of Kōmeitō's influence (*Sankei Shimbun*, 2021). The bolder anti-China campaigning does indicate a shift in Japanese politics. However, stable multi-party coalition politics are also an effective bulwark against rapid foreign policy change.

NOTE

1. The disputed territories are called the Senkaku Islands in Japan and Diaoyu Islands in China.

REFERENCES

Berton, P., and Atherton, S. (2018). *The Japanese Communist Party: Permanent Opposition, But Moral Compass*. Routledge.

Blanchard, B. (2021, December 1). *Former PM Abe says Japan, U.S. Could Not Stand by if China Attacked Taiwan* | Reuters. https://www.reuters.com/world/asia-pacific/former-pm-abe-says-japan-us-could-not-stand-by-if-china-attacked-taiwan-2021-12-01/

Catalinac, A. (2016). *Electoral Reform and National Security in Japan: From pork to foreign policy.* Cambridge University Press.

CDP. (2021). 立憲民主党 政策集2021 Constitutional Democratic Party 2021 Policy. https://change2021.cdp-japan.jp/seisaku/detail/

Chen, A. (2021, December 17). Japan Creates New Post to Handle Taiwan affairs in swipe at Beijing. *South China Morning Post.* https://www.scmp.com/news/china/diplomacy/article/3160168/japan-creates-new-post-handle-taiwan-affairs-tensions-rise

Dooley, B., and Ueno, H. (2021, October 27). Japan's Communists Are Hardly Radical, but Make a Handy Election Target. *The New York Times.* https://www.nytimes.com/2021/10/27/world/asia/japan-election-communist-party.html

Estevez-Abe, M., Takako, H., and Toshio, N. (2008). "Japan's New Executive Leadership: How Electoral Rules Make Japanese Security Policy." In F. Rosenbluth & M. Kohno (Eds.), *Japan and the World: Japan's Contemporary Geopolitical Challenges—A Volume in Honor of the Memory and Intellectual Legacy of Asakawa Kan'ichi* (pp. 251–288).

Genron NPO. (2020, November 17). 第16回 日中共同世論調査 結果. 特定非営利活動法人 言論 NPO. https://www.genron-npo.net/world/archives/9354.html

Green, M. (2022). "Foreign Policy and Defense." In Robert J. Pekkanen, Steven R. Reed, and Daniel M. Smith (Eds.), *Japan Decides 2021: The Japanese General Election.* Palgrave Macmillan.

Harris, T., and McLaughlin, L. (2021, November 4). *Komeito: The Small Pacifist Party That Could Shape Japan's Future.* Foreign Policy. https://foreignpolicy.com/2021/11/04/komeito-ldp-japan-elections-defense-policy-china/

Horiuchi, Yusaku, Smith, Daniel M., and Yamamoto, Teppei. (2018). Measuring Voters' Multidimensional Policy Preferences with Conjoint Analysis: Application to Japan's 2014 election. *Political Analysis, 26*(2), 190–209.

Igata, A., and Glosserman, B. (2021). Japan's New Economic Statecraft. *The Washington Quarterly, 44*(3), 25–42. https://doi.org/10.1080/0163660X.2021.1970334

Inagaki, K. (2021, October 4). Japan's New PM Creates Post to Address China threat. *Financial Times.* https://www.ft.com/content/7dfbd4da-344e-44b4-81ac-13daaebf5dea

Inagaki, K., and Lewis, L. (2021, October 19). Japan's Economic Security Minister Warns on Chip Industry Survival. *Financial Times.* https://www.ft.com/content/f59173b6-211c-4446-aa57-5c9b78d602c2

Japan Press Weekly. (2021, July 2). *Shii Comments on 100th Founding Anniversary of China's Communist Party—@JapanPress_wky.* https://www.japan-press.co.jp/modules/news/index.php?id=13661

Japan Times. (2021, December 2). China Summons Japan Envoy and Rips Abe for Warning About Taiwan invasion. *The Japan Times.* https://www.japantimes.co.jp/news/2021/12/02/national/politics-diplomacy/china-abe-taiwan-remarks/

JBIC. (2021). *Survey Report on Overseas Business Operations by Japanese Manufacturing Companies.* https://www.jbic.go.jp/en/information/press/press-2020/pdf/0115-014188_4.pdf

JCP. (2021). 日本共産党総選挙政策 Japanese Communist Party General Election Policy. https://www.jcp.or.jp/web_policy/2021/10/2021-sosenkyo-seisaku.html

Kim, H. N. (1976). Deradicalization of the Japanese Communist Party Under Kenji Miyamoto. *World Politics, 28*(2), 273–299.

Klein, A., and McLaughlin, L. (2022). "Kōmeitō in 2021: Strategizing between the LDP and Sōka Gakkai." In Robert J. Pekkanen, Steven R. Reed, and Daniel M. Smith (Eds.), *Japan Decides 2021: The Japanese General Election.* Palgrave Macmillan.

Komeito. (2021). 公明党2021衆院選政策集 Komeito 2021 Lower House Election Policy. https://www.komei.or.jp/special/shuin49/wp-content/uploads/manifesto2021.pdf

Kudo, Y. (2021). Impact of the US-China Conflict on Chinese Public Opinion. *Genron NPO,* 18.

LDP. (2021). 自民党政策バンク2021 Liberal Democratic Party Policy Bank 2021. https://www.jimin.jp/policy/pamphlet/

Liff, A. (2021). Japan, Taiwan, the United States, and the 'Free and Open Indo-Pacific.' In A. Denmark & L. Myers (Eds.), *Essays on the Rise of China and Its Implications* (pp. 271–299). Wilson Center.

Liff, A., and Maeda, K. (2019). Electoral Incentives, Policy Compromise, and Coalition Durability: Japan's LDP–Komeito Government in a mixed electoral system. *Japanese Journal of Political Science, 20*(1), 53–73.

Lind, J. M. (2004). Pacifism or passing the buck? Testing theories of Japanese security policy. *International Security, 29*(1), 92–121.

Lukner, K. (2022). "Covid-19: The International Dimension." In Robert J. Pekkanen, Steven R. Reed, and Daniel M. Smith (Eds.), *Japan Decides 2021: The Japanese General Election.* Palgrave Macmillan.

Maeda, Y. (2022). "Public Opinion and Covid-19." In Robert J. Pekkanen, Steven R. Reed, and Daniel M. Smith (Eds.), *Japan Decides 2021: The Japanese General Election.* Palgrave Macmillan.

McElwain, K. M. (2014). Parties and Elections in Japan. *The SAGE Handbook of Modern Japanese Studies,* 367.

Ministry of Economy, Trade, and Industry. (Various Years). *Quarterly Survey of Overseas Subsidiaries*. Ministery of Economy, Trade, and Industry. https://www.meti.go.jp/english/statistics/tyo/genntihou/index.html

Miyashita, A. (2007). Where Do Norms Come From? Foundations of Japan's postwar pacifism. *International Relations of the Asia-Pacific*, 7(1), 99–120.

NHK. (2021, October 19). 党派別集計 候補者アンケート―衆院選 2021 NHK. https://www.nhk.or.jp/senkyo/database/shugiin/2021/survey/tou habetsu.html

Nikkei. (2021, September 4). *Countering China is top priority for Japan PM contender Kishida*. Nikkei Asia. https://asia.nikkei.com/Editor-s-Picks/Int erview/Countering-China-is-top-priority-for-Japan-PM-contender-Kishida

Nippon Ishin no Kai. (2021a). 外交安保|政策|日本維新の会. 日本維新の会. https://o-ishin.jp/policy/act07/

Nippon Ishin no Kai. (2021b). 日本維新の会衆院選マニフェスト 2021 Nippon Ishin no Kai 2021 Lower House Election Manifesto. https://daikaikaku.o-ishin.jp/manifest/

Rosenbluth, F., Kohno, M., and Zinn, A. (2008). *Japan and the World: Japan's Contemporary Geopolitical Challenges—A Volume in Honor of the Memory and Intellectual Legacy of Asakawa Kan'ichi*. Council on East Asian Studies at Yale University.

Sankei Shimbun. (2021, December 20). 対中決議、再び見送り 自民、公明に熱意なく―産経ニュース. https://www.sankei.com/article/20211220-AZB 7WG2LTJN5DA5OZBVJZCEYYU/

Smith, S. (2015). *Intimate rivals*. Columbia University Press.

Smith, S. (2018). "Foreign Policy." In R. J. Pekkanen, S. R. Reed, E. Scheiner, and D. M. Smith (Eds.), *Japan Decides 2017: The Japanese General Election* (pp. 329–345). Springer.

Solis, M. (2021). The Big Squeeze: Japanese Supply Chains and Great Power Competition. *Joint U.S.-Korea Academic Studies*.

Tachikawa, T. (2021, October 25). Japan's Pick for New Economic Security Post Raises Eyebrows in China. The Japan Times. https://www.japant imes.co.jp/news/2021/10/25/business/economy-business/china-japan-eco nomic-security/

Takahashi, T. (2021, December 13). *Japan's Opaque Economic Security Policy Agenda*. East Asia Forum. https://www.eastasiaforum.org/2021/12/13/jap ans-opaque-economic-security-policy-agenda/

UN Comtrade. (n.d.). *UN Comtrade International Trade Statistics Database*. https://comtrade.un.org/

Vekasi, K. (2019). *Risk Management Strategies of Japanese Companies in China: Political Crisiand Multinational Firms*. Routled

Winkler, C. G. (2017). Right on? The LDP's Drift to the Right and the Persistence of Particularism. *Social Science Japan Journal*, 20(2), 203–224.

CHAPTER 25

The Olympics in the 2021 Election

David Leheny

Virtually none of the election round-ups in Japan about the 2021 general election focused on the role of the Tokyo Olympics. Given the punishing speed of news in the midst of a global pandemic, it is perhaps unsurprising that even a globally anticipated and closely watched event in Japan's capital seemed ultimately to play so little of a part in the national election. The vote was, after all, twelve weeks later, which seemed practically like an eternity at a time that people followed daily case counts of a pandemic, watched debates about easing and strengthening restrictions and watched warily as global trends in vaccinations and new variants of COVID-19 produced wide uncertainty. The Olympics—vilified by many, including celebrities, in the coronavirus-dominated months leading up to the Games (see, e.g., Akagawa 2021), treated with surprisingly open caution by the Emperor himself (Denyer 2001), and strongly supported by only a minority of Japanese adults in the run-up to the Opening Ceremony (*Asahi Shinbun* 2021)—had rapidly gained popular tailwind, with a substantial majority acknowledging afterward that they were glad they

D. Leheny (✉)
Waseda University, Tokyo, Japan

© The Author(s), under exclusive license to Springer Nature   375
Switzerland AG 2023
R. J. Pekkanen et al. (eds.), *Japan Decides 2021*,
https://doi.org/10.1007/978-3-031-11324-6_25

had been held (*Yomiuri Shinbun* 2021). There had been no directly-related public health disaster, no heat-related deaths in the punishing Tokyo summer weather, and, at least since the actual Opening Ceremony itself, no major gaffes that drew attention away from Japan's record medal haul. All of that could have been a boon for the incumbent government.

But there were those twelve weeks. And while public opinion remained behind the Games through that time, the initial bad news about coronavirus cases (covered in Lipscy 2022 and Lukner 2022) helped to sap any goodwill that PM Suga Yoshihide had built through his cabinet's risky decision to hold the Games. Subsequent good news about spectacular drops in the virus's hold over the country buoyed his successor, Kishida Fumio, and made the Olympics recede in public memory with a speed that seems surprising only if one ignores the context. Tokyo's Olympics had been as much of a success as anyone could have hoped on the eve of the Opening Ceremony. Expected to be financially catastrophic and producing no surge of tourists, they could not even easily shine a positive spotlight on Japan at a time that so many in the world were still struggling with new viral variants and widespread economic misery. Their visual impact—ping-pong teams, skateboarders, judo-ka, swimmers all competing in front of empty, mostly silent stands, with occasional music and loudspeaker sounds echoing erratically around arenas—was clearly going to be muted, even dispiriting. But they existed, and thousands of athletes at least had the opportunity to compete for themselves and their nations, with hundreds standing on medal podiums as their flags were raised. Myriad commentators and athletes thanked Japan for carrying out the unenviable task of hosting the Coronavirus Olympics, all of which might have been expected to be a coup for an incumbent politician. But, again, there were those twelve weeks.

This chapter examines the relationships between the 2020 Tokyo Olympics and the 2021 general election. Before the pandemic, then-Prime Minister Abe Shinzō, who placed himself at the center of the Olympic bid and their global promotion, might have expected that their triumph would have propelled his agenda and party's electoral success. By 2020, however, it became easy to imagine scenarios in which a disastrous Olympics, with scandals surrounding contagious athletes and staff causing COVID-19 clusters with Japanese victims, would have doomed the LDP's chance to hold the government in 2021. They might at least have provided the opportunity for opposition parties to focus on the LDP's recklessness in stubbornly hosting the Olympics despite widespread popular doubt, creating a more competitive political landscape. But the run-up to the Games highlighted an unspoken but seemingly shared awareness of the risk of making the Games—as political as they already are—*seem* political. That is, deploying the Olympics as a talking point would likely have paradoxically undermined any positive effect they might have had.

PRELUDE

Tokyo, with its global reputations for safety, cleanliness, and smooth public transportation, might have been viewed as a certain bet to host the Olympics. And yet the city's most recent bid, for the 2016 Games held ultimately in Rio, had foundered in 2009 in part on an apparent absence of popular support. Despite a massive public relations effort within Japan, Tokyo residents expressed misgivings, particularly given the likely cost, about hosting the Games (Kitagawa 2005). While an official Japanese government poll put nationwide support at 70%, a poll commissioned by the International Olympic Committee put local support in Tokyo at only 56%, hardly a promise of an enthusiastic welcome (Himmer 2009). Following a major public relations push four years later, the 2020 bidding committee from Japan boasted strong support for the Olympics, and even its theatrical presentation drew raves back in Japan. Popular French-born television announcer Christel Takigawa used her fluent English to explain the Japanese concept of *omotenashi* (hospitality), later noted in a television poll as one of the most memorable moments of the 30-year-long reign of Emperor Akihito.[1] By the time Abe secretly traveled to Rio de Janeiro to make a surprising and, for many, endearingly awkward appearance as Super Mario in the "handover" portion of the 2016 Rio de Janeiro Olympics' Closing Ceremony, there seemed to be little doubt about Japan's public commitment. Abe's starring role in the handover ceremony, like his assertive presence in the bidding process, might also serve as a reminder of researcher Jules Boykoff's claim that "the Olympics are political through and through" (Boykoff 2016: 2).

Even so, until 2020, the Tokyo Games were politically controversial within relatively stable and constrained boundaries. Japanese criticism of the Olympics crystallized around three themes. The first is inseparable from the ways in which Abe (the subject of Harris 2022) made himself central to the bid for the Games as well as their promotion overseas. Something of a *bête noire* for many on the Japanese Left, Abe had long made no secret of his ambition to "restore" Japan—especially through constitutional revision that would possibly gut the antimilitarist meaning of its war-renouncing Article IX—leading some to argue that the Games were designed to be used as a cover for a fundamental rethinking of the nation's identity and guiding laws.[2] Relatedly, others saw dark connections in the corporate world—especially the major advertising firm Dentsu, a key donor to major LDP figures, which had secured rights over the domestic advertising revenue streams from the Games—and its effort to enrich itself while promoting positive images of leaders (see e.g., Honma 2018). These suspicions worsened with legal investigations that uncovered company officials' part in introducing the Tokyo bid committee to the alleged channel through which putative bribes were transmitted. Finally, others publicly doubted the likelihood that the bally-hooed "Recovery Olympics" would do much of substance for the areas devastated by the 2011 tsunami that killed more than 18,000, particularly given the almost entirely predictable cost overruns and vanishingly small likelihood that the Games would turn a profit.[3]

Even when scandals toppled figures associated with the Olympics—like JOC head Takeda Tsunekazu's resignation after indictment by French authorities for a colorful bribery scheme (which he denied) in support of the Tokyo bid (*Sankei Shinbun* 2019), or Tokyo's Acting Governor Inose Naoki stepping down in disgrace after revelations of having accepted shady loans from a controversial firm (Kayatsu 2013)—they were firmly in the vaunted traditions of unsurprising money politics in the Olympics and Japanese governance. None of this threatened the viability of the Games themselves, but provided a backdrop against which critical journalists, writers, scholars, and citizens could continue to raise serious questions about Tokyo 2020.

THE TURN

On February 20, 2020—little more than a week after the first recorded COVID-19 death in Japan—bestselling author and perpetual right-wing gadfly Hyakuta Naoki tweeted to his nearly 500,000 followers, "I guess that's it for the Tokyo Olympics, huh" ("Mō, Tokyo Orinpikku wa nai ne"). Hyakuta's characteristic certainty stood in stark contrast to the official commentary to that point, like that of soccer legend Kawabuchi Saburō, who, as "mayor" of Olympic Village had pledged to make the facilities safe and secure for visitors (Chūnichi Shinbun 2020). And while government and IOC officials briefly held their the-show-must-go-on line, they soon jointly announced that the Games would be delayed until sometime no later than summer 2021.

This began, of course, a particularly dark turn for a singularly troubled Olympics. Besides the ballooning costs and likelihood that receipts from a spectator/tourist-free Games would be minimal, the delay took a toll on remaining members of the original bid committee, with Prime Minister Abe resigning ostensibly for personal-health-related reasons but as his popularity flagged under the pandemic's social and economic weight. And former Prime Minister Mori Yoshirō, an aged rugby enthusiast and perennial gaffe-maker, stepped down as head of the Tokyo Olympic Committee in early 2021 after stating that women talked too much at meetings (*Nikkei Asia* 2021), a line so outrageous even for him that one imagines that the stress and pace of dealing with a rescheduled, financially catastrophic Olympics were loosening what limited powers of restraint he had previously displayed. With many 2021 polls indicating that as many 80% of Japanese wanted the Games canceled or postponed further (*Asahi Shinbun* 2021), opposition parties called unsuccessfully for a special session of the Diet to question and criticize the government about its handling of the Games (see NHK 2021), though only the JCP openly demanded their cancellation (Shii 2021). Then-Prime Minister Suga's commitment to holding the increasingly unpopular Games was at least politically risky, even as he won plaudits from overseas leaders like U.S. President Joe Biden for going ahead with an event that at least had the possibility of generating moments of transnational enthusiasm in a grim period (e.g., Slodkowski 2021).

But the visible politics of the Games would have to change, leading to further complications. The original selection of film director Yamazaki Takashi, a favorite of PM Abe and the creator of immensely popular movies imbued with sentimental and sometimes assertive nationalism, to helm the Opening Ceremony hinted at the kind of soft national chauvinism typical of the event. But a hastily revised committee delivered on a more solemn ceremony, focused on mourning the victims of the global pandemic and even commemorating the Israeli athletes murdered by terrorists in the 1972 Munich Olympics, and lightened ultimately by jokes drawing largely from Japanese anime and video games. Whatever global goodwill these gestures—sacrificing the normal chest-beating about the host country's virtues in favor of a celebration of global resilience—might have produced were threatened by dismaying reports about the committee behind them. The creative director who had replaced Yamazaki and his partners, Dentsu advertising superstar Sasaki Hiroshi, resigned after the revelation that he floated in a meeting the possibility of having a plus-size female comedian Watanabe Naomi lowered by rope into the stadium, made up as the "Olympig." Less than a week before the Games opened, online sources began to circulate an old magazine interview with the rock star Oyamada Shinji, one of the composers of the Opening Ceremony's music, in which he had laughed about school days when he had engaged in unspeakably cruel bullying of developmentally disabled classmates (Kobayashi and Kurasawa 2021). And barely 24 hours before the Opening Ceremony, the Tokyo organizing committee fired its director, comedian Kobayashi Kentarō, after an old videotape circulated that included a joke from a 1998 sketch, when one of his dull-witted characters said "let's play we're Jews in the Holocaust" (see Iwakabe and Kawaguchi 2021). While political leaders had clearly hoped before the coronavirus pandemic that the Olympics would boost national pride and its global image, opposition politicians, like CDPJ leader Edano Yukio, took these opportunities to point again to the gaffes likely to embarrass the nation on the LDP's watch (*Sankei Shinbun* 2021).

THE AFTERMATH

A small number of off-field incidents became media stories for a short time during the Olympics, like the Ugandan wrestler who fled the Olympic Village before taking a COVID-19 test in the hope of migrating to Japan. More dramatically, a Belarusian sprinter refused to board a flight to which she had been taken by team officials against her will, securing the help of Japanese police and seeking asylum. Most of the coverage within Japan, however, focused on the athletes themselves. To a degree this was the result of an unprecedented medal haul by the Japanese team, with dozens of appealing young athletes, including sibling gold medalists in judo, taking the podium after their wins. And to some degree it was the result of the distribution of broadcast rights across all of the major Japanese national television networks, mostly owned by major national newspaper companies, ensuring that virtually all of the top media sources had a vested interest in promoting the Games. The empty stands were viewed by some to have limited enthusiasm elsewhere, making the television ratings especially disastrous in the United States, but in Japan the

Games were exceptionally popular on television. Indeed, by the end of the Games, public opinion on holding them had turned around almost entirely, returning nearly to their pre-COVID levels (*Yomiuri Shinbun* 2021). Clearly aiming to capitalize on the good news, Prime Minister Suga himself made televised phone calls to congratulate gold medalists.

Suga might have believed that this medal haul, combined with the judgment of the medical community that the Games themselves had not appreciably worsened the public health environment in Tokyo. After all, the disastrous COVID-19 wave of summer 2021, which overloaded Tokyo's hospital system in ways that earlier waves had not, began before the Olympics, and could not be attributed easily to the presence of Olympic athletes and staff, many of whom bristled against the exceptionally strict constraints on movement that the Japanese government had put in place. Indeed, as popular support for the Suga Cabinet plummeted in the midst of the alarm about the pandemic, he might have had good reason to hope that the Olympics, which seemed to have been handled safely and securely as he had promised, and for which he had received public thanks from overseas leaders, would buoy his electoral prospects in the run-up to the fall general election.

The distinguished journalist Yora Masao describes Suga as having mistakenly believed that Japan, like in 1964, was nationally interested in the image of a global underdog succeeding on the world stage, a story of striving and effort that Suga, who famously had pulled himself up from a modest background, claimed to admire. But this was not, Yora argues, an accurate description of Japan's place in the world or of public debate within Japan about the nation, making his phone calls seem like little more than desperate efforts to improve his own popularity through association with successful youngsters (Yora 2021).

As Phillip Lipscy and Daniel Smith (2021) argued on the eve of the Olympics, they could have ended up playing a dramatic role in the 2021 election. Had they gone badly, particularly with sick athletes burdening Japanese hospitals and sickening local residents, they could have ended Suga's tenure even earlier than it did. If he had expected a bounce from a successful Olympics, however, he might have reflected on the political careers of the previous prime ministers to have presided over locally-hosted Games, with Prime Ministers Ikeda, Sato, and Hashimoto all resigning within months of, respectively, the 1964 Tokyo Summer Olympics, the 1972 Sapporo Winter Olympics, and the 1998 Nagano Winter Olympics. Whether one wants to call it a "jinx," as the *Nikkei*

reports it (*Nikkei,* online edition, 2021), there is scant evidence for
the proposition that a prime minister presiding over even a successful
Games will be rewarded by voters, resembling the at-best mixed record
of post-Olympics "bounces" for other democratic governments.[4]

In her book *Theory of the Gimmick,* literature scholar Sianne Ngai
argues that the gimmick—a device that simultaneously pretends to save
labor while also seeming itself to be labored, that seems to try just a
little too hard to be a shortcut replacing real endeavor—is simultaneously an accomplishment and an embarrassment for capitalism itself (Ngai
2020), which might also be said of politics. After all, if the Olympics, the
quintessentially political celebration of the non-political, were to be politically valuable to a Japanese leader, it would almost certainly have to occur
without any reference by the leader himself or herself. Myriad voices in the
media might themselves discuss how a prime minister might benefit from
public enthusiasm about the Olympics, and might even suggest that they
depended on that politician's efforts, making no secret of the political
hopes surrounding the Games. But for a politician to emphasize or even
acknowledge it would seem both grossly transactional (I did this for you,
now you vote for my party) and deeply misplaced, expecting credit for
the success of a project whose real production rested on the work, talent,
and competitiveness of others. The Games would be exposed as political
gimmick, undermining almost whatever value they might otherwise have
had.

When news broke in 2020 that the Olympics would be delayed a year,
noted political theorist Uno Shigeki remarked that the Olympics had now
become even more politically "convenient": the delay would become a
cover story helping leaders evade responsibility for the ballooning expenditures that would have surpassed what the country would likely have
recouped even under the best of circumstances, drawing public finances
away from other, more pressing citizens' needs (Uno 2021: 143–145).
Suga's September resignation may have allowed the LDP's new leadership to sidestep criticism for the Olympics while also eliminating any
crass temptation to employ their success in the campaign. The most
durable political consequence in Japan of the delayed 2020 Olympics
might turn out to be in the limits of accountability for financial consequences that would likely have been grim under any circumstances.
Instead, they will likely be regarded as the unavoidable outcome of Japan's
bad luck in timing, with the focus placed on Japan's qualified success: in
a catastrophic moment, its Olympics avoided catastrophe.

Notes

1. Although NHK no longer maintains a webpage for their nearly five-hour-long "Yuku jidai kuru jidai – Heisei saigo no hi supesharu" (An Era Comes, an Era Goes—The Last Day of Heisei Special), which ran overnight from. April 30-May 1, 2019, it is summarized on Wikipedia, at https://ja.wikipedia.org/wiki/ゆく時代くる時代〜平成最後の日スペシャル〜. Accessed December 24, 2021.
2. Andō (2017) summarizes how this connection was made explicit in a 2017 Diet hearing in which then-DPJ leader Renhō seemed to accuse Abe of using the Olympics as a morale-boosting cover for his plan to introduce a constitutional revision bill later in 2020.
3. Renowned actor Watanabe Ken, who spent substantial time in the region in part because of his role in the film "Fukushima 50," took the unusual step in 2019 of saying in an interview that he felt that the "the Games were initially organized to show the world how Japan is able to recover from natural disasters, but I feel that only the economic effects are currently taken into account. In other words, the event only promotes Tokyo, and Tohoku is being left behind." See Asahi Shinbun 2019.
4. Most recently, then-Mayor Boris Johnson strategically used the London 2012 Games to boost his own public profile, but it was done largely at the expense of then-Prime Minister David Cameron, who enjoyed little improvement in his own polling numbers following the Games. See Shirbon 2012.

References

Akagawa Jirō. 2021. "Gorin chūshi, sore shika michi wa nai" (There's No Path Other than Cancelling the Olympics). *Asahi Shinbun*, June 6, p. 8.

Andō Kenji. 2017. "Abe shushō, 2020-nen kaiken o hyōmei⇨Renhō daihyō 'Orinpikku wa kenkō kaisei wa kankei nai'" (PM Abe Expresses Hope for 2020 Constitutional Revision – DPJ Head Renhō says "The Olympics Have Nothing to do with Constitutional Revision"). Huffington Post May 9 (online). https://www.huffingtonpost.jp/2017/05/09/renho-abe_n_16504068.html. Accessed January 5, 2022.

Asahi Shinbun. 2019. "Role that Ken Watanabe Likes Best: Helping Out in Disaster Area," February 26. https://www.asahi.com/ajw/articles/13054564. Accessed January 4, 2022.

Asahi Shinbun. 2021. "Gorin, sansei 33%-hantai 55%: Anzen, anshin no taikai 'dekinai' 68%—Asahi Shinbunsha yoron chōsa" (Olympics—33% Support, 55% Opposed, 68% Say a Safe, Secure Olympics "Impossible" Finds Asahi Poll). July 19, p. 3.

Boykoff, Jules. 2016. *Power Games: A Political History of the Olympics*. London: Verso.

Chūnichi Shinbun. 2020. "'Anzen, anshin no senshumura ni': Kawabuchi sonchōra iki komi" ("'We'll Be Making a Safe and Secure Olympic Village' say 'Mayor' Kawabuchi and Others in Morale Builder). April 4. https://www.chunichi.co.jp/article/7837. Accessed January 4, 2022.

Denyer, Simon. 2021. "Tokyo Olympics Just Got an Important No-Confidence Vote--From Japan's Emperor," *The Washington Post*, June 24.

Harris, Tobias. 2022. "Abe's Legacy." In Robert J. Pekkanen, Steven R. Reed and Daniel M. Smith, (Eds.), *Japan Decides 2021: The Japanese General Election*. New York: Palgrave Macmillan.

Himmer, Alastair. 2009. "Interview-Olympics-N.Korea Test no Threat to Tokyo Bid: Governor," Reuters, May 27. https://www.reuters.com/article/olympics-tokyo-idUST22571820090527. Accessed December 24, 2021.

Honma Ryū. 2018. *Dentsū kyodai riken: Tōkyō gorin de sakushu sareru kokumin* (Dentsū's Massive Interests: How the Tokyo Olympics are Exploiting Citizens). Tokyo: Saizō.

Iwakabe Shun and Kawaguchi Shun. 2021. "Tokyo 2020+1: Kaikaishiki enshutsu Kobayashi-shi kainin yudayajin daigyakusatsu yayu—gorin soshikiin" (Tokyo 2020+1: Olympic Organizing Committee: Kobayashi Dismissed Over Mockery of Slaughter of Jews). *Mainichi Shimbun*. July 23.

Kayatsu Setsu. 2013. "Inose chiji jishoku hatsugen e — Tōkyō gorin junbi ni eikyō — soshikii no setsuritsu kigen semaru" (Governor Inose Set to Resign: What Effect on the Tokyo Olympics, as Deadline to Establish Organizing Committee Nears?). *Yomiuri Shinbun*, December 19, C27.

Kitagawa Kazunori. 2005. "Gorin shōchi, kangei to konwaku, kokunai senkō wa Tokyo yūi ka" (Is Tokyo Leading in the Internal Selection? Confusion Over Attracting the Olympics). *Nikkei Shinbun*, November. 24, p. 19.

Kobayashi Yūta and Kurasawa Hitoshi. 2021. "Tokyo gorin: Oyamada-shi jinin kaikaishiki enshutsu chokuzen henkō e—soshikiin: 'isogi taiō'" (Tokyo Olympics: Oyamada Resigns, Moving Toward Last-Second Changes to Performances in the Opening Ceremony: Olympic Committee 'Responding Frantically'). *Mainichi Shimbun*. July 21.

Lipscy, Phillip Y. and Smith, Daniel M. 2021. "Nobody Can Go to the Tokyo Olympics. So Why is the Government Going Ahead with Them?" *The Washington Post* (Monkey Cage Blog), July 19. https://www.washingtonpost.com/politics/2021/07/19/japans-government-faces-dual-challenge-tokyo-olympics-covid-19/. Accessed January 4, 2022.

Lipscy, Phillip Y. 2022. "Japan's Response to the COVID-19 Pandemic." In Robert J. Pekkanen, Steven R. Reed and Daniel M. Smith, (Eds.), *Japan Decides 2021: The Japanese General Election*. New York: Palgrave Macmillan.

Lukner, Kerstin. 2022. "Covid-19: The International Dimension." In Robert J. Pekkanen, Steven R. Reed and Daniel M. Smith, (Eds.), *Japan Decides 2021: The Japanese General Election*. New York: Palgrave Macmillan.

Ngai, Sianne. 2020. *Theory of the Gimmick: Aesthetic Judgment and Capitalist Form* Cambridge: Harvard University Press.

NHK. 2022. "Yatō 4-tō kokkai shōshū o yōkyū 'gorin kansen taisaku fubi nado tadasu hitsuyō'" (Four Opposition Parties Call to Convene the Diet: 'We Need to Inquire about Matters Including Insufficient Measures to Prevent Outbreaks at the Olympics"). July 16. https://www3.nhk.or.jp/news/html/20210716/k10013142051000.html. Accessed January 21, 2022.

Nikkei Asia. 2021. "Meetings with Women 'Take So Much Time,' Says Japan Olympics Chief," February 4. https://asia.nikkei.com/Spotlight/Tokyo-2020-Olympics/Meetings-with-women-take-so-much-time-says-Japan-Olympics-chief. Accessed January 4, 2022.

Nikkei Shinbun. 2021. "'Goringo seihen' jinkusu yaburezu, kokunai 4 taikai, shushō taijin) "The Post-Olympic Political Change Jinx' Strikes Again: The Prime Minister Has Now Resigned After All Four Held Here," September 5, p. 5.

Sankei Shinbun. 2019. "Tōkyō gorin shōchi giwaku no kagi nigiru shingapōru no otoko, chōshuzumi ka" (Has the Singaporean Man Who Holds the Key to the Suspicions about Tokyo's Olympic Bid Already Been Questioned?). March 19. https://www.sankei.com/article/2019b0319-6GCQG36VGBLG3F6IPSMPNVIKDA/?outputType=theme_tokyo2020. Accessed January 4, 2022.

Sankei Shinbun. 2021. "Ritsumin Edano daihyô 'Nasake naku mittomonai' Sasaki Hiroshi no bujoku enshutsu mondai de" (CDPJ Head Edano Criticizes Sasaki Hiroshi's Insulting Entrance Idea as "Shamefully Uncompassionate." March 18. https://www.sankei.com/article/2021c0318-HNOWDAQ6RROHXJQFHYGSE4UXOE/. Accessed January 21, 2022.

Shii Kazuo. 2021. "We Will Continue to Call for the Immediate Cancellation of the Tokyo Olympics from the Standpoint that Life is More Important than the Games." JCP, July 23. https://www.jcp.or.jp/english/jcpcc/blog/2021/07/we-still-call-for-the-immediate-cancellation-of-the-tokyo-olympics-from-the-standpoint-that-life-is-.html. Accessed January 21, 2022.

Shirbon, Estelle. 2012. "London Mayor Uses Olympic Bounce to Taunt Government," Reuters, August 16. https://www.reuters.com/article/britain-politics-johnson/london-mayor-uses-olympic-bounce-to-taunt-government-idUSL6E8JG37E20120816. Accessed January 21, 2022.

Slodkowski, Antoni. 2021. "Biden Reaffirms Support for Tokyo Olympics to Japan's Suga," Reuters June 13. https://www.reuters.com/world/asia-pacific/biden-reaffirms-support-tokyo-olympics-japans-suga-2021-06-13. Accessed January 4, 2022.

Sponichi Annex. 2013. "Inose-shi ga shitsugen: Isutanbūru hihan? IOC ga chūi kanki" (Inose Gaffe: Criticizing Istanbul? The IOC Takes Notice." April 30. https://www.sponichi.co.jp/sports/news/2013/04/30/kiji/K20 130430005710610.html. Accessed January 4, 2022.

Uno Shigeki. 2021. *Minshushugi o shinjiru* (Believing in Democracy). Tokyo: Seidosha.

Wade, Stephen. 2021. "Why Are Olympics Going on Despite Public, Medical Warnings?" Associated Press, June 17. https://apnews.com/article/business-health-coronavirus-pandemic-olympic-games-2020-tokyo-olympics-dd49a7 aaaa6c59defea9670c5b19475c. Accessed January 4, 2022.

Yomiuri Shinbun. 2021. "Gorin saikai 'yokatta' 64% — Yomiuri Shinbunsha yoron chōsa" (64% "Glad" the Olympics Were Held, Finds Yomiuri Shinbun Poll). August 9. https://www.yomiuri.co.jp/election/yoron-chosa/2021d0 809-OYT1T50143/. Accessed January 4, 2022.

Yora Masao. 2021. "Suga shushō to tōkyō orinpikku/pararinpikku: gakai shita shushō saihen no shinario," Nippon.com. September 7. https://www.nippon.com/ja/in-depth/d00749. Accessed January 4, 2022.

CHAPTER 26

Conclusion: Voters Choose Competence in Japan's Coronavirus Election

Daniel M. Smith, *Steven R. Reed, and Robert J. Pekkanen*

There are two connected sets of questions we seek to explore in this conclusion. The first is what the results of the 2021 election tell us about the election in an immediate sense, and what they mean for the state of democracy in Japan more generally. The second connects to an issue that is likely to be one of the major comparative questions for studies of elections around this time frame: how did the coronavirus pandemic (COVID-19) affect politics and voting behavior?

D. M. Smith
Columbia University, New York, NY, USA
e-mail: dms2323@columbia.edu

S. R. Reed
Chuo University, Tokyo, Japan

R. J. Pekkanen (✉)
University of Washington, Seattle, WA, USA
e-mail: pekkanen@uw.edu

Regarding the first set of questions, the headline result of the 2021 election is that the Liberal Democratic Party (LDP) and its coalition partner Kōmeitō secured a renewed majority of seats in the House of Representatives. As the chapters in this volume chronicle, the main backdrop of the election was the ongoing coronavirus pandemic and the governing parties' handling of it. A big surprise was that the LDP-Kōmeitō coalition did so well, considering that public opinion in the summer of 2021 suggested a strong headwind against the LDP (fueled by dissatisfaction with coronavirus policy under Prime Minister Suga Yoshihide), and the fact that the opposition parties, led by the Constitutional Democratic Party (CDP), launched a successful coordination effort to avoid handing the LDP easy wins in the single-member districts (SMDs) that make up roughly two-thirds of the seats to be filled in the election.

The LDP's ability to emerge victorious in this context speaks not only to specific decisions the party made leading up to the election—such as replacing Suga as party leader with Kishida Fumio—but also to an element of luck in the timing of the vaccine rollout and voters' reluctance to place their bets on an untested opposition in the middle of the crisis. The opposition remains in disarray following the election and is now even further fragmented thanks to the seat gains made by Nippon Ishin no Kai (Ishin). This post-election situation reflects the continued anemia in Japan's opposition since the collapse of the Democratic Party of Japan (DPJ) after the 2012 general election.[1]

Our answer to the second question is that the coronavirus pandemic indeed shaped Japan's 2021 election in important ways. As noted, the key reason for uncertainty going into the election was voter dissatisfaction with the LDP's handling of the crisis. However, the replacement of Suga with Kishida helped the party to shift this narrative in the weeks prior to the poll, and a surge in vaccine doses administered by early October reinforced its image as the party that is most capable of delivering stable, competent governance in Japan. Although the opposition's coordination strategy worked in SMDs, the biggest beneficiary of anti-LDP votes was Ishin, which proved itself capable of competent governance in its handling of the pandemic response in Osaka. In short, voters' demand for competence in handling the pandemic can explain not only the LDP's lighter-than-expected rebuke at the polls, but also Ishin's surprise success among the opposition party options available.

Two Big Surprises of the 2021 Election

In one sense, the 2021 election was a clear reprimand of the LDP, which lost 15 seats. Prior to the election, the LDP-Kōmeitō coalition held 305 (of 465) seats in the House of Representatives (276 of which were held by the LDP). But the unpopularity of Prime Minister Suga, and the coordination of opposition candidates in the SMD races, led to some pre-election predictions that the party could lose as many as seventy seats. After taking over as prime minister, Kishida himself set the modest goal of winning a simple majority between the two coalition partners. In the end, the coalition's losses were much lower (Kōmeitō even gained three seats)—resulting in not just a majority, but a stable governing majority (meaning controlling all parliamentary committee chair positions) of 293 seats.[2]

When compared to the expectations set in the run-up to the election, the final voting results produced two big surprises. The first surprise is that the LDP did much better than earlier polling suggested, which we interpret as the influence of coronavirus both in the party's poor earlier polling numbers and also in the late positive bump due to a successful vaccine rollout. In the end, the LDP did significantly better than pre-election polling seemed to presage. It gained votes overall relative to the 2017 general election and increased its seat share in the proportional representation (PR) tier of the electoral system. We note that this may suggest also that Japan is joining other democracies (such as the United States and United Kingdom) where public polling is increasingly doing poorly in predicting election results (e.g., Silver 2017; Keeter et al. 2021).

The second big surprise is the huge success of Ishin in the Kinki region, both in terms of winning SMD seats and in terms of an increased PR vote share and seat share (see K. Maeda, 2022, this volume). We interpret this result as a reflection of a subset of voters being too dissatisfied with the LDP's handling of the coronavirus pandemic to stick with it, but at the same time unwilling to trust the CDP to take charge. Regional control over local offices, most notably with Governor Yoshimura Hirofumi handling the pandemic response in Osaka, allowed Ishin to publicly demonstrate its ability to govern effectively.

The Coronavirus Election: Competence and Luck

We interpret the election as indeed being shaped by the coronavirus pandemic. However, the results cannot be simply understood as voters evaluating the government's response to the pandemic and rewarding or punishing them at the polls. This was not a straightforward referendum on coronavirus policy. Rather, we think, the entire election campaign and the two years preceding it were shaped by the ongoing pandemic in three ways.

First, voters saw this election as a choice about competence and worried about putting the CDP in power in an uncertain moment. In other words, the CDP's uncertain competence was highlighted as a risk by the shadow that the coronavirus pandemic cast over the election campaign. Moreover, the LDP benefited significantly from the successful vaccine rollout just before the election. This late demonstration of competence perhaps averted a disastrous result for the LDP and suggests the particular timing of the election in the trajectory of the pandemic was quite important (see Y. Maeda, 2022, this volume). The larger point is that although it is not a straightforward endorsement of the LDP's handling of the coronavirus, the framing of the election was powerfully influenced by the context of the pandemic.

Moreover, despite the opposition's successful coordination around a common campaign message, and general avoidance of competition in SMDs, the usual distinction across government and opposition on domestic spending and redistribution was blurred by Kishida's shift away from Abenomics (see Lee, 2022, this volume). This meant that the opposition was less able to effectively compete with the LDP on an alternative vision for domestic policy because the LDP coopted these issues. With the exception of the issues of same-sex marriage and separate surnames for married couples (see Kweon, 2022, this volume), voters ended up choosing between similar domestic policies—and in this context, the LDP had a valence advantage as the party most capable of delivering them, while also handling the pandemic.

Second, we can read dissatisfaction with the LDP for its earlier handling of the pandemic (stages before the vaccine) in two ways. For one, the polling on the government policy in the earlier stages of the pandemic reflects this dissatisfaction (see Y. Maeda, 2022). Support for Suga cratered in the context of perceived failures in mitigating the pandemic, which also connected to concerns about the Olympics, a potential "superspreader event" (see Leheny, 2022, this volume). However, as Nemoto (2022, this volume) describes, the LDP choice of replacing Suga with Kishida prior to the election seems to have worked in reversing negative public opinion. Kishida proved popular enough to lead the LDP to victory, even though Kōno Tarō might have been the more popular choice.

In addition, we interpret the unexpectedly high vote for Ishin in the PR tier as driven by an undercurrent of dissatisfaction with the LDP's handling of the pandemic streaming to a seemingly competent alternative. While the pandemic meant voters were perhaps reluctant to cast their ballots for an untested CDP, Ishin had a track record to run on in regional governance (see Pekkanen and Reed, 2022; Lipscy, 2022, this volume). Thus, Ishin could emerge for this election as the most competent-appearing alternative to the LDP. Voters who wanted to punish the LDP, but fretted about CDP competence, could cast a PR vote for Ishin to reward their good record on the pandemic. Here, the high-profile governor Yoshimura in Osaka contributed greatly to the party image of Ishin, as he was perceived to be handling the pandemic well.

Third, the coronavirus situation improved with the successful vaccine rollout in fall—this happened between the expectations about a bad outcome for the LDP and the actual voting period. By October, the vaccine rollout was going well (see Lipscy, 2022). So, to the extent that there was a COVID-19-related reason for voters to punish the LDP, that was mitigated. The coronavirus pandemic had a massive effect on Japanese society and the economy, and there are many aspects and developments even to the medical story. But the timing of the election ultimately favored the LDP. As Thies and Yanai (2022, this volume) write, "had the Diet's term expired a few months earlier, the outcome might have been quite different." Our argument is that the timing of the election came at a relatively high point of perceived LDP competence. This contributed to a relatively better (and surprising) showing for the LDP.

Our overall interpretation is that the pandemic profoundly shaped the election and the election results, although not always in a simple or straightforward way. The shadow of the continuing pandemic made this a competence election, to the detriment of the CDP. A late uptick in perceived competence in the vaccine rollout led to a better-than-expected LDP victory, and to a limited extent, Ishin's perceived competence on the pandemic also contributed to its surprising showing among the opposition parties.

Putting Japan's Coronavirus Election in Comparative Context

The COVID-19 pandemic had an impact on elections around the world, with many countries postponing elections entirely, and others introducing special measures (such as mail-in voting) to mitigate the risks of voting in person (International IDEA, 2022).

The success of the LDP in the 2021 election contrasts with outcomes in several democracies that also held elections during the pandemic and witnessed voters rejecting the incumbent government and changing direction. The most obvious example is the United States, where voters ousted President Donald Trump in favor of Joe Biden (cf. Abramowitz, 2021). However, Trump's defeat can be attributed to many other failures in performance in office and personal character beyond his administration's coronavirus policy, which was polarizing but also facilitated the rapid production of vaccines. Another example is Germany, where long-serving Chancellor Angela Merkel of the Christian Democratic Union (CDU) decided not to seek reelection in 2021, and voters delivered the biggest seat share since 2005 to the Social Democratic Party of Germany (SPD), which went on to form a coalition government with its leader, Olaf Scholz, at its head. However, the German alternation in power is also difficult to pin on the coronavirus rather than differences in the personal reputations and styles of the party leaders.

Elsewhere around the world, incumbent democratic governments on the ropes prior to the pandemic seemed to bounce back to win elections thanks to competent coronavirus policies. The administration of Prime Minister Mark Rutte in the Netherlands, for example, was plagued by a childcare benefits scandal heading into 2019, but favorable views of his leadership during the COVID-19 crisis helped Rutte and his party maintain control of the government (in coalition) in the 2021 Dutch elections.[3] Prime Minister Justin Trudeau of Canada called early snap elections in 2021, hoping voters would reward his Liberal Party—in power as a minority government—with a single-party majority of seats for his government's handling of the pandemic. He failed to win the desired majority, but renewed his party's mandate to govern for another term. In South Korea, the Democratic Party was struggling to maintain support in public opinion polls in 2019, but won a large majority in the 2020 legislative elections thanks in part to public approval of the way Democratic Party President Moon Jae-in's administration dealt with the crisis—keeping case counts and deaths low in comparison with other countries (McCurry, 2020; see also Lipscy, 2022, this volume).

Ultimately, every election outcome is the product of numerous context-specific factors and the choices available to voters. That being acknowledged, our interpretation of Japan's 2021 election puts it in the company of country cases where a competent handling of the pandemic—albeit one that materialized only in the weeks prior to the campaign—saved the incumbent government from being ousted by the electorate.

WHITHER DEMOCRATIC COMPETITION IN JAPAN?

As a final reflection, what does the 2021 election tell us about the broader state of democracy in Japan? On the surface, the election was good news for the LDP. It was also a win for Prime Minister Kishida, since the better-than-expected performance strengthened his position in the party and provided him the political capital to change course from the previous administrations of Suga and Abe Shinzō. His popularity grew further in the months following the poll.

But below the surface, the LDP has several reasons not to be overly confident heading into future elections. First, support for the LDP as a party remains low (below 40% in post-election polls), and its vote share in the proportional representation tier has not surpassed 35% since the 2005 general election. To be sure, this is higher support than any other party currently enjoys, but it hardly suggests an insurmountable wall of LDP support. The CDP earned 20% of the PR vote, and Ishin is not far behind, earning 14% of the PR vote and completely defeating the LDP in SMDs in Osaka.

Second, setting aside the shellacking in Osaka, most of the LDP's majority was earned in the 289 SMDs of the electoral system, where it captured 189 seats (including two ex-post nominations given to affiliated independents). But 46 of those wins resulted from only a plurality—not a majority—of the votes. Moreover, in the remaining SMDs where the LDP's candidate won a majority, the margin of victory was less than five percentage points in 17 of them. In other words, relatively small changes in either opposition fragmentation or voter support (whether through persuasion or mobilization) could have reversed up to a third of the LDP's SMD victories. These kinds of large seat swings resulting from small vote changes occurred in the 2009 and 2012 general elections, and could happen again.

Third, turnout continues to be low, at just 56%. A majority of voters in recent years report being unsatisfied with how democracy is working, and do not agree with many of the LDP's policy positions (such as its opposition to allowing elective separate surnames for married couples). But many of these disaffected voters stay home at election time. Exit polls showed that the LDP enjoyed relatively more support among young people (under 40), but relatively less support among women. While young people are notoriously hard to mobilize (see Steel, 2022, this volume), women could be a force for increased electoral pressure on the LDP if they can be mobilized by the opposition. In 2021, women's turnout was slightly lower than men's turnout, and the share of women in the Diet declined to less than 10% (see Kweon, 2022). The LDP's share of women is the lowest among the major parties (just 7.6%), and while Kishida has promised a "regeneration" in the LDP, the party continues to be dominated by older men (and the sons and grandsons of former members). If the opposition parties can appeal to women voters and mobilize them to turn out in higher numbers in future elections, it might provide the kind of small shift in votes that can swing a large number of competitive SMDs away from the LDP-Kōmeitō coalition.

Finally, we argue that the opposition strategy of coordination worked. The CDP gained nine SMD seats. But the electoral system continues to suppress fair representation in Japan. SMDs favor larger parties, as does the D'Hondt allocation rule in the PR tier of the electoral system. So long as the opposition remains fragmented, it will continue to fare poorly under the current electoral rules. The post-election narrative in Japan painted the opposition's cooperation as a failure, and the CDP's core supporter in organized labor, Rengo, even began to make overtures toward the LDP, rejecting any future cooperation with the Japanese Communist Party (JCP). We think this reaction is premature and will only further guarantee a fragmented opposition and lack of alternation in government moving forward.

Notes

1. See the previous volumes of *Japan Decides* (Pekkanen et al. 2013, 2016, 2018).

2. The LDP later accepted former opposition-member-turned-independent Hosono Gōshi into the party after the election for an additional seat.
3. See, e.g., "Dutch elections: How COVID-19 salvaged Mark Rutte's bid amid scandal." DW, March 14, 2021. URL: https://www.dw.com/en/dutch-elections-how-covid-19-salvaged-mark-ruttes-bid-amid-scandal/a-56812885.

References

Abramowitz, Alan I. 2021. "It's the Pandemic, Stupid! A Simplified Model for Forecasting the 2020 Presidential Election." *PS: Political Science & Politics*, 54(1): 52–54.

Clarke, Harold, Thomas J. Scotto, and Marianne C. Stewart. 2021. "In Canada's Snap Election, Justin Trudeau and the Liberals were both Victims and Beneficiaries of the COVID-19 Crisis." LSE Phelan US Centre blog, October 6, 2021. URL: https://bit.ly/3BiTavQ.

International IDEA. 2022. "Global Overview of COVID-19: Impact on Elections." May 2, 2022. URL: https://www.idea.int/news-media/multimedia-reports/global-overview-covid-19-impact-elections.

Keeter, Scott, Nick Hatley, Arnold Lau, and Courtney Kennedy. 2021. "What 2020's Election Poll Errors Tell Us About the Accuracy of Issue Polling." Pew Research Center. URL: https://www.pewresearch.org/methods/2021/03/02/what-2020s-election-poll-errors-tell-us-about-the-accuracy-of-issue-polling/

Kweon, Yesola. 2022. "Women's Representation and the Gendered Impact of COVID-19 in Japan." In *Japan Decides 2021: The Japanese General Election*, (Eds.), Robert J. Pekkanen, Steven R. Reed, Daniel M. Smith. Palgrave Macmillan.

Lee, Yeon Ju. 2022. "Does Income Inequality Matter in Japan?" In *Japan Decides 2021: The Japanese General Election*, (Eds.), Robert J. Pekkanen, Steven R. Reed, Daniel M. Smith. Palgrave Macmillan.

Leheny, David. 2022. "The Olympics in the 2021 Election." In *Japan Decides 2021: The Japanese General Election*, (Eds.), Robert J. Pekkanen, Steven R. Reed, Daniel M. Smith. Palgrave Macmillan.

Lipscy, Phillip Y. 2022. "Japan's Response to the COVID-19 Pandemic." In *Japan Decides 2021: The Japanese General Election*, (Eds.), Robert J. Pekkanen, Steven R. Reed, Daniel M. Smith. Palgrave Macmillan.

Maeda, Ko. 2022. "The 2021 Election Results: Continuity and Change." In *Japan Decides 2021: The Japanese General Election*, (Eds.), Robert J. Pekkanen, Steven R. Reed, Daniel M. Smith. Palgrave Macmillan.

Maeda, Yukio. 2022. "Public Opinion and COVID-19." In *Japan Decides 2021: The Japanese General Election*, (Eds.), Robert J. Pekkanen, Steven R. Reed, Daniel M. Smith. Palgrave Macmillan.

McCurry, Justin. 2020. "South Korea's Ruling Party Wins Election Landslide Amid Coronavirus Outbreak." *The Guardian*, April 16, 2020. URL:https://www.theguardian.com/world/2020/apr/16/south-kor eas-ruling-party-wins-election-landslide-amid-coronavirus-outbreak

Nemoto, Kuniaki. 2022. "How the Liberal Democratic Party Avoided a Loss in 2021." In *Japan Decides 2021: The Japanese General Election*, (Eds.), Robert J. Pekkanen, Steven R. Reed, Daniel M. Smith. Palgrave Macmillan.

Pekkanen, Robert J. and Steven R. Reed. 2022. "The Opposition in 2021: A Second Party and A Third Force." In *Japan Decides 2021: The Japanese General Election*, (Eds.), Robert J. Pekkanen, Steven R. Reed, Daniel M. Smith. Palgrave Macmillan.

Pekkanen, Robert J., Steven R. Reed, and Ethan Scheiner (Eds.), 2013. *Japan Decides 2012: The Japanese General Election*. Palgrave Macmillan.

Pekkanen, Robert J., Steven R. Reed, and Ethan Scheiner (Eds.), 2016. *Japan Decides 2014: The Japanese General Election*. Palgrave Macmillan.

Pekkanen, Robert J., Steven R. Reed, Ethan Scheiner, and Daniel M. Smith (Eds.), 2018. *Japan Decides 2017: The Japanese General Election*. Palgrave Macmillan.

Silver, Nate. 2017. "Are the U.K. Polls Skewed?" FiveThirtyEight. URL: https://fivethirtyeight.com/features/are-the-u-k-polls-skewed/

Steel, Gill. 2022. "Are the Kids Alright? Young People and Turnout in Japan." In *Japan Decides 2021: The Japanese General Election*, (Eds.), Robert J. Pekkanen, Steven R. Reed, Daniel M. Smith. Palgrave Macmillan.

Thies, Michael and Yuki Yanai. 2022. "Did COVID-19 Impact Japan's 2021 General Election?" In *Japan Decides 2021: The Japanese General Election*, (Eds.), Robert J. Pekkanen, Steven R. Reed, Daniel M. Smith. Palgrave Macmillan.

INDEX

Printed by Printforce, the Netherlands